W9-BQW-007

INTRODUCTION
to
CRIMINAL EVIDENCE
and
COURT PROCEDURE

Seventh Edition

◆

Julian R. Hanley
County Judge, Retired
Wyoming County, New York

Wayne W. Schmidt
Operating Director of
Americans for Effective Law Enforcement, Inc.

Larry D. Nichols
Retired Professor of Law Enforcement Technology and
Coordinator of Police Academy
South Plains College, Levelland, Texas

McCutchan Publishing Corporation
3220 Blume Drive, Suite 197, Richmond, California 94806

In Memory of Ray K. Robbins

ISBN 978-0-8211-0738-6
Library of Congress Catalog Card Number 2001012345

Printed in the United States of America

To Betty
—J.R.H.
To Nancy and Andrew
—W.W.S.
To Micheline
—L.D.N.

McCutchan Publishing acknowledges the substantial contributions of Ray K. Robbins, retired professor of criminal justice at Western Texas College, to creating and updating all the previous editions of *Introduction to Criminal Evidence and Court Procedure*. Professor Robbins's expertise in law enforcement has resulted in an extremely popular and effective criminal justice textbook.

Contents

3. Arrests, Searches, and Seizures   25

4. Interrogations, Confessions and Nontestimonial Evidence   113

A. INTERROGATIONS AND CONFESSIONS

11. Articles and Exhibits of Evidence   297

Preface

This seventh edition of *Introduction to Criminal Evidence and Court Procedure* reflects changes in the law since the sixth edition was published in 2006.

This revision reorganizes the text into a logical order that starts with an overview of the criminal justice process from arrest through sentencing. By sequencing the chapters to correspond to the specific steps of the criminal justice process, a student logically moves through the evidence gathering and court procedures necessary to achieve justice in our judicial process, which seeks not only to prosecute the guilty but also to protect the innocent. Presented in a clear, concise, comprehensive, and forceful manner, this text is organized to address one-semester or two-quarter undergraduate courses in criminal evidence and court procedure.

This revision also incorporates various websites available through the Internet that allow students to access various resources, including numerous court cases, courts, and current research material.

Designed to further understanding that will assist officers in effectively performing a vital criminal justice function, the book is dedicated to all law enforcement officers—past, present, and future—as well as to students and teachers of the subject, all of whom are involved in service to their fellow man—the noblest and most satisfying of all human endeavors.

The Bill of Rights
(Ratified 1791)
and the Fourteenth Amendment

Amendment I

> Congress shall make no law respecting an establishment of religion, or prohibiting the free exercise thereof; or abridging the freedom of speech or of the press; or the right of the people peaceably to assemble and to petition the Government for a redress of grievances.

Amendment II

> A well regulated Militia, being necessary to the security of a free State, the right of the people to keep and bear Arms, shall not be infringed.

Amendment III

> No Soldier shall, in time of peace be quartered in any house, without the consent of the Owner, nor in time of war, but in a manner to be prescribed by law.

Amendment IV

> The right of the people to be secure in their persons, houses, papers, and effects, against unreasonable searches and seizures,

shall not be violated, and no Warrants shall issue, but upon probable cause, supported by Oath, or affirmation, and particularly describing the place to be searched and the persons or things to be seized.

Amendment V

No person shall be held to answer for a capital, or otherwise infamous crime, unless on a presentment or indictment of a Grand Jury, except in cases arising in the land or naval forces, or in the Militia, when in actual service in time of War or public danger; nor shall any person be subject for the same offense to be twice put in jeopardy of life or limb; nor shall be compelled in any criminal case to be a witness against himself, nor be deprived of life, liberty, or property, without due process of law; nor shall private property be taken for public use, without just compensation.

Amendment VI

In all criminal prosecutions, the accused shall enjoy the right to a speedy and public trial, by an impartial Jury of the State and district wherein the crime shall have been committed, which district shall have been previously ascertained by law, and to be informed of the nature and cause of the accusation; to be confronted with the witnesses against him; to have compulsory process for obtaining witnesses in his favor, and to have the Assistance of Counsel for his defense.

Amendment VII

In suits at common law, where the value in controversy shall exceed twenty dollars, the right of trial by jury shall be preserved, and no fact tried by jury shall be otherwise reexamined in any Court of the United States, than according to the rules of the common law.

Amendment VIII

Excessive bail shall not be required, nor excessive fines imposed, nor cruel and unusual punishments inflicted.

Amendment IX

The enumeration in the Constitution, of certain rights, shall not be construed to deny or disparage others retained by the people.

Amendment X

The powers not delegated to the United States by the Constitution, nor prohibited by it to the States, are reserved to the States respectively, or to the people. . . .

**14th Amendment
Ratified 1868**

Amendment XIV

Section 1. All persons born or naturalized in the United States, and subject to the jurisdiction thereof, are citizens of the United States and of the State wherein they reside. No State shall make or enforce any law which shall abridge the privileges or immunities of citizens of the United States; nor shall any State deprive any person of life, liberty, or property, without due process of law; nor deny to any person within its jurisdiction the equal protection of the laws. . . .

1

The Criminal Justice System

The American criminal justice system is uniquely organized to protect both the constitutional rights of a person accused of a crime and the safety of all our citizens. To achieve these goals, and the delicate balance between the rights of the accused and the rights of society, our states have created a system of checks and balances through penal codes, codes of criminal procedures (CCP), and other specific codes.

(1.1) The Criminal Justice System

The American criminal justice system is designed to incorporate the principles of *justice* (which can be defined as "basic fairness") in three main cooperating government groups, each of which has separate, but integrated, purposes in handling criminal behavior. The groups are (1) law enforcement; (2) courts; and (3) corrections. In addition, various other governmental agencies, such as women's protective services, children's protective services, juvenile probation offices, state and county adult probation (community supervision), and parole divisions, play major roles in the criminal justice system.

The term *system* implies separate entities or parts that work together to accomplish a specific purpose. For example, consider an air-

1

conditioning and heating system. To cool or heat an area, there must be a separate working unit (or mini-system) that works to cool or heat the air. However, the unit is unable to complete the mission without additional parts such as ducts and vents (to carry the air to the location) or temperature-control gauges (to determine the precise amount of cooled or heated air needed to complete the required task). If any of the various parts fails, the whole system fails.

The criminal justice system also demands that each element of the whole system accomplish its goals and objectives to successfully attain the required outcome—*basic fairness* to individuals accused of committing criminal violations. Balancing the constitutional rights of the accused and the need to protect citizens in communities from the illegal acts of those who choose to violate the law requires professionals dedicated to following *due process of law* (guaranteed by the Fifth and Fourteenth Amendments to the U.S. Constitution). Another word for *process* is *procedure*. Only when the criminal justice system follows the required procedures outlined in the federal and state governments' codes of criminal procedure does the required result—that is, *justice*—occur.

Law enforcement is charged with the responsibility to investigate crimes, collect evidence of criminal acts, establish probable cause regarding who committed the criminal acts, make arrests, and file criminal charges with the appropriate state attorneys. In addition, grand juries perform similar functions and work with law enforcement agencies and sheriffs to formally charge individuals with offenses. Grand juries have additional responsibilities in the process, including conducting independent investigations of criminal allegations. Grand juries can, therefore, conduct their own investigations that include gathering input from numerous resources in a community.

The court system integrates states' attorneys (municipal, county, and district), who evaluate reports of crimes submitted by law enforcement agencies, with the grand jury to ascertain probable cause and whether there is sufficient evidence to go forward with criminal proceedings. In felony and *infamous crimes* (see the Fifth Amendment to the U.S. Constitution), a grand jury may be commenced to determine if there is sufficient evidence to warrant a trial. Once the accused is formally indicted or charged by a grand jury, the case is filed in the appropriate court with jurisdiction and venue to determine guilt or acquittal. In the event that the accused waives the right to a grand jury investigation, the appropriate district attorney may file an *information* (a formal accusation of guilt that brings the case to trial) with the court with jurisdiction. The accused has the right to an attorney (the Sixth Amendment to the U.S. Constitution) at the earliest time she or he requests such assistance (*Escobedo* v. *Illinois*). In misdemeanor cases, the city or county attorneys determine whether a *complaint* (or formal accusation of guilt) will be filed to bring the case to trial without consulting a grand jury. The trial involves a judge, with or without a *petit jury* (trial jury), who hears evidence in an adversarial process to determine whether or not the accused person committed the criminal violation as alleged in the indictment, information, or complaint.

The chapters in this text examine the specific processes involved in each step of the criminal justice system to determine whether a person committed a crime to the level of proof (that is, beyond a reasonable doubt) required by law.

(1.2) The American Court System

To understand the criminal justice process, you must first understand the organization of the American court system (described in detail in Chapter 2). To begin with, which court has jurisdiction must be determined. The term *jurisdiction* means having the authority to *adjudicate* (that is, to bring a case to judgment) both the type of offense and the person charged with criminal responsibility. For example, if a person is charged with committing a violation of federal law, then she or he would be tried in federal, not state, court, providing that the federal court has authority over the individual charged. If the person has *diplomatic immunity* due to his or her status as a diplomat, or has other immunity under law, the court may not adjudicate the person even though he or she committed a federal crime; such a person may be deported back to his or her own country. If a crime is both a federal and a state offense, the federal court has original jurisdiction. State courts' jurisdiction is generally divided by various courts (county courts, justice courts, municipal courts) that have specific statutory jurisdiction over felony or misdemeanor offenses. Here again, however, the courts must have jurisdiction over the offense *and* the person. For example, the adult court would not have jurisdiction if a person suspected of a crime is a *child* as defined by state statutes; the child's case would be adjudicated in a civil trial under the juvenile justice system rather than in a state criminal court.

There are numerous Internet sites that describe U.S. courts. For example, the United States Supreme Court's website is http://www.supremecourtus.gov. A vast array of information on various courts under the federal system (circuit courts of appeal, U.S. district courts, etc.) is found at http://www.uscourts.gov. Information on a specific state court can be found by designating a specific state court. For example, the Texas court system is found at http://www.Texasonline.com or http://www.courts.state.tx.us. California courts can be accessed at http://www.courtinfo.ca.gov, and Florida courts can be found at http://www.flcourts.org. Each of the state websites contains a vast amount of information that will enrich your understanding and appreciation of the organization and structure of the American court system. In addition, students can locate various U.S. Supreme Court cases at http://laws.findlaw.com/us.

(1.3) Arrest, Search, and Seizure

Chapter 3 of this text details the appropriate actions of peace officers as they investigate criminal offenses. When a crime occurs, the officer's initial actions are to *make the scene safe* and to *protect any victims* on the scene. Acting appropriately to preserve evidence and to effectively investigate the scene is necessary in order to obtain physical and testimonial evidence that may be later introduced into a court of law.

Peace officers follow specific guidelines of federal and state codes of criminal procedure (CCP) to conduct investigations. Their investigations are evaluated by a court to confirm that they meet the court's "rules of evidence," which determines whether the evidence gathered in the investigation will be admissible in a court of law. When the facts and circumstances of the investigation lead a peace officer to believe that a specific person *probably* committed a crime, and such facts and circumstances would also convince a magistrate of this conclusion, the officer has *probable cause* to arrest in accordance with the Fourth Amendment to the U.S. Constitution. Probable cause exists when the "facts and circumstances within their (the officers') knowledge and of which they had reasonably trustworthy information (are) sufficient in themselves to warrant a man of reasonable caution in the belief that an offense has been or is being committed (by the person to be arrested)" *(Brinegar* v. *U.S.,* 338 U.S. 160 [1949]*).*

States' codes of criminal procedures outline the specific details or procedures that justify an "arrest with warrant" and specific probable cause situations when an officer may "arrest without a warrant." To obtain a warrant, an officer files an *affidavit* (a sworn statement that details the probable cause facts and circumstances) with a complaint to seek an arrest and/or search warrant from a magistrate with jurisdiction. When an arrest is made without a warrant, the probable cause will be scrutinized in either a preliminary hearing or during a grand jury review of the facts and circumstances of the arrest. To justify arrests, searches, and seizures under the U.S. and state constitutions, officers must follow specific due-process-of-law requirements outlined in the Bill of Rights, state CCP guidelines, and court case precedents (known as s*tare decisis)* that govern police procedures.

(1.4) Interrogations, Confessions, and Nontestimonial Evidence

Chapter 4 of this text reviews the guidelines and precedents involving officers' actions regarding gathering nontestimonial evidence, including conducting interrogations and obtaining confessions. The admissibility of such evidence will be determined by the officers' actions to ensure that the accused person's constitutional rights have been protected and that the accused understands such rights during the interrogation process. The accused must understand that he or she does not have to incriminate him- or herself and that anything said may be used against the accused (Fifth Amendment, U.S. Constitution); that the accused has a right to an attorney (Sixth Amendment, U.S. Constitution); and that if he or she cannot afford an attorney, the state will provide representation *(Miranda.* v. *Arizona).* Confessions must be given voluntarily without *coercion* (which is a threat, *however communicated,* by the officers conducting the interrogation).

Once arrested, an accused is entitled to an initial appearance before a magistrate without unnecessary delay, or *forthwith*. State codes of criminal procedures define the specific time periods governing this appearance. Generally, if the person is arrested at a time when the court is in session, the initial appearance is required before any interrogation can be conducted by the arresting officers. If the court is not in session, then the accused is entitled to such an appearance the next day that the court is in session. The appearance may be made in person or by means of interactive television between the court and the jail where the person is in custody.

The initial appearance before the magistrate is the first time during the accused's contact with the criminal justice system that he or she *must* be informed of his or her constitutional rights. Generally, the accused is positively identified (to ensure that the correct person has been arrested), he or she is provided the warning defined by the code of criminal procedure (*Miranda* warning*)*, and bail is set if the offense warrants bail. The accused person may also request that an attorney be provided if she or he is indigent or cannot afford an attorney. If a person fails to meet bail or bond, he or she is committed to jail pending the next steps in the process. This proceeding is generally limited to these administrative actions and does not deal with any other issues of probable cause, pretrial procedures, or trial issues.

(1.5) Pretrial Procedures, Discovery, and Privileged Communications

Chapter 5 overviews issues of pretrial procedures, and Chapter 6 looks at the process of discovery and privileged communications. Whether or not a person chooses a preliminary hearing is a strategy decision of the defense. This action generally occurs when an individual was arrested without a warrant. Because the judiciary did not review the officer's probable cause to arrest prior to the arrest, the preliminary hearing is conducted as a "probable cause hearing" to determine whether the officer's facts and circumstances warranted an arrest. In such a hearing, the accused is normally represented by a defense attorney who cross-examines the state's evidence and calls witnesses to support the case for the accused. Note that the hearing does not deal with the question of the guilt or nonguilt of the accused, but is held to determine only if there was justification for the arrest. If the defense is successful in challenging the probable cause to arrest, the defendant is released from custody. If the state is successful in presenting a valid probable cause case, the defendant is bound over for trial.

In the event that the defense decides to waive the preliminary hearing, the case proceeds to the next step in the process, which is defined by the type of offense alleged to have been committed.

a. Felonies and Other Infamous Crimes

The Fifth Amendment to the U.S. Constitution guarantees an accused person the right to a grand jury. A defendant may choose to have a grand jury determine whether the state has sufficient evidence to proceed to trial. One difference between the grand jury proceeding and the preliminary hearing is that the defense attorney is not permitted to be inside the grand jury room during its proceedings. During the grand jury proceedings, the state's attorney presents the state's case and calls witnesses to testify under oath regarding their knowledge of facts and circumstances. The grand jury is not obligated to follow the general "rules of evidence" and may listen to hearsay and other evidence that might not be admissible in a trial. A defendant can be called to testify before a grand jury but is not obligated to answer any questions that might incriminate him or her (Fifth Amendment to the U.S. Constitution). In such a circumstance, a defendant is generally entitled to visit with counsel outside of the grand jury room before answering any questions and return to the room (without counsel) to resume proceedings. Refusal by the defendant to answer questions that might incriminate him or her cannot be used as a presumption of his or her guilt.

Each state's CCP statutorily defines which courts have jurisdiction over felonies and other offenses considered to be "infamous crimes." In Texas, for example, the district court has original jurisdiction over all felony offenses and the offense of "official misconduct," which is a Class A misdemeanor offense. The grand jury is convened by the district court (in some states this may be called a "superior court"). The grand jury is made up of a jury of citizens from the county in which the offense occurred or that has *venue* (the location of the court having jurisdiction) in the case. Members of the grand jury hear evidence from witnesses and investigate allegations of criminal activity. If the grand jury determines that there is insufficient evidence to proceed to trial, the grand jury issues a *no bill,* and the defendant is released from custody. If the grand jury determines that sufficient evidence exists to formally accuse the defendant, an *indictment* (also called a *true bill*) is issued and signed by the foreperson of the grand jury.

In some cases, the defendant has the right to waive his or her right to a grand jury proceeding and go straight to trial. In this case, the state's attorney issues an *information,* which is a formal accusation of guilt that brings the case to trial. This choice is frequently used when a defendant seeks a speedy trial and does not desire the delay that a grand jury proceeding would necessitate.

b. Misdemeanor Offenses

Most misdemeanors do not go before a grand jury for review. The state's attorney reviews the evidence presented by a peace officer and issues a complaint or other legal document that formally accuses the person of an offense against the law. This document serves to formally bring the case to trial in the same manner that an indictment or an information does in the felony trial. In Texas, for example, the county court (or county court-at-law) generally has jurisdiction over Class A and Class B misdemeanors. Justice and municipal courts have jurisdiction over Class C (or "petty") misdemeanors. Students should understand the jurisdiction of courts in their individual states.

c. Arraignment

The arraignment is the step in the criminal justice process that permits the accused an opportunity to hear and understand the formal charges and enter a plea. The defendant enters a plea of "not guilty" if he or she does not accept culpability for the offense charged and decides to place the burden of proof on the state to prove guilt. A plea of guilty, if accepted by the court, will cause the court to move into the sentencing phase of the criminal justice system. A plea of *nolo contendere* ("no contest") means that the defendant accepts ceremonial, but not civil, responsibility for the offense charged; this plea is treated as a guilty plea for criminal court purposes.

d. Pretrial Motions

The court of original jurisdictions frequently conducts hearings to consider various pretrial motions from both the state and the defense attorneys. These hearings include motions for *discovery,* which permits each side to review evidence that may be used at trial. This procedure allows both state and defense attorneys an opportunity to look for alternative evidence that either corroborates or challenges the evidence to be presented in court. In the interest of justice, such actions ensure that a trial will proceed smoothly and without challenges that would slow down the trial.

In addition, motions may be considered to challenge evidence that might be presented at trial. A motion to suppress evidence arises because the evidence was obtained in violation of the Fourth Amendment rules that govern reasonable searches and seizures. This motion generally alleges that officers conducted an illegal search and seizure or that evidence does not meet one of the tests of admissibility (relevant, material, competent) under the rules of evidence. Other motions might be to ascertain the sanity of an accused through an examination by medical experts. Each of these motions is designed to prevent surprises during the trial and to ensure that it will proceed efficiently.

(1.6) Prosecution and Defense

Chapter 7 provides an overview of the specific roles of the prosecution and the defense in the criminal justice system. While considered adversaries, the prosecution and defense are vital components of a system designed to ensure justice. The prosecution must prove each element of the state's case beyond a reasonable doubt. The defense seeks to raise a reasonable doubt about the state's evidence and bring witnesses to testify on behalf of the defendant.

(1.7) The Trial, Rules of Evidence, Examination of Witnesses (including Courtroom Demeanor and Testimony), and Other Proceedings Before the Court

The fact that a person is *guilty* (or is in jeopardy of "loss of innocence") or *not guilty* is determined through presentation of evidence at the trial. States' CCPs govern the processes that will be followed to arrive at a reasonable conclusion. These processes are divided into various chapters to concentrate attention on specific areas of the trial process. Chapter 8 of this text reviews the trial process, including how a petit jury (trial jury) is seated, and the order of procedures, including the manner of presentation of the case, is also covered. Chapter 10 looks at questions, answers, impeachment, and cross-examination of witnesses. This chapter also reviews a witness's courtroom demeanor and testimony. Chapter 11 considers the rules of evidence regarding various articles and exhibits of evident. Finally, Chapter 12 is a review of "opinion evidence," and Chapter 13 is a comprehensive study of "hearsay evidence."

(1.8) The Jury Process and Verdict

The jury process and verdict is one of the most unique elements of the U.S. system of justice. Countless novels and nonfiction accounts focus on the specific processes involved in finding verdicts. At least one cable network, *Court TV,* devotes its programming to involve the public in courtroom trials, and commentators seek to "read the jury's mind" to guess what verdict a jury will eventually reach. Following a verdict, the same commentators do in-depth inquiries to understand how the jury deliberations proceeded and what factors the jury used in forming its verdict. *Court TV's* website (www.courrtv.com; see also www.crimelibrary.com) recaps many interesting cases and provides in-depth analysis of recent trials. Chapter 14 overviews the jury process and looks at jury verdicts in a clinical sense.

(1.9) Sentencing

A criminal trial is a bifurcated, or two-part, process. The first part determines the facts of the case presented to a jury (or judge if no jury is present) that decides on the guilt or nonguilt of the accused. When the defendant is found guilty of the charges, the second part of the trial begins—sentencing. During this phase, the judge or jury determines what degree of punishment provides justice or "basic fairness." In making such decisions, the court can ask for various studies and reports about the defendant's background, prior criminal record (if any), and mitigating factors (if any), and it can require penalties that range from fines to death, depending on the specific law related to the criminal offense and the judgment of the court.

(1.10) Appeals Before the U.S. Supreme Court

Chapter 16, the new chapter in this edition, explores the process of *writs of certiorari* and the protocol for appeals to the U.S. Supreme Court. A detailed outline explains the processes attorneys must follow in planning the argument in front of the Supreme Court. They include: timelines for the appeal, filings, and submissions of documents; processes for the day of oral argument; various protocol issues; and general information relative to the physical location and facilities relative to the U.S. Supreme Court. Individuals who may one day become attorneys for petitioners and other entities, including *amicus curiae* attorneys, may find this information revealing and informative.

(1.11) United States Supreme Court Cases

Numerous websites are available for case law research, and U. S. Supreme Court cases can be accessed via the Internet. The following is a brief list of some of these websites.

•www.laws.findlaw.com
•www.lawlibrary.state.mn.us
•www.fbi.gov/publicationshtm

Discussion Questions

1. Using an Internet-connected computer, open *www.crimelibrary.com* and review cases from one or more of the following categories: Serial Killers, Gangsters & Outlaws; Notorious Murder Cases; The Criminal Mind, Premium Content; or Terrorists, Spies & Assassins. Form discussion groups to review the facts of various features in the news.
2. Draw a diagram that depicts the criminal justice process from arrest to sentencing; include all the steps for the felony and misdemeanor processes.

2

The American Court System

No man is above the law and no man is below it; nor do
we ask any man's permission when we require him to
obey it.

—Theodore Roosevelt
Speech, December 7, 1903

No other judicial system in the Western world is as complex as
the court system in the United States. Part of our courts' complexity
in structure and function can be attributed to the fact that the nation's
founders established a federal form of government with powers constitutionally divided between two levels of authority. This is the over-
riding feature of the American system. Because two distinct sets of
laws exist—those of the national government and those of the individual states—some arrangement was necessary to handle cases arising
from such a system. The solution to this dilemma was to establish a
dual court structure, each with its own trial and appellate courts, a
unique characteristic of the American system. Additionally, each of
the fifty states has its own court organization, personnel, and procedural rules. Constitutionally, the federal and state court systems are
autonomous and equal in their particular provinces.

Article III, Section 1, of the United States Constitution provides
that the "judicial power of the United States shall be vested in one
Supreme Court, and in such inferior courts as the Congress may from
time to time ordain and establish." Thus, the Supreme Court is the
only court specifically established by the Constitution, with other
federal courts being products of legislation.

The federal court system is a hierarchy. The United States district courts stand as the base, with federal appellate courts in the middle, and the Supreme Court at the top. United States magistrates and a variety of specialized courts are part of the federal judicial system. Among these specialized courts are the U.S. Court of Military Appeals, the U.S. Court of Claims, and the U.S. Customs Court.

(2.1) The Supreme Court

The United States Supreme Court is comprised of nine justices. They are appointed by the President, subject to approval of the Senate. One member of the Court is appointed to serve as the chief justice, also subject to Senate confirmation. The chief justice, as chairman of the Court, has no formal coercive powers over the associate justices; however, he or she presides over the Court's public sessions, assigns caseloads, directs the writing of judicial decisions, and has supervisory authority over the nation's courts.

Supreme Court justices hold their office "during good behavior," as provided by the Constitution, and can be removed only by voluntary retirement or impeachment. The Constitution even prohibits the Congress from reducing the salaries of the justices. The term of the Court varies; however, statutory law mandates that it begin on the first Monday of October each year. Because no closing date is fixed, the Court continues in session as long as it has business to conduct.

Over the years, the Court's work load has steadily increased with the expansion of the federal and state judiciaries. The principal way in which cases reach the Supreme Court is through the *writ of certiorari*, an order directed to the lower court whose decision is being disputed to send up the records of the case so that the Supreme Court can ascertain if the law has been appropriately applied. Although the Court gets most of its cases on appeal from these courts, the number of justices has not been correspondingly increased to deal with the expanding caseload, which has now reached over three thousand cases annually.

As specified in the Constitution, the Supreme Court is the court of original jurisdiction in cases involving diplomatic officials of foreign nations and in controversies to which a state is a party. Nearly all cases the Court hears under its powers of original jurisdiction involve disputes between states or between a state and the national government.

By far, the greatest amount of the Court's business comes within its appellate jurisdiction. It reviews cases from lower federal courts and state courts when the issues involved pertain to the Constitution or to federal law.

The Court does not have to hear a case unless it wants to. In fact, it has almost absolute power to control its docket, thus allowing it to be highly selective in the cases it reviews and to assume jurisdiction only in those cases that present an issue it wishes to consider. This discretionary power of the Court to decide which cases it will consider allows it to regulate its work load. Over half the cases that reach the Court come from disappointed litigants in the U.S. Courts of Appeals, with most of the remainder coming from the losing parties in state courts of last resort. If the Court accepts jurisdiction in an appeal, it will carefully examine the constitutional question at issue and either sustain the state court's ruling or overrule the decision and release the appellant.

In deciding which cases it will hear, the Court employs the *rule of four*; that is, four of the justices must vote to hear a case before it is placed on the agenda. The Court hears only a small percentage of the requests for appeals. A set of prerequisites has evolved that must first be met before a writ is granted. First, the litigant must have exhausted all other avenues of appeal. Second, the legal issue must involve "a substantial federal question" as defined by the particular court. Thus, state appeals courts' interpretations of state law can be appealed to the U.S. Supreme Court only if there is an alleged violation of either federal law or the U.S. Constitution.

Due in large measure to careful screening by the Court for cases that involve specific issues it wishes to address, the Court reverses rulings in about 60 percent of the cases it hears.

(2.2) The U.S. Courts of Appeals

The United States Courts of Appeals are the intermediate appellate courts below the Supreme Court of the United States. They were created in 1891 to relieve the high court of considering all appeals in the cases originally tried in the federal trial courts. These courts are empowered to review all final decisions and certain interim decisions of the district courts within their circuit except in those very few cases where the law provides direct review by the Supreme Court. They also stand between the U.S. magistrates and the specialized federal courts and the Supreme Court. They have principal responsibility for reviewing judicial decisions in the lower courts.

Thirteen U.S. Courts of Appeals, including one for the District of Columbia, have jurisdiction over a specific geographical area of the country called a judicial circuit (see Figure 2.1). The number of judges in each court, which varies with the size and population of the area served, ranges from three to fifteen. Decisions are generally made by a three-judge panel, and a minimum of two must sit in each case. Group composition varies from case to case, with the presiding judge in each court making assignments. Occasionally, disagreements on some important point of law may arise among the judges. When this happens, the issue may be resolved by the entire court in an *en banc* decision. The tenure of judges of the U.S. Courts of Appeals, like Supreme Court justices, is during life and good behavior.

(2.3) The United States District Courts

There are ninety-four U.S. District Courts, with eighty-nine in the fifty states and one each in the District of Columbia, Guam, Puerto Rico, and the Virgin Islands (see Figure 2-2). Until 1979, when its sovereignty was turned back to the government of Panama, a U.S. District Court served the Canal Zone. The federal district courts are courts of original jurisdiction. They hear the majority of civil lawsuits arising under federal law, such as postal difficulties, copyright violations, patent rights, and bankruptcy. They are also the trial courts for crimes committed against the federal government (that is, those offenses defined by federal statute and made punishable by the federal government). Each state has at least one U.S. District Court, some with several divisions. Sixteen states have two courts, eight have three, and New York and Texas have four each. Every district court has at least one judge, and some districts have as many as twenty-four, depending on the work load. Trials held in these courts are heard by one judge except in cases involving the constitutionality of federal or state laws. In such cases, three judges must preside at the trial.

(2.4) State and Local Courts

The vast majority of cases are processed by the state courts. The courts in one medium-sized state handle more cases than the entire

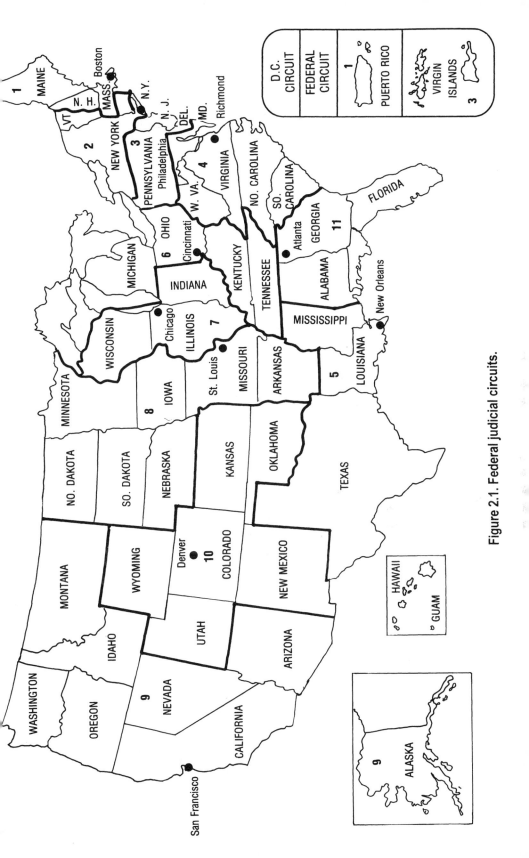

Figure 2.1. Federal judicial circuits.

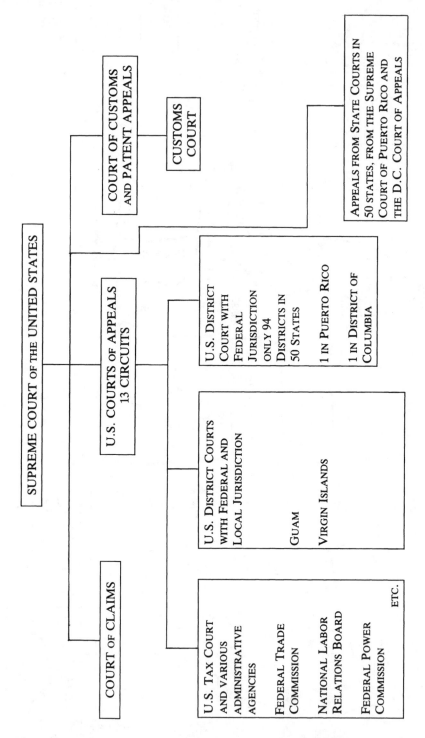

Figure 2.2. The United States court system.

federal system. No generalizations can be made about the jurisdictions, functions, and titles of state and local courts. The structure in any given state may include two, three, four, or more levels of courts. To complicate matters, many local courts have overlapping jurisdiction. In examining the vast array of state courts, it is useful to divide them into four levels: trial courts of limited jurisdiction, trial courts of general jurisdiction, intermediate appellate courts, and courts of last resort.

a. Courts of Limited Jurisdiction

At the bottom of the hierarchy are the courts of limited jurisdiction. These minor courts, numbering more than thirteen thousand, are called by such titles as municipal courts, police courts, justice of the peace courts, magistrate's courts, and small claims courts. Although they have a wide range of duties and responsibilities, all but a few of them are not courts of record. Consequently, appeals from these courts usually amount to a completely new trial before the next level in the state system. For example, appeals from justice of the peace and municipal courts in the state of Texas are *trial de novo* in the county court. Jurisdiction in these lesser courts is limited to minor offenses, usually those punishable by fines or by jail time of less than one year. Such offenses as disorderly conduct, traffic violations, and civil suits involving small amounts of money are heard in these courts.

In some states, magistrates and justices of the peace hold preliminary hearings in criminal cases to determine whether accused persons should be bound over for trial in higher courts.

b. Courts of General Jurisdiction

Trial courts, also referred to as courts of general jurisdiction, are those that have original jurisdiction in most criminal cases. They are the lowest courts of record at the state level and are called district, circuit, superior, or courts of common pleas. These courts are structured differently from state to state, with some providing for separate civil and criminal divisions, a few with equity divisions, and still others with special probate and domestic relations courts. These trial courts handle the vast majority of felony grade criminal trials, and all significant civil suits originate in them. In many states, they also serve as appellate courts for cases originally heard in courts of limited jurisdiction. However, such appeals are tried as though they had not previously been heard, and further appeals generally rest with a higher tribunal.

c. Intermediate Appellate Courts

Twenty of the most populous states have intermediate appellate courts corresponding generally to the U.S. Courts of Appeals. Like the federal system, these intermediate courts serve as courts of last resort for the majority of appeals coming from the state trial courts. In this way, they are able to relieve the overburdened state supreme courts.

Known by such various titles as appellate courts, superior courts, and supreme courts, in some states, courts of appeals may have both original and appellate authority. In others, jurisdiction is limited to special kinds of cases. In some states, the defendant is assigned the right of appeal regardless of whether or not the court wants to hear the case. Following a criminal conviction, the defendant may appeal the trial court's decision. The process of appeal is fragmented and cumbersome; however, a basic procedure may be applied to most jurisdictions.

First, there must be a finding of guilt by some court at the municipal, county, state, or federal level. The procedure for appeal in each case is determined by the court of record. In most cases, the defendant initiates the appeal because states are highly restricted in their efforts to appeal decisions. The result of an appeal, appropriately introduced, is a postponement of the carrying out of the original sentence until the appeal is heard and decided. Immediately following the trial court's sentence, the defense attorney must either file a motion for a new trial or make an appeal based on some legal question. Frivolous appeals are usually quickly recognized and readily disposed of by appellate courts.

In many cases a convicted defendant is allowed out on bail pending his appeal, and that automatically delays the sentence. Defendants unable to make bail must begin their sentences regardless of the pending appeal. Defendants often abuse the appellate process by filing repeatedly for appeal or by using other legal moves, which sometimes puts off the original sentence for years. The death penalty, as now constituted in this country, can be delayed almost indefinitely by making repeated appeals to both federal and state courts.

In most state court systems, a court of appeal reviews the trial court decision for judicial error. Facts of a case are not questioned, and the appellate court is bound by the trial court's decisions concerning them. The appeal is considered on the basis of the trial record, and evidence is not presented to the court of appeals. An appellate court has no authority to overturn the factual findings of the trial court unless the facts are entirely false or inaccurate. In states having a second level of review, both the trial court's record and the intermediate court's ruling are scrutinized. Generally, refusing to consider an appeal from a lower appellate court's ruling amounts to concurring with the decision. The process terminates at this point unless the appellant is able to produce some constitutional ground upon which to file a separate appeal in federal court.

d. Courts of Last Resort

At the apex of a state's court system stands the court of ultimate review. In some states, it is called the court of appeals, the supreme judicial court, or the supreme court of appeals. In most states, however, it is known as the supreme court. Regardless of its name, the court of last resort has ultimate jurisdiction over controversies involving the interpretation of the state constitution or state statutes.

The relationship of the state court of last resort to the lower state courts is basically the same as that of the United States Supreme Court to the lower federal courts (see Figure 2.3). As the ultimate tribunal of the sovereign states, these high courts exercise broad discretion in selecting the cases they will review. For this purpose, the state's high court, in much the same way as the U.S. Supreme Court, uses a *writ of certiorari*, a writ of review ordering a lower court to "send up the record" of a specific case for review.

(2.5) Summary

Courts are organized on a separate basis, with each state and the federal government having its own system. Trial courts function on two levels: one for minor offenses, the other for felonies. More than twenty thousand judges preside over misdemeanor courts, many serving part-time, some having no legal training. These courts, many of which are poorly funded and staffed, are often targets of criticism.

Each court system has two higher levels of appellate courts, the

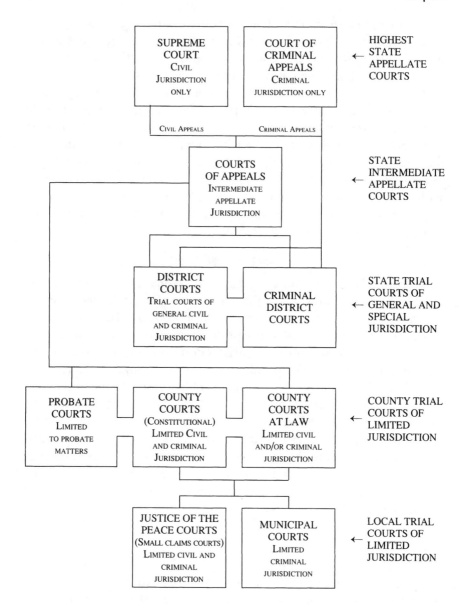

Figure 2.3. Texas court structure and jurisdiction.

highest usually being called the supreme court. As a further complication, the federal courts have the power to overturn state decisions.

Limits on every court's jurisdiction add further problems. Local court jurisdiction extends only to the boundaries of its area. State courts have no power beyond state lines. Federal and state jurisdictions sometimes overlap. Division and procedural delay are two of the system's greatest problems.

Discussion Questions

1. Discuss the concept of a dual court system.
2. What is the term of office of a U. S. Supreme Court Justice?
3. Discuss *writ of certiorari*.
4. Which courts are included in the category of courts of limited jurisdiction.
5. How many justices serve on the U. S. Supreme Court?

3

Arrests, Searches, and Seizures

No man is justified in doing evil on the grounds
of expediency.

—Theodore Roosevelt
Speech, December 7, 1903

(3.1) Detention in General

A detention is not an arrest and is a lesser intrusion on an individual's rights. It is a temporary curtailment of personal freedoms and is justified for limited purposes. The most common form of temporary detentions are those associated with "stop-and-frisk" practices.

For many years conscientious police officers have stopped suspicious individuals to ask them questions about their conduct. These stops are frequently accompanied by frisks, a limited form of searching the person's outer clothing. In 1968 the Supreme Court, in an eight-to-one decision, upheld the right of police officers to detain suspicious individuals temporarily and to frisk those who appear to be dangerous. The landmark case was *Terry* v. *Ohio*, 392 U.S. 1 (1968).

Terry was one of three men who was pacing back and forth in front of a jewelry store in downtown Cleveland. Police Detective McFadden, who was highly experienced in foot patrol surveillances, believed they were casing the store in contemplation of an armed robbery. He confronted the men and asked them their names, but their reply was not understandable. He grabbed Terry, turned him around, patted his overcoat, and removed a pistol he found there. A companion had a bulge in his coat that also turned out to be a weapon. Terry was convicted of carrying a concealed weapon, and he appealed.

The question was whether McFadden had probable cause to believe Terry was armed. The Supreme Court agreed with Terry that McFadden's actions constituted a "search." In justifying a temporary detention and pat-down, a lesser standard of proof is required for a determination of probable cause. The Supreme Court enunciated for the first time the existence of a sliding scale: the greater (or lesser) the physical intrusion, the greater (or lesser) the amount of proof necessary to sustain police action under the Fourth Amendment.

The Supreme Court clearly acknowledged the duty of police officers to investigate suspicious conduct and to attempt to question persons acting in a peculiar fashion. Once a legitimate detention is made, an officer may have the right, on the basis of the particular circumstances, to pat down a suspect for a weapon. The court, with Justice Douglas dissenting, felt it could not "blind" itself to the increasing dangers to police officers from armed assault. Weapons confiscated during a properly conducted stop and frisk would, therefore, be admissible in evidence against the accused.

(3.2) Evidentiary Facts Justifying Stops

Police officers have a sworn duty to investigate crimes that have been committed, to investigate crimes that are in the process of being committed, and to prevent crimes that are about to be committed. The *Terry* case involved a crime that was about to take place—a robbery. Though an officer has probable cause to believe a crime is about to take place, if no offense has occurred he cannot arrest anyone at this stage. Nevertheless, as a peace officer, he must use whatever constitutional powers he has to prevent the forthcoming occurrence. This is the power of temporary detention and questioning.

A police officer does not have to have reasonable suspicion or probable cause when his or her encounter with a citizen is consensual. (*Florida* v. *Bostick*, 501 U.S. 429, 1991). The courts have held that mere questioning by police is insufficient to establish coercion on the part of the officers. The courts consider whether the words or conduct used by an officer would lead a reasonably objective innocent person to believe that he or she is not free to leave, refuse the officer, or otherwise terminate the encounter.

To justify a valid stop, an officer need only show that he suspected an individual of criminal conduct and that his suspicion was reasonable. These are two separate criteria, one subjective and the other objective. The *subjective* test is the officer's belief, in good faith, that the suspect is involved in criminal activity: past, present, or future. The *objective* test is that the officer's belief, which is based on commonly accepted standards of conduct, was reasonable under all the circumstances. Many factors alone, or in conjunction with other factors, will satisfy the objective test. Some of them are listed below.

1. Does the suspect resemble a person who is wanted for a past offense?

2. Does the officer know the suspect, and does the latter have a record or reputation for criminal conduct?

3. Is the suspect behaving peculiarly, under all of the circumstances? Is he running, sneaking down an alley, hiding in bushes, or carrying a flashlight and bag?

4. Did the suspect attempt to conceal himself or to avoid contact with the officer when the latter came into view? Is he trying to conceal or discard something?

5. Is the suspect's clothing unusual? Examples would include denims in the parking lot used by opera patrons or a deliveryman with neither merchandise nor a delivery truck. The combination of neighborhood, sex, race, and age of the person might provide sufficient reason to justify a stop.

6. Is the suspect in a peculiar place, such as on the roof, near the delivery entrance of a store at an unusual hour, or under a car in a parking lot?

It is impossible to give a comprehensive list of such factors since circumstances alone will justify or excuse "suspicious" activity. The Supreme Court made clear, however, that in determining the objective test of reasonableness an officer's training and experience may enter into the record. Thus, it is not relevant if a judge, defense lawyer, or ordinary citizen thinks a suspect's behavior is or is not peculiar. An officer, such as McFadden who had thirty-nine years of experience, may draw on his specialized knowledge of criminal behavior in deciding whether to stop and question a person. The court must respect an officer's training and experience, but the burden remains with the prosecution to elicit this information. An example follows.

In justifying a stop and frisk, Officer Jones testifies that the suspect looked "suspicious." He explains that he has patrolled the particular neighborhood—an upper-class, white, residential area—for three years. While many residents employ members of minority groups as maids, gardeners, or handymen, none of them live in their employers' homes, and, to the officer's knowledge, none work at night except as butlers and cooks. The suspect is black. He was dressed in a leather jacket, motorcycle boots, and jeans. Officer Jones states that in three years he has never seen a black man walking the streets at this time of night, dressed in this manner. In all likelihood, an appellate court would rule that the officer's subjective belief of suspicion was reasonable. And while the race and clothing of the suspect might not seem peculiar to the average citizen, Officer Jones's three years of experience in patrolling the neighborhood must be taken into account in justification of his actions in stopping and frisking the suspect.

(3.3) Evidentiary Facts Justifying Frisks

The power to stop is not the power to frisk. Each activity must be justified on separate and distinct bases. To be specific, officers must reasonably suspect that the person they are dealing with is armed and dangerous in order to frisk him. The Supreme Court made clear that an officer "need not *be* absolutely certain that the individual is armed" because his suspicion is enough, if his suspicion is reasonable. Again, it is a two-fold test of subjective and objective belief. Not certainty, not probable cause, but reasonable suspicion is the critical test.

The suspected danger need not be imminent. It can be a future danger (after the officer leaves the scene). It can be a danger to others—potential victims of violence. As the court said, the power to frisk is justified upon the need to protect the safety of officers "or that of others." For example, four armed officers might approach a suspicious person with their guns drawn. The fact that there are four officers and a single suspect is not the test. If the officers depart without frisking the suspect, he would be free to accost unarmed citizens.

Thus, at a suppression hearing, cross-examination of officers as to their "degree" of apprehension is simply not relevant to the proof at issue. An officer is not required to testify that he was "afraid" or that the defendant posed an actual or imminent threat to him. It is sufficient for the officer to express a belief that he suspected the defendant of being armed and to articulate sufficient facts to indicate that his belief was reasonable under the circumstances.

Below are some of the factors that would be relevant in determining whether a frisk is appropriate.

1. Is the suspected offense one that is associated with weapons?

2. Does the suspect have a reputation for violence or use of weapons?

3. Does the suspect have adequate identification? Does he present a plausible explanation for his whereabouts and actions?

4. Is the suspect overly "nervous" or overly nonchalant about the confrontation?

5. Is there a noticeable bulge in his clothing?

6. If the suspect is in a vehicle, does he make any "furtive" movements prior to the stop?

Valid stop-and-frisk procedures are not, of course, restricted to pedestrians. Suspicious persons are often encountered in automobiles. A gun is just as dangerous when hidden under the seat, in an unlocked glove compartment, above a visor, or under papers on the seat as when it is in the suspect's pocket. An officer who has the right to conduct a pat-down of the suspect's clothing may also check these areas in the vehicle for a secreted weapon. The frisk normally cannot be extended to a locked glove compartment or a trunk. It would make no difference if the suspect jumped out of his car just prior to the encounter. An officer would still have the right to make a preliminary check of the vehicle for weapons. If this were not so, the suspect could get back into the car, and the law would be frustrated.

There has been much discussion over what is an acceptable pat-down. The frisk is usually restricted to outer clothing. But, in winter, when heavy overgarments are worn, an officer may not be able to detect a bulge, and the coat may have to be unbuttoned to frisk sweaters or work clothing worn underneath. In the absence of secretive movements, an officer may not reach into a suspect's pockets without first feeling a bulge. If it appears that the suspect is stashing a gun when he sees the officer, the gun should, of course, be immediately retrieved. Nothing in the Fourth Amendment requires an officer to jeopardize his safety while performing a ritualistic ceremony, if it can be assumed there is adequate reason to believe the suspect is armed. As an example, a citizen approached Officer Connolly in a high-crime area and told him that Williams, who was seated in an auto, was carrying a firearm. Connolly knew the citizen, and the citizen knew the suspect. Connolly walked over to Williams's car and asked him to open the door. Instead, Williams rolled down the window. Connolly immediately reached through the window and pulled a loaded revolver from Williams's waistband. The Supreme Court affirmed the legality of the immediate frisk in a six-to-three decision *(Adams* v. *Williams,* 407 U.S. 143 [1972]).

In the above case, it would have been dangerous for Connolly to interrogate Williams, forcibly pull him from the car, conduct a pat-down, then remove the weapon. It is clear that, under certain circumstances, the stop and frisk may be coterminous. In unusual cases the officer may have enough information—coupled with the suspect's conduct—to justify a frisk without any formalities.

Two presidential assassination attempts by women in 1975 should make it clear that females are not exempt from stop-and-frisk procedures. In addition to an examination of their outer clothing, their handbags may be squeezed and opened if they are firm. Discretion should, of course, be used in pat-down procedures executed by male officers.

Stop-and-frisk procedures cannot be used to prevent the destruction of evidence or to escalate a minimum number of facts into a situation of probable cause. The crinkle of cellophane in the pockets of a known narcotics peddler is a prime example.

In every case where the frisk results in an arrest, the officer must be prepared to document his activity step by step in his report. The report should include why he stopped the suspect, why he frisked him, and why he reached into his clothing or pockets. These progressive steps must be elicited one by one by the prosecutor during the suppression hearing. If this is not meticulously done, the court will conclude that the search was illegal.

There should be no mistake about it. The stop-and-frisk procedure constitutes a search and is judged by the Fourth Amendment. The standard is, however, less rigid. It is reasonable suspicion, as opposed to probable cause.

There is nothing consensual about stop-and-frisk procedures. It should be remembered that the suspect is not under arrest, but the power to detain him is, nevertheless, a fact of law. Reasonable force, but never deadly force, may be used to detain and frisk a suspect. Suspicious persons cannot be compelled to answer questions, and, unless a statute or ordinance provides otherwise, they are not legally compelled to produce identification. California, for example, has a provision in its penal code requiring that identification be produced, on demand of police officers, when the citizen is encountered under suspicious circumstances.

Courts scrutinize this type of situation very closely. In *Brown* v. *Texas,* 443 U.S. 47 (1979), police stopped two men in an El Paso alley in the afternoon in a high-crime area. One of the men, Brown, refused to identify himself. He was arrested and convicted under a Texas law that made it a crime not to identify yourself to a police officer "who has lawfully. . .stopped and requested the information." The Supreme Court reversed his conviction saying that a stop is a "seizure" of one's person and while not requiring "probable cause," it does require "reasonable suspicion." The court said that simply being in a high-crime area did not give rise to reasonable suspicion. The stop being illegal, Brown could not be punished for refusing to identify himself.

The unprovoked flight of a citizen upon seeing a police officer, while in a high crime area, is sufficient to establish reasonable suspicion to make an investigatory stop (*Illinois* v. *Wardlow*, 528 U.S. 119; 2000). Officers must be able to articulate factors, beyond mere flight, in order to justify the stop. In the case cited, the court found articulation of "high crime" area sufficient to meet the statement of facts required for the stop. In a footnote to this case, the court asserted that it was not deciding whether a frisk would be justified under these circumstances. The officer would still need to articulate facts that would justify a frisk for weapons based on "fear" that the suspect possessed a weapon. In addition, an anonymous tip is insufficient to establish the requisite reasonable suspicion to support a valid frisk.

In *Florida* v. *J.L.*, (529 U.S. 266 [2000]) the court held that where a tip is such that any passerby could pass along the information that fails to predict future conduct of the suspect being informed upon, the anonymous tip is not sufficient reason for an officer to conduct a frisk. Again, an officer must articulate the specific facts that led him or her to believe the suspect had a weapon that could be used against an officer at that time to build "reasonable suspicion."

In *Ybarra* v. *Illinois* (444U.S. 85 [1979]), the court held that an officer may not frisk patrons of a commercial establishment where officers are executing a search warrant unless each individual officer has reasonable suspicion to believe that the person to be frisked is armed and poses a danger to officers.

A recent Supreme Court decision (argued December 9, 2008, and decided January 26, 2009) found that an Arizona officer's pat down of a defendant did not violate the Fourth Amendment's prohibition on unreasonable searches and seizure. While patrolling near a Tucson neighborhood associated with the Crips gang, police officers serving on Arizona's gang task force stopped an automobile for a vehicular infraction warranting a citation. At the time of the stop, the officers had no reason to suspect the car's occupants of criminal activity. Officer Trevizo attended to respondent Johnson, the back-seat passenger, whose behavior and clothing caused Trevizo to question him. After learning that Johnson was from a town with a Crips gang and had been in prison, Trevizo asked him to get out of the car in order to question him further, out of the hearing of the front-seat passenger, about his gang affiliation. Because Trevizo suspected that Johnson was armed, she patted him down for safety when he exited the car. During the pat down, she felt the butt of a handgun. At that point, Johnson began to struggle, and Trevizo handcuffed him. Johnson was charged with, *inter alia*, possession of a weapon by a prohibited possessor.

The trial court denied his motion to suppress the evidence, concluding that the stop was lawful and that Trevizo had cause to suspect that Johnson was armed and dangerous. Johnson was convicted; the Arizona Court of Appeals reversed. While recognizing that Johnson was lawfully seized, the Court found that, prior to the frisk, the detention had evolved into a consensual conversation about his gang affiliation. Trevizo, the court therefore concluded, had no right to pat Johnson down even if she had reason to suspect that he was armed and dangerous. The Arizona Supreme Court denied review. Upon appeal to the U. S. Supreme Court, Trevizo's actions were upheld as a lawful "stop and frisk." The Supreme Court relied on both *Terry* v. *Ohio* as well as *Brendlin* v. *California* (551 U.S. 249, 255 [2007]), in which the court recently confirmed that a police officer effectively seizes "everyone in the vehicle," that is, the driver and all passengers (*Arizona* v. *Johnson*, 555 U.S ____ [2009]).

(3.4) Collateral Evidence Found

Although the stop-and-frisk procedure is justified on the basis of the need to protect investigating officers and others from assaults with weapons, anything found in a *properly conducted* frisk is admissible as evidence against the accused. Many suppression hearings based on frisks do not involve weapons; narcotics are often located by this procedure. The scope of the frisk determines whether narcotics will be admissible. If the frisk was restricted to a pat-down for hard objects, and the object turns out to be narcotics or paraphernalia, the confiscation will, in all likelihood, be upheld. Tightly wrapped tinfoil packets and hypodermic needles may feel like a switchblade knife, which is, of course, a concealed weapon. Glassine or cellophane packets would, on the other hand, crinkle and not feel like a gun or knife; it is likely that these items would be suppressed.

(3.5) Elements of an Arrest

A person is arrested when he is taken into custody for the purpose of answering to a court. In criminal cases, arrests can be made with or without an arrest warrant. In civil cases, the warrant is always used. There are a number of views concerning arrest. One holds that a person is "arrested" whenever his freedom is significantly curtailed in some manner. The rationale for this view is that the act of arrest is part of an "imprisonment." Imprisonments, of course, can result from natural as well as human causes and may be accidentally, negligently, or intentionally caused. A person who is kidnapped, for example, has been wrongfully imprisoned, but not falsely arrested.

It is generally agreed that there are four elements to every arrest: authority, intent, custody, and knowledge. The first assumes that the "officer" must be acting under real or assumed authority. There must be either a right to make the arrest or a claim of right on the part of the officer or the person acting in place of the officer. It may be that the person making the arrest has not qualified as a peace officer, that the warrant he holds is defective on its face, or that the law being enforced has been repealed or held unconstitutional. In each of these instances there has been an arrest, albeit an illegal one.

For the second element, intent, there must be a bona fide intention to take the person into actual custody for the purpose of his appearance in court. Thus, if a person is temporarily stopped for the purpose of investigation or is issued a notice to appear in court, he has not been arrested since there was no intent to take him into custody. While the purpose of an arrest is to take a person before a judicial body (or to an executive agency upon judicial order), peace officers can suspend the process and release the person in custody. Though, in terms of paperwork, a person can be "unarrested," in fact, there have been an arrest and a release.

The third element of an arrest—custody—requires actual or constructive restraint of the person arrested. Needless to say, it is not necessary to handcuff or otherwise physically restrain a person to arrest him. Physical contact is not needed if the arrestee voluntarily submits to the arresting officer. It is said that the slightest touching of a person satisfies the requirement of custody. But physical contact alone will not make an act an arrest, without the additional factor of knowledge.

To satisfy the fourth element of an arrest, a person must know—recognize or understand—that he is being arrested. It is usually sufficient to tell an individual he is under arrest. Other words and other acts, however, have the same effect. Thus, the suspect is told to put his hands up, he is handcuffed by a uniformed officer, and he is led away. Knowledge of the arrest is only important when there is no physical contact by the officer, that is, no actual custody. Voluntary submission, as mentioned, constitutes constructive custody. One's knowledge that he has been arrested need not be simultaneous with the act of custody, and there can still be a lawful arrest. Otherwise there could not be a valid search, incidental to an arrest, of an unconscious person.

Most arrests take place when an officer informs a person of his intention to take him into custody, coupled with the voluntary submission of the arrestee. But words alone will not constitute an arrest, unless physical force or voluntary submission follows.

(3.6) Probable Cause

The Fourth Amendment states that "no warrants shall issue, but upon probable cause . . . ." The standard for arrests, without warrant, is the same. State, county, and municipal law enforcement officers are bound to enforce the U.S. Constitution. Their arrests are judged by the same criteria as those applying to federal officers. This is because the Fourth Amendment is made applicable to the states through the Fourteenth Amendment.

To state the matter simply, an officer must have knowledge of sufficient facts and circumstances to form the belief that, first, a crime *probably* was committed and that, second, the arrestee *probably* perpetrated the acts constituting the suspected offense. The test involves both the facts that existed at the time and what the officer reasonably believed. The court must agree that a man of reasonable caution would have made such an arrest, and thus had probable cause.

The question of probable cause is normally one of law, not of fact, and is to be decided by the judge, not the jury. The question is occasionally one of mixed law and fact, and thus a judge—sitting as a trier of fact—would decide whether to believe the officer. The determination of probable cause is made at a preliminary or suppression hearing, preceding a full trial. There is no jury at this phase of the criminal justice system. In a civil case alleging false arrest, the judge decides whether the facts upon which the officer relied constituted probable cause, which is a question of law. If, however, the officer's credibility is at issue, a question of fact arises, and that is decided by a civil jury.

In common-law states, an officer can make a misdemeanor arrest without a warrant if the crime takes place in his "presence"; that is, he either saw the offense or became aware of it through any of his senses such as sound (a shot), smell (marijuana), or taste (liquor). In these common-law states, if the misdemeanor did not take place in his presence, the officer must get an arrest warrant in order to make a legal arrest. In case of a warrantless felony arrest, an officer may act on "information and belief." Many states have abolished this distinction by statute and permit warrantless arrests for either misdemeanors or felonies if done on information and belief.

The courts have now added restrictions to police actions in felony arrests even where there is "probable cause" if they enter a private home to make the arrest. In *Payton* v. *N.Y.*, 445 U.S. 573 (1980), the police had probable cause to believe that Payton had committed a homicide. They went to his apartment and broke in when there was no response to their knock and found a shell casing in plain view.

In a companion decision, *Riddick* v. *N.Y.*, the police had probable cause to believe that Riddick was guilty of armed robbery. They went to his house and saw him inside when his young son opened the door. The officers went in without a warrant and arrested him. The court reversed the convictions of the lower court in both the *Riddick* and *Payton* cases, holding that a nonconsensual entry into a suspect's home to make a routine felony arrest *without a warrant* violates the Fourth Amendment right to privacy.

Several state decisions have followed this same rule, requiring warrants to make felony arrests in private residences of the suspect, but they have also added a requirement that there be exigent circumstances for such entries. The Supreme Court, in *Welsh* v. *Wisconsin*, 466 U.S. 740 (1984), went farther and ruled that it is unconstitutional to make a warrantless arrest in a private home for a nonjailable traffic offense unless exigent circumstances exist. The best police procedure is to obtain an arrest warrant whenever possible since there is no way of knowing where the suspect will actually be when the arrest takes place.

As implied in the phrase itself, "probable cause" is a question of probabilities. Officers need not be legal specialists, and the courts ordinarily will not require precise legal analysis from them. Each arrest will be judged on the facts and circumstances known to the officer at the time a warrantless arrest is made or when an affidavit for an arrest warrant is written. Some of the factors that may lead an officer to conclude that he has probable cause are the same as those that would also justify a stop. The amount of proof needed to justify an arrest is, of course, necessarily higher than that required to justify a temporary detention. Such elements as knowledge that a crime was recently committed and a complete description of the offender and his car will normally support a conclusion of probable cause. Less information, which will justify a temporary detention, may be used to build probable cause, such as admissions made during questioning or the finding of a weapon during a frisk.

In determining the existence of probable cause, an officer may use evidence that is legally inadmissible in the trial of the accused, but is admissible at the suppression hearing. Common among this type of evidence are statements obtained from a confidential informant that implicate the accused. Other factors of restricted admissibility include flight, furtive movements, evasive answers, records of arrest or of conviction, lack of identification, known criminal associations, and otherwise "suspicious" conduct. Factors that establish probable cause and that are admissible in the actual trial include knowledge the crime was recently committed, coupled with the location of the accused at the time of his apprehension; the time of the day or night; the clothing worn; the vehicle used (if it has been identified); evidence seized as the result of a lawful frisk; inculpatory (incriminating) statements made prior to custody of the accused.

The degree of proof necessary might be depicted schematically on a scale from 0 to 100. A slight amount of proof indicating guilt would be evident when it appears that an officer has a "mere hunch" (MH) that a suspect is guilty. This occurs when the officer knows something is "wrong," but cannot adequately particularize his suspicions. It is sometimes called "police intuition." At the next level is the standard required to justify a valid stop and frisk, a "reasonable suspicion" (RS). This is based on facts that the officer can articulate, but that, admittedly, do not fall into the category of probable cause. Probable cause (PC) is that amount of proof necessary to justify a warrantless arrest (or search) and to obtain an arrest warrant (or search warrant). At this stage an arrest (or search) becomes reasonable and lawful. It is still not sufficient for a conviction, however, since in criminal cases proof must be shown beyond a reasonable doubt (BRD), which is represented near the far end of the spectrum.

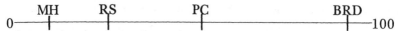

Because officers can initiate an arrest at the stage of probable cause, they may be able to obtain the additional evidence necessary to support a conviction through their efforts in the postarrest period. It may be that physical evidence is found at the time an officer makes a search incident to a custodial arrest. The subject may respond to lawful questioning and confess. A witness may identify the suspect after his apprehension. In such cases the amount of proof will escalate from probable cause to proof beyond a reasonable doubt.

A number of factors can invalidate an otherwise lawful arrest. For instance, an officer cannot obtain the necessary probable cause by illegally secreting himself on someone's property or by making a forcible entrance. If an officer is lawfully on the premises for another reason, anything seen may be used to formulate probable cause. Thus, an officer responds to a fire alarm and sees smoke inside a building. He makes a forcible entry to determine if anyone needs aid. When he gets inside, he observes a burglar on the premises. He would be justified in apprehending the burglar. Alternatively, if he had observed illicit activity on the premises, such as contraband in plain sight, he could later charge the owner or occupant with illegal possession.

(3.7) Collective Information and Radio Broadcasts

Officers may rely upon information that they give to each other. It is presumed to be valid until proven otherwise. For example, one officer may obtain statements from a confidential informant, another may make a surveillance, a third may obtain a records check, and a fourth may actually investigate the scene of the crime. Any officer, after discussing these things with each of the other officers, may swear out an arrest warrant or make a warrantless arrest, if there are no additional legal barriers.

One of the principal applications of the rule relates to serving arrest warrants. If probable cause exists for the issuance of an arrest warrant, the apprehension will be valid regardless of who serves the warrant. The arresting officer does not need to learn the particulars of the offense and investigation. If, however, the warrant was issued on less than probable cause, the arrest would not be lawful. Moreover, anything found incident to an unlawful arrest cannot be used in evidence later on.

Suspects are often apprehended on the basis of information relayed in an all points bulletin (APB) or a "be on look out" (BOLO) message. Once again, the transmission of information, like the existence of an arrest warrant, must be buttressed by probable cause. If the evidence supporting the broadcast does not rise to the level of probable cause, the arrest will be unlawful.

In 1971 the Supreme Court decided the case of *Whiteley* v. *Warden*, 401 U.S. 560 (1971). A local sheriff, investigating a burglary, swore out a warrant on the defendant. The sheriff was acting on information received from a confidential informant. The affidavit in support of the arrest warrant was conclusory and did not incorporate the informant's information, upon which the sheriff had relied. Whiteley was subsequently arrested in another town by an officer who was aware of the outstanding warrant. Tools and coins taken in a burglary were found in his possession. The Supreme Court ruled, however, that this evidence had to be suppressed.

The following rules apply in an analysis of the *Whiteley* case.

1. Assuming the underlying reliability of the confidential information, the sheriff could have arrested Whiteley without a warrant. The actual knowledge that an offense occurred, coupled with information from a reliable informant, could furnish the basis for a reasonable person to conclude the existence of probable cause.

2. Even though the sheriff had probable cause to make a warrantless arrest, he chose to have a warrant issued. The warrant was defective, however, because the affidavit upon which it was based did not recite enough facts to conclude the existence of probable cause.

3. The officer who arrested Whiteley had a legal right to rely on the legitimacy of the arrest warrant. The existence of the warrant, though it was defective, protected that officer from civil claims for false arrest, but it did not furnish him with probable cause. The sheriff had such knowledge. The arresting officer did not. Because

the affidavit upon which the warrant was issued was defective, the warrant should not have been issued by the magistrate.

4. If the sheriff, in addition to broadcasting information concerning the issuance of the warrant, had also added facts that would have constituted probable cause, the subsequent arrest would have been lawful. Such an arrest would not be based on the defective warrant alone, but would be a warrantless arrest using the facts and circumstances relayed to the arresting officer by the sheriff.

The rule is a rather simple one. If an officer has probable cause to make an arrest and swears out a valid warrant, anyone can make a valid arrest in the constitutional sense. But if the warrant is defective because of an insufficient affidavit, only the officer who swore out the warrant can make a lawful arrest; the legality of that arrest would be the underlying probable cause that would justify a warrantless arrest. Finally, should the arresting officer in a distant location learn additional information supporting a conclusion of probable cause, the subsequent apprehension would be a valid warrantless arrest. The additional information could come from either of two sources: the original officer, or facts learned by the arresting officer. The following example demonstrates the point.

A radio bulletin alerts city officers to be on the lookout for Smith, who is wanted for the burglary of a TV repair shop. A full description of Smith's station wagon is included by the sheriff of a nearby county where the alleged crime took place. Officer Jones, on seeing the vehicle, pulls it over and asks the driver for his license. In the back of the wagon Officer Jones sees six TV sets.

In this example we simply do not have enough information to know whether the local sheriff had probable cause to order the arrest of Smith. A warrant, based on an affidavit indicating the existence of probable cause, was not obtained. A warrant issued on a conclusory affidavit would have the same effect. Officer Jones did, however, sufficiently corroborate the information he received, which would lead a reasonable man to conclude that Smith had, indeed, taken the TV sets in the reported burglary.

The principal exception to the *Whiteley* rationale is that officers are lawfully furnished with an excuse to investigate the accused and to make good use of anything seen or of statements made to them in the course of the investigation. If these factors, added to an insufficient radio broadcast, add up to a finding of probable cause, the subsequent arrest and search incident to arrest would be valid.

There are two major exceptions to the rule in *Whiteley*: exigent circumstances and fresh pursuit. Thus, if several officers appear on the scene, and one officer asks the others to assist him in making the apprehension, the legality of the arrest will be based on the information known to the officer requesting assistance. This would be true even if, for example, the officer who apprehends the suspect is in a back alley while the officer who requested assistance is in the front. Courts will not require officers who locate and take custody of a suspect at or near the scene of the crime to explain laboriously why they concluded the existence of probable cause.

Officers may lawfully assist each other in the apprehension of a fleeing suspect who is being pursued by another officer. Since time is of the essence, the law does not require the officer, in the heat of chase, to confide fully in all those assisting him in the capture.

(3.8) Federal Offenses and Immunity

State and local officers are sworn to uphold the Constitution and the laws of the United States. They frequently make arrests for offenses that are both state and federal in nature, such as bank robbery, possession of narcotics, interstate theft, and certain crimes concerned with weapons. Either the federal or state government may decide to prosecute the crime involved. If a county prosecutor refuses to charge the suspect, the U.S. attorney can act instead, and vice versa. Selection of the forum is a matter of comity between sovereigns.

Some offenses are solely federal in nature. Many involve the postal service, the Internal Revenue Service, or crimes committed on federal reservations. Pursuant to 18 U.S. Code, Sec. 3041, a state or local officer may swear out a warrant in either state or federal court for individuals suspected of federal offenses. While a state court judge cannot try the offense charged, he can order the defendant held for trial or discharge him from custody. A state or local officer may arrest, without warrant, a person who commits a purely federal offense if a warrantless arrest is permitted by state law.

Certain classes of persons are, by federal law, immune from arrest. Ambassadors, foreign ministers, their families, members of their official households, civil and military attachés, personal servants, and personal secretaries have full diplomatic immunity. Delegates to the United Nations, the Organization of American States, and the North Atlantic Treaty Organization also have official immunity. Foreign nationals and U.S. citizens employed as clerical staff, as well as all ranks of consuls, do not have diplomatic immunity except when they are on official foreign business. To ascertain whether a person has full or partial immunity, the chief of protocol of the U.S. Department of State should be contacted.

Law enforcement officers should, as a matter of courtesy among friendly nations, notify the closest embassy, consulate, or legation of the arrest of any foreign national. The imprisonment or assault of a foreign ambassador or minister is a federal crime punishable by up to ten years of imprisonment in accord with 18 U.S. Code 112.

The Constitution prohibits the arrest of all U.S. senators and representatives, except for treason, felonies, and breach of the peace, during their attendance at a session of Congress and while they are traveling to and from such sessions. Thus, they are immune from arrests for misdemeanors and traffic violations during the entire time Congress is in session, and not just during their working hours.

Many state senators and representatives have immunity from state misdemeanors and traffic offenses, similar to members of the U.S. Congress. Members of the state militia who are on duty, judges, lawyers, and jurors attending court, and other classes of persons may be given limited immunity under state law.

(3.9) Particular Types of Arrests

Not every arrest is for a criminal offense. Persons may be arrested on civil process, issued by a court of competent jurisdiction. For example, bench warrants may be issued for contempt of court, as when a witness fails to appear on a subpoena that has been served in a civil case. The ancient writ of *capias* is a civil arrest process and is sometimes used to bring in a person for a mental examination. The writ of *ne exeat*, which is rarely used, orders the detention of a person until he posts an appearance bond in a civil case; this will "guarantee" his appearance. According to common law, an officer may not use deadly force or forcibly enter a dwelling to execute a civil arrest. Other degrees of reasonable force are permissible.

Citizens are authorized to make arrests in criminal cases, without warrant, when the offense is committed in their presence. This power does not normally extend to offenses concerned with municipal ordinances, but is reserved for felonies and breach of the peace. Citizens may also be "deputized" to assist officers in making an arrest. This is not a new procedure. The *posse comitatus* is of ancient origin, and no one who has seen a Western can fail to have witnessed posses in action. The common law recognizes that it is the duty of all male adults to come to the aid of officers who request it; recent statutes have included women when the rule has been codified. As a matter of fact, in some cases it is a criminal offense to refuse to assist law enforcement officers in the execution of their office.

Under statutes existing in most states, merchants are given powers of arrest or detention with respect to shoplifting offenses. They may, if they have sufficient information and belief, detain and sometimes arrest suspected shoplifters. Under such laws police officers need not view misdemeanors committed only in the presence of shopkeepers and security personnel hired by the store.

An individual who is on parole does not enjoy the civil rights of ordinary citizens. He may be apprehended, without warrant, for parole violations. He may be searched without warrant, without probable cause, and without first being placed under valid arrest. This is because he is still *legally* confined under the conditions of parole. Probationers may also be searched by their probation officer.

Bondsmen, under common law, have an absolute right to retake those for whom they have posted bond should those individuals attempt to skip town or otherwise impair the conditions of their appearance in court. They may cross state lines and, without warrant or other legal process, capture and return the accused to the jail from which he was released on bond.

Police officers may arrest and detain a person who is wanted, on warrant or bulletin, to answer for the commission of an offense in another state. This power is granted by the U.S. Constitution, which requires that each state give "full faith and credit" to the legal processes of sister states. Except in exigent circumstances, however, resident police officers should not apprehend suspects on a bulletin alone, unless the request indicates a warrant has been issued. In situations where the suspect is fleeing, an officer can, of course, detain him until a warrant has been obtained. Officers may promptly pursue a fleeing suspect across state lines to make the apprehension, but the offender may not be returned to the state in which he is supposed to have committed the crime without due process of law. Nearly all states have adopted the Uniform Fresh Pursuit Act and the Uniform Extradition Act. These statutes give an accused the right to a hearing before the governor of the state to which he has fled before he can be returned to the state that issued the warrant.

In 2004, the court held in *Hiibel* v. *Humboldt County* (2004 U.S. LEXIS 4385) that police may enforce state laws that require a person to identify him- or herself during a valid "Terry" stop, provided that

- the officer has a valid "stop- and-frisk" situation;
- an officer can ask the subject for his or her name (*note*: the court did not go any further in deciding whether a demand for a valid and credible identification could be made and suggested that such a demand cannot be made); and
- there must be a state statute requiring that a person validly stopped for criminal activity must identify him- or herself in order to make such an arrest for "failure to identify."

(3.10) Use of Force

Police officers may use reasonable and necessary force to apprehend a criminal suspect. They are not required to retreat from an assault, as is an ordinary citizen in most cases. They are not required to time their arrest so that it can be effected with the least amount of resistance. They are not bound to use psychology or to wait for hours or days before flushing out an armed suspect who offers resistance. What is good police policy and what is good law may surely differ. Thus, an officer may be fired for escalating or not defusing a situation, but ordinarily he cannot be sued or prosecuted for immediately apprehending a suspect who is resisting arrest.

If the offense is a misdemeanor, an arresting officer may not use deadly force to apprehend a fleeing suspect. In every state an officer may—as a last resort—use deadly force to apprehend a suspect who is believed to have committed a dangerous felony. In most states this applies to all grades of felonies. It makes no difference that the offense is minor. To state the matter simply, the law will not permit felons to flee from justice.

In *Tennessee* v. *Garner,* 471 U.S. 1 (1985), the Supreme Court has put some limits on the use of deadly force, holding that it may be used (1) only where necessary to prevent the escape of a fleeing felon and (2) where the officer has probable cause to believe that the suspect poses a significant threat of death or serious injury to the officer or others.

A physical seizure occurs only when physical force to stop a person is used through a means intentionally applied (*Brower* v. *Inyo County,* 289 U.S. 593; 1989). Force that is accidentally applied to innocent third parties is not a seizure or use of force under the Fourth Amendment to the U.S. Constitution. Force intentionally applied to an innocent third party because of a mistaken belief that the third party is a suspect does constitute a Fourth Amendment seizure.

Regardless of whether the offense is serious or whether the suspect's arrest is attempted or not, a police officer may use deadly force to defend himself against the use of deadly force. This principle does not escalate in degrees. An attacker with a knife, with a broken beer bottle, with a fireplace poker, or with an automobile that he is using as a weapon may be shot dead with an elephant gun. Even though there may be twenty-five armed officers against one armed suspect, any officer may return the fire as though the suspect were taking aim against him individually.

Most cases where excessive force has been alleged do not involve the use of deadly force. An officer is not only privileged to use a reasonable and necessary amount of force to make an apprehension; he is obligated to use more force than the person resisting arrest. Here, then, the law will examine the degrees of responsive force. There are no ready answers, and the progression is not necessarily from pebbles to boulders or from table lighters to chairs.

Entry of dwellings and other premises by force in order to effect an arrest is limited to two situations. The first occurs when officers are in hot pursuit or the criminal acts are of a continuous nature. The second takes place when officers who are armed with an arrest or search warrant have first requested consensual entry, which is refused.

Handcuffs may be used to restrain or transport arrested persons who are suspected of felonies, breach of the peace, or minor offenses when it is thought that they might escape or assault the arresting officers. Some departments use them routinely on all offenders.

a. On-Scene Identification and Use of Force [1]

The issue with all identification procedures is that the conduct of the police while carrying out the procedures cannot be overly suggestive. The following considerations should be taken into account:

- What were the witness's opportunities to view the suspect at the time of the crime?
- Where was the witness's focus of attention at the time of the crime?
- What was the accuracy of the witness's description of the suspect prior to identification procedures?
- What was the level of certainty exhibited by the witness in making the identification?
- What was the length of time that passed between the crime and the identification?

Police officers should articulate these points when documenting an identification procedure. All uses of force in an arrest and seizure of a free citizen are judged by the Fourth Amendment standard of objective reasonableness *(Graham* v. *Connor,* 490 U.S. 386; 1989). Objective reasonableness includes:

- The severity of the offense suspected.
- Facts that support that the suspect posed an immediate threat to the officer or to others.
- The suspect's actions to actively resist or attempt to escape.

The officer's actions are judged by a totality of circumstances known to the officer at the time that the force was used. The actions are based on what another officer would do under the same circumstances.

---

1. Material in this section is summarized from Jack Ryan, "Case Law for Critical Tasks in Law Enforcement," July 2004–June 2005, Legal & Liability Risk Management Institute, 2004. Officers using this text are encouraged to read the cases on which the principles in the manual are based. Cases can be found by using free Internet databases such as www.findlaw.com. Officers can also subscribe to the Public Agency Training Council's bi-weekly, electronic briefing at www.patc.com. The briefing regularly provides updates on law enforcement topics and is a free service to law enforcement officers.

Once an arrest is complete, some courts have followed a different standard in subsequent uses of force based on the "due process" standard of the Fourteenth Amendment *(Brother* v. *Klevenhagen,* 28 F. 3d 452; 1994). This court standard is more protective of officer conduct. An officer's use of force must have inflicted unnecessary and wanton pain and suffering and must not have been applied in a "good-faith effort" to maintain order or restore discipline. A violation does occur when the officer acted maliciously or sadistically for the very purpose of causing harm. For example, handcuffing too tightly and failing to double-lock the handcuffs may lead to a claim of excessive force, particularly when the officers have been placed on notice by a suspect's complaints *(Baskin* v. *Smith,* 50 Fed. Appx. 731; 6th Cir., 2002). In *Martinez v. New Mexico Dept. of Public Safety* (47 Fed. Appx. 513; 10th Cir. 2002), the court held that it is unreasonable to use pepper spray as a pain-compliance techniques when the suspect is restrained in handcuffs and is being only verbally resistant. Pain compliance techniques can be immediately stopped when the suspect responds with compliance. The effects of pepper spray cannot be immediately stopped upon compliance. (*See also Vineyard* v. *Wilson,* 311 F. 3d 1340; 11th Cir., 2002, for a similar conclusion.) Furthermore, pointing a firearm toward the head of an apparently unarmed suspect during an investigation can be a violation of the Fourth Amendment, especially when the individual poses no particular danger *(Robinson* v. *Solano County,* 278 F. 3d 1007; 9th Cir., 2002).

The courts have also ruled on the use of canines as force. In *Kuha* v. *City of Minnetonka* (328 F. 3d 427; 8th Cir., 2003), the court ruled that a jury could properly find it objectively unreasonable to use a police dog trained in the bite-and-hold method without first giving the suspect a warning and opportunity for peaceful surrender. In *Robinette* v. *Barnes* (854 F. 2d 909; 6th Cir., 1988), a suspect died when a canine seized the suspect's neck because it was the only part of his body exposed. The court ruled that the use of a properly trained police dog to apprehend a felony suspect does not constitute a use of deadly force.

In *Cruz* v. *Laramie* (239 F.3d 1183; 10th Cir., 2001), the court ruled that an officer may not use a hog-tie when the suspect's diminished capacity is apparent and the hog-tie is likely to result in a significant risk to the arrestee's health or well-being. Diminished capacity may include severe intoxication, the influence of a controlled substance, discernible mental condition, or any other condition apparent to the officer that would make use of a hog-tie a significant risk to the arrestee's health.

A strip search requires the removal or rearrangement of clothing that results in the exposure or observation of a portion of a person's body when that person has a reasonable expectation of privacy. In *Mary Beth G.* v. *City of Chicago* (723 F. 2d 1263, 1983), a court held that a police officer may only strip search arrestees when the officer has a reasonable suspicion to believe that the arrestee has evidence or contraband hidden on his or her person. Body cavity searches are more intrusive and must be supported by probable cause and a search warrant in the absence of exigent circumstances *(Fuller* v. *M.G. Jewelry,* 950 F.2 d 1437, 1991). Body cavity searches must be done in accordance with medically approved procedures and in sanitary conditions *(Rodriquez* v. *Furtado,* 950 F. 2d 805, 1991).

(3.11) False Arrest

Civil action may be taken against a police officer, and in most cases the unit of government that employs him, for false arrest, false imprisonment, and malicious prosecution. The gist of a suit for false arrest is that the officer arrested the civil plaintiff without probable cause. It is of no consequence whether the officers acted maliciously, recklessly, or for personal gain. While such factors might subject an officer to punitive damages if the plaintiff prevails, they have nothing to do with liability. In a suit for false arrest a complete defense is that there was probable cause for the arrest to be made. If a felon is bound over in a preliminary hearing in criminal court, or if the civil court determines the existence of probable cause, the judgment will be in favor of the officer, who is the defendant.

In most cases the existence of probable cause is a question of law for the judge. There is, consequently, little a sympathetic jury can do for the officer other than limit the amount of damages. Recently, however, many federal courts and several state courts have adopted the doctrine of "good faith." When it is viewed schematically on the diagram appearing in the section on "Probable Cause," above, good faith is to the left of probable cause and to the right of reasonable suspicion. If an officer makes an arrest without probable cause, but *reasonably* believes in good faith that he has probable cause and that the arrest is lawful, he will be immune from any damages.

Good faith is thus both a subjective and an objective test. First, the officer must in honest good faith believe in the legality of his actions. Second, this belief must be reasonable under the circumstances. The jury answers these questions, which provide added protection to officers. A foolish officer, for example, might honestly believe he can arrest blue-eyed, blond-haired males only because they have those characteristics. His belief would not be reasonable and would fail the objective part of the two-part test.

False imprisonment is the unlawful incarceration of a person. Though it often follows a false arrest automatically, it could arise because of a failure to release someone after his bond was posted, after the charges were dropped, or after he served his term. This charge can be used to sue officers who detain persons *without* justification in a stop-and-frisk situation at the scene of a crime or the place where a raid has taken place. Good faith is normally not a defense in an action alleging false imprisonment when the plaintiff is held in jail beyond the proper time.

Malicious prosecution is the actual prosecution of criminal charges against the accused when probable cause is absent and when the charges were brought for malicious reasons. The circumstances prompting this action usually arise when police officers learn that the accused is no longer a good suspect, but fail to notify the court or prosecutor of the person's innocence or his ironclad defense.

Civil claims of excessive force often accompany arrests. These allegations are, in reality, for civil assault and civil battery. They are common-law claims. Since a lawful arrest may be accompanied by excessive force, the existence of probable cause or proof of guilt beyond a reasonable doubt is not involved in the claims or their defense.

Plaintiffs who prevail in personal injury litigation are generally entitled to compensatory damages, both special and general. Special damages are those capable of setting a dollar figure: loss of earnings, cost of bond, attorneys' fees, and medical expenses, if any. General damages are those assessed for the pain or suffering, humiliation, and defamation of the plaintiff. A jury has wide discretion in imposing damages for general purposes. In cases of flagrant police misbehavior, a jury can award punitive damages to "teach and punish" the civil defendant. In most jurisdictions neither cities nor insurance companies will indemnify an officer for punitive damages, and they cannot be discharged through the bankruptcy courts. Thus an officer may have to pay such damages for the rest of his life.

An officer who merely serves a regular arrest warrant is immune from liability for false arrest. He can rely absolutely on the determinations made by the court that issued the warrant and the regularity of the proceedings upon which it is based.

In *Kaupp* v. *Texas* (538 U.S. 626; 2003), the court held that, for Fourth Amendment purposes, a person involuntarily transported to a police station has been arrested. No person can be involuntarily transported to a police station unless the police have probable cause to believe that person has committed a crime. A confession obtained as the result of such an arrest is invalid unless (1) the proper *Miranda* warning has been administered; (2) there has been a passage of time between the illegal arrest and the confession; and (3) intervening circumstances occur.

(3.12) Entrapment

Entrapment has been defined as the procurement of a person to commit a crime that he did not contemplate or would not have committed, for the sole purpose of prosecuting that person. "It is not entrapment of a criminal upon which the law frowns, but the seduction of innocent people into a criminal career by its officers is what is condemned" *(People* v. *Braddock,* 41 Cal. 2d 744). Though it is not recognized as a defense against prosecution at common law, most states acknowledge it as a defense in their codes of criminal law and procedure.

In *U.S.* v. *Russell,* 411 U.S. 423 (1973), the Supreme Court affirmed the conviction of a manufacturer of methamphetamine (speed). An undercover agent delivered a necessary component to the suspect and agreed to split the profits. After the drug was produced, the federal agents raided the laboratory and arrested the suspect. The Supreme Court held that:

1. the defense of entrapment is not a constitutionally protected right;
2. in the absence of "shocking" conduct on the part of law enforcement officers, a conviction would not be set aside merely because the government participated in the crime;
3. a predisposition to commit the crime, on the part of the defendant, precludes the defense of entrapment.

States are free to adopt their own rules concerning the entrapment defense, and the rules may be more rigorous in some jurisdictions than others. At the local level, entrapment is often raised in vice cases. In some jurisdictions, for example, a plainclothes police officer can offer to purchase the services of a prostitute, but cannot set the price, which must be fixed by the suspect.

Entrapment poses problems of enforcement when officers deal with first offenders. As noted, a predisposition to commit the offense will usually prevent a successful defense based on entrapment. To ensure a conviction, officers frequently do not make an arrest immediately after the commission of the first crime, but wait until a second offense has taken place. This usually establishes predisposition. In cases charging the sale of narcotics by first offenders, however, it may not be necessary to wait for a second transaction before making an arrest. If, for example, a large quantity of narcotics is seized, a jury would probably believe that the defendant intended to engage in narcotics transactions as a business. In any event, the crime of possession of narcotics would not be subject to the defense of entrapment, and a conviction for this less serious offense would usually follow.

It is not improper for a police officer to give a suspect marked money, to misrepresent his true identity, or to pose as an addict or hoodlum. In *Sherman* v. *U.S.*, 356 U.S. 369 (1958), however, the Supreme Court found "shocking" police conduct. Federal agents had persuaded an addict, who was in the process of breaking himself of the habit, to obtain heroin and to readdict himself. The defense has also been successfully raised when prior to the commission of a planned crime, police officers have discouraged a participant from withdrawing.

Though entrapment as a defense must be raised by the defendant, in some cases a judge will rule as a matter of law that officers encouraged the defendant's participation in the offense. In most cases, however, it will also be a question for the jury because of variances in testimony between the officer and the defendant.

(3.13) The Fourth and Fourteenth Amendments

Two phrases of the Fourth Amendment to the U.S. Constitution contain the real substance of its protections. The first is the prohibition against "unreasonable" searches. The second is the requirement of "probable cause." In regard to the first prohibition the amendment states that the people have the right to be secure in their persons, houses, papers, and effects from unreasonable searches and seizures. Thus, the amendment protects people, not corporations, animals, or inanimate objects. Although it specifies "houses," the word has been interpreted to include barns, warehouses, offices, and other structures. No mention was made of boats, which, of course, existed in the eighteenth century, or of automobiles, trucks, and aircraft, which did not. Nevertheless, the protections of the Fourth Amendment have been extended, by interpretation, to these forms of personal property. Thus, the gist of the amendment is that people are protected from unreasonable searches, regardless of what is searched.

Only a few types of searches can be considered unreasonable. If a search is reasonable, other things being equal, the search is constitutional. It is sometimes claimed that a warrantless search is unreasonable and therefore illegal because there was ample time to procure a warrant. That is not, however, the proper test. The real question is whether it was reasonable to require a warrant under the circumstances of the case.

The second major prohibition of the amendment states that no warrants shall be issued except on "probable cause." This requirement has also been extended to warrantless searches, warrantless arrests, and arrest warrants.

The Fourth Amendment also requires that warrants be based on an oath or affirmation, which particularly describes the place to be searched and the persons or things to be seized.

The Fourteenth Amendment is important in constitutional history because it was originally thought that the first eight amendments only applied to congressional enactments and to federal officers. But the "due process clause" of this amendment makes it clear that these amendments also apply to state enactments and to locally constituted law enforcement officers.

(3.14) The Exclusionary Rule

The single most important rule of evidence is the one that suppresses and rejects otherwise admissible evidence because it was obtained in an "illegal" manner, in this case, in violation of the Fourth Amendment. In earlier times it made no legal difference to the courts how physical evidence was obtained. But in 1914 the

U.S. Supreme Court changed that. In *Weeks* v. *U.S.*, 232 U.S. 383 (1914), it ruled that evidence gathered by federal officers to be introduced in a federal criminal trial was subject to exclusion if it was obtained in violation of the Fourth Amendment.

The *Weeks* decision stated that courts should not sanction convictions obtained by "unlawful seizures and forced confessions." In order to force the police to comply with the Fourth and Fifth Amendments, it was necessary to exclude "tainted" evidence from the criminal trial itself. Thus, a "guilty" man might go free because, as one jurist has said, the "constable has blundered." The rule applies equally to intentional abuses and negligent omissions. A number of people feel that the rule has had unfortunate results. They believe that it detracts from the main purpose of a criminal trial—the search for the truth and the determination of the guilt or innocence of an accused. Further, they see it as encouraging police officers to commit perjury in order to secure the admission of probative evidence. Finally, they think that it causes considerable delays in the prosecution of offenses and an enormous expense, particularly at the appellate stage.

Many states followed the federal courts in adopting the exclusionary rule. But for over thirty years nearly half of the states did not recognize it. This gave rise to the "silver platter doctrine." Thus, if a federal agent uncovered evidence through an illegal search, the evidence could be admitted in a state court that did not have an exclusionary rule. Moreover, during one period of time, even states that recognized the rule applied it only to state searches and still admitted evidence that had been illegally seized by federal agents. So, too, the federal courts admitted evidence illegally seized by state officers. The "illegal evidence" was thus "served up" on a "silver platter."

The Supreme Court addressed itself to the issue in the famous case of *Mapp* v. *Ohio*, 367 U.S. 643, decided in 1961, by which time twenty-six states had fashioned some form of an exclusionary rule. That decision marks the beginning of what is known as "The Criminal Law Revolution." The Ohio courts had sustained the conviction of Mrs. Mapp for possession of obscene matter. The evidence brought forth to prove her guilt was seized during an unlawful search of her home. In reversing the conviction and ordering the suppression of that evidence, the Supreme Court relied on the Fourteenth Amendment. It felt that a citizen had a right to be "free from unreasonable state intrusion." The failure of a state to observe its own laws, said the court, would eventually destroy the government itself.

The exclusion of tainted evidence is not automatic. The defendant must affirmatively raise the issue before the court in a "motion to suppress." It is normal for the motion to be made before the actual trial begins. In some cases, in fact, a person can institute an action to suppress evidence that might be used to procure an indictment against him. Even if an accused fails to raise the motion before the trial, he can still object to the admissibility of the evidence at the time of trial. Most courts have held, however, that the issue cannot be first raised at the time of an appeal, unless good cause can be shown for not doing so previously.

Evidence that is suppressed is not necessarily returned to the accused. Things that are not returnable include the following:

1. contraband per se, which, by its nature, is illegal to possess, such as narcotics;
2. derivative contraband, which a statute has outlawed, such as automatic firearms;
3. evidence held pending an appeal, since a court of appeals can overrule a motion to dismiss that was granted below and order a new trial;
4. stolen property, which the rightful owner can obtain by a court order;
5. forfeitures, to which the exclusionary rule may not apply and which can be forfeited to the state, such as money gained from illegal activities, a weapon used to commit a crime, or a vehicle used to transport contraband.

It should be noted that the exclusionary rule also applies to "derivative evidence." This extension of the rule is called the "Fruit of the Poisoned Tree Doctrine." For example, through an illegal search of a suspect, officers find a key to a storage locker in a bus station. They open the locker, hoping to find evidence of the offense under investigation. The purpose of the rule would be defeated if it did not apply to evidence *derived* from an illegal search as well as to evidence seized from an illegal search. Thus, the exclusionary rule applies to direct and derivative evidence, seized as the result of an illegal arrest or search.

An exception to the Poisoned Tree rationale is operable when the police can show that they would have found the evidence anyway, and in a lawful manner. We can demonstrate this by returning to the example of the storage locker. If the officers already knew that the suspect had secreted evidence in a certain locker, but they did not have the key, they could have obtained a search warrant for the locker and forcibly opened it. Thus, the use of the illegally seized key would not have affected the outcome of the subsequent search, and the evidence should be admitted in spite of the use of the key.

Currently, there is a general trend to weaken the exclusionary rule both by legislative action and by various court decisions. The Supreme Court, in *U.S.* v. *Leon,* 468 U.S. 897 (1984), has ruled that evidence found under a defective warrant or an unconstitutional state statute can still be used if obtained in "good faith." State decisions on "good faith" vary. New York and North Carolina refuse this exception. Arizona allows it by statute.

Herring v. *United States* (555 U.S. _____ [2009]) was argued October 7, 2008, and the Supreme Court issued its decision on January 14, 2009. In this case, officers in Coffee County arrested petitioner Herring based on a warrant listed in neighboring Dale County's database. A search incident to (or following) that arrest yielded drugs and a gun. It was then revealed that the warrant had been recalled months earlier, though this information had never been entered into the database. Herring was indicted on federal gun and drug possession charges and moved to suppress the evidence on the grounds that his initial arrest had been illegal. Assuming that there was a Fourth Amendment violation, the District Court concluded that the exclusionary rule did not apply and denied the motion to suppress. The Eleventh Circuit Court affirmed, finding that the arresting officers were innocent of any wrongdoing, and that Dale County's failure to update the records was merely negligent. The Court therefore concluded that the benefits of suppression would be marginal or nonexistent and that the evidence was admissible under the "good-faith rule of *United States* v. *Leon* 468 U S. 897 (1984). The Court held that when police mistakes leading to an unlawful search are the result of isolated negligence attenuated from the search, rather than systemic error or reckless disregard of constitutional requirements, the exclusionary rule does not apply.

Many objections to the impact of the rule on law enforcement have been raised. A few of these objections are set forth below. The first four were mentioned above, but are elaborated on here.

1. *It punishes all transgressions alike.* Police misconduct is a nebulous term that embraces a broad range of acts and omissions. It can be an affirmative act of substantial injury, such as kicking in the front doors of every home in a subdivision, without cause. Or it can be a minimal intrusion, such as a pat-down that goes beyond the suspect's outer clothing. It could be an omission, such as the failure to date a search warrant affidavit. It might be an intentional wrongdoing, such as the strip search of an innocent female suspect by a male officer; it could be negligence, such as mixing up warrants and their affidavits. Whatever the "misconduct" charged, all mistakes suffer the same penalty: the exclusion of probative evidence.

2. *The rule runs counter to the basic purpose of a trial, which is the search for truth.* Every trial, whether civil or criminal, has as its purpose the goal of determining the truth of the matter in dispute. In criminal trials, it is the guilt or innocence of the accused that should be determined. All of the rules of evidence are supposedly fashioned to facilitate that goal. Thus evidence is excluded when it is irrelevant, immaterial, or, by rule of law, incompetent. Evidence that suffers no inherent disability and is probative in nature is normally admissible, and it should be. Yet the exclusionary rule discards evidence that is probative and otherwise competent, but is not based on a desire to give an accused a fair trial; it is fashioned to deter police misconduct.

3. *The exclusionary rule encourages perjury by the police.* Few police officers would seriously consider framing an innocent defendant by giving false testimony on the issue of guilt or innocence. Testimony given at an evidence suppression hearing, however, relates to the method used to gather physical or testimonial evidence, and not to the presence or absence of evidence. Thus, perjury at a suppression hearing will not make a truly innocent suspect seem guilty; it will only decide whether a factually guilty suspect should be tried on the merits of the evidence. Simple misstatements of fact, such as whether

an officer knocked before forcing open a door or whether he limited his pat-down to the suspect's outer garments, are examples of police perjury that do not affect the guilt or innocence in the nonlegal sense. Officers are therefore pressured, by the nature of their assignments, to misstate these events. This is, of course, perjury.

4. *The exclusionary rule causes significant delays in the process of punishment.* Many criminologists and behavioral psychologists believe that the certainty and alacrity of punishment create a stronger deterrent effect than the severity of punishment. The pretrial suppression hearing causes but another delay in the process from arrest to incarceration. It is followed, in many instances, by a further delay at the trial stage. The introduction of physical or testimonial evidence often forms the exclusive basis for an appeal to an intermediate court of appeals, then to the state's supreme court. The usual methods of appeal are exhausted when the Supreme Court refuses to hear the case. But that does not end the appellate process. A collateral attack on the judgment may be made, in some instances, through a writ of habeas corpus at the U.S. district court. This writ is appealable to the U.S. circuit court, in a three-judge panel, followed by an *en banc* appeal before the entire circuit bench, and, once again, to the Supreme Court. It is not unusual for a defendant who was convicted ten years before to continue to file appeals based on illegal search and seizure.

5. *The rule causes an added expense to society.* Each appeal and each collateral attack brought by a defendant must be briefed and argued. In addition to the time spent in researching each point of law that is appealed, sufficient copies of the final brief must be reproduced (and often printed) at considerable expense. Lawyers for the state must prepare their oral arguments, travel to the court that is hearing the matter (often in a distant city), and present their arguments. A certified copy of the transcript, purchased from court reporters, must accompany the briefs at the first levels of appeal.

In many cases the appealing defendant is indigent. He must, therefore, be provided with a free copy of the transcript, free legal counsel in preparing his appeal, free printing of the briefs concerning his case, and free representation before the appellate court. "Free" to an indigent means paid for by the state. It is not unusual for the entire cost of processing numerous appeals to exceed the total cost of confining that defendant in a correctional institution for his entire life. It has been estimated that an appeal to the Supreme Court can cost as much as $50,000. And that is but one stage of the appellate process.

6. *Application of the rule does not prevent many types of police "misconduct."* There are many areas of enforcement activity where the time necessary to conduct a foolproof investigation prior to a raid or an arrest is so excessive compared to the punishments imposed by the penal code that there is no incentive to make the investigation. For example, to corroborate properly an informant's disclosures might require three surveillances utilizing three officers and two cars. Coupled with the cost of conducting a raid, the total expenditures would probably exceed $1,000. The maximum fine for keeping a bawdy house, running a gambling house, engaging in lewd behavior, possessing dangerous drugs, or participating in disorderly conduct may be $200. In many cases the maximum fine is not imposed, or the fine is suspended. If a jail term is possible, it may not be imposed, or it, too, may be suspended. Besides the factor of expense, a limited number of vice officers can raid four times as many people by dispensing with legally sufficient surveillances.

In one city it was learned that vice officers made arrests with no intention of prosecuting the offenders. These officers were pressured to "clean up" the city. A raid would result in the closing of a place where illegal activity was being carried out, the identification of suspects, the posting of bonds, the employment of legal counsel, and the investigation of reported crimes. Such activity gets narcotics, pornography, and gambling paraphernalia off the street and makes them unavailable for sale. It drives the cost of these goods up, makes trading in them less profitable, and creates additional expenses for "doing business." These factors may impose more dissuasion than the sanctions of fines and potential incarcerations. The exclusionary rule will not deter police officers who find that nonjudicial sanctions are equal to or more effective than judicial ones.

Police officers also know that they must exceed the bounds of permissible searches if they are to confiscate the maximum number of concealed weapons. Only a few convicted defendants are ever incarcerated for this offense in major cities, and yet the number of shootings continues to rise because of the legal difficulties encountered in properly seizing handguns. Again, the number of guns confiscated dramatically increases when the protections of the Fourth Amendment are relaxed. Those found with weapons are arrested, are identified in the records systems, and are required to post bond and employ legal counsel. The nonjudicial sanctions may be more effective when broadly applied than are judicial sanctions selectively applied. Thus, there are fewer guns in the community when the exclusionary rule does not serve as a deterrent to patrol officers.

7. *The exclusionary rule punishes society, not a misbehaving officer.* Society suffers every time a dope peddler or an armed robber is turned loose because of the exclusionary rule. The defendant is free to continue his illegal activity, to make sport of the system of criminal justice, and to harm society. But when, if ever, is a policeman demoted, suspended, or otherwise punished because he lacked probable cause to make an arrest or conduct a search? Even in those few cases where a defendant subsequently sues a police officer for false arrest or illegal search, the officer escapes punishment. In the first place, less than 4 percent of such suits are successful (Schmidt, *Survey of Police Misconduct Litigation, 1967-1971* [Evanston, 111.: Americans for Effective Law Enforcement, Inc., 1974], 6). In the second place, the police department employs an attorney for the officer in 99.6 percent of the cases. In the third place, the city almost always pays a judgment in behalf of the officer. On the other hand, it is common knowledge that if an officer leaves his post, becomes intoxicated while on duty, or wears an improper uniform he will suffer disciplinary suspension and, sometimes, dismissal. But in our larger cities a vice squad can serve over 5,000 search warrants a year that are later thrown out as lacking probable cause, and not a single instance of police misconduct will be administratively prosecuted.

Alternatives to the exclusionary rule that would probably be more effective include:

1. mandatory civil liability for improper police conduct;
2. use of contempt of court procedures by the courts against errant officers;

3. implementation of an effective system of discipline, internally administered against police misconduct.

(3.15) Searches, Distinguished from Plain View

In one sense a "search" is, at least in the layman's terms, the examination of things for the purpose of finding something. To the courts, it is something quite different. A search is the seeking of something that is not in plain sight, in places where the object (or person) sought might be concealed. As stated by the Supreme Court in *Harris* v. *U.S.* (390 U.S. 234 [1968]), "It has long been settled that objects falling in the plain view of an officer who has a right to be in the position to have that view are subject to seizure and may be introduced in evidence." Simply stated, the "plain view rule" holds that readily observable things, seen by an officer (in a place where he has a right to be), are not the product of a "search" and are not subject to exclusion from evidence.

The plain view rule frequently arises in the course of police duties. Every time a police officer talks with a pedestrian, stops a motorist, or questions a suspicious person, the rule applies. For example, a patrol officer stops a motorist for speeding. While writing a notice for the motorist to appear in court, the officer observes the barrel of a gun protruding from under a newspaper on the seat of the car. Noticing the barrel is not a search, and the officer has probable cause to remove the newspaper and seize the weapon.

Observations within the rule are not limited to sightings with an unaided eye. Flashlights and vehicular spotlights may be used at night or in dark places. Thus, a foot patrolman, walking down the sidewalk at night, might routinely shine his flashlight into parked cars. If he observes narcotics paraphernalia on the backseat of an unoccupied sedan, he would have probable cause to seize the vehicle and arrest the driver on his return.

a. Open Fields

The "open fields doctrine" is an integral part of the plain view rule. Officers may enter private outdoor property to look for evidence, without a warrant or other justification, and anything seen in the course of their expedition falls within the plain view exception. A typical example of the application of the doctrine occurs in the pursuit of the growing of marijuana. An anonymous telephone call, a story told by hikers, a rumor—each could be the impetus for surveying hills and meadows. None of these, standing alone, would constitute probable cause. Yet, since a walk through fields and woodlands is not a "search," no violations of the Fourth Amendment arise because police officers are looking for marijuana that is being grown in open fields.

Though the doctrine appears to run counter to the concepts of private property and trespass, which are firmly rooted in Anglo-American law, such observations are, nevertheless, lawful. Even the presence of a fence is not determinative. Even a fence with a locked gate and a "No trespassing" sign cannot legally bar police from seizing evidence in open fields (*Oliver* v. *U.S.*, 466 U.S. 170 [1984]).

Numerous cases affirming the open fields doctrine arose during Prohibition, when federal revenue agents sought out and destroyed illegal stills.

Recent case law has added a new dimension to the open fields doctrine. If the occupant or landowner has an "expectation of privacy" over the fields, the search might be unlawful. The question for the courts to determine is whether, under all the circumstances, the occupant's expectation of privacy was reasonable. Thus, a farmer would not have a reasonable expectation that his plowed fields near a state highway are private. Conversely, a homeowner might reasonably expect that his fenced backyard would not be spied upon from the roof of a nearby building. Court decisions in many cases are now allowing aerial searches for marijuana. Evidence found by police helicopters flying as low as 400 feet over open fields has been approved as not being found during a "search" (*Florida* v. *Riley*, 109 S.Ct. 693, 102 L. Ed. 2d 835 [1989]).

b. Curtilage

Another concept of the law of property is that of curtilage. It includes the area immediately surrounding a person's home and has the same protections as the actual home. Trespass onto the curtilage is not within the exception of the open fields doctrine. It violates the Fourth Amendment and thus requires the issuance of a search warrant, absent exigent circumstances. It is difficult to define a building's curtilage. It is often considered the area that is a part of the "domestic economy" of the household. It always covers the immediate area surrounding a home and all attached structures.

Though it may include a nearby barn, it probably will not include a distant outbuilding. There is no hard-and-fast rule that defines precisely the number of feet that the curtilage is from the home. Each case is decided on its own facts and circumstances.

The use of telescopes, binoculars, or night scopes, by themselves, does not render an observation unlawful. Police officers can, therefore, position themselves in a location where it is lawful for them to be and observe suspicious activities using magnifying lenses, except in Hawaii.

Police officers are not free, however, to accomplish illegal searches with the use of mechanical devices and stand on technical concepts of trespass. For example, an officer cannot stand outside the bedroom window of a suspect and peer inside, because this is a violation of the curtilage. He could stand across the street on a sidewalk and look through an open window, as could any citizen. He could not climb to the roof of a nearby office structure and, with the aid of binoculars, look down into an apartment bedroom, if the only other way to look through the window was by standing just outside the window, within the curtilage. There is no "expectation of privacy" that a neighbor will not look out his window, but there is a reasonable expectation that one will not be spied upon from a nearby roof.

Thus, officers, by sitting in a parked car on the street, would be able to look into the front window of a home and see illegal activity because the occupants had carelessly left the drapes open. If the neighborhood is predominantly black and the officers are white, they may feel it prudent to park in an alley away from but in the line of sight of the windows. Anything they would see with the aid of binoculars is lawful because anyone parked on the street could see the same activities. There is no "search," and the events observed fall within the plain view rule.

c. Semiprivate Places

Another area of considerable litigation is the definition of a public place. If an officer sees incriminating evidence or actions in a public place, no search is involved, and the observations are admissible as evidence against an accused. If, however, an officer is in a private place without consent or without a warrant, his observations are not admissible against the accused.

Not every place is clearly public or private. Many are semi-private. If, for example, a police officer walks through a department store during business hours, he is in a public place. This is because the store by implication invites the public to enter the premises, and the public has ready access to the store through unlocked doors facing a street or parking lot. When the officer enters an unlocked rest room, he is still in a public place. But if he enters a commode stall, stands on the plumbing, and looks over into another stall, he is conducting a search of a semiprivate area. It is easy to see the reason for this. First, if the stall has doors, the occupant has a reasonable expectation of privacy from intrusions. Second, a locked rest room stall does not provide the general public with ready access. If, therefore, an officer observes an addict taking a fix under these conditions, the observations will be excluded at the trial. To illustrate further the principle involved, suppose the activity is conducted in a doorless commode stall or in front of a urinal. In this case anyone who enters the rest room, including a police officer, could see the activity. It would make no difference if the officer had concealed himself behind a false air vent in order to observe the illegal actions since they were performed in plain view of anyone who entered the room.

d. Execution of Search Warrants

The plain view exception often takes effect during the course of searches conducted pursuant to a warrant. Thus, a warrant might command an officer to search for stolen goods. In the course of the search he finds narcotics. The contraband, although not named in the warrant, is admissible and should be seized because it was observed in plain view, within the course and scope of a lawfully conducted search. Officers executing a search warrant are in a place where they lawfully have a right to be. Anything they see of an evidentiary nature, therefore, can later be related in the courtroom. To state the matter simply, the officers do not have to close their eyes to contraband, weapons, instrumentalities of a crime, or fruits of other crimes.

Similarly, officers who enter a home or business to serve an arrest warrant need not blind themselves to the contents of the premises during the course of apprehending the defendant. As an example, officers enter a person's home to arrest him for failure to appear in court for a traffic violation. While in his living room, they see twelve television sets bearing a bill of lading stacked in a corner. The officers are free to investigate the circumstances of the defendant's possession of the sets, including tracing them to determine if they were stolen.

e. Inventories

Pursuant to departmental regulations or standing custom, officers usually check the contents of impounded vehicles. The routine taking of an inventory is not a search as defined by the Fourth Amendment. It is conducted for the purpose of safeguarding any valuables found in the vehicle, and it protects the officers from false claims of theft or from liability from mysterious disappearance. Police officers would be derelict in their duties if they failed to remove weapons or valuable property from vehicles that are impounded, stored in an unprotected lot, or left parked beside a roadway.

In most states, any items found in the course of conducting an inventory of a vehicle are admissible in court. This is because an inventory is not a search, and items found inadvertently come within the plain view exception. The courts in California have rejected this philosophy and thus exclude items found during the course of an inventory. In spite of this interpretation, it would be wise for officers in California to continue to conduct inventories in order to reduce losses by theft. While evidence fortuitously found would be inadmissible, officers can protect themselves against civil claims for negligent custody of personal property.

(3.16) Abandoned Property Rule

Property that has been abandoned belongs to no one. It has been defined as the voluntary relinquishment of possession, right, title, and claim to something, accompanied by an apparent intention of not reclaiming it. Law enforcement officers have occasion to use the rule of abandonment in four contexts.

First, objects that are thrown away by a pedestrian or a motorist may be picked up by an officer. Thus, an officer might not have probable cause to stop a suspect and search him for contraband, but he can legally retrieve the contraband if the suspect discards it. These are the so-called "dropsie cases," which are often encountered by uniformed officers who see known narcotics users in public. Defense attorneys commonly engage in vigorous cross-examination of arresting officers, seeking to prove that the narcotics were recovered by an illegal search rather than by abandonment.

Second, officers are sometimes called by the management to such places as hotels or motels when the housekeeping staff finds contraband or a weapon in a rented room. If the occupant has abandoned the premises, the search is lawful. If, on the other hand, the "abandonment" was temporary (that is, the occupant intended to return), the search is unlawful. Serious problems arise when the management has asked the occupant to leave for nonpayment of rent and later takes possession of the premises. The law cannot presume an occupant has abandoned the premises simply because he has been asked to leave for this reason.

Third, abandoned homes and apartment houses are frequently found in larger communities, often having been condemned for redevelopment purposes. They may be inhabited by drug addicts, criminals seeking refuge, and others. Police officers may enter these places without the consent of the occupants and without a search warrant. Occupants do not have a reasonable expectation of privacy and lack standing to object to the search on the grounds of the Fourth Amendment. This aspect of the rule also applies to abandoned automobiles.

A seizure based on a show of authority does not occur until the person who has been subjected to the show of authority complies with that show of authority by submitting to the officer's commands (California v. Hodari D., 499 U.S. 621, 1991). Until submission takes place or there is a physical seizure, an officer's actions need not be justified by some level of proof, and items discarded by the suspect prior to seizure under these rules are "abandoned" prior to seizure.

Finally, officers working on cases related to narcotics and intelligence sometimes sift through trash and garbage deposited in refuse cans. If this can be accomplished without a physical trespass on the property of the occupant, the search is lawful. Officers may also enter into community-occupied space in an apartment building to search commonly used trash barrels. California, however, has refused to recognize the validity of these searches and holds that they violate the occupants' expectation of privacy.

(3.17) Searches Incident to Arrest

One of the most important exceptions to the requirement that officers have probable cause to search suspects is the incident to a legal arrest exception. In the past police officers would search an entire house or automobile when they placed an occupant under arrest. No further showing of cause was necessary.

In one of the most revolutionary cases decided by the Supreme Court under Chief Justice Earl Warren, the scope of searches incident to a legal arrest was dramatically curtailed. In *Chimel* v. *California*, 395 U.S. 752 (1969), the court announced that, thereafter, officers could only search the arrestee and the area immediately around him. The court said:

> It is reasonable for the arresting officer to search the person arrested in order to remove any weapons that [might be used] to resist arrest or effect his escape. Otherwise, the officer's safety might well be endangered, and the arrest itself frustrated. In addition, it is entirely reasonable for the arresting officer to search for and seize any evidence on the arrestee's person in order to prevent its concealment or destruction. And the area into which an arrestee might reach in order to grab a weapon or evidentiary items must, of course, be guided by a like rule. A gun on a table or in a drawer in front of the one who is arrested can be as dangerous to the arresting officer as one concealed in the clothing of the person arrested. There is ample justification, therefore, for a search of the arrestee's person and the area "within his immediate control" —construing that phrase to mean the area from within which he might gain possession of a weapon or destructible evidence.
>
> There is no comparable justification, however, for routinely searching rooms other than in which an arrest occurs, —or, for that matter, for searching through all the desk drawers or other closed or concealed areas in that room itself. Such searches, in the absence of well-recognized exceptions, may be made only under the authority of a search warrant.

The *Chimel* rule initially gave rise to the "arm's reach" doctrine. Most courts have more liberally construed the case and have adopted variants of the "lunge" doctrine. In its simplest analysis, the case restricts searches to those areas of a room where the arrestee can reach or jump over to.

Chimel also applies to arrests made when the suspect is apprehended in a motor vehicle. Officers may search the seat tops, under the front seats, the floorboard, above the visor, and an unlocked glove compartment.

A more serious question arises over whether an otherwise acceptable search can be continued after the suspect has been restrained or removed from the area where he was arrested. If the search of the room or the car is contemporaneous with the arrest, the search is proper. If the suspect has been placed in a transport vehicle or has been physically removed from the premises, the searching process must be discontinued. Inquisitive officers might think it wise to permit an arrestee freedom to move around unrestrained as long as possible. Not only is this dangerous to the officers, but the courts would find it a sham to avoid the restrictive consequences of the *Chimel* ruling.

No justification need be shown for a search of the clothing and accessories of the arrestee. They may be thoroughly searched if the search is conducted contemporaneous with the arrest and transport of the accused. Courts have disagreed over whether an officer can search a suitcase that an accused was carrying at the time of the arrest. Such inspections can often be justified on the theory that its contents are being inventoried, particularly when the accused was apprehended on the street or in a car.

Two qualifications of the *Chimel* ruling must be made. First, officers may, in many cases, walk into adjacent rooms, open closets, or peek under beds. This is to ensure that cohorts of the arrestee are not hiding in wait. These individuals might assault the arresting officers and prevent the arrest. Even stronger justification arises when accomplices in the crime are still at large, and their whereabouts are unknown. Second, under the plain view exception, officers need not ignore contraband, weapons, and evidence observed in open places while they are apprehending the accused and ensuring themselves against attack by concealed cohorts.

Finally, it must be noted that, long before the *Chimel* case was decided, courts condemned the so-called timed arrest. That is, officers may not unreasonably delay the apprehension of an accused merely to invade his home in the hope of extending their search to the premises he had occupied. If, however, a residential arrest is justified on the basis of other factors, the delay is reasonable. Thus, officers, armed with an arrest warrant for Smith, observe him walking home. Smith is part of a suspected drug ring, and his arrest on the streets would alert his accomplices. If the officers delay apprehension until he is inside his residence, the delay is reasonable and justified. Anything seen in plain view, once the officers are inside, is admissible as evidence. Items within Smith's reach, in the room where he is apprehended, can be lawfully searched.

Tensions in a community, which sometimes result in civil disturbances, can often be avoided by inconspicuous apprehensions. If hostile attitudes are prevalent in a neighborhood, delayed residential arrest of a local resident would be justified.

(3.18) Searches of Vehicles

Vehicular searches are, in most cases, an exception to the rule requiring issuance of a search warrant. This is because vehicles can be easily moved and concealed (*Carroll* v. *U.S.*, 267 U.S. 132 [1925]).

In addition, the Supreme Court has pointed out that people have less expectation of privacy in a motor vehicle because of the public nature of travel and because the automobile itself is ruled by various governmental regulations.

If the stop is justified, a vehicular search without a warrant may be legal under the following set of circumstances:

1. The officer has probable cause to search the vehicle.
2. The officer has probable cause to arrest the driver for a custodial offense of an evidentiary nature. That is, the offender must be booked, not released on citation, and the offense is one in which physical evidence may be present.
3. The officer has probable cause to arrest the driver for a custodial offense of a nonevidentiary nature. Here, the scope of the vehicle search is limited by the *Chimel* ruling.

In 1982, the U.S. Supreme Court clarified the rule relating to containers found inside a vehicle. The High Court, in a six to three decision, concluded that police, acting under the automobile exception to the Fourth Amendment warrant requirement, may search every part of a vehicle, including closed containers that might conceal the contraband they are seeking. In this case (*U.S.* v. *Ross*, 456 U.S. 798 [1982]), the Court held, in effect, that officers having probable cause to search an occupied vehicle for a specific type of evidence (for example, contraband or stolen property) are authorized to conduct a warrantless search of all compartments, including closed containers, inside the vehicle where the evidence sought might reasonably be found.

The Court stated in *Ross* that

The scope of the warrantless search authorized by (the *Carroll*) exception is no broader or narrower than a magistrate could legitimately authorize by warrant. If probable cause justifies the search of a lawfully parked vehicle, it justifies the search of every part of the vehicle and its contents that may conceal the object of the search.

In a significant subsequent case, some nine years after *Ross,* the High Court addressed the questions of whether the Fourth Amendment requires police to obtain a warrant to open a closed container in a vehicle if they lack probable cause to search the vehicle but *do* have probable cause to believe that the container itself contains contraband. The Court concluded in *California* v. *Acevedo*, 500 U.S. 565, 580 (1991) that probable cause to believe that a container in a vehicle holds contraband or seizable evidence justifies a warrantless search of that container even in the absence of probable cause to search the vehicle.

Lower courts have been split on the legality of police use of road blocks to stop cars. A vehicle road block stop is a "seizure" within the meaning of the Fourth and Fourteenth Amendments, and random stops are unconstitutional. Now, under present Supreme Court rulings, the police may legally set up sobriety road blocks as long as they follow regular police guidelines (*Michigan* v. *Sitz*, 496 U.S. 444 [1990]).

a. Custodial and Evidentiary Offenses

When an officer makes a custodial arrest for a crime of an evidentiary nature, it is possible that the fruits of or the evidence of the offense, such as weapons or contraband, will be in the car. No special proof of the existence of these items is necessary to justify a complete warrantless search of the vehicle.

When a custodial arrest is made for a nonevidentiary offense, however, the scope of the permissible search is limited by the *Chimel* decision to the area immediately around the arrestee. Thus, officers see Smith, who is wanted on an outstanding warrant for nonsupport, driving a car. At the time the officers apprehend him, they may search the area around the front seat. This is done for their own safety since Smith could have secreted a weapon in the vehicle. But, because Smith is not being charged with an evidentiary offense, the officers cannot open his trunk or a locked glove compartment.

A custodial arrest is occasionally made for a traffic offense. They are normally of a nonevidentiary nature. If, however, the apprehension is for drunk driving, the arresting officers may search for intoxicants.

Most traffic offenses are handled by the issuance of a citation, and a custodial arrest is not involved. In these cases a search "incident to arrest" is not justified. If, however, the officer issuing the citation reasonably suspects that the driver may be armed and dangerous, he may frisk the occupant. Though the scope of the frisk of someone occupying a vehicle is broader than that permitted of a pedestrian, it parallels that allowed in searches incident to arrest. A gun kept under the driver's seat is just as accessible and as dangerous to the officer as one concealed in the driver's clothing—perhaps more so.

(3.19) Hot Pursuit and Exigent Circumstances

Two exceptional situations make a search warrant unnecessary. The first is the so-called hot pursuit exception. An officer who chases a fugitive, or is in fresh pursuit, does not need a search warrant to continue his chase into homes or offices, and anything found in the course of the pursuit and is incident to it is an admissible item. In order for the incident to qualify as this type of exception, the officer must have legal grounds to make an arrest, the suspect must be fleeing to avoid imminent capture, and the pursuit must be promptly started and continuously maintained. It is not necessary that the fugitive be constantly in sight of the officer or, for that matter, in sight at all. Certain interruptions are justified, such as calling for assistance, temporarily resting, if the pursuit is on foot, or stopping for gas or directions, if it is in a car.

Since fresh pursuit, in the absence of a statute, is a common-law rule, an officer must stop at the territorial limits of his jurisdiction. If, during the course of the pursuit, the officer finds incriminating evidence, contraband, or weapons, he may seize these items without a warrant.

The second exception is exigent circumstances. If a true emergency exists, or is reasonably believed to exist, officers may enter the premises without a warrant. The most common example is the situation in which there is the threat of a bomb. Another is when officers believe a person may be in need of aid. The urgency of the incident justifies entry without a warrant, and, in most jurisdictions, anything seen inside in plain view may be seized without a warrant. In a few states the officer must return with a warrant for the actual seizure, but the entry and search without a warrant are lawful when they occur. The Supreme Court has made it clear that police officers cannot create their own exigent circumstances. These circumstances must exist independently. The following is an example of this. Officers had an arrest warrant for Vale and knew where he lived. Outside his home they witnessed him conduct an apparent narcotics transaction. They arrested Vale and searched his house. The search could not be justified on exigent circumstances since the police themselves created the circumstances (*Vale* v. *Louisiana*, 399 U.S. 30 [1970]).

(3.20) Consensual Searches

Nothing in the Fourth Amendment requires the issuance of a warrant when the party in possession of that which is to be searched validly consents to the search. There is nothing immoral or unethical about asking a suspect to give his consent. As a matter of fact, the majority of police searches are made on this basis. The "waiver" is simply the voluntary relinquishment of a known right—the right to demand a search warrant. Consensual searches are convenient because of several factors.

1. The search need not be based on probable cause or a lesser amount of proof.

2. The search does not have to be related to a valid arrest.

3. The officer does not have to name or particularly describe the property sought.

4. The search may be commenced long after the leads have become stale.

5. The premises to be searched do not have to be particularly described.

6. Extensive paperwork and judicial approval are unnecessary.

7. The search may be conducted outside the officer's jurisdiction.

a. Voluntariness

The consent must be freely given, without coercion or deceit. Once incriminating evidence or contraband is found, the suspect's only realistic defense is to challenge the legality of the consent itself. It is important, therefore, that officers document facts surrounding the giving of consent. It may not be enough simply to warn a suspect that he has the right to refuse to give his consent. Below are some factors that tend to prove the voluntariness of the consent.

1. The suspect actively assists the officers in conducting the search.

2. The suspect verbally incriminates himself.

3. The suspect expresses a belief that nothing incriminating will be found.

4. The suspect is the first to suggest that a search be made.

5. The suspect is well educated or holds a responsible position.

Factors that tend to prove a consent was not given voluntarily include the following.

1. The suspect is an alien or is semiliterate.

2. The original entry into the premises was illegal.

3. The consent was taken while the subject was at gunpoint and was handcuffed.

4. The officers made "implied threats" such as "You'll be better off if you cooperate."

5. The suspect was forcibly arrested and suffered minor injury, such as lacerations.

Exculpatory statements expressing belief that nothing will be found tend to support a finding of voluntariness. This is so because of the recognition that many suspects use affirmative means to suggest their innocence. Similarly, a suspect might believe that the items sought are well hidden and will not be discovered. The courts have also recognized that denials of ownership or a stated lack of authority to give consent are simply efforts to use an alternative defense.

The Supreme Court has held that an officer may not falsely state that he possesses a search warrant in the hope that he will obtain consent. Such action constitutes coercion and would invalidate the consent as "freely given." Officers may state that if consent is not given they will apply for a search warrant. They may also express the belief, if it is reasonable, that a warrant will be issued at their request. They can, moreover, advise the suspect that, unless he voluntarily consents to an immediate search, his premises will be placed under surveillance while they attempt to secure a search warrant. As stated in *U.S.* v. *Faruolo*, 506 F. 2d 490 (2d Cir. 1974), "In our view . . . the well founded advice of a law enforcement agent that, absent a consent to search, a warrant can be obtained does not constitute coercion. There is an admission by the officer that he has no right to proceed unless the defendant consents." This situation must be distinguished from a consent obtained by deceit, which would just as surely invalidate a consensual search as coercion. If a detective posed as a building inspector and sought to search a place for "building code violations," the search would be illegal.

Deceit differs from "infiltration," which rests on another theory. If an officer works undercover or poses as a criminal, such action does not legally constitute deceit. Although deception is necessary, it is the "misplaced trust" put in the officer that leads to the finding of evidence or contraband. The officer is actually *invited* onto the premises. In the incident of the building inspector he is *permitted* to enter the place to be searched. As an example, officers, posing as customers, enter a pawnshop and ask to see "better buys." The owner takes them into the back room and displays stolen wares. The officers were invitees the owner mistakenly believed were genuine customers. The items observed in plain view are thus admissible.

The simplest method of ensuring that a suspect knows he has the right to refuse his consent is to tell him so. It is not essential that this be done. The Supreme Court has stated that the "prosecution is not required to demonstrate such knowledge as a prerequisite to obtaining a voluntary consent." A distinction should be made when the suspect is under arrest and in custody. At that stage a suspect is entitled to a recital of the *Miranda* warnings because of the "inherently coercive atmosphere" associated with custodial questioning. It is recommended that officers obtain written consents to search from suspects who have been arrested. Such waivers indicate that the suspect knows he has the right to refuse his consent.

The burden of showing that a consent was involuntary rests on the defense. Nothing in the *Miranda* decision applies to consensual search cases. Some courts have, nevertheless, enlarged on a suspect's rights under the Fourth and Fifth Amendments as they are embodied in their respective state constitutions.

b. Scope and Capacity

Officers frequently assume that once consent is given it applies to all of their subsequent actions. This is untrue, and the courts will limit the areas of permissible search to the scope of the given consent. Authority to look in a glove compartment does not extend to a locked trunk. Consent to frisk a suspect does not include the right to rummage through his wallet. A suspect may limit the places that can be searched, define the time limits, direct the numbers or classes of searching officers, and revoke his consent at any time.

Consent may be given by juveniles as well as adults. Courts often hold, however, that a person lacks the capacity to give his consent when he is drunk, high on drugs, very youthful, mentally retarded, injured or in pain, illiterate, or hysterical.

Consensual searches are not limited to goods and chattels. A suspect can lawfully consent to the taking of his fingerprints or footprints; urinalysis; hair, blood, and seminal samples; handwriting and voice exemplars; paraffin and other skin tests; breath and pupillary examinations; and nalorphine injections (the nalline addiction test).

c. Third-Party Consent

At common law, a husband, as head of the household, could consent to a search of the family residence. Over half of the states have ruled that the wife can also consent to a search of the family residence. Five states (Arizona, Florida, Mississippi, North Carolina, and Oklahoma) have ruled, however, that wives lack the authority to allow police officers to enter the family's premises to search for evidence. It is generally felt that one spouse has as much right as the other to control the household, in the absence of the partner. The Supreme Court has recently held that a wife may consent to the search of the family home under the Fourth Amendment, but states are free to fashion a more restrictive rule based on their state constitutions.

Some courts have examined the subject's marital situation to see if it was harmonious or antagonistic. Most courts have upheld the legitimacy of the consent if both parties live on the premises, since they have equal control or right of control over the property. It may be another situation when the spouse has moved out of the suspected home. If the vacating party has retained a key and has lawful access to the home, the consent is probably valid. On the other hand, if the vacating party returned the key to the other spouse on separation, a forcible entry based on the consent of the vacating spouse is of dubious validity.

So-called common-law marriages and temporary liaisons often result in relationships of convenience. The test of the validity of a consent is control and access. It is unnecessary to prove that one person authorized another to give his or her consent to a search. The following serves as an example. William Matlock lived with a woman in a large home. Officers who were investigating a bank robbery asked the woman for her consent to search Matlock's room, which she shared with him. Matlock was in custody, and his consent was not sought. The woman pointed out Matlock's room, and the officers confiscated a large quantity of money. The Supreme Court upheld the woman's consent and the subsequent seizure. Although the woman's statements were hearsay, the court found them inherently believable, made against her interests because she could have involved herself, and were thus admissible in a suppression hearing.

It is possible that one spouse may not have access and control over some property of the other, regardless of the length of time they have been married and cohabiting. Examples include a safe, a safe-deposit box, or a file cabinet that is locked and exclusively used by one spouse.

Regardless of the age of a child, his room may be searched with the consent of a parent who owns or leases the premises. Even if the child pays his parents something for support, the room he uses does not, in most cases, take on the context of separately rented property. When, however, a child lives with his spouse in separate quarters over which the parents have voluntarily relinquished control, the situation is different. The situation is similar when a parent moves in with an emancipated child. In that case the parent can only give consent to the search of his room and jointly occupied rooms. On the other hand, if the child owns or leases the home, he can usually grant consent to officers to search the entire premises, including rooms occupied by a parent, brother, or sister. Normally a brother or sister could not consent to the search of a sibling's private room, only to shared and commonly occupied rooms.

Roommates can give consent for the search of their own rooms and those occupied in common, such as the kitchen, bathroom, basement, garage, and hallways. This situation frequently arises in college towns and in communes.

Hosts may normally consent to the search of rooms occupied by visitors. If, however, the houseguest has a reasonable expectation of privacy, the consent will not be binding. Things left on the dresser of an unlocked bedroom are not within the zone of privacy. Things put in drawers or left in suitcases normally would be. Jointly used drawers, closets, and storage space do not create an expectation of privacy.

The concept of the expectation of privacy is a limited one. The expectation is not that a roommate, host, or cotenant will not consent to a police search. The expectation must be that this person will not have access to these places. Thus, the question is an expectation from an intrusion by the other party, not an expectation that his consent will not be given the police.

Landlords do not have the right to consent to a search of occupied property they have leased to another person, even if the tenant is in arrears. Once the tenant has vacated or given up occupancy, the landlord may consent to a search. Although a landlord might have a right to enter a tenant's premises to make repairs, to inspect for damage or hazards, and to show the premises to future tenants, this right is a limited one, and it cannot be extended to police officers for another purpose.

Hotel rooms that are occupied by guests, even past checkout time, are treated no differently than premises leased for longer durations. If a maid, bellhop, valet, or any other employee sees contraband or weapons in a room and notifies the police, the police should refrain from entering the room until a search warrant is obtained. If the officers responding to a call reasonably believe that evidence or contraband will be destroyed or removed, they may, of course, act immediately because of the exigent circumstances surrounding the event. Courts do not lightly uphold exigent searches and will often demand strict compliance with the warrant requirement.

Employers normally have the right to inspect lockers and work areas that are assigned to employees for the mutual convenience of workers and employers. Employees usually cannot expect immunity from employer-instituted searches of company property, including desks, file cabinets, and company-owned vehicles.

Employees do not have an unrestricted right to consent to the search of an employer's property. A manager, of course, has broader discretion in authorizing a search than a clerk. Partners, who at law are joint owners, may consent to the search of the company's premises, files, books, and other property. Silent partners in a limited partnership ordinarily do not have unlimited access and authority and cannot authorize such a search.

Schools, which are somewhere between employers and parents, have the power to authorize a search by police of lockers and other areas that are used by or assigned to a student. Dormitory rooms occupied by college-age students do not fall within this exception, and the school is relegated to the status of a landlord in these situations.

Parolees are released from prison on the condition that they, their automobiles, and their homes may be searched without further consent, and even against their will. Because parolees remain in "constructive custody" of the state, correctional officials and probationary and parole officers may conduct such searches over the objection of the former convict. This right may not be delegated to police officers investigating a crime. These officers may, however, instigate such a search and accompany correctional or parole officers at the time the search is made.

(3.21) Border Searches

Several federal statutes authorize searches at our nation's borders. It is unnecessary to demonstrate the existence of probable cause to justify such searches. This does not mean, however, that the border patrol and customs and immigration officers have complete freedom to conduct warrantless searches. They still must comply with the test of reasonableness as set down in the Fourth Amendment.

The mere fact that a person crosses a border is justification for a customs search. Officers may not subject an individual to indignities and intrusions on human privacy unless there is a reasonable suspicion that he is smuggling contraband or items subject to duty.

Recent court decisions have restricted the right of federal agents to conduct random searches at some distance from the actual border. For example, the occupants of a vehicle seen near but not crossing the Mexican border may appear to be Mexican nationals. This is not sufficient reason for federal agents to stop them to determine whether they are actually aliens. Probable cause is not necessary, however, at a fixed checkpoint some distance from the border.

(3.22) Airport Searches

Airports present unique concerns with their diverse operations and the volume of passenger traffic passing through them daily. Renewed and intensified attention to possible hijacking has brought increased security at airports worldwide.

Recognizing the gravity of safety interests and reduced privacy expectations associated with airline travel, courts have made clear their positions regarding electronic scanning of *all* passengers and their carry-on possessions. If such examinations indicate the presence of metallic objects, physical searches are conducted to discover what they are.

For example, one appellate court, acknowledging that such searches are administrative measures essential to the interest of public safety, said, "The need to prevent airline hijacking is grave and urgent . . . a pre-boarding screening of all passenger and carry-on articles sufficient in scope to detect the presence of weapons or explosives is reasonable to meet . . . the administrative need that justifies it (*U.S. v. Davis,* 482 F. 2d 893 [9th Cir. 1973]).[1]

A person who refuses to submit to the limited search may be denied entry to the boarding area even to the point of detention and questioning.

(3.23) "Shocking" Searches

Some types of searches may "shock" the conscience of the reviewing court and are therefore illegal. The landmark case is *Rochin*

---

1. *Rolando v. Carmen, Criminal Procedure Law and Practice,* second edition (Pacific Grove, Calif.: Brooks/Cole, 1991), p. 178.

v. *California*, 342 U.S. 165 (1952), where the Supreme Court invalidated the use of a stomach pump to retrieve narcotics the suspect had swallowed. The use of an emetic, given by medical personnel, has, however, been upheld. This is particularly true when the suspect swallows a balloon filled with narcotics, the contents of which could have fatal effects.

The Supreme Court also allowed, in *Schmerber* v. *California*, 384 U.S. 757 (1966), the extraction of blood from a suspect, under medically supervised conditions. Another case in California, *People* v. *Kraft*, 84 Cal. Rptr. 280 (App. 1970), held that the application of a scissors lock on the suspect's leg and holding his arm immobile constituted excessive force and was, therefore, an impermissible search.

Several courts have maintained that a successful attempt to prevent a suspect from swallowing apparent contraband is not an illegal search. This includes choking the suspect or inserting fingers into his mouth.

Searches of a suspect's rectum or vagina have been upheld when they are done in a "dignified manner" and when police have reasonable grounds to believe contraband has been concealed in these body cavities. Routine inspections of these areas are not permissible.

"Strip searches" of suspects arrested for minor offenses are generally held to be unreasonable, but strip searches and visual inspection of body cavities after a contact prisoner visit have been approved by the Supreme Court.

(3.24) Standing

"Standing" refers to the legality of a person's status to file a motion or seek other relief. Before 1960, if a defendant denied possession or ownership of seized items of evidence, he had no "standing" to move the court to suppress it. The rule was then changed by the Supreme Court decision of *Jones* v. *U.S.*, 362 U.S. 257, which gave any defendant an automatic "standing" and allowed defendants to move to suppress evidence without having to admit either that they owned it or possessed it.

In one of the moves that further weakened the exclusionary rule, the Supreme Court has overruled the *Jones* case and in a series of decisions now holds that a *suspect must have standing* before he can move to suppress evidence in that he must (a) have a privacy interest in the article seized and (b) he must also have a personal right of privacy in the *place* searched.

The defendant's testimony at the suppression hearing, where he must admit an interest in the items seized, cannot be used as evidence against him at the subsequent trial, but it is still an open question whether his suppression evidence can be used to impeach his testimony if he chooses to take the stand at his trial.

(3.25) Miscellaneous Searches

Police are now faced with the problem of how to legally obtain computer records. Gamblers, drug dealers, and financial con men have gone modern and now widely use computers. Computers can be set to erase whenever they are shut down; or while data are still in the computer, access may be barred to police unless they have the access code. Employees can refuse to reveal the code, relying on their protection from the Fifth Amendment. Once data are stored on disks, the data are hard to find because all disks look alike. Which disk must authorities ask for in applying for a search warrant? Prosecution and police have to develop innovative techniques to cope with this new problem.

When a search warrant is used, can individuals found on the premises be personally searched? *Ybarra* v. *Illinois*, 63 L. Ed. 2d 838 (1979), involved an Illinois search warrant for narcotics in a tavern and on the bartender. In executing the search warrant, the police also did a pat-down for weapons on customers and found narcotics on one of them.

The Illinois statute allowed a search of any person on the premises. The Supreme Court, however, suppressed the narcotics evidence in spite of the Illinois statute, pointing out that the bar customers had a "legitimate expectation of privacy" of their persons while in the tavern, and that there was not even a "reasonable suspicion" in this case to justify a *Terry* type pat-down.

The widespread use of administrative searches done for building inspections, industrial inspections, and the like has been restricted by decisions regarding OSHA inspections. For the latter, the courts now require either a consent from the owner or else a showing of probable cause from the government and the issuing of a warrant authorizing the search.

Police and customs officials now widely use "sniffer dogs" to locate drugs and other contraband in school lockers, luggage, vehicles, and cargo containers. Most court decisions uphold such use of dogs, holding that the sniffing action of the dog is not a "search," because only the surrounding air space is used, the suitcase or other container not being opened *(U. S. v. Place,* 462 U. S. 696 [1988]). Other court opinions have discussed the legal basis necessary to justify using the dogs. One circuit court ruled that a "reasonable suspicion" rather than "probable cause" is all that is required *(U.S. v. Whitehead,* 849 F. 2d 849 [C.A.4, 1988]).

Physical evidence is not admissible unless it has been lawfully collected. In many cases, the defendant goes free because of a faulty seizure of evidence. To avoid the consequences of the exclusionary rule, officers must be expert in the law of arrest, search, and seizure. The subject of arrest and search warrants has never received more attention than now. In recent years the U.S. Supreme Court has emphasized the importance of interposing the determinations of a "neutral and detached magistrate" between the police officer and the citizen. Early in 1976 the California Supreme Court said that, unless there are exigent circumstances, police officers must obtain a warrant before arresting a person in his home; failure to do so will result in the suppression of evidence seized incident to the arrest.

In 1980, the Supreme Court ruled in this same area that a *warrantless* nonconsensual entry into a *suspect's* home to make a *routine* felony arrest violates the Fourth Amendment. This decision did not consider whether exigent circumstances would validate such an arrest. *Steagall* v. *U.S.,* 451 U.S. 204 (1981), did rule that unless there are exigent circumstances, the arrest of a suspect is illegal if done in the course of a warrantless search of a third party's home. However, other decisions have collectively held that probable cause, warrantless felony arrests, in *any* private home can be done only if there is an emergency situation. Warrantless arrests in *public* places are always valid if on probable cause.

Another key court case regarding search and seizure was *In re* I.R.T., 647 S.E.2d 129, 132 (N.C. App. 2007). In 2007, juvenile I.R.T. was standing in a group of people outside an apartment building on Beamon Street in Durham, North Carolina, when two patrol officers approached. One of the officers testified that I.R.T turned his head away when the officer approached him. The officer asked I.R.T if he lived in the building, and IRT said that he did not. The officer testified that he thought I.R.T turned his head away so that the officer could not see that his mouth did not move when he talked, as through he had something inside his mouth he was trying to hide. The officer told I.R.T to spit out whatever was in his mouth, and I.R.T spit out a rock of crack-cocaine wrapped in cellophane. For the purpose of determining whether a "seizure" took place, the juvenile's age was a relevant factor in determining whether a reasonable person in his position would have felt free to leave. In this case, there were two officers present, both of whom arrived in marked police cars. Second, the guns they were carrying were visible. Third, the officers had a gang unit emblem on their shirts. Fourth, the juvenile was fifteen years old at the time of the alleged offense. Given this show of authority, the officer's "request" could have been construed by a reasonable person of the juvenile's age as an order, compliance with which was mandatory. Under these circumstances, the Court did not believe that a reasonable person would feel free to leave. Here the court held that there was reasonable suspicion to stop I.R.T because he acted suspiciously in a high-crime area and that there was probable cause to conduct the search. The Court did remand on the adjudication for possession with intent to sell or deliver because the amount of cocaine recovered was relatively small.

The standards for a warrantless arrest or search are, moreover, the same for the issuance of an arrest or search warrant. There is one important difference between warrantless arrests and searches and those authorized by a magistrate, and it is this difference that ties warrant requirements into the substantive law of criminal evidence. A police officer must demonstrate the existence of probable cause at the time he applies for an arrest or search warrant. This demonstration must be full and unequivocal. All the supporting facts and circumstances must be set forth in the affidavit itself, which means the facts must be in writing or otherwise recorded.

In cases where a warrant was issued, the prosecution is bound by the contents of the affidavit. This is the so-called four corners rule, which means the demonstration of probable cause must be contained within the four corners of the piece of paper given to the magistrate. Something forgotten or unintentionally omitted is lost forever. No matter what evidence of guilt a police officer may have had at the time the warrant was sought, only the facts set forth in the affidavit will be considered when the motion to suppress is introduced. Deficient affidavits cannot be cured later by facts that the officer possessed but did not articulate at the time the warrant was issued. In many jurisdictions, oral statements made under oath cannot be considered by the issuing magistrate, who must consider only the written statements of the officer.

In the case of warrantless arrests and searches, an officer need not establish the existence of probable cause until the preliminary hearing stage (or trial, if the crime is a misdemeanor). This gives him additional time to gather the facts that point to the guilt of the accused. He cannot, of course, use after-acquired information (that is, information acquired after an arrest or search), but he is under less pressure once the arrest has been consummated.

(3.26) Searches by School Officials

Searches and seizures involving students in school has also been a topic of Supreme Court rulings. The case of *New Jersey* v. *T.L.O.,* 469 U.S. 325, 83 L.Ed.2d 720 (1985) involved a New Jersey high school teacher found a 14-year-old student smoking in the bathroom. Under questioning from an assistant principal, the student denied smoking. Not believing the student, the principal opened the student's purse and found a pack of cigarettes and cigarette rolling papers. The principal kept searching, and also found a small amount of marijuana, a pipe, a number of empty plastic bags, a lot of one-dollar bills, an index card listing other students who owed the student money, and letters that implicated the student as a marijuana dealer. The Supreme Court held that the pivotal question in any search and seizure case involving a student in school is: Was the search conducted by a police officer or by a school official? School officials are still subject to some theoretical limits under the Fourth Amendment, but not the same that govern police officers. More specifically, the majority of the Court held that for school officials, "the legality of the search of a student should depend simply on the reasonableness,   under all the circumstances, of the search.... Under ordinary circumstances, a search of a student by a teacher or other school official will be 'justified at its inception' when there are reasonable grounds for suspecting that the search will turn up evidence that the student has violated or is violating either the law or the rules of the school. Such a search will be permissible in its scope when the measures adopted are reasonably related to the objectives of the search and not excessively intrusive in light of the age and sex of the student and the nature of the infraction." This precedent has been called the "T.L.O. reasonableness" standard.

In 1998, an assistant principal noticed that a school bank bag was stored under the office counter. The principal also saw Nicole Phillips in the office, while the secretary was not at the counter. When the secretary returned, Phillips left the office. The secretary found that the bank bag was missing. When the assistant principal began to search for the money, he saw Phillips leave a women's bathroom. The principal and a female teacher searched the bathroom and found the bank bag in the trash can. The principal asked the student to lead him to the money, and the student went in a bathroom stall and retuned with the cash. The court here did not cite T.L.O., but used suspiciously similar reasoning to reach its decision in this case. The court acknowledged that custodial statements obtained without a *Miranda* warning are inadmissible, and that a custodial interrogation may be conducted by an individual acting as an agent of the police. However, the Court held that the defendant in this case was not "in custody" when she was questioned by the principal, because the principal was not acting as an agent of law enforcement authorities. The Court also noted that the principal did not question the defendant to "obtain information to be used in criminal proceedings" but simply "for school disciplinary purposes" (*In Re* Krystal Nicole Phillips, 128 N.C. App. 732, 497 S.E.2d [1998]).

In a 2000 North Carolina case, a student told a middle school assistant principal that the defendant had something is his bag that he should not have at school. The principal questioned the defendant, who first told her that he did not have a bag and then denied that there was anything inappropriate in his bag. The defendant would not let the principal search the bag, and asked to call his father. The assistant principal contacted the dean of students and the school resource officer. The officer handcuffed the defendant when he still refused to turn over the bag, and the principal opened the bag and found a pellet gun. At this point, the principal called the defendant's father. In applying the "T.L.O." ruling to these facts, the Court of Appeals decided that the search was conducted by a school official (the principal) and not a police officer (the resource officer). As such, the court applied the T.L.O. "reasonableness" standard and upheld the search because the tip from the other student, combined with the defendant's lie claiming that he did not have a bag, provided "sufficient grounds for a reasonable person" to believe that something in the bag would yield evidence that the defendant had "broken a school rule or law." Significantly, the court noted that the resource officer "acted to enable (the principal) to obtain the bag and search it. He did not search the bag himself, nor did he conduct any investigation of the bag on his own" (*In Re Jason Patrick Murray*, 136 N.C. App. 648, 525 S.E.2d 496 [2000]).

In 2001, the Court also applied the T.L.O. reasonableness standard to actions of school officials and police officers. In the case of *In Re D.D.*, 146 N.C. App. 309, 554 S.E.2d 346 (2001), a substitute teacher overheard a student say that a group of girls was coming onto campus to fight at the end of the school day. The substitute told the school's principal. About ten minutes before the end of the school day, the principal contacted the school resource officer, and they positioned themselves at opposite ends of the school building. The principal saw four female students, including one of his students, standing in the parking lot. The principal, together with the resource officer and two other uniformed officers, approached the girls; the officers had hand guns in their possession. In the parking lot, the principal asked the students why they were there, and the defendant said she was waiting at the public bus stop to catch a bus to go an appointment. When the students tried to walk away from the principal and the officers, the officers told them to "hold on." The principal asked the girls their names, and called other schools to try and find out what school they attended. The school resource officer asked one of the students for permission to search her purse. The student testified that the officer grabbed the purse before she could give permission. The officer found a box cutter in the purse. The principal took the students to the office and asked the girls to empty their purses. The defendant had a knife in her pocket. The principal and one of the officers (not the resource officer) testified that they both made the decision to charge the defendant. The court determined that the T.L.O. "reasonableness" standard applied, not only to searches by school officials, but also to searches where police officers work "in conjunction with" school officials, so long as they do so "to maintain a safe and educational environment." The court applied the reasonableness standard and found that the search was both "justified at its inception" and "reasonably related in scope to the circumstances which justified the interference in the first place." Further, the court ruled that the officers' involvement was "minimal" relative to the principal's actions. The court held that the officers did not initiate the investigation, nor did they direct the principal's actions. The court believed that the officers simply held the girls in place so that the principal could act. The court also noted that the school resource officer performed the function of "maintaining a safe and proper educational environment."

In 2005, a school resource officer (also a Forsyth County, North Carolina, sheriff's deputy) was investigating a fight at school involving T.B. When the officer saw T.B. leaving the school, he told T.B. to stop, but she did not listen. Later, at about 3 P.M., the officer saw T.B. standing at a bus stop on school grounds. The officer told T.B. to come back to the school office to talk to the school administrator about the fight and find out if she would be suspended. T.B. refused, and her sister told the officer to get his hands off her. T.B. ran, and the officer grabbed her sister, J.M., who resisted and then also ran. The two sisters were apprehended a short time later. Relying heavily on the *In Re* D.D. case described in the previous paragraph, the court held that the T.L.O. "reasonableness" standard applies to cases where "a resource officer, acting in conjunction with a school official, detains a student on school premises." In this holding, the Court noted that the officer was still on duty and on school property (the bus stop) when he attempted to detain T.B. The court also held that the officer's sole purpose in detaining T.B. was to bring her to the school administrator (*In Re* J.M.F and T.J.B., 168 N.C. App. 143, 607 S.E.2d 304 [2005]).

Also in 2005, S.W. was walking through the hall of his school with another student. When the students passed by the school's resource officer (a Durham County sheriff's deputy), the officer smelled marijuana. The officer stopped S.W., took him from the hallway to the school's weight room, and asked him if he had anything on him. S.W.

said he did not, and the officer asked, "Do you mind if I search?" S.W. said that he did not mind. There were two assistant principals present, but they did not question or search S.W. The officer found marijuana during the search. In light of the above cases, the real questions here were whether the officer was acting as a law enforcement officer, as a school official, or at the direction of a school official. The Court held that the officer was "not an outside officer that was conducting an investigation" into a nonschool crime. The court applied the T.L.O. standard, and upheld the search based on the officer's smelling marijuana. In reaching the conclusion that T.L.O. applied, the court noted that the officer was an employee of the Durham County Sheriff's Department, but that he "assisted school officials with the school discipline matters and taught law enforcement related subjects." Also, the officer "was exclusively a school resource officer, who was present in the school hallways during school hours and was furthering the school's educational related goals when he stopped the juvenile" (*In Re* S.W., 171 N.C. App. 335, 614 S.E.2d 424 [2005]).

(3.27) Probable Cause

Although arrest and search warrants require a judicial finding of probable cause, they involve different probabilities. Both warrants necessitate demonstration that a crime has taken place. An arrest warrant, however, requires an identification of the probable perpetrator; a search warrant does not. A search warrant presumes the existence of tangible evidence of the offense; an arrest warrant does not. The search warrant affidavit must go still further and demonstrate the likelihood that the things sought will be at a stated location during an identifiable time. Table 3-1 graphically illustrates the different probabilities.

As has been said, the first probability, common to both warrants, is that an offense has taken place. The existence of an offense report will, in routine cases, establish this fact. It is not necessary that the officer who swears out the warrant be the same one who completed the offense report. In larger departments a patrol officer completes the preliminary report of the theft burglary, robbery, or other crimes; a detective is then assigned to follow up the investigation and obtain

Table 3-1
Probabilities in arrest warrants and search warrants

Prerequisite judicial findings	Arrest warrants	Search warrants
A crime was probably committed.	Yes	Yes
An identified suspect probably committed the act.	Yes	No
Tangible evidence of the offense exists.	No	Yes
Such evidence will be found at or in a described place.	No	Yes
Such evidence will be found at a certain time.	No	Yes

necessary warrants. The individual who swears out the warrant (the affiant) need not communicate directly with the patrol officer for he is entitled to accept the written report at face value and to presume its correctness. A conscientious detective will, of course, call the victim, witnesses, and the uniformed officer who took the initial report, verifying all relevant details. In drafting the affidavit, the affiant should state the existence of the initial report, summarize its details, and indicate that he is swearing out the affidavit "on information and belief."

Specialized enforcement units usually do not receive citizen complaints; they produce their own reports to demonstrate the existence of an offense. This is usually true in the so-called inspectional services units, such as narcotics, gambling, and other vice squads. Reports of informants' interviews, surveillance reports, and undercover operational accounts furnish the necessary presumption of criminal activity. In the affidavit these documents are referred to in the same manner as offense reports.

In some states by statute and also under the federal rules, a search warrant may be issued for a crime in progress, but not yet committed. This is true of certain possessory offenses.

Only arrest warrants need identify a suspect. This is usually by name, but John Doe warrants, coupled with a description, are permissible. The affidavit must show that the suspect is the person who committed an act that is alleged to be illegal. As mentioned, a search warrant may be issued for a home, business, auto, boat, or airplane without naming a suspect. Nearly all states provide, however, that a search warrant may be issued for a described person. The affidavit must show why there is probable cause to believe that evidence will be found on him.

Search warrants require a demonstration that what is sought probably exists. This is simple when officers seek to recover stolen television sets, a murder weapon, or other specifically identifiable items. In addition, certain offenses, by their nature, employ tangible items describable by their generic nature. For example, bookmakers keep written records, narcotics dealers keep an inventory, addicts keep paraphernalia, and burglars keep tools.

The affiant should state his belief, which is based on stated facts, that the things sought will be found in the location to be searched. *People* v. *Prall*, 145 N.E. 610, 612 (Ill. 1924), described below, is an example.

The defendant, Prall, was arrested by a deputy sheriff for possession of automobile tires taken from a railroad siding. A search warrant for Prall's home was defective, because it was necessary for the deputy sheriff to allege that more tires were taken than had been recovered.

In general, the longer the time between the crime and the search, the greater is the likelihood that the items sought have been destroyed, sold, concealed, or otherwise disposed of. The nature of the offense, the type of item sought, and the individual who seems to be involved must, however, always be considered. If a professional burglar took six television sets, it is unlikely that he will have any of them after several months. If, however, the suspect is a rather young, nonprofessional criminal, he might keep one set for his personal use.

It is not necessary to assume that particularly described goods will exist if the crime, by its nature, involves a turnover of items, and these items are of the same generic class. Surveillances may indicate, for example, that a suspect has taken bets on horses over a period of several weeks. Officers do not have to assume that records of older transactions still exist; they need only allege that the crime requires the keeping of records. They have probable cause to believe, therefore, that recent entries are kept at a named location and that the newer records have replaced the older ones.

It is important in cases where there is a turnover of the items sought that the affiant demonstrate the continuing nature of the offense. This may be done in one of two ways: by two or more surveillances conducted on different days, or by disclosures from a reliable informant that the activity is continuing.

Though staleness is always a significant factor in search warrants, it is not in arrest warrants. Subject only to the statute of limitations, officers may possess probable cause for an indefinite period of time before seeking the issuance of an arrest warrant. Delays can, on the other hand, imperil the validity of search warrants unless continuity is shown.

(3.28) Grounds for Issuance

Search warrants are not among the warrants, writs, and other processes recognized by common law; they are wholly statutory. The Fourth Amendment requires that all warrants must be supported by probable cause, under oath, and they must particularly describe the person or things sought and the person or place to be searched. Most states require the request to be written, but transcribed testimony is constitutionally acceptable if it is allowed by statute. It is imperative that the affiant, sometimes called a complainant, state that he has been placed on his oath or affirmation. Some states are streamlining the warrant process by using facsimile (fax) machines to send the application to the judge, which allows for quick processing and a return of the signed warrant in the same fashion.

Although the oath is normally administered before an officer presents his facts, it may follow unless a state law forbids this practice. It is also customary to sign a form affidavit without raising one's hand and stating aloud, "I swear the truth of these matters so help me God." It is not an unforgivable error to do so, but it is important for officers to comply with formalities

Search warrants can only be secured for enumerated offenses, whereas arrest warrants can be issued for any crime unless a statute demands issuance of a summons or citation. Only the things listed in the statute can be named in the warrant. Recent legislation tends to simplify the list to include the following:

1. contraband, the possession of which is unlawful;
2. instrumentalities used to commit any crime;
3. fruits of a crime;
4. items that are evidence of the commission of a crime or the identity of the perpetrator.

Prior to 1967 some states did not allow the issuing of search warrants that sought "mere evidence," which might be a blood-stained undershirt, mud scrapings from shoes, a diary or plans, powder burns on a cuff, or innumerable other things that could only be listed in a statute by category. These things could only be seized incidental to a valid arrest. A serious problem arose because of the restrictions imposed on the scope of searches incident to arrest in the *Chimel* case. The Supreme Court made clear in *Warden* v. *Hayden*, 387 U.S. 294 (1967), that "mere evidence" could be seized by warrant, assuming there was a statute authorizing such searches. Unfortunately, not all states acted promptly after the *Hayden* case and relied on pre-*Chimel* standards.

(3.29) Particular Description

The requirement that an item be particularly described is flexible. It means the best-known description of the thing sought, not necessarily a unique description. Officers should mention the specific things sought plus the generic name so as to authorize seizure of similar items found but not named in the warrant. For example, contraband can be loosely described as narcotics, illegal weapons, or counterfeit currency, but it is preferable to state heroin, cocaine, and other narcotics, a sawed-off shotgun, automatic rifle, and other illegal firearms, or counterfeit twenty-dollar notes and other U.S. tender.

Some courts have permitted a vague description in the warrant if a more precise description appeared in the affidavit and vice versa. Ordinarily, however, care should be used to repeat the descriptions exactly.

Many of the cases with suppressed warrants involve misdescribed premises to be searched. A street address is sufficient where a single-family residence is involved, but it is preferable to state that the premises are a one- or two-storied single-family residence and to describe the home. One might state, for example, "a red brick structure with a front and rear entrance, green front door, and pitched roof covered by gray shingles." Rural property must be so clearly described that there can be no doubt about which place was meant, such as "a two-storied white frame farmhouse on Route 31, approximately 400 yards south of the intersection with Highway 7, on the west side of the road, surrounded by a white picket fence and behind a rural mailbox marked 'The Smiths.'" Some rooming houses do not number floors, much less rooms, and so they must be described in a way similar to the following: "past the front door and up two landings, south thirty feet and up one landing, south down the hallway to the third door on the left (east side of hall)." At least one court decision has approved of the inclusion of a photograph of the premises, attached to the affidavit, and referred to in the warrant. A minor defect in the description will not invalidate the search unless it means that two or more places fit the description. Even in that case, if the affiant or other officer who conducted the surveillances also serves the warrant, the search will be upheld in most jurisdictions.

The Supreme Court now takes a less restrictive view on the use of search warrants. The court upheld a Maryland search where police were armed with a search warrant for a third-floor apartment, but discovered on arriving that there was more than one third-floor apartment. They proceeded to search the wrong apartment and found contraband. The court overlooked the error because the warrant itself was valid when issued; the police discovered their error only after the contraband was found, and they immediately then stopped the search. The court found the search to be "reasonable" and allowed the contraband in evidence (*Maryland* v. *Garrison*, 480 U.S. 79 [1987]).

It is important that the affidavit and warrant list the parts of the building to be searched, unless there is probable cause to believe the things sought could be anywhere in it. This becomes critical when two or more unrelated persons or families share a residence. Only ingenuity can identify which person or family lives in the back, the basement, or the attic. If the officers learn they have named the wrong portion of the building once they have entered it, they should seal the exits and obtain a new warrant quickly.

As mentioned previously, search and arrest warrants may be obtained for persons as well as places. A name is ordinarily sufficient for an arrest warrant, and the name and address for a search warrant. If a physical description is known, however, it is preferable to include it in the warrant and the supporting affidavit. A physical description, photograph, or other method of identifying the individual must be part of a John Doe warrant. For example, a search warrant could be issued for the following: "a negro male, dark complected, balding, middle aged, who accompanies [name] on Monday mornings when money is picked up, and sits on the right side, front seat, of the red over white 1976 Mustang Lic. ASD-701."

The affiant should be described in such a manner as a police officer, victim, or eyewitness. In cases where only circumstantial evidence is present, it is essential that the affiant's background be set forth in detail. It is one thing for a priest or postman to see two people conversing; it is quite another for an experienced narcotics officer to observe this same conversation. Police officers may rely on their specialized training and experience when they are interpreting their surveillances and disclosures by informants. Chief Justice Warren Burger, speaking for two other justices in *U.S.* v. *Harris*, 403 U.S. 584 (1971), stated: "We cannot conclude that a policeman's knowledge of a suspect's reputation—something that policemen frequently know and a factor that impressed such a 'legal technician' as Mr. Justice Frankfurter—is not a 'practical consideration of everyday life' upon which an officer (or magistrate) may properly rely in assessing the reliability of an informant's tip."

The following are typical recitations of expertise. They include the kind of information that officers should keep in their memo books, such as number of arrests, raids, and other law enforcement activities. The numbers in parentheses should always be kept up to date.

"I have been a police officer for (47) months and have been assigned to the gambling unit for (13) months; during this period I have made (74) arrests for gambling, (12) of which were for possession of gambling paraphernalia. I have participated in (53) gambling raids and have testified in (28) trials or suppression hearings involving gambling charges."

"I have been a police officer for (19) months and have been assigned to the narcotics unit for (3) months. I attended a five-day school for narcotics enforcement officers conducted by the Drug Enforcement Administration; I also attended a fourteen-hour in-service seminar on narcotics enforcement sponsored by the Metro Enforcement Group (MEG). I have participated in (28) narcotics arrests, (14) of which followed (8) narcotics raids."

An officer does not have to compile an impressive arrest record personally; it is sufficient that he participated in arrests or raids in order to gain the necessary expertise to give an opinion in a search or arrest warrant affidavit. Certain activities give important clues to the individual with expertise. The following examples illustrate what such a person might ascertain.

1. A gambling detective observes a suspected bookmaker carrying sheets of an off-white colored paper into an apartment. This

could be nitrocellulose fibered rag, known as "flash paper," which instantly burns without residue; it is frequently used by wire room operators.

2. A gambling detective observes a suspected bookmaker carrying a plastic bucket, wooden salad fork, and bottle of liquid drain opener into an apartment. Gelatin paper, which is used extensively by wire room operators, rapidly dissolves in water. Decomposition is assisted by liquid drain openers. A large wooden fork quickens destruction in a plastic bucket.

3. A narcotics detective observes a suspected pusher giving tinfoil packets to a suspected addict and receiving money. Heroin and cocaine are often sold in aluminum foil or cellophane packets.

4. A narcotics detective observes a suspected pusher buy a large bottle of sleeping capsules at a drugstore. These capsules can be easily taken apart, filled with cut heroin, and recapped.

Burglars are known by their tools; gamblers and addicts are known by their associates; prostitutes and some homosexuals are known by the parts of town they frequent. Even if an officer-affiant is not personally acquainted with such facts, he can include them in his affidavit. The collective wisdom of the entire police department can be referred to in supporting pleadings. To reiterate, the important point to remember is that an officer's background should be particularized in the affidavit.

(3.30) Use of Informants

Generally speaking, there are three motives of informants. Television dramas highlight the underworld informer who implicates others for financial gain, revenge, the elimination of competition, or in the hope that his illegal activity will be overlooked. "Stoolies" are typically portrayed as disreputable characters. The motive of the second type of confidential informant is to be a good citizen. Someone who is not involved in criminal activities, but is motivated by a sense of right and wrong, falls into this category. Citizens often report neighbors, acquaintances, business contacts, or friends, and, therefore, they desire total anonymity. The third type of informant is a police officer, federal agent, or other law enforcement employee, and his motive is to perform his duty. Because of their dealings with certain groups or individuals, they are reluctant to take forthright action or to complain about suspects. Law enforcement officers are sometimes called "automatic informants" because they are automatically supposed to report criminal behavior.

All three types of informants may demand confidentiality. The underworld character may fear death, assault, or a lesser form of retaliation. A citizen may fear social ostracism, ridicule, or contempt. An officer may fear impairment of his efficiency or credibility.

Police agencies should keep careful records on confidential informants. For reasons of security, records of identity are normally kept in safe custody, accessible to only a few senior officers, and informants are customarily referred to in reports by number only. Each time an informant furnishes information, a report should be written, and an attempt should be made to verify the substance of the disclosures. A running record should be kept on all criminal informants because their tips cannot furnish the basis for probable cause unless prior reliability is demonstrated. This credibility is important because a confidential informant cannot be cross-examined like other witnesses. His information constitutes, therefore, hearsay evidence and is admissible at a suppression hearing, but not at a trial.

Proving an informant's reliability can be accomplished in a number of ways. The usual method is to allege that the informant has provided information in the past and that he has proved himself trustworthy. A single arrest that results from prior information can provide the necessary reliability, if one of two conditions are met: First, a conviction resulted from the arrest. Second, evidence was seized at the time of the arrest even though a conviction was not obtained for some reason or the prosecution is still pending.

Multiple arrests, regardless of whether evidence was seized and although the prosecution of the cases is still pending, also demonstrate reliability. Surveillances provide another way of verifying an informant's disclosures. If independent observations by police officers corroborate the information, reliability is established, as it is when a second informant independently corroborates the facts of the first informant.

A preeminent case on disclosures by an informant is *Spinelli* v. *U.S.*, 393 U.S. 410 (1969). The Supreme Court affirmed prior decisions that held that a police officer may obtain a warrant, based on the word of a confidential underworld informant, if, first, the affidavit states how the informant obtained his information, and, second, the word of the informant is sufficiently corroborated from past instances of reliability, surveillances, or other supporting sources. The problem is particularly acute when an informant who does not qualify for good citizen status is being used for the first time.

Courts abhor "hearsay on hearsay." Even if an informant has provided good leads a hundred times, the investigating officers must determine whether the latest disclosure is based on personal knowledge. Without such assurances, the information will not in itself support a conclusion that probable cause exists. The problem facing law enforcement officers is that an informant cannot always permit this information to be written into an affidavit without jeopardizing his anonymity. If, for example, an informant was the only person who saw a suspect in possession of stolen goods, the affidavit might as well give the informant's name to indicate how he knows the suspect to be in possession of the goods. There is no problem if several individuals saw the suspect in possession of the goods, unless, of course, the exact time was stated.

An affidavit can be intentionally vague concerning the way an informant obtained his information if the facts disclosed are in sufficient detail that a court can presume the knowledge is firsthand. The following is an example of such a statement. "A confidential informant told me that Jones has a quantity of heroin in his apartment at 234 Main, suite B. He said that the heroin is kept in red balloons and is concealed in a green vase. The vase is on a walnut bookshelf on the east side of the living room of said apartment. The informant has personal knowledge of the truth of this information."

Informants usually provide information in a particular area such as gambling, narcotics, or hijacking, but if they are reliable in one area they are usually reliable in another. It is not necessary that the informant's reliability be based on past experience in the activity under investigation.

The so-called good citizen informant receives greater respect from the courts. Thus, it is not necessary for the police to establish tested reliability, and the person's disclosures do not need independent corroboration. The Supreme Court concluded in *U.S.* v. *Harris*, supra, that a person who lacks experience as an informer and is not part of the criminal community can furnish probable cause to law enforcement officers. As with the *Spinelli* case, he would have to disclose how he learned of the suspected activity. The affidavit, in such cases, must affirmatively establish that the citizen is not a part of the scheme, does not have a criminal record, fears for his safety, and witnessed evidence of the offense. Statements from witnesses that they participated in an illicit act are also entitled to credibility since, in the words of the Supreme Court, "people do not lightly admit a crime . . . ." In the *Harris* case, which involved bootlegging, the citizen informant stated that he had recently purchased moonshine from the suspect.

a. The Gates Case

The 1983 case of *Illinois* v. *Gates*, 462 U.S. 213 (1983) provided an opportunity for the U. S. Supreme Court to establish the "totality of circumstances" test in determining the existence of probable cause where the basis for it includes information from an informant.

On May 3, 1978, the Bloomingdale, Illinois, Police Department received by mail an anonymous handwritten letter that read:

> This letter is to inform you that you have a couple in your town who strictly make their living selling drugs. They are Sue and Lance Gates, they live on Greenway, off Bloomingdale Road in the condominiums. Most of their buys are done in Florida. Sue his wife drives their car to Florida, where she leaves it to be loaded with drugs, then Lance flys down and drives it back. Sue flys back after she drops the car off in Florida. May 3 she is driving down there again and Lance will be flying down in a few days to drive it back. At the time Lance drives the car back he has the trunk loaded with over $100,000 in drugs. Presently they have over $100,000 worth of drugs in their basement.
>
> They brag about the fact they never have to work, and make their entire living on pushers. I guarantee if you watch them carefully you will make a big catch. They are friends with some big drug dealers, who visit their house often.
>
> Lance & Susan Gates
> Greenway in Condominiums

The Bloomingdale police chief forwarded the letter to Detective Mader, who decided to investigate further. Mader verified from official records that an Illinois driver's license had been issued to one Lance Gates, residing at a stated address in Bloomingdale. He contacted a confidential informant who determined from certain financial records a more recent address for the Gates. Mader also learned from a police officer at O'Hare Airport that "L. Gates" had made a reservation on Eastern Airlines flight 245 to West Palm Beach, Florida, scheduled for departure from Chicago on May 5 at 4:15 P.M.

Detective Mader then made arrangements with an agent of the Drug Enforcement Administration for suveillance of the May 5 Eastern Airlines flight. The agent later reported to Mader that Gates had boarded the flight and that federal agents had observed him arrive at West Palm Beach and take a taxi to a nearby Holiday Inn. They further reported that Gates went to a room registered to Susan Gates. Then, the following morning at 7:00 A.M., Gates and an unidentified female left the motel in a Mercury bearing Illinois license plates and drove northbound on an interstate frequently used by travelers to the Chicago area. In addition, the DEA agent informed Mader that the license plate number on the Mercury was registered to a Hornet station wagon owned by Gates. He also advised Mader that the driving time between West Palm Beach and Bloomingdale was approximately 22 to 24 hours.

Based on the foregoing facts, a search warrant was issued for the search of Gates' automobile and residence.

At 5:15 A.M. on March 7, only 36 hours after he had flown out of Chicago, Lance Gates and his wife returned to their home in Bloomingdale, driving the car in which they had left West Palm Beach some 22 hours earlier. The Bloomingdale police were awaiting them, searched the trunk of the Mercury, and uncovered approximately 350 pounds of marijuana. A search of Gates' home revealed marijuana, weapons, and other contraband. The Illinois Circuit Court ordered suppression of all these items on the ground that the affidavit submitted to the Circuit Judge failed to support the necessary determination of probable cause to believe that the Gates' automobile and home contained the contraband in question. This decision was affirmed in turn by the Illinois Appellate Court and by a divided vote of the Supreme Court of Illinois, which concluded that, standing alone, the anonymous letter sent to the Bloomingdale Police Department would not provide the basis for a magistrate's determination that there was probable cause to believe contraband would be found in the Gates' car and home.

The Illinois Supreme Court also properly recognized that Detective Mader's affidavit might be capable of supplementing the anonymous letter with information sufficient to permit a determination of probable cause. In holding that the affidavit in fact did not contain sufficient information to sustain a determination of probable cause, the Illinois Court applied a "two-pronged test," derived from the U. S. Supreme Court's decision in *Spinelli*.

According to this view, the letter, as supplemented by Mader's affidavit, first had to adequately reveal the "basis of knowledge" of the letter writer—the particular means by which he came by the information given in his report. Second, it had to provide facts sufficiently establishing either the "veracity" of the affiant's informant or, alternatively, the "reliability" of the informant's report in this particular case.

The Illinois Court, alluding to an elaborate set of legal rules that have developed among various lower courts to enforce the "two-pronged test," found that the test had not been satisfied.

The U. S. Supreme Court agreed with the Illinois Supreme Court that an informant's "veracity," "reliability," and "basis of knowledge" are all highly relevant in determining the value of his report. The High Court did not agree, however, that these elements should be understood as entirely separate and independent requirements to be rigidly exacted in every case, which the opinion of the Illinois Supreme Court would imply. Rather, they should be understood simply as closely intertwined issues that may usefully illuminate the commonsense, practical question of whether there is "probable cause" to believe that contraband or evidence is located in a particular place.

This totality-of-circumstances approach is far more consistent with the High Court's prior treatment of probable cause than is any rigid demand that specific "tests" be satisfied by every informant's tip. Perhaps the central teaching of the High Court's decisions bearing on the probable-cause standard is that it is a "practical, nontechnical conception" (*Brinegar* v. *U.S.*, 338 U.S. 160, 176 [1949]). The court went on, "In dealing with probable cause, . . . the very name implies, we deal with probabilities. These are not technical; they are the factual and practical considerations of everyday life on which reasonable and prudent men, not legal technicians, act" (*Brinegar*, at 175). Finally, the High Court, in reversing the judgment of the Supreme Court of Illinois, concluded that ". . . probable cause does not demand the certainty we associate with formal trials. It is enough that there was a fair probability that the writer of the anonymous letter had obtained his entire story either from the Gateses or someone they trusted. And corroboration of the major portions of the letter's predictions provides just this probability. It is apparent, therefore,

that the judge issuing the warrant had a substantial basis for
. . . concluding that probable cause to search the Gates home and car
existed."

The *Gates* case preserves the "two-pronged test" rooted in *Aguilar* v. *Texas*, 378 U.S. 108 (1964) and *Spinelli* v. *U.S.*, 393 U.S. 410
(1969); however, these two aspects are not treated as separate independent concerns. Rather, the "totality-of-circumstances" concept is
employed. The conclusion here is that if one prong is lacking, it can be
satisfied by the other when considered in combination with other
evidence.

The courts preserve the confidentiality of informants. To do
otherwise would jeopardize their lives, their safety, and their privacy.
In 1967 the Supreme Court clearly held that confidential, nonparticipating informants may establish probable cause for the police to
make an arrest or to conduct a search. Their identities should not be
disclosed as a matter of public policy. Though their disclosures may
furnish underlying probable cause to support the search or arrest
upon which the prosecution is predicated, they may not be used
against an accused at his trial. In limited cases, however, courts will
order production of an informant or revelation of his identity. Should
this situation arise, the prosecution can either comply or drop the
charges. The informant's confidentiality will not be breached unless
disclosure is necessary to a fair trial or the informant actually participated in the offense being prosecuted.

Confidential information received from other police officers is
intrinsically reliable. It is unnecessary to establish a history of tested
disclosures or to corroborate the information through surveillances.
The knowledge of one officer, at law, is the knowledge of the whole
police department, and officers are presumed, at law, to be truthful
and to have a duty to exchange information. They are more likely
to use care in repeating things overheard, and their hearsay is more
likely to be valid. Information furnished among officers does not
lose any credibility because of repetition; such exchanges are merely
conduits of "official" knowledge. Though police officers normally
want to testify against a suspect, there are valid reasons for preserving
confidentiality. Undercover agents might be identified, working relationships with other informants might be impaired, and other unpleasant consequences might result.

The law distinguishes between named and confidential informants. This is because a named informant may be subpoenaed to a
deposition, and he can be called to testify at the trial by either side

and can be cross-examined. Most victims of and witnesses to a crime are named informants. They may, however, be treated as confidential informants. If they are credible public citizens, no showing of prior reliability is necessary, particularly when the victim or witness will be produced at the trial or when the information will only be used to develop probable cause for a search warrant.

In larger communities an anonymous informer may occasionally give information to police officers through the mails or over the telephone. Such informants cannot be accorded the good citizen presumption, and prior reliability must be shown. Reliability can be established where, in repeated instances, the anonymous informant is recognized by his handwriting, his voice, or through the use of a code name.

(3.31) Surveillances

Surveillances are conducted by the police for a variety of purposes. They often provide the tactical information necessary to conduct an efficient and safe raid. Sometimes they are strategic, as when they are conducted to keep tabs on a known criminal or terrorist. They may explain motives of suspects or ensure that no other persons are involved. In addition, they may be necessary to aid in developing probable cause preparatory to the issuance of a search or arrest warrant. Surveillances standing alone, if sufficient, can, in fact, furnish the sole basis for a conclusion that probable cause exists. They are also necessary to corroborate information obtained from an underworld informant being used for the first time or informants who may have provided untrustworthy information in the past.

Police officers may lawfully follow a criminal suspect in public areas and make still or motion pictures of his activities. Binoculars, telescopes, and infrared scopes may be used to observe criminal suspects in public and semi-public places. Fluorescein powder, which is excited and becomes visible under ultraviolet light, may be employed. Electronic tracking devices (such as bumper beepers) can be attached to a private car; some courts have found, however, that a suspect's reasonable expectation of privacy may be invaded by their use, and so they should be employed only with the advice of counsel. Surveillances conducted by helicopters and covert rest room observations may, by their nature, be a violation of a suspect's reasonable expectation of privacy.

Police may enter open fields to observe property, and a fence designed to keep animals in or erected for apparently aesthetic reasons will not change an open place into a closed one. Areas in multiple-unit dwellings, such as common garages, hallways, and jointly used trash containers may be lawfully observed without a warrant.

A person living on the ground floor in a populous area who leaves his shades up and drapes open does not have a reasonable expectation of privacy. Officers may not peer into windows if doing so involves trespassing. It is also illegal for them to look from a rooftop, use a fire department snorkel truck, or utilize a telescope from a distant building. An officer should not completely rely on these generalized guidelines; he should, rather, seek the advice of a prosecutor in all important investigations.

Nothing prevents an officer from assuming the identity of an addict or other criminal, a salesman or customer, or ordinary citizen and from visiting a criminal suspect. A person who carelessly places his trust in another does so at his own peril. Deceptive pretenses, including the furnishing of the motive, opportunity, and means to commit a crime, are all lawful police activities.

A famous case, decided by the Supreme Court, involved former Teamster's Union official James Hoffa (*Hoffa* v. *U.S.*, 385 U.S. 293 [1966]). A government informant named Partin was invited into Hoffa's hotel suite and heard conversations that led to the latter's conviction for jury tampering. On appeal, Hoffa claimed that Partin's misrepresentations vitiated the invitation and consent. Mr. Justice Stewart, writing the court's opinion, stated: "Neither this court nor any member of it has ever expressed the view that the Fourth Amendment protects a wrongdoer's misplaced belief that a person to whom he voluntarily confides his wrongdoing will not reveal it."

The court went on to say that the Fifth and Sixth Amendments also were not violated by this practice. "The police are not required to guess at their peril the precise moment at which they have probable cause to arrest a suspect, risking a violation of the Fourth Amendment if they act too soon, and violation of the Sixth Amendment if they wait too long." In the same term of court, Chief Justice Warren, writing for the majority, upheld the practice of using an undercover agent who concealed his identity and misrepresented his true purpose.

Most surveillances do not involve police participation in an offense or overt observations. They usually consist of a list of names, addresses, and license plate numbers, information that is, on the surface, neutral. Once such observations have been completed, corroborative detail must be added by checking available records. Occupancy of a premise can be established through subscription records to telephone, newspaper, water, trash, electric, or gas services, tax rolls, licenses, and building permits. Vehicle registrations are available from the department of motor vehicles, secretary of state, or department of public safety. The identification of persons as "known" gamblers, narcotics users or peddlers, burglars or fences can be made through checks of criminal history with the FBI and state law enforcement agencies. Arrest records of suspects or their associates can assist in the development of probable cause, even though such information is hearsay and is inadmissible in a subsequent trial. Expert opinion of police officers can be used to interpret otherwise innocent facts.

In 1968 in Chicago police detectives had information that a named parking garage was used as a place for high-stakes crap games, policy ticket sales (numbers racket), and narcotics transactions. Surveillances showed that numerous persons entered and left the premises. A substantial number of these individuals, however, walked in and walked out or drove in and drove out. This activity is inconsistent with parking operations where customers walk in and drive out or vice versa. Many of the license plates were traced to persons with long records for gambling offenses. Some of the vehicles were traced to women. Records of marriage licenses, tax rolls, or subscriber services showed that these women were the wives of men who had similar criminal records. This case vividly demonstrated the importance of surveillances that corroborated informant disclosures of unknown reliability. The information acquired through surveillances was, by itself, insufficient. Extensive checks of records and experienced police interpretations were necessary to demonstrate the existence of probable cause.

Post-Watergate morality has had its effects on surveillance practices. There is a growing tendency for courts to expand concepts concerning privacy. As noted earlier, if a person has a reasonable expectation of privacy, the surveillance is illegal under the *Katz* decision (*Katz* v. *U.S.*, 389 U.S. 347 [1967]). Efforts to corroborate or add to visual surveillance methods have also been changed. A banker's association has recently challenged unsuccessfully the right of federal agents to inspect customers' bank records without legal process. Certain telephone companies and other utilities systematically refuse to divulge information to local police departments. The Buckley Amendment to the General Education Provisions Act, 45 U.S. Code, Sec. 438, passed in 1974, forbids access to students' records by law enforcement personnel unless they possess a court order.

New methods in the fields of surveillance and search are continually being developed, and the courts deal with these. For example, many retail stores now use electronic sensory devices to detect stolen merchandise when the customer passes the cash register without paying. At least one court decision has held this is not an unreasonable search or surveillance.

(3.32) Administrative Search Warrants

A search warrant may be necessary for the enforcement of public safety laws. In its 1966 term, the U.S. Supreme Court forbade warrantless, nonconsensual searches of commercial places to enforce building and fire codes. Probable cause in the usual sense is, however, unnecessary. If the officers are acting pursuant to a reasonable legislative or administrative standard, if the search is necessary for the protection of the public, and if the occupant has refused admission, a warrant can be issued. A form affidavit could be used for this purpose, leaving only the address to be filled in. This procedure seems to cheapen the prestige of warrants. Six members of the Supreme Court made clear, however, that the Fourth Amendment protects people and places from unreasonable searches, regardless of the purpose for which they are made.

Not all administrative searches are unreasonable without a warrant. Establishments that serve alcoholic beverages and other licensed premises may, for example, be inspected as a condition of the special privilege license.

(3.33) Execution and Use of Force

Arrest and search warrants are limited to a class of officers named in the statutes. There is no inherent right of a municipal or state police officer to serve all classes of criminal process, and, in some jurisdictions, only the sheriff and his deputies can serve warrants. A warrantless arrest can be made, using an arrest warrant as the basis for believing probable cause exists for the apprehension. Evidence seized incident to that arrest would be admissible in another case. Serving a search warrant, without legal authority to do so, would nullify the warrant.

Statutes or rules of court set the durational limits on serving search warrants, usually 72 to 240 hours. There is no similar restriction on arrest warrants. Some jurisdictions forbid serving any warrant at night unless it is so specified by the court on the warrant.

A warrant does not have to be promptly served, if there are good reasons for delay. A search warrant, for example, is normally served when an individual, usually the suspect, is on the premises. This makes it easier for the prosecution to prove a possessory offense, if contraband or fruits of a crime are located. On the other hand, officers may want to delay serving a search warrant until the suspect leaves, if they believe this would lessen the possibility of resistance. It is not improper to delay serving an arrest or search warrant so that more suspects will be present or so that other evidence will be found. Gambling detectives, for example, could legitimately delay the timing of a raid on an accounting station until all runners had turned in their collections.

A police officer is required to identify himself, announce his purpose, and request entry into the premises, unless those acts would be futile or dangerous. If his knock is unheeded or if entrance is refused, he may forcibly enter the premises. If the officer has a search warrant, it makes no difference whether or not the items sought are dangerous, whether or not they are feloniously possessed, or whether or not the offense under investigation is a misdemeanor or a felony. In the case of an arrest warrant, the crime can be of any magnitude, and it is not necessary to obtain a search warrant to enter the residence of the accused.

Occasionally a defendant, named in an arrest warrant, is believed to be staying at or hiding in the home of a third party. If officers have reasonable grounds to believe this to be the case, they may enter that home without procuring a search warrant.

Under the laws of some states, an elaborate procedure has been established for the procurement of "no-knock" warrants. Once the requirements are complied with, a warrant so endorsed can be served by an unannounced forcible entry into the premises.

(3.34) Scope of Search

The scope of a search incident to an arrest is the same in warrant situations as in warrantless arrests. Search warrants specify the rooms, floors, and areas that may be searched. Officers must restrict themselves to the items sought, even though they suspect other evidence might be found. This does not mean that they must close their eyes to the obvious. If they are lawfully in a place looking for one class of goods or contraband and they see in plain view another class of seizable goods or contraband, the search is lawful. It is advisable in cases where "mere evidence" of an offense is fortuitously seen to secure the premises and to obtain a second search warrant. Contraband, weapons, and fruits of a crime can be immediately seized. This type of seizure is not by authority of the warrant, however; it is due to necessity.

A wise officer will always list small items to be sought with a search warrant. For example, currency is the fruit of many crimes; in possessory offenses, evidence of occupancy, such as rent receipts and mail addressed to the occupant, can be sought. Inclusion of these items will authorize officers to search desks, files, and storage boxes in minute detail. Once, however, officers have located the principal items sought and have established occupancy, the search must cease.

An officer would not ordinarily be authorized to remove paneling, rip up carpeting, or tear open chair cushions, but when he is dealing with experienced drug dealers, extreme measures may be called for. In one case, federal agents removed outer shingles, parts of the roof, and dug trenches in the yard of a house worth $65,000. They found nothing and were later sued; the Justice Department paid $160,000 to the owner for physical and mental damages.

It is important that all items seized be properly inventoried on the search warrant, which is returned to the clerk of the court that issued it. A copy of the warrant, together with a receipt for all items taken, must be given to the owner or party in possession of the premises.

(3.35) Electronic Surveillance Warrants

Title III of the Omnibus Crime and Safe Streets Act of 1968 regulates the issuance of warrants authorizing wiretapping and bugging. Most serious offenses are mentioned in the statute, including kidnapping, murder, sabotage, extortion, bribery of public officials, and certain other federal offenses. State attorneys general and district attorneys may personally apply for intercept orders, or authority to wiretap or to bug, in state court.

Not all eavesdropping situations require an intercept order. A person can unilaterally permit police officers to overhear conversations on his telephone. Warrantless radio monitoring of cordless telephone conversations has been allowed.

A citizen or an officer can wear a concealed radio transmitter or tape recorder without an intercept order. Normal conversations can be taped in this fashion.

Use of a pen register (a device that records the numbers called on a telephone) has been approved by the Supreme Court, which held that it was not a "search."

Videotape surveillances have generally been court approved, all the way from the Abscam investigations to their use in such situations as videotaping a police officer in a bar talking with known criminals. A dentist was suspected of sexually molesting his women patients after injecting them with drugs for tooth extraction. Police obtained a warrant to secretly install a TV camera in his office and then videotaped his actions with a female undercover policewoman. The Federal Rules of Evidence 1001 (2) now includes the use of videotapes.

Whenever police officers or federal agents have bugged or tapped a defendant in a criminal case without legal sanction, neither the conversations nor derivative evidence obtained by listening to the conversations can be admitted into evidence. A defendant is entitled to discover the tapes or transcripts and to have a hearing to determine whether any evidence presented against him was tainted by the illegal surveillances. *Kolod* v. *U.S.*, 390 U.S. 136 [1968], mandates an adversary hearing, and a dismissal will be granted if the prosecution fails to produce the transcripts.

Motions to suppress evidence obtained by electronic surveillance are handled in the same manner as motions to suppress physical evidence. An overheard party has standing to challenge the evidence if he can show a violation of *his* rights under the Fourth Amendment. A defendant could not usually challenge with any success the illegal interception of another's home or telephone.

(3.36) Qualified Immunity

In 2001, the U.S. Supreme Court established a two-step sequence for resolving government officials' qualified immunity claims. The

Saucier procedure stated that a court must decide (1) whether the facts alleged or shown by the plaintiff constitute a violation of a constitutional right, and (2) if so, whether that right was "clearly established" at the time of the defendant's alleged misconduct. Qualified immunity applies unless the official's conduct violated such a right (*Saucier v. Katz,* 533 U.S. 194 [2001]).

In a case decided January 21, 2009, the Supreme Court considered the case of *Cordell Pearson, et al, Petitioners* v. *Afton Callahan* (555 U.S. ___ [2009]). After the Utah Court of Appeals vacated the respondent's conviction for possession and distribution of drugs (which he sold to an undercover informant he had voluntarily admitted into his house), he brought suit in federal court, alleging that petitioners, the officers who supervised and conducted the warrantless search of the premises that led to his arrest after the sale, had violated the Fourth Amendment. The District Court granted summary judgment in favor of the officers. Noting that other courts had adopted the "consent-once-removed" doctrine—that permits a warrantless police entry into a home when consent to enter has already been granted to an undercover officer who has observed contraband in plain view—the court concluded that the officers were entitled to qualified immunity because they could reasonably have believed that the doctrine authorized their conduct.

The Central Utah Narcotics Task Force is charged with investigating illegal drug use and sales. In 2002, Brian Bartholomew, who became an informant for the task force after having been charged with the unlawful possession of methamphetamine, informed Officer Jeffrey Whatcott that respondent Afton Callahan had arranged to sell Bartholomew methamphetamine later that day. That evening Bartholomew arrived at Callahan's residence at about 8 P.M. Once there, Bartholomew went inside and confirmed that Callahan had methamphetamine available for sale. Bartholomew told Callahan that he needed to obtain money to make his purchase and left. Bartholomew met with members of the task force at about 9 P.M. and told them that he would be able to buy a gram of methamphetamine for $100. After concluding that Bartholomew was capable of completing the planned purchase, the officer searched him, determined that he had no controlled substance on his person, gave him a marked $100 bill and a concealed electronic transmitter to monitor his conversations, and agreed on a signal the he would give after completing the purchase.

The officer drove Bartholomew to Callahan's trailer home, and Callahan's daughter let him inside. Callahan then retrieved a large bag containing methamphetamine from his freezer and sold Bartholomew a gram of methamphetamine, which he put into a small plastic bag. Bartholomew gave the arrest signal to the officers who were monitoring the conversation, and they entered to trailer through a porch door. In the enclosed porch, the officers encountered Bartholomew, Callahan, and two other persons; the officers saw Callahan drop a plastic bag. Officers entered the residence and conducted a warrantless search that revealed the methamphetamine in the residence. Relying on the "consent-once-removed" doctrine, the officers believed that the consent given to Bartholomew's entry also allowed them to enter and conduct a warrantless search.

Following the procedure mandated in the *Saucier* v. *Katz* precedent, the Tenth Circuit Court held that petitioners were not entitled to qualified immunity. The court disapproved broadening the consent-once-removed doctrine to situations in which the person granted initial consent was not an undercover officer, but merely an informant. It further held that the Fourth Amendment right to be free in one's home from unreasonable searches and arrest was clearly established at the time of Callahan's arrest, and determined that, under this court's clearly established precedents, warrantless entries into a home are *per se* unreasonable unless they satisfy one of the two established exceptions for consent and exigent circumstances. The court concluded that petitioners could not reasonably have believed that their conduct was lawful because they knew that (1) they had no warrant; (2) the respondent had not consented to their entry; and (3) his consent to the entry of an informant could not reasonably be interpreted to extend to them.

The Court held that the *Saucier* procedure should not be regarded as an inflexible requirement. *Saucier* mandated a two-step sequence for resolving government officials' qualified immunity claims: a court must decide (1) whether the facts alleged or shown by the plaintiff make out a violation of a constitutional right, and (2) if so, whether that right was "clearly established" at the time of the defendant's alleged misconduct. Qualified immunity applies unless the official's conduct violated such a right (*Anderson* v. *Creighton,* 483 U.S. 635, 640 [1987]). In a unanimous decision, the Court reversed the lower-court ruling that qualified immunity should not apply, stating that petitioners were entitled to rely on the "consent-once-removed" entry doctrine.

(3.37) Summary

Not every time a police officer deprives a citizen of his freedom is there an arrest in the legal sense. The Supreme Court has made clear that a temporary detention, although it constitutes a seizure within the meaning of the Fourth Amendment, is not an arrest. Police officers may stop citizens, forcibly if necessary, to conduct a preliminary investigation in order to determine whether a crime has taken place, is in progress, or is about to take place.

To justify a stop, a police officer must be able to articulate facts that would lead a prudent person to believe that the officer reasonably suspects a person of criminal activity. This detention is incident to his power to investigate. Moreover, if the officer reasonably suspects that the person with whom he is dealing might be armed, a limited search can be conducted. This search, called a frisk, is restricted to a pat-down of the suspect's outer clothing for weapons. If the frisk is properly conducted and is not a generalized search of the person, evidence fortuitously found is admissible in a criminal trial.

To consummate an arrest, an officer must have the authority to make an arrest and the intention to arrest the suspect. There must be some restraint of the suspect, either physical or mental, and the suspect must understand that he has been arrested. The Fourth Amendment requires that police officers have probable cause before a lawful arrest can be made. This means that an officer must reasonably believe that a crime has been committed and that the suspect is the perpetrator.

The law recognizes that police officers have unique experience and specialized training that make them more proficient in their field than the normal citizen. They may use this combination of education and experience in determining whether there are sufficient grounds to justify a stop or an arrest. They must, however, be able to recount fully the underlying facts and circumstances in court, or the detention or arrest will be found unlawful.

The Fourth Amendment, made applicable to the states by the Fourteenth Amendment, applies to people, not to things or places. It has been continuously interpreted in light of modern phenomena, such as motor vehicles. Aside from its literal meanings, it prohibits unreasonable searches and allows those that are reasonable. There is no absolute warrant requirement, for example, and the test of reasonableness applies. The amendment is enforced by the most important of evidence in criminal cases: the exclusionary rule. It is an absolute rule. There are no gradations in sanctions based on the gravity of the unlawful character of a policeman's acts. The rule does not consider either the good faith of an officer or its total absence. It only theoretically deters police "misconduct."

Not every act that uncovers evidence, contraband, or other seizable items is a "search." Open lands are quite different from homes. Moreover, an officer does not have to close his eyes to things he observes in plain view, in a place he has a lawful right to be. He may use technical aids, such as field glasses, in his surveillances and accomplish lawfully what he could not do directly through trespass.

Decisions related to the Fourth Amendment no longer follow strict concepts of property. If a person has a reasonable expectation of privacy, any warrantless intrusion upon this right will give rise to the exclusion of evidence. Again, the test is the reasonableness of an individual's expectation of privacy, and no absolute lines are drawn. Officers can no longer justify their actions on the basis that they had a legal right to be where they could observe illegal activity.

Concepts of property are still important when they involve abandonment or consent. The Supreme Court has relaxed many of the technical aspects surrounding consent searches and has imposed the overall standard of reasonableness.

Vehicles are still treated differently than homes. Because they are movable and because their contents are more readily subject to removal, concealment, and destruction, a warrant is usually unnecessary. Though the Fourth Amendment still protects people without regard to the place searched, the rule of reasonableness recognizes the exigent circumstances that surround a vehicular search. Two types of searches are covered by distinct rules. Border searches do not require evidence of suspicious conduct unless the suspect is asked to disrobe or other significant intrusions are attempted. Inventory inspections are not really searches at all, at least in the criminal sense; they are justified by the duty of officers to safeguard property in their keeping.

Standing is an important, but not always the final, factor in determining the application of the exclusionary rule. It is of prime relevance when consent searches are sought, but should not be used to subvert the rights of a suspect.

Although warrantless arrests and searches are judged by the same standards as those conducted pursuant to warrants, the courts have always expressed a preference for the latter. The procedure requires a police officer to seek out a neutral and detached judicial officer, usually a lawyer, and establish a prima facie case against a suspect.

Warrants are issued upon a statement made under oath, usually a written affidavit. Most courts have adopted the four corners rule, which requires that all elements that comprise the underlying probable cause be within the four corners of the written affidavit. Once a warrant is issued, it is too late for an officer to add additional facts he mistakenly overlooked. The warrant process forces police officers to arrange their facts and arguments carefully.

The Fourth Amendment requires "particular descriptions" of the person to be seized or searched, the place to be searched, and the things that are sought. The supporting investigations must be complete, and skill in verbal expression is demanded.

Informants and surveillances are often needed to come to the conclusion that probable cause exists. Often the two are intertwined, since neither an informant's disclosures nor a raw surveillance may alone be sufficient.

Care must be used in the execution of warrants, and statutory procedures cannot be avoided. Even a search warrant is a limited authority to intrude upon a suspect's rights. The scope of a search warrant is restricted to the items named and the nature of the offense under investigation.

Discussion Questions

1. Discuss the "exclusionary rule" of evidence.
2. Name three ways to legally search.
3. Define "search incidental to a lawful arrest."
4. Discuss consent search. Who may consent?
5. Explain "fruit of the poisonous tree" doctrine.

4
Interrogations, Confessions, and Nontestimonial Evidence

Time will explain it all. He is a talker, and
needs no questioning before he speaks.
—Euripedes

A. INTERROGATIONS AND CONFESSIONS

(4.1) The Exclusionary Rule in General

In 1964 the U.S. Supreme Court revolutionized the law of confessions and interrogations, with the famous case of *Escobedo* v. *Illinois*, 378 U.S. 478 (1964). Danny Escobedo was a murder suspect who was being held in custody by the Chicago police. He had an attorney, but the officers concerned with the case refused the attorney access to his client. Escobedo made damaging admissions, which were later used at his trial. He was thus convicted of the crime. In reversing his conviction, the Warren Court ruled that once an investigation had "focused" on a particular suspect, he was entitled to specific warnings before he could be interrogated.

Two years later, in *Miranda* v. *Arizona*, 384 U.S. 436 (1966), the court ordered an addition to the warning. The "focus" test was all but abolished. Instead, the court adopted the concept of "custodial interrogation." This means that a defendant's pretrial statements are not admissible in evidence to prove his guilt if those statements were obtained by state officers during an interrogation and while the defendant was in custody, *unless* he was warned of his rights under the Fifth Amendment and properly waived them.

The penalty for failure to comply with the requirements of the *Escobedo* and *Miranda* decisions is the exclusion of the statements from the trial, which could prove the guilt of the accused. In the past, trustworthy statements were always admissible, regardless of the ignorance of the accused, his ability to pay for a lawyer, or the hopelessness of his custody.

(4.2) Voluntariness of Statements

As was indicated above, prior to the *Escobedo* case, trustworthy statements voluntarily given were always admissible. Needless to say, if a confession was beaten out of a suspect, or if he was coerced into confessing under the duress of a threatened beating, lynching, or other violence, the confession was tainted. Some of the circumstances that would always invalidate a confession include the following:

1. brutality or threatened brutality;
2. promises to drop the charges or to forgo prosecution of other suspected crimes;
3. threats to arrest members of the suspect's family or to cut off welfare assistance to them;
4. threats to contact the suspect's employer and have him fired should he not cooperate;
5. holding the suspect on false charges;
6. refusing the suspect the right to make bail;
7. using false or illegally seized evidence to induce a confession.

Sometimes there is a fine line between "clever tactics" and coercion. Police officers are not required to be "friendly" with a suspect. They may ask questions in an indignant or hostile manner. They may express belief that the suspect is lying. They can interrogate a suspect using teams of officers, some friendly, some antagonistic. They can play on the suspect's conscience. Officers may act confident that the suspect is guilty and suggest reasons why they believe him to be lying. They may sometimes even express sympathy for the suspect and contempt for the victim. When two suspects are in custody, one can be played against the other.

Statements made by persons who have been falsely arrested are subject to exclusion by the courts. The fact that a false arrest is followed by valid *Miranda* warnings and that the interview was free from physical duress is not enough to remove the taint of illegality. In *Brown* v. *Illinois*, 95 S. Ct. 2254 (1975), the Supreme Court ruled that the mere recitation of *Miranda* warnings does not sufficiently interrupt the process to render a confession legal. As in a prior Supreme Court case, the officers had made an arrest without probable cause and had forcibly entered the defendants' homes. Such actions, said the justices, affect the voluntariness of confessions, which cannot, therefore, be the products of a "free will."

Not every statement taken following a false arrest should be excluded, however. As the court said:

> It is entirely possible, of course, . . . that persons arrested illegally . . . may decide to confess, as an act of free will unaffected by the initial illegality. But the *Miranda* warnings, *alone* and *per se* cannot always make the act sufficiently a product of free will to break, for Fourth Amendment purposes, the causal connection between the illegality and the confession . . . . While we therefore reject the *per se* rule which the Illinois courts appear to have accepted, we also decline to adopt any alternative *per se* or "but for" rule . . . . The question whether a confession is the product of a free will . . . must be answered on the facts of each case. No single fact is determinative . . . .
>
> The *Miranda* warnings are an important factor . . . but they are not the only factor to be considered. The temporal proximity of the arrest and the confession, the presence of intervening factors . . . and, particularly, the purpose and flagrancy of the official misconduct are all relevant.

The court went on to say that the burden of proving that an illegal arrest did not taint a subsequent confession falls on the prosecution.

(4.3) The *Miranda* Warnings

In its 1966 decision the Supreme Court spoke of four distinct warnings, but did not specify the exact wording. As a result, several acceptable versions are in use today. A suggested warning that is used by many police departments appears below.

ADVICE OF RIGHTS

It is my duty to inform you that you are under investigation by the _____Police Department.

1. You have the right to remain silent.

2. Anything you say can and will be used against you in court.

3. You have the right to consult a lawyer before answering any questions, and have him present during any interrogation.

4. If you cannot afford to employ a lawyer, one will be provided for you at no cost to yourself.

Once these admonitions are given, before proceeding further, the officer should state the following:

A. Do you understand your rights, as I have explained them?

B. Are you willing to answer questions at this time, without consulting a lawyer, or having a lawyer present?

C. If at any time during the questioning you want to stop answering questions, you may do so and remain silent.

Some law enforcement agencies state the contents of "C" as a fifth warning. Though it is not legally necessary to warn a suspect that he may discontinue the questioning process, once he has expressed this desire all interrogation must cease. It is obvious that the suspect must answer "yes" to "A" and "B" before the interrogation process can begin.

If all four warnings are properly given, a valid waiver by the suspect can be presumed from facts and circumstances other than specific responses to "A" and "B." Officers are *not required* to ask these questions, but should do so if they begin a formal interrogation. A waiver may legally result, and often does, from the mere fact that the defendant freely answers questions put to him. The burden of showing a valid waiver is, however, more difficult for the prosecution in such cases.

Officers should always *read* the warnings from a printed card that they carry at all times. A jury is more likely to believe that the warnings were complete if they were read, as opposed to their being recited from memory. The *Miranda* card is also admissible into evidence at the trial. The card should be read to the suspect and not simply handed to him to read for himself.

Some courts have split hairs over the second warning. A few departments warn suspects that statements "may" be used against them. Others say they "can" be used. A few state they "will" be used. The theory is that "may" implies that leniency is possible, or even likely, if the suspect confesses.

Miranda applies to both exculpatory and inculpatory statements. Thus, should a suspect admit to being present when a criminal act was committed but not having taken part in the act, officers cannot later testify that the suspect acknowledged his presence at the scene of the crime, if the warnings were absent or defective.

If the warnings are defective, the procedure should be repeated, and anything said after the correct warnings are given will be admissible. When officers begin the interrogation process they should make sure that proper warnings were given recently and that the waivers were obtained. If there is any doubt, the admonitions should be repeated. The officers who first gave the warnings will have to appear in court if the waiver is challenged. It is preferable, therefore, for them to conduct the questioning since it minimizes the number of witnesses needed to prove a confession.

(4.4) What Is Custody?

Not every admission or confession must be preceded by warning of rights. As was mentioned above, the *Escobedo* case used the "focus test," that is, whether the investigation focused on the suspect. *Miranda* reinterpreted a suspect's rights under the Fifth Amendment and applied the rule to "custodial interrogations." The court defined this phrase as meaning those circumstances when an accused "is deprived of his freedom in a significant way."

Usually the arresting officers read a suspect the warnings at the time of his actual arrest. It should be noted that an accused does not have a constitutionally protected right to receive these warnings. Rather, his induced statements will be inadmissible in the absence of the warnings. Most departments require that arrested felons be promptly advised of their rights, at the time of the arrest. This does not mean, however, that a person who forcibly resists arrest should be warned during the time of his resistance.

Arrests are often made because a police officer observes the offense taking place in his presence. In many such cases, statements received from the suspect are of little value, and it is unnecessary to question him at the time of the arrest. For example, if a demonstrator smashes a window in front of an officer, the individual should be arrested and booked without interrogation. After the arrest and booking, he should be read the warnings before he is questioned. Nothing in the Fifth Amendment requires an officer to demean himself in the presence of a group of demonstrators.

Should the officers who are transporting the suspect engage in conversation with him, they ought to warn him of his rights unless they are sure this has already been done and by whom. Prisoners frequently become talkative at this stage of the process. They may, for example, express regret that they struck an officer. If they later plead self-defense, accusing the officers of aggressive acts, such statements are invaluable.

In a narrow interpretation of *Miranda* (*Illinois* v. *Perkins*, 52 L.W. 4737 [1990]) the Supreme Court upheld the legality of a jail inmate's murder confession made to an undercover policeman posing as another inmate. The defendant was in jail on another charge and was not then being held on the murder he confessed to, so there was no need for a *Miranda* warning and there was no "coercial atmosphere" to the questioning.

Miranda causes the most problems when the suspect has not been placed under formal arrest. A police station may create an inherently "coercive atmosphere." Warnings should always precede questioning at the station house, even if the person is not a strong suspect, or if he or she voluntarily came to the station without invitation. This does not mean, of course, that everyone who visits a police station should receive *Miranda* warnings. Persons who are reporting the theft or loss of property, who are completing accident reports, or who are seeking assistance obviously should not. But if the visitor is a potential suspect in an unsolved crime and officers plan to question him about that crime, the warnings should be given. Sometimes the existence of a crime will be unknown when an individual goes to a station house. For example, Smith goes to a police station to report a stolen car. During the time his report is being taken, a desk officer learns that the car, driven by a man matching Smith's description, was involved in a holdup. Smith should be given the *Miranda* warnings at this time, and questioning should cease until a valid waiver is obtained. Anything said up to this point would, however, be admissible later.

Miranda warnings should always be given when a suspect is asked to go to a station house to be fingerprinted, to take a polygraph examination, to appear in a lineup, or to give a physical specimen (such as hair or blood).

Persons are frequently asked to get inside a police car for the purpose of giving preliminary information about an incident. Whether the interrogation is custodial or not does not always depend on whether the person was arrested. A coercive atmosphere can also exist in a squad car. If, however, cold weather, rain, darkness, or convenience dictate the location of the questioning, the interrogation is less likely to be considered "custodial."

Most sidewalk confrontations are not covered by *Miranda* until the suspect has been formally arrested. If an officer intends to arrest a suspect regardless of what he says, or if he is questioning him at gunpoint or while the suspect is spread-eagled against a wall or made to lie facedown, coercive factors will, of course, be present and will probably invalidate statements made without the warnings.

When a crime occurs, the officers on the scene often direct everyone present to remain on the premises or at the location and not leave without permission. The Supreme Court made clear in the *Miranda* decision that they did not intend to "hamper" the "traditional function of police officers in investigating crime." Thus, general "on-the-scene questioning" as to facts surrounding a crime is not covered by the *Miranda* ruling. This is true even though the exits are sealed temporarily. Circumstances will affect this rule. A possible suicide at a crowded party will be handled differently from the case where the victim is shot six times in the back and only one person is present at the scene.

Though it was originally thought that residential questioning was never covered by the *Miranda* decision, a case in 1969 (*Orozco* v. *Texas*, 394 U.S. 324 [1969]) made clear that this was not always true. Four officers entered the suspect's bedroom at 4:00 a.m. and interrogated him there. They asked him about a shooting that had taken place earlier and sought to inspect his gun. The lateness of the hour, an uninvited intrusion, and the number of officers present, each standing alone, will not require the admonition of the *Miranda* rights. In combination, however, these factors can create a coercive atmosphere that would require the warnings.

In many cases, the fact that the arrest occurred sometime later than the questioning will avoid the necessity of *Miranda* warnings. Though no rigid rule exists, the courts look more favorably on admitting statements if the arrest occurs on a subsequent day rather than shortly after the crime is committed. If, however, interrogating officers already have probable cause to make the arrest and delay the actual apprehension for reasons of convenience, the statements will be inadmissible.

In the case of *State v. Bunnell,* 340 N.C. 74, 455 S.E.2d (1995), Bunnell, a fourteen-year old boy, was charged with the first-degree murder of his father by shooting him in the back of the head after an argument. Bunnell lived with his mother, and his father was frequently drunk and abusive. After the killing, Bunnell and his girlfriend drove from North Carolina to Daytona Beach, Florida, where Bunnell got in a traffic accident and was arrested. Along the way, Bunnell disposed of some evidence at a South Carolina welcome center. An FBI agent questioned Bunnell in an airport office while he waited to fly back to North Carolina. The officer went over a "juvenile rights form" with Bunnell before they went to the airport. Bunnell made incriminating statement to the FBI agent. On appeal, Bunnell challenged the voluntariness of his statement. The North Carolina appeals court held that one must look at the "totality of the circumstances" in evaluating the voluntariness of juvenile statements, including (1) custody; (2) mental capacity; (3) physical environment; and (4) manner of interrogation. The court found important that Bunnell could read at a ninth-grade level (even though he had failed three grades in school), had apparently normal intelligence, was not deprived of food or sleep, and seemed familiar with his *Miranda* rights when they were administered by Florida police officers. The court also held that later statements are not tainted by problems with earlier, unlawful statements.

Places of employment are sometimes the sites of police questioning. An employee under the scrutiny of superiors, subordinates, and fellow workers is in a compelling—if not a coercive—atmosphere. The situation is less coercive if the crime being investigated took place on the premises, and everyone understands why police officers are present. This is particularly true if the investigation results from the officers' appearance on the scene immediately after the commission of the crime.

Routine business inspections do not come under the protection of the *Miranda* decision. These include such occurrences as visits to pawnshops by the theft and burglary details, ID checks in establishments licensed to dispense intoxicating beverages, and the like.

Persons who are present where a search is being conducted pursuant to a search warrant should be advised of their *Miranda* rights, if they are prevented from leaving, if they are asked to participate in the search, or if they are questioned by officers who are making the search. Once contraband or other evidence is found, there is a more compelling reason to warn persons at the scene of the search.

(4.5) What Is Interrogation?

Not every question asked by a police officer constitutes interrogation. There should be some connection between the question and the offense or suspected offense. General questions asked before an officer discovers that a crime has been committed are less likely to be considered interrogation than similar questions asked after a crime has been discovered. This is often the case when suspicious persons are encountered on the streets and in alleys.

Interrogation has been defined as "any questioning likely or expected to yield incriminating statements." General on-the-scene questioning, as mentioned above, is not likely to be held "interrogation." Thus, officers responding to a silent burglar alarm notice a man sitting in a van near the premises. The hour is late, and the street is dark. They ask the man to explain his presence. Such generalized questioning is only preliminary and does not constitute "interrogation." The man's initial answer would be admissible, even if the officers blocked his van and detained him temporarily.

At some point, general questioning may become accusatorial questioning. This comes about in one of two ways. First, the questions become less general and focus on incriminating conduct. Second, the conversation systematically eliminates noncriminal explanations, leaving only a conclusion of criminal conduct. For example, officers respond to a call concerning a shooting. They find a young man, seriously wounded and comatose, and an older man. General questioning reveals the wound was not self-inflicted, that no other persons were present, that the shooting was not accidental, and that self-defense was not involved. As the various noncriminal alternatives are eliminated, suspicion deepens that the older man shot the younger man, without apparent justification. At this stage all questioning should cease until the *Miranda* warnings are given. The conversation is no longer general and therefore constitutes interrogation.

Statements that are volunteered are admissible, even though the person making the statement is in custody. This is because volunteered statements are not the product of interrogation. A "volunteered" statement is different from a "voluntary" statement. The first means the utterance came forth without elicitation. The second refers to a statement that is free of duress and coercion, but is usually elicited by questioning. Volunteered statements are frequently spontaneous and may take officers by surprise. Also called *res gestae* (Latin for "things done"), such statements are admissible as an exception to the hearsay rule because they are spontaneous and concurrent. The following are examples of volunteered *res gestae* statements.

1. A man walks into a police station and says, "I just murdered my wife."

2. Police officers knock on a suspect's door, seeking permission to search the premises for narcotics. The suspect says, "That won't be necessary. The dope is under the front seat of my car."

3. A man being driven to the morgue to identify a woman thought to be his wife suddenly says to the officer accompanying him, "Stop. I can't bear to see her. I killed her, and I'm sorry."

"Threshold confessions" are also admissible since they are not the product of an interrogation. They are so called because they are often made as officers cross the threshold of the premises and ask, "What happened?" Once an incriminating statement is volunteered or made in response to a threshold question, further questioning must cease, and the *Miranda* warnings must be given. Anything said up to this point is admissible, without the admonitions. Most courts have held that an officer does not have to interrupt a person who is in the process of volunteering a story or responding to a threshold question. But the longer the story continues, and the more pauses contained in it, the more likely it is that an officer must interject with the *Miranda* warnings.

One of the exceptions to *Miranda* is the situation in which an officer is working undercover at the time a crime is being perpetrated. The person talking or answering questions will not be under arrest, but he will be arrested immediately after the conversation is completed. The officer is not required to interrupt the progress of the crime to warn the person of his *Miranda* rights. There must, however, actually be an offense in progress, or about to take place, for this exception to apply.

Miranda warnings need not be given to persons responding to questions in an accident report or a similar incident. This is true even if the citizen is suspected of having committed a felony. The purpose of the interview must, of course, be legitimate, such as the completion of a report form. If, during the interview, the citizen makes damaging admissions that are unconnected with the report, the *Miranda* warnings must be given at that point.

(4.6) Statements During Detention

When a suspect is taken into custody, the person should be taken before a magistrate "without unnecessary delay" so that the magistrate may advise the accused person of his or her constitutional rights under the Fifth and Sixth Amendments. However, many detentions occur when a magistrate is not immediately available or under circumstances that cause reasonable delay in bringing the suspect before a magistrate.

McNabb v. *United States* (318 U.S. 332) and *Mallory* v. *United States* (354 U.S. 449) "generally render inadmissible confessions made during periods of detention that violate the prompt presentment requirements of Federal Rule of Criminal Procedure, 5(a)." The Court ruled in *United States* v. *Alvarez-Sanchez* (511 U.S. 350, 354) that Rule 5(a), in turn, provides that a "person making an arrest...must take the defendant without unnecessary delay before a magistrate judge...." Congress enacted 18 U.S.C., Article 3501, in response to *Miranda* v. *Arizona,* and some applications of the *McNabb-Mallory* rule. In an attempt to eliminate *Miranda,* Article 3501(a) provides that "a confession...shall be admissible in evidence if it is voluntarily given;" Article 3501(b) lists several considerations for courts to address in assessing voluntariness. Subsection (c) of the article, which focuses on *McNabb-Malory,* provides that "a confession made...by...a defendant..., while...under arrest...shall not be inadmissible solely because of delay in bringing such person before a magistrate judge...if such confession is found by the trial judge to have been made voluntarily and...within six hours (of arrest)"; it extends that time limit when further delay is "reasonable considering the means of transportation and the distance to...the nearest available (magistrate)."

The case of *Corley* v. *United States* (555 U.S. ___ [2009]) was argued January 21, 2009, and the Supreme Court decided the case April 6, 2009. Petitioner Corley was arrested for assaulting a federal officer at about 8 A.M. Around 11:45, FBI agents took Corley to a Philadelphia hospital to treat a minor injury. At 3:30 P.M. he was taken from the hospital to the local FBI office and told that he was a suspect in a bank robbery. Though the office was in the same building as that of the nearest magistrate judge, the agents did not bring Corley before a magistrate judge, but questioned him, hoping for a confession. At 5:27 P.M., some 9½ hours after his arrest, Corley began an oral confession that he robbed the bank. He asked for a break at 6:30 P.M., and was held overnight. The interrogation resumed the next morning, ending with his signed written confession. He was finally presented to a magistrate judge at 1:30 P.M., just over 29 hours after his arrest, and charged with armed bank robbery and related charges. The district court denied his motion to suppress his confessions under Rule 5(a) and *McNabb-Mallory.* It reasoned that the oral confession occurred within Article 3501's six-hour window because the time of Corley's medical treatment should be excluded from the delay. It also found the written confession admissible, explaining there was no unreasonable delay under Rule 5(a) because Corley had requested the break. Corley was convicted of conspiracy and bank robbery; the Third Circuit Court affirmed the holding, relying on Circuit precedent to the effect that Article 3501 abrogated *McNabb-Mallory* and replaced it with a pure voluntariness test. It concluded that if a district court found a confession voluntary after considering the points listed in Article 3501(b), it would be admissible, even if the presentment delay was unreasonable.

The U.S. Supreme Court held that Article 3501 modified *McNabb-Mallory* without supplanting it. Under the rule as revised by Article 3501(c), a district court with a suppression claim must find whether the defendant confessed within six hours of arrest (unless a longer delay was "reasonable considering the means of transportation and the distance to be traveled to the nearest available magistrate"). If the confession came within that period, it is admissible, subject to the other rules of evidence, so long as it was "made voluntarily and...the weight to be given it is left to the jury." If the confession occurred before presentment and beyond six hours, however, the court must decide whether delaying that long was unreasonable or unnecessary under the *McNabb-Mallory* cases, and if it was, the confession is to be suppressed.

The Court ruled in the Corley case that the Third Circuit did not apply this rule and consequently never conclusively determined whether Corley's confession "should be treated as having been made within six hours of arrest," as the district court held. The Supreme Court stated that the circuit court did not consider the justifiability of any delay beyond six hours, and if the oral confession should be treated as given outside the six-hour window; the Court noted that the circuit court did not make this inquiry with respect to Corley's written confession. The U.S. Supreme Court, therefore, vacated the judgment of the Court of Appeals and remanded the case for consideration of those issues in the first instance, consistent with the opinion of the Supreme Court.

(4.7) What Is a State Officer?

The *Miranda* decision only applies to "state action." This means that interrogation by nongovernmental personnel falls outside its mandates. With the exception of Maryland, private security officers in all states are exempt from the *Miranda* decision, even if they possess a commission as a special officer or deputy sheriff. Shopkeepers, under many state shoplifting laws, are granted powers of arrest or detention, but these laws do not transform private action into state action. Citizens' arrests are wholly outside the protection of *Miranda*.

Statements made by an arrested felon, in response to questions asked by civilians, are similarly admissible. Some courts have ruled suspects' statements as inadmissible when an officer requested the civilian to ask certain questions or even when the officer was present at the time the questions were asked. To state the matter simply, the courts will not tolerate subterfuge.

Also outside the scope of *Miranda* are statements made to non-police officials, such as physicians and nurses in city hospitals, school administrators, firemen, and similar personnel. It would be a travesty of justice to exclude such admissions because nonpolice officials and employees would not know the *Miranda* warnings or when to give them. Exclusion of these statements would not punish police misconduct, but would only allow inculpatory remarks to be made outside the "coercive" atmosphere of police interrogation.

(4.8) Applicable Offenses

A survey by the International Association of Chiefs of Police in 1972 indicated wide variance among law enforcement agencies in the interpretation of *Miranda*. Though the decision applies to all felonies, many states have ruled that misdemeanors are excluded from its protections. There is merit to this interpretation if the offense is a petty one, punishable by fine only, or a jail term of short duration (less than six months). Nearly everyone agrees that traffic offenses are outside the scope of *Miranda*, although some courts have extended its protections to serious traffic offenses, such as driving while one is intoxicated.

Officers in states that have not resolved this issue should give the *Miranda* warnings to all persons with an offense punishable by incarceration. This policy will eliminate unnecessary appeals and avoid problems with civil liberties groups.

(4.9) Capacity of Suspects

Statements taken from the insane, persons who are drunk, under the influence of drugs, or who do not speak elementary English may not be admissible. A suspect must make a knowing and intelligent waiver. At what age and level of intelligence a person becomes legally capable of understanding his rights and knowingly waiving them is not subject to definition. The mere fact that a suspect is a juvenile will not invalidate the waiver. In one case a waiver by a thirteen-year-old boy was upheld, as was, in another case, a confession by a fifteen-year-old who was "mildly retarded." In other cases, courts have failed to find a knowing and intelligent waiver when the suspect had an IQ of sixty, an IQ of seventy-two at age fifteen, and when age and retardation or other factors impaired the suspect's judgment.

The testimony of a psychiatrist that the suspect understood the warnings will go a long way in validating the confession.

Insanity may be a complete or partial defense in a crime, but it does not automatically invalidate a confession. One case upheld a waiver by a paranoid schizophrenic. Another admitted statements by a suspect who had the mental state of a six-year-old.

Most courts have refused to exclude statements made under the influence of alcohol or mild tranquilizers. Addiction to heroin is more likely to invalidate a confession, depending on the amount used, the degree of withdrawal, and other factors.

Whether a suspect was suffering from impaired capacity at the time he made incriminating statements is based on the "totality of the circumstances test." There is no "per se" rule unless it it enacted in the penal or evidentiary code. For example, a law in Colorado forbids the police to question juveniles in the absence of their parents.

Police officers who have custody of a suspect who is willing to talk but whose capacity is dubious, should use the following procedure. First, the statement should be taken, accompanied by other questions that tend to indicate the suspect's mental capacity. If the statement is later excluded from evidence, no harm has been done since the alternative is not to interrogate at all. If the impairment is temporary, officers should attempt to take a second statement at a later time. If this can be done, the second statement should not be induced by reference to the prior statement. This is because the first statement might be excluded. The court might conclude that the second statement was obtained by referring to the first statement, and thus the second statement could be excluded.

Even if the statement is of dubious validity, it might encourage a suspect to plead guilty in the hope of being given a lesser punishment, which is certainly better than a straight acquittal.

(4.10) Impeachment and Other Derivative Uses of Inadmissible Confessions

The Supreme Court decided in *Wong Sun* v. *U.S.*, 371 U.S. 471 (1963), that police could not use the results of inadmissible statements to garner additional evidence. In that case federal agents forced their way into the residence of a man named Toy, arrested him without probable cause, and obtained a statement that implicated Wong Sun and Johnny Yee. The statements led to the arrest of Yee and Wong Sun. Wong Sun later confessed his guilt to the agents.

The court concluded that the case against Yee was the result of illegal police conduct, the "fruit of the poisoned tree." Wong Sun was convicted because his subsequent confession was so "attenuated" from the original illegality that all "taint" was "dissipated."

Thus, evidence that is seized or statements that are subsequently obtained as a result of an inadmissible confession are themselves subject to exclusion, as the "poisoned fruit" of the initial illegality. In order for evidence to be admissible, the prosecution must show one of two things: that the police would have obtained the evidence anyway and without the use of the tainted statements, or that the connection between the original misconduct and the subsequent evidence was too remote to require its exclusion.

Another example of the use of evidence derived from statements made in violation of *Miranda* came to light in *Michigan* v. *Tucker*, 94 S. Ct. 2357 (1974). In its decision the Supreme Court upheld the following evidentiary scenario: Tucker, the accused, was given defective *Miranda* warnings. His alibi involved Henderson. When Henderson was questioned, he did not support Tucker's alibi; rather, Henderson's testimony further incriminated Tucker. The court ruled that although Tucker's statements were inadmissible, the police could properly use this information to gain additional evidence against the accused.

In its majority opinion, the Supreme Court said that the law does not require that policemen "make no errors whatsoever. The pressures of law enforcement and the vagaries of human nature would make such an expectation unrealistic." Most lawyers interpret the result in *Tucker* as a loosening of the harsh results of the exclusionary rule rather than as a relaxing of the Poisoned Tree doctrine.

Statements taken in violation of *Miranda* may be introduced at the criminal trial for the purpose of impeaching the credibility of the defendant as a witness if he takes the stand. Suppose, for example, a suspect admits selling heroin, but later denies it at the time of his trial. If the statement is tainted because of a *Miranda* violation, it nevertheless may be read to the jury. The purpose of the prior statement is to impair the believability of the accused, not to prove his guilt. It is admitted to contravene his testimony because, said the Supreme Court (*Harris* v. *New York*, 401 U.S. 222 [1971]), "The shield provided by *Miranda* cannot be perverted into a license to use perjury by way of a defense, free from the risk of confrontation with prior inconsistent utterances." An involuntary confession is different. Such a "confession" has no validity whatsoever and cannot be used for any purpose (*People* v. *Walker*, 110 App. Div. 2d 730 [N. Y. 1985]). However, should an illegal confession be used at a trial, the Supreme Court has ruled that the conviction may still stand if there is other sufficient proof of guilt beyond a reasonable doubt (*Arizona* v. *Fulminante*, 59 LW 4235 [1991]).

(4.11) Effect of Immunity or Conviction

The basis for all restrictions on confessions and admissions is the Fifth Amendment, which prevents a person in a criminal case from being a witness against himself. Once an individual is given immunity from prosecution, he can be compelled, under penalty of contempt, to answer questions put to him. The immunity usually takes effect at the time the person is called before a grand jury. The process is later repeated in the criminal trial.

The Supreme Court has ruled that a person is not entitled to "transactional" immunity; he is limited to "use" immunity. This means that the individual still may be prosecuted for the offense, if the police gain their evidence from sources independent of the self-incriminating statements. This has happened occasionally. Thus, under use immunity, the statement itself and the fruits of the statement cannot be used against the accused in a criminal trial. An example follows.

Bruno is granted use immunity before a grand jury and admits that he participated in a counterfeiting scheme. He reveals the location of the printing press (in New Jersey) and the plates (in New York). An accomplice later surrenders himself and brings in the plates from New York. The surrender is not connected with Bruno's statement. Federal agents could not introduce Bruno's statement against him in a criminal trial, but they could introduce it in prosecuting the accomplice. And the accomplice can testify against Bruno. The printing press, if seized on the basis of information in Bruno's statement, cannot be used in Bruno's trial, but could be used in the prosecution of the accomplice. The plates could be used in Bruno's trial since they were turned over to the agents independent of the immunized statement. Had the accomplice been located by using information in Bruno's statement, nothing could be used against Bruno. Had the agents been able to find the accomplice and the plates anyway, Bruno's use immunity would not have prevented the admission into evidence of the plates and the testimony of the accomplice.

Although prosecutors rarely use this technique, a convicted

defendant can be called to the witness stand and be required to give testimony that incriminates himself and others. This tactic has been employed occasionally when one party to the offense has received a light sentence and the others are yet to be prosecuted. The reason it is seldom used is because, in most cases involving multiple defendants, one of them offers to plead guilty and testify against the others in the hope of receiving a reduced sentence.

B. EYEWITNESS IDENTIFICATION

(4.12) Lineups and the Sixth Amendment

In 1967 the Supreme Court under Chief Justice Warren ruled in three cases (*Wade, Gilbert,* and *Stovall,* at 388 U.S. 218, 263, 293 [1967]) that an indicted defendant is entitled to the presence of counsel at a lineup. The rationale behind this rule was that the lineup process is subject to abuse; the abuse might be irremediable; and the presence of a lawyer would help ensure the basic fairness of the procedures utilized. In 1972 the Supreme Court under Chief Justice Burger clarified its original position in *Kirby* v. *Illinois*, 406 U.S. 682 (1972), saying that the right to counsel attaches "only at or after the time that adversary criminal proceedings have been initiated." This means after indictment, arrest by warrant, or arraignment.

In the intervening five years between these decisions, many state courts ruled that the right to counsel is operative at all lineups. While most state courts have reversed themselves in light of the 1972 decision, others have declined to do so. *Kirby* was a plurality decision (that is, two concurring opinions resulting in a holding); because of this, it has not been totally followed by those courts that fail to make a distinction between pre- and postindicted felons.

The rationale for the limitation in the *Kirby* decision is that the government has not committed itself to the prosecution of a suspect until he has been "formally charged." Thus, the right to counsel does not apply before this event since it is not a critical stage of the prosecutory procedures. The rule in *Kirby* will not serve to admit lineup evidence without benefit of counsel if the arraignment is negligently or purposefully delayed.

There is no reason why a defendant cannot waive his right to counsel. Waivers are routinely given in police departments of large cities, often on the advice and with the consent of the public defender. It must be assumed, however, that certain rudimentary records are kept of the proceedings. They include the following:

1. a frontal and profile color photograph of each participant and the entire group assembled;
2. the name, address, race, age, height, weight, and clothing worn by each participant;
3. the names of all witnesses and police officers present;
4. the time and place of the lineup;
5. information on whether the participants were required to wear specified clothing or masks, assume certain postures or walk, repeat directed words or phrases, and so forth;
6. a tape recording, should the lineup contain verbal identification procedures.

In addition, a very thorough written report should be made immediately following the lineup. Questions asked of each witness and their response should be transcribed or recorded. Officers must use great care not to suggest the identification of any particular participant. Each witness should be interviewed separately and told not to discuss possible identifications with each other.

Rare is the lineup that includes five whites and one black suspect. Serious problems have resulted, however, when the police attempt to find five or six people with peculiar characteristics. It would be difficult indeed to find six Oriental males in their thirties, who are six feet tall, have brown hair, walk with a limp, speak with a lisp, and have a French accent. Obviously, some matches cannot be done, and professional reasonableness must be the ultimate test. If, for example, the suspect is very fat, everyone should wear a coat. If the suspect has a large mole on his nose or a tattoo on his cheek, special effects, makeup, or bandages can be used. Several courts have held that officers do not have to go to such lengths when truly unique features are involved.

Police are now trying a different kind of lineup—a "scent" lineup using police dogs. Evidence from a crime scene, such as a murder weapon or sheets from the bed of a sexual attack, are lined up with other objects including some with the suspect's scent. A suspect's cigarette pack or paper towels or linens used by the suspect while in jail are often used. The dog is allowed to smell the suspect's objects and is commanded to search the things in the lineup. The dog then identifies the defendant's scent with the crime scene evidence. Courts have found this method of a "scent lineup" to be constitutional but have not accepted the dog's findings on the basis that there was insufficient expert evidence at the trial level of the dog's reliability. Tracking dogs have long had court approval as have the "sniffer dogs" that locate contraband. The use of dogs in a "scent lineup" is something new, and so is in need of further proof of the dog's reliability. As police gain experience in this new type of lineup, a proper foundation proving the dog's ability will be found.

To avoid problems of suggestive lineups, officers should arrange to have five or six persons participate. If one individual has to wear jail clothing, all should do so. It is never permissible for a suspect to wear garments resembling the clothing worn by the perpetrator, unless all participants do so. Similarly, five detectives in conservative suits will impair the effectiveness of a lineup if the suspect is wearing casual attire. Finally, the suspect or suspects should be randomly placed in the lineup.

In many communities, particularly smaller ones, the jail population will not have a sufficient number of inmates who resemble the suspect. Citizen participants must be recruited for this purpose. Even if they are paid, they should be advised that they are under no compulsion to participate and are not suspects in the proceedings; a written consent form can be established for this purpose.

To minimize the number of officers who will have to appear in court, it is advisable that a single officer conduct the lineup, complete the reports, interview the witnesses, take the photographs, and perform the clerical tasks. Polaroid photographs will minimize the problems concerned with the chain of evidence, and the officer in charge should initial the print and staple it to the reports.

To avoid unexpected problems connected with the viewing procedures, it is recommended that witnesses be given a printed sheet explaining the system. A typical information sheet would advise the witnesses not to speak unless asked a question by an officer and not to display recognition of anyone until those individuals in the lineup are interviewed by an officer. It would, in addition, explain that they are under no obligation to identify anyone and that, if they do, certainty of identity is not required.

The attorney representing the accused should be permitted to view the entire proceedings, including the interview of the witnesses. This will help ensure that the lineup and the subsequent interview process are free of suggestive influences. Attorneys for suspects ought to be told that they should communicate any suggestions or objections to the officer in charge of the lineup, but that they will not be permitted to obstruct the procedures. They should not be allowed to interview the witnesses before, during, or after the procedures. If they want to take the deposition of a witness, they should follow the state's rules of criminal procedure designed for that purpose.

An attorney will occasionally be late. The lineup should be delayed for a reasonable time, but for no longer than an hour. If the attorney calls the station and gives a valid excuse, the lineup should be postponed. If, however, no valid excuse is provided, the public defender's office should be contacted, and arrangements should be made for a substitute defense lawyer to appear. A court order can be secured for the purpose of appointing an alternate counsel for a lineup.

A different situation exists where a photographic lineup is used, that is, a witness looks at a number of photographs, which includes one of the suspect in order to identify the suspect. Police often do this before and after an arrest and indictment. Attorneys have attempted to exclude such evidence, claiming that they were not notified of the lineup, and so the defendant was deprived of his right to counsel. The court has denied this claim, pointing out that this was not a "confrontation" but a gathering of evidence at which even the defendant is not required to be present (*U.S.* v. *Ash*, 413 U. S. 300 [1973]).

(4.13) Right to Compel Attendance

A suspect does not have a constitutional right to refuse to appear in a lineup, providing there is sufficient cause to believe he is a suspect. This does not mean that police officers can conduct a dragnet for dozens of persons who fit a description and forcibly detain them for the purpose of putting them in a lineup. Not only would innocent persons have a right to bring a civil suit for damages, but the perpetrator, if identified, would be entitled to have his identification suppressed because of an illegal "dragnet-type" arrest. This does not mean that the police must have the same quantity or quality of proof required to justify an arrest in order to compel attendance of suspects at a lineup. A lesser standard of proof is sufficient and will support the legality of the proceedings.

It is not uncommon to reduce the number of suspects in a

case to not less than three or five individuals. In these cases, officers should apply to a court of competent jurisdiction for an order compelling the attendance of these persons if they do not appear voluntarily. An affidavit, in support of the order, must be filed. The affidavit is similar to that required for the issuance of an arrest warrant, though the proof may be substantially diminished. For example, to obtain an arrest warrant, the affidavit must indicate that there is probable cause to believe that X, a named suspect, committed the offense. In a lineup order it is only necessary to allege that there is probable cause to believe that X, Y, or Z committed the offense, coupled with facts supporting that conclusion.

A lineup order may be issued for several suspects, when only one of them could be guilty, or issued for a single suspect based on less proof than is required for an arrest warrant, because the intrusion on the rights of a participant in such a lineup is less than the intrusion on the rights of an arrested suspect. The lineup procedure takes about an hour; it can be arranged to take place at a convenient time. A suspect is not booked, individually photographed, jailed, or required to post bond. The stigma of guilt associated with an arrest is not present.

As an example of the above, a drugstore was robbed by a gunman who was dressed in the uniform used by deliverymen of the Baker Department Store. Three drivers for that company fit the description and were in the area of the drugstore at the time of the holdup. A court order should be obtained requiring each of the three drivers to appear in a lineup in order that employees of the drugstore might determine whether one of them was the robber.

There are at least two other ways to accomplish the same result. The first is to obtain photographs of each of the three drivers, mix them in with several other photographs of individuals who are similar in appearance and who are dressed in uniforms of the department store, and show these to the witnesses. This is a lesser intrusion on the rights of the innocent drivers and is similarly free of any suggestive techniques. On the other hand, photographs may not truly represent the identity of the accused. Body movements and mannerisms, height and weight, voice and expressions, and other factors cannot be portrayed in pictures. A second way to accomplish this purpose is to conceal a witness on the premises of the department store. As each driver reports to work and leaves, the witness can observe him. This will only be free from improper suggestions when more than one driver is observed.

Although a suspect cannot lawfully refuse to appear in a lineup, there is no practical way to force him physically to do so. What if he must be dragged onstage, screaming and cursing? This will clearly focus attention on him and away from the other participants. On the other hand, a resisting suspect misbehaves at his peril, and he should not be allowed to complain later that he was identified solely because of his performance. Thus, each participant is free to appear as nonchalant and obedient as he chooses. If he intentionally misbehaves, he waives any rights he might have to object to an identification tainted by his own behavior.

(4.14) Confrontations with Single Suspects

Although identifications of single suspects tend to be suggestive, there are three situations where they are completely lawful. The first is when the suspect is located near the scene of the crime at about the time the crime was committed. Most police departments define this time as sixty minutes and set the location as the distance that can reasonably be traveled in that period. The greater the distance from the scene and the greater the time elapsed since the crime, the stronger is the case for a full due process lineup. There is also less likelihood of a faulty identification when the suspect is presented shortly after the commission of the offense. That is, the process is more reliable. Sometimes several suspects may be stopped because they fit a general description. It would be unfair to hold a half dozen persons until a lineup could be put together.

If, on the other hand, a single suspect is stopped, and there is other evidence that he committed the crime, it is a better practice to book him and arrange for a formal lineup. Such other evidence would include a large amount of money or a gun found on his person or in his car, or a confession. A lineup of a single suspect should be avoided when the witness is injured or is extremely upset. It would be a bad practice, for example, to take a suspect back to a grocery store for identification by a woman whose husband was fatally shot by the robber. If this is the only choice without risking a false arrest, it must, of course, be done. When suspects are returned to the scene of the crime, they should not be hauled in at gunpoint or wearing handcuffs. Both of these practices are too suggestive of guilt. If there is more than one witness, each should be asked to step outside to make an identification. This avoids the risk of one witness shouting out his or her identification in the presence of others and thus influencing them.

The second situation justifying a confrontation with a single suspect occurs when a witness is in danger of dying. In these cases the suspect should be taken to the hospital or wherever the witness is for immediate identification.

The third situation is the accepted police practice of having a witness get into a patrol car while the officers ride around the neighborhood looking for the suspect.

It is sometimes thought that a single-suspect confrontation is permissible when the witness knows the identity of the suspect. Examples of this would include a former employee, a resident of the building in which both live, or a relative. It is permissible for the witness to point out such a suspect for the purpose of apprehending him. If the suspect is already in custody, however, the prosecutor should be consulted before allowing a confrontation with the single suspect.

(4.15) Use of Photographs

Police have resorted to the rogues' gallery since the invention of the photograph. There are many reasons why books of photographs are used instead of lineups. First, the police may not know the identity of the suspect, and it is thought that he may be a prior offender. Second, the suspect may have fled, or his whereabouts are unknown. Finally, the police may have the person under surveillance and not want him to know he is suspected of the crime.

Photographs only portray how a person looked at a particular time. Aging, facial hair, a different hairstyle, baldness, and a number of other factors tend to make the process less reliable than a lineup. Nevertheless, such viewings of photographs frequently take place in larger police departments. If no particular person is a suspect before the viewing takes place, it is proper to permit the witnesses, on an individual basis, to look through a book consisting of known burglars, robbers, rapists, or other categories of criminals.

If, however, a particular person or persons are under suspicion, the following procedure should be utilized.

1. All photographs of the suspects should be removed from the books or files in which they are kept.

2. The suspects' photographs should be mixed with pictures of persons with similar features. It is not absolutely necessary that these individuals have been arrested for the crime under investigation, but, if at all possible, they should be.

3. "Mug shots" should not be mixed with other photographs unless there is no alternative.

4. The date of arrest and other ID data that might appear in a mug shot should be covered up. This will minimize the chance that the witness will pick out a recent arrestee when the witness knows that a suspect has been picked up.

5. If a particular person is suspected of the offense, and he is in jail or facing charges, the prosecutor should be consulted. He may want to notify the suspect's attorney of the scheduled viewing.

6. After an identification is made, the officer in charge should record the ID numbers of each photograph shown the witness, if the photographs are displayed separately. If the witness picks the suspect from a book, the pages viewed should be noted. This procedure will enable the officer to reconstruct the viewing process in court, if it becomes necessary.

Many police agencies use a photocomposition process to build a likeness of the perpetrator. Several identification kits are on the market and employ drawings of many types of eyes, ears, noses, and mouths that can be placed together. Their usefulness and legality have been upheld in several court decisions. The officer using such devices should be trained or educated in the proper techniques, and he must be prepared to be cross-examined on this process.

C. OTHER NONTESTIMONIAL EVIDENCE

(4.16) Blood and Breath Samples

When the procedure is done by or under the direction of a licensed physician, blood samples may be taken from the body of a suspect, even if he objects. Because it is an extraordinary remedy, probable cause is a necessary condition when the individual makes an objection. Samples are usually taken to determine the influence of alcoholic beverages or of narcotics. In order to avoid civil liability and not violate the prerequisites of the Fourth Amendment, a court order should be sought and obtained before a suspect is forcibly strapped down and blood drawn from him. If the objections are merely verbal and not physical, a court order is not necessary. The motor vehicle code may provide for forcible samplings under certain conditions. A person can, of course, always consent to the taking of a blood sample. Moreover, it is wise to administer such a test if the suspect insists on it.

A person may be required to breathe into a device that measures his intoxication or other conditions. Again, the motor vehicle code may provide that such a test be given, and a court order can be obtained if he forcibly resists.

In justifying such actions, courts have said the following:

1. There is no privilege against self-incrimination since the evidence is obtained by the labors of the prosecution.

2. There is no right to counsel. Since the suspect does not have a right under the Fifth Amendment to refuse a blood or breath test, he cannot have the right to counsel under *Miranda*, which was decided on the basis of the Fifth Amendment.

3. The action is not an unlawful search and seizure. There is reason to believe the evidence will be destroyed by natural bodily processes unless the tests are administered promptly, and the methods used in extracting the evidence are not unreasonable. No body cavities are searched, and the process does not shock the conscience of the courts.

Not all courts agree on the issue of the degree of force that may be used. In a California case decided in 1970 the officers kept a scissors lock on the suspect and held his arm immobile while he was lying on the floor. Though the suspect was "defensive," the officers were aggressive beyond all need. Thus, in California, if excessive force is applied, the evidence will be suppressed.

New York's highest court has rejected the argument that *Miranda* warnings should be given a suspect before he is asked to perform physical tests such as walking a straight line, putting finger to nose, and the like. The court pointed out that the Fifth Amendment applies only to thought process; physical performance tests show physical condition and thus *Miranda* warnings are inapplicable (*People v. Hager*, 69 N.Y. 2d 141 [1987]).

(4.17) Other Physiological Measurements and Evidence

Samples of hair can be taken over the objection of a suspect. The Supreme Court recently upheld the forcible taking of fingernail scrapings from a suspect. The rationale for this case was that the evidence could be quickly destroyed by cleaning. The warrantless scrapings were based on probable cause.

The so-called moral and privacy considerations surrounding the taking of seminal smears will preclude their use unless the individual gives his consent. A suspect's clothing may, however, be forcibly taken and examined for seminal stains.

For several years legal philosophers have debated whether a bullet could be forcibly removed. Suppose that a policeman is found shot to death, with his gun in hand and a single bullet missing. Suppose, further, that a former offender is found a few minutes later in the next block, suffering from a bullet wound. Suppose, finally, that the gun that fired the fatal shot was found next to the officer, wiped clean of prints, and, again, with a single bullet missing. On the basis of such evidence, could a search warrant or court order be obtained to extract the bullet from the suspect? If the bullet is removed to preserve his life or well-being, it would, of course, be admissible. By the same token, if removal of the bullet would imperil his life, the court cannot order that it be done. If a decision is made by the prosecutor not to seek a court order, if the suspect refuses to consent to an operation, and if medical evidence all concurs that the bullet could be removed safely, would it be lawful for the prosecution to introduce these facts into evidence against the accused?

Police may not forcibly pump the stomach or forcibly examine the rectal cavity of a suspect. Cases have upheld the administration of an emetic by a physician and the use of such evidence derived from the procedure. If, however, a stomach pump or rectal probe is administered by a physician as a necessary procedure to save the life or preserve the well-being of a suspect, anything recovered during these processes would be admissible.

In general, urine samples may be required of a suspect (for alcohol or narcotics tests). They cannot, however, be forced by inducing the suspect to drink liquids. Because of the problems of dilution, a suspect may be required to urinate in the presence of an officer, with his back toward him.

(4.18) Summary

Prior to 1964 the only test governing the admissibility of a confession or admission was the voluntariness of the statement. The *Escobedo* and *Miranda* decisions put the lawyer in the middle of the interrogation process. They mandated a litany of warnings that must be recited when the suspect is in "custody."

In recent years the lawbooks have been filled with cases that have searched for the "proper" warnings and have speculated at what point in time the warnings were necessary. Recitation of the warnings is not enough; a "knowing and intelligent" waiver must precede an admissible statement. At what age and in what mental condition a suspect must be have never been precisely defined. Jurisdictions have differed on whether misdemeanors and traffic offenses are includable under the *Miranda* decision.

The Warren Court seemed to infer that full compliance with *Miranda* in every respect was a necessary prerequisite to the admissibility of a statement. The Burger Court has been more flexible and has carved out several exceptions to *Miranda*. For example, statements in violation of *Miranda* may be admitted to impeach a suspect's credibility if he testifies at his trial. The Poisoned Tree doctrine will no longer be automatically applied to tainted confessions.

The Warren Court also put lawyers into the lineup procedures in police stations. The Burger Court qualified that holding and limited this requirement to situations following the initiation of adversary criminal proceedings.

Lineups, blood tests, and other physiological measurements are nontestimonial in nature. A person does not have a constitutional right to refuse to participate in these procedures, if there are reasonable grounds to compel his participation.

Discussion Questions

1. What is meant by the statement "a confession or admission must be voluntarily given?"
2. What are the *Miranda* warnings?
3. Who determines the admissibility of a confession as evidence?
4. What effect does a grant of immunity have on self-incrimination?
5. Outline procedures for conducting a lineup.

5
Pretrial Procedures

The history of liberty has largely been the history of the observance of procedural safeguards.
—*McNabb* v. *United States,*
318 U.S. 332, 347 (1943)

(5.1) Misdemeanors

Arrest is the activity that initiates the process of bringing a criminal offender to justice. It is the taking into custody of a person so that he or she will be available to answer for an alleged crime. Arrests on criminal charges can be made on authority of a warrant; however, a warrant is not absolutely necessary, and most arrests are made without them. A valid warrant may be executed by any law enforcement officer or private individual to whom the warrant is directed.

A misdemeanor, being a less serious offense, may be punished by a fine or by confinement in a city or county jail for a period of less than one year. A misdemeanor prosecution is initiated by the issuance of a complaint, usually made by the victim of, or a witness to, the crime. Frequently, the arresting officer is the complaining witness. After the suspect is arrested, he or she is brought to the police station and detained. Such persons may be released for lack of evidence of a crime or booked on formal charges.

After booking, a suspect may be released on his or her own recognizance with a signed promise to appear in court, released on presentment of bail, or confined to await trial. The decision is based on the suspect's reputation and the seriousness of the offense.

The complaint is the basis for proceeding with the prosecution of misdemeanors following arrest. Actually, the complaint may be misleading because it suggests an action taken by the injured party or victim of a crime. Although the victim of the crime may be the complainant, the plaintiff is actually the people of the state acting through their legal representative, the district or county attorney. The public prosecutor therefore issues the complaint in a written document that (1) alleges the commission of an offense and the intent of the accused; (2) identifies the time, place, and jurisdiction of the court involved; and (3) is sworn to and signed by the complainant. A complaint is essentially a justification for the arrest of a defendant so he or she can be arraigned—that is, allowed to enter a plea.

Procedural law requires that a suspect be brought before a magistrate or justice of the peace without unnecessary delay after the arrest. Excessive delays can affect the outcome of the trial and provide grounds for dismissal of charges.

A magistrate may determine guilt or innocence and can impose minor penalties for petty offenses. Many states allow the accused to request a jury trial. In more serious crimes, the magistrate holds a preliminary hearing to determine the sufficiency of evidence presented to justify holding the suspect for further action.

Felony offenses are serious crimes punishable by confinement for a year or more in a state prison or by death in the case of capital offenses. Some felony offenses are settled by dismissal or by a guilty plea early in the criminal justice process. Cases not settled in one of these ways progress through a series of stages, beginning with the preliminary hearing.

(5.2) Preliminary Hearing

Following arrest, a felony suspect is brought before a lower court for a preliminary hearing. At this stage, the state is obliged to show "probable cause" for binding the accused over for trial. The term "probable cause" sounds like legal jargon because it is extremely unlikely that a prosecutor would initiate judicial proceedings without a reasonably strong case. Nevertheless, the legal view persists that the preliminary hearing is beneficial to the accused.

Occasionally, a prosecutor may ask for a *nolle prosequi*, which indicates that no further action will be taken by the prosecution. A "nolle pros," as it is commonly called, usually means that the prosecution's case is weak; for example, an important witness died or disappeared before making a deposition, or a key piece of evidence was lost or stolen. Regardless of the reason, the prosecutor decides not to pursue the prosecution.

The state reveals only enough of its evidence against the accused to support the contention that further prosecution is warranted. Defendants represented by effective counsel may be able to gather additional information from the preliminary hearing, such as the strength of the case presented by the state. Preliminary hearings tend to favor the prosecution and have been criticized as a needless procedure amounting to little more than a dress rehearsal for the prosecution. Because defendants in many jurisdictions are allowed wide pretrial discovery, preliminary hearings in their cases are seldom used.

The prosecution presents evidence, and a judge decides whether there is probable cause to believe that the accused person committed the alleged crime. An affirmative answer binds the defendant over for trial; however, if the answer is no, charges are dismissed, and the defendant is released from custody. When the decision is to bind the accused over for trial, the prosecution files an information with the court where the trial is to be held. The time for filing varies from jurisdiction to jurisdiction, but it is generally within fifteen days following the preliminary hearing.

(5.3) Arraignment

At a scheduled time and after prior notice, the accused is summoned into court and informed of the charges against him, for the purpose of eliciting a plea. This process is known as arraignment. More precisely, it means the appearance of an accused person in a felony case before the magistrate who has the authority to hear the accused's plea. Arraignment usually takes place in the court where a case will be tried.

The prosecutor formally reads in open court the bill of indictment that charges the accused, and the accused is informed again of the constitutional right to have an attorney. In the case of an indigent defendant who has not already been assigned counsel, an attorney will be appointed at this time.

Generally, the defendant may plead guilty, not guilty, or *nolo contendere*. The plea of *nolo contendere* in a criminal proceeding is treated the same as a guilty plea, although in some jurisdictions it means simply that the defendant does not understand the charges. The principal advantage of a *nolo contendere* plea is that it may shield the defendant from certain civil penalties that might result from a guilty plea. Thus, a *nolo contendere* plea may benefit the defendant in situations in which, in addition to criminal sanctions, he or she may be liable for civil damages (e.g., driving while intoxicated). The *nolo contendere* plea can be entered only at the discretion of the prosecutor and the judge. However, in many jurisdictions, if the accused fails to enter a plea of any kind, the court will automatically enter a plea of not guilty.

Before a court will accept a guilty plea, certain conditions must be met. The plea must be entered voluntarily, and the defendant must be aware of its implications. A guilty plea is considered equivalent to a verdict of guilty, and the court may impose sentence at the time of the plea or set a date for sentencing.

(5.4) The Grand Jury

The function of the grand jury is to investigate criminal charges to determine if a defendant should be brought to trial. The Fifth Amendment of the United States Constitution provides that " no person shall be held to answer for a capital or otherwise infamous crime unless on a presentment or indictment of a grand jury." This applies to all federal crimes. In many states, on the other hand, the grand jury is no longer used for most cases. A prosecutor's information is used instead.

The grand jury does not determine guilt or innocence. If it is convinced by the prosecution's evidence that a *prima facie* case has been made, the grand jury will return a "true bill" of indictment, indicating probable cause to proceed to trial. If, however, the grand jury is not convinced by the prosecutor's evidence, it can ignore the charges by returning a "no bill" finding. In such cases, the prosecution may charge the defendant with a lesser offense. In the majority of indictments, the grand jury follows the prosecutor's inclination. Most states require a preliminary examination prior to charging in a felony case. Grand jury indictments are required by law in about half the states.

(5.5) Pretrial Motions

Generally, defense attorneys move for the dismissal of charges against their clients even before a plea is entered. The general strategy is to attack the information or indictment, claiming improprieties in the organization or methods of the grand jury. Other possible grounds for a motion to dismiss are prior jeopardy and the statute of limitations. A more effective pretrial motion, a bill of particulars, requests the state to reveal information or evidence that the prosecution has gathered against the defendant. If some or all of the evidence was obtained illegally—as has been the case in some prosecutions of illegal drug cases—the case will probably be dismissed.

If, due to pretrial publicity, the accused and the defense attorney believe it is impossible to receive a fair trial in the area where the crime was committed, the defense attorney may move for a change of venue. Despite the attention paid to such motions in media coverage, this motion is made rather infrequently. Equally infrequent are motions seeking a separate trial in cases of codefendants.

(5.6) Bail

Bail is the security required by the state and given by the accused to ensure that he or she appears before the proper court at the scheduled time and place to answer the charges.

In theory, the only function of bail is to ensure the defendant's appearance at the scheduled time for trial. In practice, however, bail has also been used to prevent the release of an accused who might otherwise be dangerous to society or whom the judge might not want to release. This latter practice is called "preventive detention."

In mere misdemeanor cases, most courts have bail schedules pursuant to which the arrested person can post bail with the police or clerk of the court in an amount designated in the schedule, without having to see the magistrate.

In felony cases, if the offense is bailable and no bail has been set, the magistrate will determine the amount of bail if sufficient evidence exists to justify charging the accused with a felony.

The amount of bail is usually determined in light of the facts then known to the magistrate, including the nature and seriousness of the offense, the accused's previous criminal record, his or her conduct at the time of arrest, and the likelihood of escape.

The magistrate's setting bail is not subject to review by a higher court unless there is flagrant violation of the Eighth Amendment prohibition of excessive bail. Unfortunately, what constitutes excessive bail is difficult to define; this, of course, makes the constitutional right difficult to invoke.

In most states, the magistrate or any judge of the court in which the charge is pending can—for good cause shown—increase or decrease the amount of bail.

Bail is usually posted by a bail bondsman who demands cash payment of anywhere between 5 and 20 percent of the set amount of bail. This amount is not refundable even if the defendant shows up for trial. The bondsman also demands collateral in the form of property, which he can confiscate if the accused should "jump bail."

Bail practices by bail bondsmen have been severely criticized in recent years, and several projects have attempted to make bail more available to and less damaging for the accused. One widely sanctioned project is a court-administered bail system in which the state, through the court, serves as bondsman but refunds the cash deposit (except for a small fee) if the accused appears for trial. This, or a similar bail system, may provide a greater incentive for the accused to show up, knowing that he or she will get the refund.

One unfortunate result of the bail system is that the poor waiting for trial remain in jail while the affluent are set free. Various attempts have been made to liberalize the system so that fewer defendants are confined during trial.

By statute in a number of states, the magistrate or judge before whom the proceedings are pending may release any accused "on his own recognizance" (that is, without monetary bail). This usually happens when the accused is one who, because of community ties, employment, and reputation, will likely appear for trial. If he fails to do so, however, a warrant may be issued for his arrest.

Finally, the federal courts and most state courts deny bail to persons charged with a capital offense (offenses punishable by death or life imprisonment) when indications of guilt are strong.

After a forfeiture of bail, the bondsman or surety has 180 days in which to adjust the forfeiture. Three procedures are available: (1) The defendant and the bondsman appear in court and provide an acceptable explanation or justification for the defendant's neglect or satisfactorily indicate to the court that the absence was not with the connivance of the bondsman or surety. (2) The bondsman may appear in court and certify that the defendant is dead or physically unable to appear during the time period allowed. (3) The defendant may be turned over to the court.

(5.7) Summary

Procedures for handling cases prior to the trial stage include filing a complaint, setting bail for felonies and misdemeanors, conducting preliminary hearings, and posting bail. Bail is the security posted to assure the defendant's appearance in court. Preliminary hearing or examination is the process for "testing the evidence," and a grand jury may consider the basic evidence to decide whether the accused should be tried by a petit jury.

Discussion Questions

1. What is arraignment? When does it occur?
2. Discuss *nolo contendere*.
3. What is the role of the grand jury?
4. What Constitutional Amendment protects against excessive bail?
5. What is the function of a preliminary hearing? How does it differ from a grand jury?

6

Discovery and Privileged Communications

It is not what a lawyer tells me I *may* do; but what humanity, reason, and justice tell me I ought to do.

---Edmund Burke
Speech, March 22, 1775

(6.1) Discovery in General

For many years the common-law rule was always that the accused could not inspect any prosecution evidence before trial. This inspection is termed "discovery." "At common law, discovery before trial was generally unavailable in both civil and criminal cases." Even in relatively recent judicial history, the criminal trial was usually run with neither side revealing anything to the other in advance. Secrecy of the prosecution was upheld on the theory that pretrial revelation of police witnesses or prosecution evidence could lead to intimidation or possible physical danger or death of witnesses. There was also a subconscious reason for secrecy. Everyone considered the criminal trial a legal contest with prescribed rules in which each side tried to beat the other—not as a vehicle for seeking the truth.

Even in civil cases, pretrial discovery of evidence was only narrowly allowed. This attitude in civil suits has now been completely reversed. Experience has shown that, if each side understands the strengths and weaknesses of the other, cases are often settled without necessity of a trial.

This experience in civil cases has greatly affected the court's attitude toward pretrial discovery in criminal matters. As a matter of fact, the old idea against pretrial criminal discovery is now rapidly being discarded. The U.S. Supreme Court decision of *Jencks* v. *U.S.*, 353 U.S. 657 (1957), started this trend. In that case the convicted defendant was denied access to statements made previously by a prosecution witness. The court ruled that the defense must be given the witness's statements for purposes of cross-examining him at the trial. Though the *Jencks* decision involved the trial use of prosecution material, it led to a general recognition of the propriety of allowing the accused to see such material before trial. The present attitude on pretrial criminal discovery is best summarized in a statement from *Williams* v. *Florida*, 399 U.S. 78 (1970): "The adversary system of trial is hardly an end to itself, it is not yet a poker game in which players enjoy an absolute right always to conceal their cards until played."

Coupled with this changing attitude toward pretrial criminal discovery has been an increased emphasis in the courts on protecting the criminal defendant's rights. Now by court decision, rules, and statutes, criminal defendants are being allowed much wider pretrial access to the prosecution's evidence.

The more liberal discovery rights in criminal trials should not be confused with depositions. "Discovery" and "depositions" are not the same. According to *Kardy* v. *Shook*, 237 Md. 524 (1965), " 'Discovery' has long been one of the working tools of the legal profession . . . . Discovery suggests the disclosure of facts resting in the knowledge of a party to a suit or the production of . . . things in his possession or under his control . . . . 'Depositions,' on the other hand, indicate the *testimony of a witness reduced to writing* [emphasis added]."

Many older court decisions deny criminal pretrial discovery. These cases should be relied on only with caution, in view of the changing attitude allowing broad pretrial criminal discovery. Because of this changing attitude, the only safe conclusion is that a defendant's right to pretrial discovery of the prosecution's evidence will get broader and broader. The prosecution's right to pretrial discovery of defense evidence will lag behind considerably, but it, too, will gradually be enlarged by court decisions and rulings.

(6.2) Power to Compel Disclosure

Because pretrial criminal discovery was not accepted in common law, the older cases held that the courts were without power to order it. As late as 1958, the U.S. Supreme Court held that denial of pretrial criminal evidence to the defendant did not violate due process. A general rule now adopted by state courts is that the court can compel pretrial discovery of prosecution evidence.

The court can also, within constitutional limits, allow prosecution discovery of defense criminal evidence. Discovery in federal cases is detailed in the Federal Rules of Criminal Procedure.

(6.3) Propriety of Compelled Disclosure

The accused, even in the modern view, is not entitled to discovery as a matter of right or as a constitutional guarantee. In some jurisdictions, however, it is now spelled out by statute.

In general, discovery by the criminal defendant will be allowed if it is a matter of fairness and if it is a factor in the search for truth. Thus the trial court determines whether to allow the defendant to employ discovery, and the judge is not in error if he refuses to do so unless he has clearly abused his discretion.

The defense counsel must show that the evidence sought is actually needed and is not being requested in the hope that he can learn something useful. The courts have, in fact, denied a blanket request by the defense that the state supply copies of all statements in its possession. A subpoena to the prosecutor requiring him to bring all statements from his files was also disallowed. A defense request for all police reports resulted in the same decision.

Courts still consider carefully, however, valid arguments by the prosecution that pretrial discovery of prosecution witnesses or evidence might be dangerous to a witness, might improperly reveal the name of an informant, or might otherwise be unfair. In these situations prosecution matters will be protected. There must be a balance of the right of a defendant to discover potentially material witnesses with the probability that such discovery might lead to the elimination of an adverse witness or the influencing of his testimony. In balancing these competing factors the trial court must be allowed great discretion.

(6.4) Matters in the Prosecutor's Files

a. Statements by the Accused

Older case law withheld any pretrial discovery of the defendant's own confession. Under present-day practice, he can gain access to it in almost every court. Part of this change came about as a result of *Jackson* v. *Denno*, 378 U.S. 368 (1964). This decision by the Supreme Court required the judge to hold a separate hearing to determine the voluntariness of the confession. Decisions in various states have followed this decision, and now pretrial hearings on the voluntariness of confessions are common. Because of such hearings before the trial, defense counsel usually has access to the confession itself. Federal Rule 16 now requires that the U.S. attorney give the defendant access to his statements. A number of states have enacted similar statutes. Aside from these statutory requirements, courts now generally recognize that, as a matter of fairness, the defendant should be allowed to have a copy of his own confession before he goes to trial. Even corporations charged with criminal offenses have been allowed access to pretrial testimony of their employees before the grand jury.

Typical of the modern trend is a decision that allowed a defendant to have copies of his codefendant's statement (*People* v. *Garner*, 57 Cal. 2d 135, cert. den. 370 U.S. 929 [1962]). In that case a man and his wife shot and killed a fellow robber, left his body in the California desert, and fled to Mexico. When arrested, the man made a handwritten statement, which was followed by a joint statement that he and his wife made on tape. The court gave the male defendant his own statement and allowed him to hear the recorded one made with his codefendant. It also granted him permission to make copies.

In a federal charge of criminal conspiracy to steal foreign freight and transport it interstate, the defendant sought statements of coconspirators and codefendants whom the government did not intend to use as witnesses. (A coconspirator is jointly involved, but is not indicted; a codefendant is tried with the defendant.) The court decided that he was entitled to the coconspirators' statements because they were admissible in evidence against him as an exception to the hearsay rule. Thus, they would have the same effect as his own statement. Any statements by codefendants could be given him at the trial court's discretion only if he showed a "particularized need."

Unless there is a rule or statute to cover the situation, the courts are split on the question of discovery of statements by a codefendant or an accomplice.

b. Statements of Witnesses

Once a witness testifies at a trial, opposing counsel has the right to a copy of any prior statement the witness has made. He can then use this information on cross-examination for impeachment purposes. This rule is accepted everywhere by all courts.

The more important question is whether the defendant can obtain the statements of a prosecution witness before trial. Some courts relax pretrial inspection and give the defense access to statements of all witnesses that the state has obtained. An example of this is illustrated by *People* v. *Garner*, 18 Cal. Rptr. 40 (1961). In this case the defendant was charged with performing illegal abortions. Two women and a man testified at the preliminary hearing. Cross-examination showed that they had given prior statements to the police. The defendant demanded copies of these statements, which were either recorded or taken down in longhand from the police files before the case went to trial. The court granted the defense request. It declared that such statements are always allowed at the trial itself for impeachment purposes, and so there was no valid reason why the defense should not have access to them before the trial.

Accessibility of information before a trial takes place can indeed endanger prosecution witnesses. Some courts will, therefore, not allow *pretrial* defense examination of statements by prosecution witnesses, and it is forbidden by statute in federal courts.

c. Statements of Victims

Neither rule nor statute generally differentiates between the availability of a victim's statement and that of any other prosecution witness. Where the court has discretion, it is reluctant to require the pretrial availability of a victim's statement. Should there be a preliminary hearing at which the victim testifies, the defense can, of course, obtain a transcript of the testimony before the trial begins. If there is not such a hearing, the court will usually protect the victim by refusing the defense access to his statement. This is particularly true for victims of sex crimes.

d. Statements of Police

If a police officer was a *witness*, his statement in the departmental files is as that of any other witness. A statement by a police officer concerning his investigation and a summary of evidence are different matters. They are not generally given to the defense in advance of trial. The court may, however, make them available at the trial itself to be used in cross-examination of an officer. Indeed, the Federal Rules of Criminal Procedure, 16 (e), expressly mentions these matters. Thus, except for such things as the defendant's statements, criminal record, and reports of physical and mental examinations, "This rule does not authorize the discovery or inspection of reports, memoranda, or other internal government documents made by the attorney for the government or other government agents in connection with the investigation or prosecution of the case . . . ."

Police statements summarizing evidence are exactly what they say they are—summaries. They are not actual statements of witnesses. They can be used in evidence only as possible tools for cross-examination impeachment of the officer making the report. Police statements often discuss problems of prosecuting the defendant. Such material will not, of course, be allowed defense discovery.

e. Transcripts and Recordings

Investigators are making increased use of tape recordings for taking statements. The fact that the statement is done electronically rather than in writing has no legal effect on its availability to the defense. If the defendant is entitled to a copy, he may be furnished his transcript or be allowed to hear the recording and make his own copy from it. This rule goes as far back as 1950. An undercover agent posing as a coburglar took secret recordings of the planning for the burglary. Court decisions made his recordings available to the defense.

In a case in California the defendant was charged with a sex crime involving children. As part of their interrogation of the man, the police had him listen to a taped conversation between them and the victim. The defendant claimed that he could not remember what he had said. The court ordered that the accused be allowed to hear the recording of himself as well as that of the child. It is safe to say that tape recordings are normally now made available to the defense.

f. Medical Reports

A report by a coroner or medical examiner is admissible evidence in most courts. In jurisdictions where this is true, the court can make such a report available to the defense before trial. In some jurisdictions, however, the coroner's report may not be made available for technical reasons. Reports of physical or mental examinations ordered by the prosecution can normally be obtained by the defendant as a necessary tool in preparing his defense.

g. Laboratory Findings and Reports by Experts

Courts will usually order that the defendant be given copies of police laboratory reports. This is true even when the report itself cannot be used in evidence and the technician must testify in person.

There are innumerable kinds of these reports. The prosecution can normally use photographs as evidence, and pretrial access to such materials will be given the defendant. Reports by experts and technicians on handwriting, ballistics, fingerprints, and blood will also be ordered shown to the accused. Even organs and bodily specimens may be made available to the defense for examination and testing.

A defendant accused of manslaughter was charged with running over a two-and-a-half-year-old girl with his car. His defense was that he was completely unaware that he had hit anything. Scrapings were taken from the car and examined by the F.B.I. laboratory. The court gave the defendant pretrial access to the report, stating that he was entitled to know whether it was positive or negative. If it was positive, the circumstantial evidence would, of course, be used against him.

Another accused allegedly killed a man by kicking him in the head. When he was arrested, he had on the same pair of shoes he had worn at the time of the fight. The shoes were taken from him and sent to the laboratory. He argued that the condition of the shoes had been altered; his own laboratory tests would, therefore, be useless. He demanded a copy of the state's laboratory report so that it could be determined if any hair or other material had been found on the shoes. Even though the report was not admissible in evidence, the court granted his request in the interest of justice.

Today only an unusual set of circumstances would persuade a court to refuse a defendant access to a laboratory report held by the prosecution.

h. Grand Jury Transcripts

Grand jury proceedings are confidential hearings at which only the state's evidence is normally given. The purpose of the hearing is to determine if the prosecution has sufficient evidence to accuse the defendant of a felony. This process is designed to prevent an individual from being unjustly accused by the state.

There are a number of reasons why grand jury hearings are secret. One is for the protection of witnesses. Another is to provide a way of charging the accused and issuing an arrest warrant for him without his knowledge, should he not be in custody. Most jurisdictions consider unauthorized revelation of grand jury testimony contempt of court or even a criminal offense.

Once a witness has testified at the actual trial, a copy of his testimony before the grand jury will be given to the defense counsel. He may use it as possible impeachment material in cross-examination.

Though pretrial access to grand jury transcripts will not usually be allowed by the court, in some cases a witness who has given evidence before a grand jury may be allowed to see his own testimony before trial.

i. Names of Witnesses

According to the old rule, neither side in a criminal trial was required to reveal the names of its potential witnesses. Modern procedure requires the prosecution to supply the names of its witnesses unless it can show a valid reason for concealing them. The court must balance the arguments and decide whether to keep the names confidential.

A case in Illinois, *People* v. *Martin*, 74 Ill. App. 2d 431 (1966), illustrates the kind of problem that still can arise over the names of witnesses. In this case the prosecution supplied the defendant with a list of names of the state's witnesses, but did not include the name of a confidential informant. The defendant was told orally about the informant and was given a chance to interview him. The informant refused, however, to talk to the defense counsel. Though the defense objected, the trial court allowed the informant to testify. The appellate court upheld this ruling. It pointed out that the defense counsel had the name before the trial and that the informer could not be required to talk to him if he chose not to do so.

j. Criminal Records

If the prosecution is allowed to keep secret the records it has of criminal convictions of the defendant or of any potential witness, the defendant is at a disadvantage. Knowing that a criminal record can have an adverse effect on a jury, the accused may have a problem in determining whether he can safely use a potential witness or even take the stand in his own behalf. Because of this, the defense should have pretrial information on such criminal records. Courts ordinarily grant a defense request for such information. As a matter of fact, several states (such as Arizona, Vermont, and New York) now have statutes requiring the prosecution to furnish such information without a request by the defense.

k. Work Product

The "work product" of an attorney consists of such matters as summaries of evidence, trial strategy, and research. It is part of the pretrial investigation and is not subject to pretrial discovery by either side. Sometimes it is debatable whether an item is evidence or a work product. If the court determines it is the latter, it will be protected.

(6.5) Police Files and Records

In the past, defendants were denied access to reports and records compiled by police officers, whether the reports were official or investigative. As with other aspects of discovery, the courts have increasingly liberalized the rules concerning these reports. Some reports, such as those sent to the state after an automobile accident, in some jurisdictions, are available to anyone on the payment of a fee. In other jurisdictions, they are restricted to the persons involved, to owners of the vehicles even if they were not involved in the accident, and to attorneys or insurance adjusters who represent one of the parties involved.

The report on a breath test is usually made available to the person tested if he requests it. As a matter of fact, the report is customarily released on subpoena to any party requesting it, along with photographs of the accident and statements by witnesses. An exception is vehicular homicide, in which matters in police files are protected in the same manner as in other felony cases.

In some jurisdictions, routine police reports sent to the prosecutor will also be turned over to the attorney for the accused; in other jurisdictions, the defense attorney must demand that these items be produced and show that they have some relevancy for the defense effort. The incident report (such as for a burglary, robbery, or theft) is the initial document prepared by police officers; it is usually completed in the field on a standardized form by the patrol officer assigned to respond to the call. It contains little more than bare facts concerning the time of the call and the address where it was received, identity of the victim and his address, one or two sentences describing the event, a description of the alleged perpetrator, a list of witnesses, and other neutral but germane facts. It usually includes additional information for police statistical purposes, such as the amount of light, weather conditions, day of the week, type of property involved, and similar factors that, when aggregated, show criminal patterns.

The follow-up report is written by detectives assigned to the case. It is not neutral because it discloses investigative processes, indicates leads, states conclusions, and generally describes the events and personalities involved. Except for information that can be presented in a strictly factual form, such as data on arrest and loss of property, investigative reports are narrative and therefore vary by the unit and the officer reporting.

A third kind of report is prepared by technicians who are specialists in the field of evidence. They verify the existence of contraband, confirm the identity of fingerprints, conduct paraffin tests, and make comparative ballistic examinations and other scientific studies. Their reports are strictly factual. Thus, if a technician is likely to testify, there is no reason to keep the report from the defense attorney.

The report by a specialized unit such as vice, narcotics, or intelligence is a chronological summary of events leading up to an arrest. These units prepare surveillance reports, reports on interviews with informants, corroborative reports, and investigative summaries. The essential portions of these reports are usually included in affidavits seeking arrest or search warrants. The reports are highly confidential, particularly in investigations that are likely to continue for an indefinite period of time. Gambling, extortion, narcotics, and terrorism are often the offenses investigated. Confidentiality is important because other offenders may be at large, police techniques could be compromised in future cases, and informants might be revealed. Courts should be extremely reluctant to order discovery of these files.

A fifth kind of report is made for the police personnel department or for the purpose of an internal investigation. An officer's personnel dossier lists chronologically all complaints made against the officer and gives a summary of the investigations concerned with the complaints, and conclusions drawn from the investigations, including disciplinary action taken against him, if there was any. These reports are highly sensitive because they may impair the effectiveness of an officer who has been the subject of past investigations, invade his privacy if they are disclosed, and adversely affect police morale.

As was indicated previously, the initial case report is routinely turned over to defense counsel in many jurisdictions and, therefore, does not pose a discovery problem for either side. The follow-up report is sometimes made available if the detective who completed it is to testify on matters contained in it. The theory behind such discovery is that the defense should be allowed access to matters that might impeach the credibility of the officer and prevent a surprise at the trial. Many courts will not require that these reports be produced even if they contain notes of conversations with the accused.

Because they constitute the work product of the state, they are privileged. If, however, defense counsel is able to show inconsistencies in the testimony of one or more officers, there is a stronger likelihood that a court will order them produced. Such inconsistencies may arise at a preliminary hearing or at a suppression hearing.

Surveillance reports are privileged, and a court ordinarily will not compel disclosure. If, however, law enforcement officers used illegal electronic surveillances in conducting their investigation, the accused is entitled to inspect the evidence that was gathered illegally. The purpose of the inspection is to determine whether evidence gathered against him is the fruit of the poisoned tree. The U.S. Supreme Court has ruled that an accused is entitled to obtain records of illegal electronic surveillance without a prior in camera (secret) screening by the court. But he must have standing to object to the act; that is, he must be the party who was overheard illegally or who owned the property on which the surveillance occurred. The court may enter semiprotective orders against disclosure by the accused or his attorney to third parties, such as coconspirators.

Personnel files and reports of internal investigations are ordinarily not discoverable by an accused. In cases where an officer is the complaining witness (such as a charge of assaulting an officer), the accused can obtain a copy of the officer's personnel dossier. The purpose of such discovery is to locate incidents that might bear on the officer's credibility as a witness.

No prior showing of relevance is necessary and that production is not limited to those matters in the officer's file that report on sustained instances of misconduct. Although there is no common-law privilege concerning officers' personnel files, courts in other jurisdictions do not compel production of police dossiers. It is generally felt that such a file is not relevant to the case being prosecuted, even if the officer will be called to testify.

A privilege against disclosure can ordinarily be waived. This is not necessarily true in the case of certain police records, such as arrest sheets. By federal regulation, law enforcement officers may not disclose an individual's arrest record or juvenile record unless it is allowed by statute, executive order, court order, or court rule. Violation of the regulation subjects police officers to a maximum fine of $10,000. A court can order a police agency to turn over criminal history information to the attorney for the accused, but a particularized need must be shown. For example, if a prosecution witness had ever been arrested for perjury or committed to an institution for the criminally insane, the attorney for the accused needs this information in order to conduct an effective defense.

(6.6) Matters in Defense Files in General

The idea of letting the state discover matters from the defense has been slow to develop. Some of the older cases, which are probably now obsolete, refused discovery on grounds it would violate the defendant's right against self-incrimination as set forth in the Fifth Amendment. In addition to this reason, there was the argument that the prosecution has sufficient pretrial weapons, such as police investigations, grand jury proceedings, and preliminary hearings.

The growing area of pretrial criminal discovery is now allowing both sides more latitude, and it is becoming necessary for the defense to give up information. Statutes in some states require defendants to appear in lineups, give physical samples such as blood and submit to physical examinations, and provide samples of handwriting. Federal rules can require both sides to give the names of their witnesses.

a. Alibis

Most states have statutes requiring prior notice by the accused of a proposed defense based on an alibi. The defense can be required to give the names of proposed alibi witnesses as long as the state, in return, must furnish the names of any witnesses it proposes to use to rebut the claimed alibi.

b. Defense Witnesses

There is, as noted, a growing tendency of each side to furnish the names of its witnesses. Unless there is some compelling reason against it, such as possible danger for a prosecution witness, the courts will generally require that the names be revealed to the other side. The courts have moved so far in the direction of allowing the prosecution discovery that in one case the state was furnished copies of a statement by a defense witness for cross-examination, even though the defense counsel had written out the statement and his witness had not signed it.

c. Fingerprints, Handwriting, and Photographs

Fingerprinting and photographing the defendant can be constitutionally required in all felony cases. If these things are not done initially, the courts will order them on application from the state.

The accused can also be ordered to give examples of his handwriting, blood samples, and the like. In one case the state was working on a possible criminal charge involving $25,000 in faked automobile insurance claims. The prosecution moved to require a suspect to appear in his office and give handwriting samples. The court ordered that this be done. It pointed out that, while no criminal action was pending, the state's moving papers showed probable cause to identify the suspect as the defendant. He could, therefore, be required to furnish the handwriting samples.

As early as 1962, the courts in California allowed wide discovery to the prosecution. A rape charge was involved. The defendant claimed that he was impotent and asked for time to get medical evidence and reports on an old injury that had caused his condition. A discovery order was granted the prosecution. It made the defendant surrender the names of the doctors he planned to call and any doctors' reports or X rays he intended to use in evidence. The court excluded only medical reports that had been made for the defense counsel. In its decision, the court gave the pioneering statement on prosecution criminal discovery. It is now generally regarded as the proper rule.

(6.7) Depositions of Third Parties

In criminal actions the courts are reluctant to grant the right to take pretrial depositions of third parties (that is, anyone other than the victim or the defendant). Some states grant it by statute or rule. Various decisions, however, refuse to allow the taking of such depositions, as is routinely done in civil cases.

The reluctance to order free use of pretrial depositions in criminal cases is partially grounded on the argument that fear motivates many witnesses where a crime is concerned. Also, witnesses can develop adverse feelings toward the prosecution if they are subjected to giving additional pretrial depositions. Thus, while pretrial depositions are acceptable in some cases, there are limits to what the courts will allow.

(6.8) Effect of Noncompliance

If either side refuses a court-ordered pretrial discovery, contempt of court is always an available remedy. Though contempt of court can result in fine or imprisonment, this alone might not deter some individuals. The court, therefore, has additional remedies. It can adjourn proceedings until the court order has been followed. If the state has failed to grant discovery, the charges may be dismissed. This has been done, for example, in espionage cases, where the government has felt it could not reveal its informant. What is most common is for the trial judge to refuse to receive the evidence where a discovery order has not been complied with. The court may, in addition, use any other legal remedy it deems appropriate.

(6.9) Privileged Communications

A variety of privileged communications cannot be revealed in court. They range from military secrets to communications between husband and wife. The rule of evidence that communications between certain parties should be confidential and immune from testimonial compulsion is based on public policy. Some, such as confidential communications between attorney and client, are historical and part of the common law. Others, such as the confidentiality between doctor and patient, are of modern origin and are usually found in statutes.

"Communication" in these situations is not confined to what one person has told another, but may include such things as written material or observations that could be seen and heard by the person involved in the confidential relationship.

From time to time interested groups seek to enlarge the field of privileged communications by having new laws passed that grant them testimonial immunity. Newspaper reporters, for example, are promoting legislation in some jurisdictions that grants them limited immunity for refusing to reveal their news sources.

For any communication to be excluded from court, the general rule is that it must have some aura of confidentiality about it, and there has to be the required relationship between the parties. If, however, only part of the testimony is privileged, this does not bar the witness from testifying, but only excludes the part that is privileged.

The rule of confidentiality applies to all proceedings, pretrial hearings, grand jury sessions, and the actual trial. There are various exceptions and legal refinements in all areas of privileged communications. Though no constitutional problems are involved, local statutes and court decisions must be consulted in every case to be sure of the particular rule.

(6.10) Marital Privilege

An old English rule disqualified one spouse from testifying *for* the other. This has been completely changed through the years so that now in some cases a spouse cannot testify *against* the other. Only a few remnants of this outmoded English rule remain in a small number of states. The general rule of evidence that forbids one spouse from testifying against the other in criminal proceedings known as "confidential communication" grew up by court decision and became part of our common law. Though the reasons for the rule are obscure, the usual rationale is that "it prevents disruption of the home." In this day of women's liberation, equality of the sexes, and divorce by consent, there is no longer any real basis for retaining the husband-wife immunity rule.

It is interesting that a brother was always allowed to testify against a brother and a father against a child without the court feeling that this was socially disruptive, and yet this could be equally disruptive of family harmony as a situation involving a husband and wife.

The husband-wife testimonial privilege does, however, cause problems for law enforcement personnel, and it promotes more injustice than almost any other rule of evidence. Law books are full of frustrating examples where the rule suppressed the truth and freed guilty defendants. Following is one such example.

In a case in Ithaca, New York, a policeman was charged with stealing from the Montgomery Ward retail store. The store's janitor testified that Officer Daghita often drove him to work in the early morning hours and would go in the store and take merchandise. Many times he carried it away in cardboard boxes. At his larceny trial the state called Daghita's wife and, over objection by the defense, had her testify against her husband. She said that he often brought home articles in his own car or in the police car at 4:00 or 5:00 a.m. She further told how he carried in rugs, clothing, jackets, pillows, and bath towels, often in cardboard boxes. He hid them in the cellar and brought them upstairs later in the day. The husband was convicted and appealed. In New York a statute barred a husband or wife from testifying as to a "confidential communication between them." The appellate court held that even if no word is spoken, the husband's acts done in the presence of the wife were covered and that her testimony in this case was barred. Thus, the conviction was reversed.

Most states do have laws providing for the marital privilege in criminal cases. Following are factors that these statutes generally have in common.

a. Valid Marriage

The parties must actually be married. A mistress or paramour will not qualify, neither will the partner to a bigamous or incestuous marriage or one where there was no marriage license. A common-law marriage, where recognized, does, however, qualify for the exclusionary rule.

The general rule is that no privilege attaches to communications before the marriage takes place or after it has been terminated. There are, nevertheless, exceptions. In many jurisdictions a marriage ceremony after the crime will make the earlier communications privileged. Some states even preserve the confidentiality of marital communications after a divorce. The law of the locality must, of course, be consulted in case of a premarital or postdivorce situation.

b. Necessity of Confidentiality

Court decisions are split as to just what husband-wife communications are protected. Most state statutes have attempted to narrow the privilege to cover "confidential communications" only. The prosecutor's problem is that various courts have given a wide interpretation as to the meaning of both "confidential" and "communication." A police investigator may think he has an airtight case because the wife saw some of her husband's criminal activity and no confidential words came from him. When the case comes to trial, the officer may be shocked to find that her testimony is not allowed because it is considered to be privileged.

Many court rulings have regarded conduct observed by a spouse as a "communication." Further, since the acts were done in the presence of the spouse, they are "confidential" because the other spouse committed them in the confidence that he was in the privacy of the marriage situation.

Thus, in barring the testimony of Officer Daghita's wife when she testified about her husband's bringing home the stolen goods, the court stated: "Confidential communication . . . means more than oral communications or conversations between husband and wife. It includes . . . disclosive acts done in the presence [of] the other which would not have been performed except for the confidence so existing."

A criminal indictment was dismissed by a court because a wife testified that she found a pistol in her husband's pocket. In another, the wife called police to her home and gave them a loaded pistol her husband had hidden in their liquor cabinet. She was not allowed to so testify. One wife was forbidden to testify that she had found a bag of checks that her husband had hidden in the house. The court held that he must have hidden them there because of his reliance on his marital status. In a murder case an important clue was a piece of cloth found near the victim's body. The defendant's wife testified that her husband left home in the morning of the murder wearing an overcoat of similar cloth and that he had come home that night wearing a different coat. The state's highest court considered this privileged communication, and the testimony was stricken.

Courts have argued over whether a wife's diary is privileged and even over whether she should be allowed to identify her spouse's handwriting. There is further division concerning the legality of a spouse's testimony in regard to the other spouse's intoxication or mental condition. Merely calling the spouse to the witness stand and making her claim the privilege may be ruled as prejudicial, unless it is done in good faith.

Courts agree that the marital privilege disappears when a third person capable of understanding what is going on is present. In such a situation, confidentiality is lost. Courts quibble, however, when, for example, the husband was talking to a third party and the wife overheard it. A court in Texas even barred a wife from testifying that she had heard her husband threaten to kill a third person.

c. Exceptions

There are some court-approved exceptions where the marital privilege does not apply. If, for example, a husband commits a crime against his wife, she may testify freely against him. In most jurisdictions this exception has been extended to cover any offense against a family member, such as incest, child abuse, or assault. The exception is based on the theory that such a family offense is in reality an offense against the other spouse. According to the same theory, one spouse has been allowed to testify against the other regarding sexual misconduct with any third party. The privilege does not apply when the husband and wife are joint participants in a crime. A criminal cannot use a spouse to engage in a crime with the idea that she could not be a potential witness.

d. Waiver

The protected person can always waive his privilege and allow the testimony to be used, but the waiver has to be made by both parties. The federal rule is that the marital privilege belongs to the witness alone, and in a few jurisdictions the protection belongs to the defendant.

(6.11) Medical Privilege

Privileged communication between doctor and patient was unknown in common law. The idea began with a nineteenth-century statute in New York. Most states have passed similar laws, so that, in general, communications between doctor and patient are privileged. The term "doctor" includes psychiatrists and other medical specialists. As is to be expected, the privilege has produced many unjust results. An example of this is shown in *People* v. *Decina*, 2 N.Y. 2d 133 (1956).

At 3:30 p.m. on a bright, sunny day Decina was driving alone in his car on a city street. Suddenly he swerved to the wrong side of the road and then to the right and mounted the sidewalk at fifty to sixty miles per hour. On doing so, he plowed through a group of young schoolgirls, killing four of them. The car finally crashed through a brick wall. When he was pulled out of the car, he appeared "dazed" and said "I blacked out from the bridge." The police took him to the hospital under guard. An intern examined him and took his history, all of which was overheard by a police officer stationed at the door of the hospital room. The accused told the doctor, who later testified, that he had suffered from convulsions since childhood when he had sustained a brain injury. Further, for nine years he had been subject to seizures in which his right hand "jumped." Just prior to the accident his right hand acted in that way. Decina was convicted of criminal negligence. The appellate court ruled, however, that, even though the intern was not hired by the defendant, the doctor-patient relationship existed and the information the doctor received was privileged. The conviction was reversed.

Thus, four people were killed by a driver with a long history of epilepsy, and this information was kept out of court. Such a result vividly illustrates the need to reexamine this rule for criminal cases. There is now less reason than in times past to bar evidence of a person's physical condition during a criminal proceeding. Little harm, if any, can come to the individual and much public good can result from revealing the truth where a crime has been charged.

In criminal cases the statutory rule against revealing information that passes between a doctor and his patient is, nevertheless, widespread. Only a few states do not let the medical privilege apply to criminal cases.

Where the doctor-patient privilege is upheld in criminal trials, there are certain general requirements.

a. Relationship with Patient

There must first be a genuine doctor-patient relationship. The doctor must either be a duly licensed physician or the patient must have, in good faith, believed him to be such. In respect to the privilege, a consulting physician stands in the same position as the regular doctor. The doctor's nurse or the paramedical assistant is generally included.

b. Privileged Subject Matter

Medical privilege is based on the idea that the patient is confiding in the doctor in order that he might be treated. Where the patient is seen for observation only, not to be cured, the information is normally not privileged. A court-ordered physical or medical examination falls into this category. Blood alcohol tests, for example, are not given for treatment. The results are, therefore, admissible. The same is true of autopsies, since the doctor obviously is not going to treat the corpse.

The doctor-patient privilege covers much more than any confidential matter the patient discusses with him. It includes all information the doctor obtains from the patient that enables him to act.

c. Exceptions

Some results from applying the doctor-patient privilege have been so extreme that the courts have made exceptions. One of these exceptions is given below.

A physician operated on and removed the bullet from a woman who had been shot. The state had a statute concerning the doctor-patient privilege. It also required doctors to report all gunshot wounds to the police, which the physician did. At the criminal trial the prosecution called the doctor to testify. The defense objected on the basis of privilege, pointing out that the doctor was testifying about treatment. The court overruled the objection and allowed the testimony to stand, stating that the privilege statute was not intended to protect the criminal and that the matter was public information anyway since the physician had to report the wound to the police.

Another doctor treated an individual who was poisoned. The patient died, and the doctor was allowed to testify rather than protect the murderer.

d. Waiver

Only the patient can waive the doctor-patient privilege, since he is the one protected. A stranger to the privilege will, therefore, not be allowed to claim it. In a criminal prosecution for driving while intoxicated, the defendant moved to inspect the hospital records of the deceased accident victim. The prosecution claimed that the victim's death resulted from an embolism that developed from a leg fracture. The defendant wanted his medical expert to examine the hospital records in order to determine whether the blood clot was the result of a nonaccidental factor. The district attorney objected on the grounds of doctor-patient relationship. The court allowed the inspection, holding that the People were strangers to any claim of medical privilege and had no standing to object.

The patient can either expressly waive the privilege or he can fail to object at the trial. He may also lose his privilege by voluntarily disclosing the information to a third party. The courts do not unanimously hold that the privilege is lost if a third party is present during the examination by the doctor. They do agree, however, that the presence of the doctor's nurse or other employee does not waive the privilege.

The patient can lose his privilege if he "opens the door" at his trial by introducing evidence concerning his physical or mental condition, where this is an issue. If his defense is insanity, and he introduces medical evidence to demonstrate his condition, the state will even be allowed to bring in a psychiatrist who previously treated him for insanity. The rationale is that the introduction of defense evidence on mental condition opens the entire field for full exploration.

e. Miscellaneous

Medical privilege generally applies to all matters within the hospital, such as hospital records, X rays, and nurses' notes. Interns and hospital residents are within the area of privilege if they treat the patient, even though they are employed by the hospital. Police may, for instance, overlook the fact that a resident in an emergency room who treats a drunken driver and takes a blood sample in the process may be prevented from testifying.

(6.12) Legal Privilege

The rule of confidentiality of communications between lawyer and client is of ancient origin and does not depend on statute. It is found in civil law in the codes of continental Europe. In English law its history can be traced to the time of Queen Elizabeth.

The rule originated to maintain the honor of the attorney, not to protect the client. At first the counselor was the only one who could waive it, because his honor was involved. As time went on the idea of protecting the lawyer was rejected, and the theory evolved that the privilege belongs to the client. Indeed, the lawyer is now duty bound not to reveal privileged information given by his client and can do so only if the latter consents.

The privilege applies whenever legal advice is sought from a lawyer and the client makes a confidential communication to him for that purpose. Such information is permanently protected from disclosure, unless the client consents to its revelation.

a. Attorneys within the Rule

"Lawyer" here includes any attorney who is admitted to practice in any state, not necessarily the state where the crime was committed or where the communication was made. The modern trend is to allow the privilege if the client believes that the individual he consults is a licensed attorney. If the communication was made to the attorney's agent, such as his legal secretary, investigator, or clerk, it is also protected. A law student is not, however, within the protection of the rule, nor is the judge who is consulted as a judge.

b. Relationships within the Rule

The lawyer must be consulted as a lawyer, though it is not necessary that he actually be retained or later hired. "Curbstone advice" is thus not protected.

c. Confidential Communication

Any information the client gives the lawyer for consultation purposes is protected. It need not be labeled "confidential." "Communication" includes words, conversations, or letters from the client.

"Acts" or observations the attorney makes of his clients are somewhat more difficult to classify. An accused thief may pay his lawyer from a large roll of bills. Can the attorney refuse to reveal this? If insanity is an issue, can the lawyer refuse to testify concerning his observation of his client's mental condition? Usually these two questions must be answered in the negative. Facts that anyone could observe are not immune simply because the lawyer saw them. If, for the purpose of consultation, the client gives his attorney a voice sample or exhibits a scar, this would be protected.

At times the client may ask a lawyer to do things a layman could do just as well, such as having him witness a bank deposit or listen to a conversation. In this situation there is no privilege.

Attorneys have even claimed that the name of their client was protected. This situation is demonstrated in *People ex rel Vogelstein*. Vogelstein, a New York attorney, appeared in magistrate's court on behalf of fifteen clients who had been arrested for running an illegal lottery. Twelve of these defendants pleaded guilty, and the trial of the other three was pending. Meanwhile, on the theory that organized crime was involved, a grand jury began an investigation. Vogelstein was subpoenaed to appear before the grand jury and was asked who retained him to defend the gamblers. Claiming the attorney-client privilege, he refused to testify. He argued that the information sought by the grand jury might incriminate his client. The judge found him in contempt and had him jailed. Vogelstein appealed. The appellate court affirmed the contempt conviction and held that he must name his client. The names of the fifteen defendants was a matter of public record, the court noted, and so it strongly suggested that there was a wholesale scheme to avoid the law. The decision added that there was no way for the court to know a privileged relationship existed if the attorney would not name his client. It was pointed out, in addition, that the privilege against self-incrimination is personal and does not extend to the attorney. Thus, even that claim did not prevent revelation of the client's name.

A more difficult area is one in which a lawyer receives information regarding physical evidence of a crime. For example, Robert Garrow was charged with the knife slaying of an eighteen-year-old boy. His defense was insanity. During preparation for trial, Garrow told his lawyers that he had killed two other people about a year before, and he described the location of their bodies. Though the lawyers located the bodies, they did not notify the authorities. The police did not find either body until three months later. At that time Garrow publicly confessed to the two slayings when he testified in his own behalf at his murder trial. Criminal charges were brought against the lawyers, but were later dismissed at the trial court level.

Defense lawyers have opposed the federal prosecutor's seizure of drug money used to pay the attorney's legal fees for defending accused drug violators. Defense counsel argue that this violates the confidential attorney-client privilege and that seizure of fee money prevents the defendant from getting a fair trial. Generally, they have been unsuccessful in preventing the seizure.

It is still the law, however, that a lawyer cannot conceal actual physical evidence of a crime that his client has given him. A lawyer was suspended from practice because he saw a sawed-off shotgun and money that came from an armed robbery and intended to conceal this information until after the trial, under a claim of attorney-client privilege.

d. Exceptions

Lawyer-client communication ceases to be protected and loses its confidentiality if there is a third party present who is not in the attorney's employ, who is not a codefendant, or who is not closely associated with the defendant. A letter from a third person delivered to the attorney is not confidential, nor is a message from the client to the attorney directing him to deliver it to someone else.

If a lawyer is a party to a crime, or if he is a participant in a conspiracy, there is no privilege. The same is true if the client communicates with the attorney about a proposed crime.

If the communication itself is criminal, it is, of course, not protected, as illustrated by the case of *People* v. *Farmer*, 194 N.Y. 251 (1909). Mrs. Farmer was indicted for murdering Sarah Brennan.

Evidence was presented that she passed herself as Sarah Brennan and signed that name to a deed of Sarah's property. At Mrs. Farmer's murder trial the attorney who prepared the deed was called by the prosecution. He testified that Mrs. Farmer pretended to be the deceased and signed the name Sarah Brennan before him in his capacity as a notary public. The court approved of the testimony, stating that the communication itself was a criminal act on the part of Mrs. Farmer and that "the seal of personal confidence can never be used to cover a transaction which is in itself a crime."

e. Waiver

Since immunity belongs to the client, he must be the one to waive it. In a case in Minnesota, a prosecution witness was being cross-examined by defense counsel regarding inconsistent statements the witness had made to an attorney. Because the witness made no objection to the questions, the prosecutor did, saying that whatever the witness had told the lawyer was privileged. The court overruled the objection, stating the privilege belonged only to the witness and not to the prosecutor.

If a defendant chooses to take the stand, his act of testifying does not waive any attorney-client communication that he may have had. Should part of his testimony concern a communication with his lawyer, he has then "opened the door" on the whole subject and has, in effect, waived his privilege.

The privilege survives the death or the discharge of the attorney. Once a communication is protected, it is protected forever, unless it is waived.

(6.13) Paraprofessional Privilege

Some professional fringe areas claim the right of privileged communications. These are occasionally the subject of court decision. Newspaper reporters, as mentioned earlier, are trying to claim the privilege. A privilege of this type ordinarily exists only because a statute grants it.

a. Nurses and Other Medical Personnel

No common-law privilege exists for either of these groups. In some jurisdictions the doctor's nurse is covered under the physician's protective privilege, but the outside registered or practical nurse has no communication privilege unless it is granted by statute. A nurse is allowed to keep a patient's information confidential only when that information is necessary for her to act in her professional capacity.

Medical technicians have been excluded from coverage. Psychologists, psychotherapists, or dentists are not included unless they are specified by statute.

b. Hospital Records

Records of hospitals, both regular and mental, are generally included by statute in the area of medical privilege. The rationale is, of course, that these records contain in written form most of the communications between doctor and patient.

c. Miscellaneous

As was said previously, psychologists and psychotherapists are, from time to time, included in statutes concerning privileged communications. This may affect prosecution of juveniles in cases where the school psychologist is barred from testifying.

Accountants have tried without success to be included. A Florida statute, however, now grants the privilege to confidential information exchanged between clients and accountants. Other jurisdictions may do likewise.

With the increase of prosecutions concerning drugs and drug-related matters, the question of confidentiality of pharmacists' prescription records occasionally surfaces. Unless he is included by statute, the druggist cannot claim exemption from revealing his records.

Telephone and telegraph employees, who are generally forbidden by statue from revealing customers' messages, have occasionally been required to disclose such information as trial witnesses.

Private detectives have at times been compelled by the court to reveal information regarding their clients even when a statute requires them to respect their clients' confidentiality.

A parent-child privilege has been recognized by some jurisdictions. Some now grant the privilege in such matters to counselors who advise victims of rape or sexual assault.

(6.14) Divinity Privilege

Privileged communication between priest and penitent was unknown in common law, but it is now granted by law in most states. The privilege seems, in fact, to be interpreted in the courts more strictly than any of the others.

a. Relationship of the Parties

The usual statute provides confidential protection if the clergyman involved is a minister of any religion and if the rules of his order forbid him to disclose a confession made to him in his professional capacity.

b. Material Protected

Not every communication with a recognized clergyman is barred. An individual must be consulting him professionally, as he would a physician, and the information must have been given with the understanding that it was to be confidential. No promise of confidentiality need be given by the minister, however, as that is understood.

Not every message from penitent to priest is covered. Statements regarding a confederate, codefendant, or other third party are not confessions of the speaker and therefore have no protection. In the same class would be a message that the priest was to give to someone else. By the same interpretation, the privilege does not protect observations the clergyman made.

c. Who Is a Clergyman?

Statutes name "clergymen or priests" and a "clergyman, minister or other person or practitioner authorized to perform similar functions." Problems arise with people who are not officially ministers, but are closely related to religious matters. In a homicide trial in New Jersey, refused to testify about a conversation she had carried on with a youth. She was convicted of contempt, and the appellate court agreed with the conviction. It was ruled that she did not perform the functions of a priest and that nothing in Catholic doctrine gave her the right to claim the privilege. Presbyterian elders have been included in the area of religious privilege because in that denomination they are "ministers." Elders of other Christian churches, however, are not included.

d. Waiver

The divinity privilege is generally conceded to be two sided. The person who confesses has the privilege to protect his confession, and the clergyman has a separate privilege because the rules of his church forbid him to speak. Even if the person who confesses waives his right, the law will not force the clergyman to reveal the confession if it violates the rules of his order. Thus, even if the penitent is dead, absent, or does not claim his privilege, the clergyman may still refuse to testify.

(6.15) Privilege of the Police Informant

There are three kinds of police informants: the good citizen informant, the nonparticipating underworld informant, and the participating informant. Although the identity of the good citizen informant is kept confidential, his reliability must be affirmatively demonstrated in an affidavit establishing probable cause.

a. Nonparticipating Informants

Nonparticipating informants are those who learn of criminal activity and report it to the police, but also desire confidentiality. Their motives for anonymity may be based on a number of factors, such as fear of retaliation or cultural and social ostracism. Many of these informants are paid for their services, and others hope to receive "favors" from officers. The value of such information is significant. Many cases, in fact, could not be solved without it.

In criminal trials, disclosures by informants are not admissible because the accused cannot confront his accuser—a right guaranteed by the Sixth Amendment. Such disclosures are, moreover, hearsay and do not fall within one of the recognized exceptions. Such information may, however, be used to support an arrest or search warrant or in a suppression hearing that attacks the legality of an arrest or search.

In *McCray* v. *U.S.*, 386 U.S. 300 (1967), the Supreme Court held that the confidentiality of unnamed, nonparticipating informants should be preserved. To guard against perjury by the police, however, the judge at the suppression hearing retains the right to examine the informant, in chambers and outside the presence of the accused and his attorney.

b. Participating Informants

Participating informants are those who actually take part in the offense. They may, for example, have bought the capsule or bag of heroin upon which an arrest warrant is based. Because their testimony bears on the ultimate outcome of the trial, an accused may be entitled to learn the identity of these informants. This exception poses a real dilemma for an investigating officer. If he intends to arrest and prosecute the accused for the crime in which the informant participated, he must be prepared to produce him at a later time. To avoid that situation, another alternative is available. The offense under investigation may be changed to one of a possessory nature. Thus, the informant might purchase narcotics from the suspect, and his information can be used to support a search warrant to look for contraband, which is a continuing and possessory offense. The eventual prosecution of the suspect could take place on the charge of possession of narcotics, which were found pursuant to a search by warrant. If, however, the officer prefers to pursue the more serious offense of sale, the informant would have to be produced in most jurisdictions. In this situation the informant is in a strategic position to exonerate or incriminate the accused, even though substantive circumstantial evidence might also exist.

When offenses are possessory, the officer can testify and respond to cross-examination respecting the existence of contraband on the premises. In determining whether the informant should be identified or produced, courts generally apply a balancing test. Where the informant was the sole participant in the transaction for which the accused is being prosecuted, his confidentiality ordinarily will not be preserved. If, however, there was sufficient evidence in addition to his confidential disclosures, his identity will not be revealed.

For example, an informant is searched and given ten dollars in marked money. The suspect's home has been under surveillance all day, and it is believed that he is alone. Several people have visited under suspicious circumstances; all of them stayed only a few moments. Many are known addicts. The informant is observed as he goes to the suspect's door and is then seen to leave. When he is searched again, the police find that the money is missing and that he has a glassine bag containing a substance that tests reveal to be heroin. To make sure that the informant's identity remains confidential, the surveillance continues until a few more visitors come and go.

In the above example, the officers would have probable cause to arrest the suspect and search his person for the marked money; or they could obtain arrest and search warrants for the suspect and his residence. If heroin was found on the premises, the informant's confidentiality could be preserved. There may even be sufficient corroborating evidence to support a conviction for sale, which evidence would also help contravene any claims that the informant was mistaken in his identity or the events that took place. Should the court rule, however, that the suspect could not get a fair trial without disclosure of the informant's identity or his production as a witness, the charge of sale would have to be dismissed, and the officers would have to be content with the remaining charge of possession.

(6.16) Official Privilege

Matters of state, which, by their very nature, are confidential, are subject to a claim of privilege. When a general is asked questions about a missile, or when a Secret Service agent is asked about precautions taken to protect the President, both may claim executive privilege. If, however, the agent is asked what steps the Secret Service is taking to locate another fugitive or a missing witness, the answer is protected by investigatory privilege. Often the same information will be sought, not in a courtroom, but through interrogatories, by depositions, or by subpoenas duces tecum. The same principles of privilege will often prevent discovery.

Several of the Watergate defendants attempted to call former President Richard Nixon as a defense witness. He resisted their subpoenas to testify on the grounds of executive privilege. The Supreme Court stressed, with respect to the presidential tapes, that a court must accord a high degree of deference to such evidence. A judge must balance this solemn responsibility, however, against the needs of criminal defendants.

In the Poindexter criminal trial arising out of the Iran-Contra scandal, Poindexter sought to subpoena former President Reagan's diary entries and to require Reagan to testify at the trial. The diary material was denied to him, but the ex-president voluntarily testified at a taped pretrial deposition, thus sidestepping the issue of executive privilege.

It appears, therefore, that there are varying degrees of official privilege, as is the need to know. At the highest level are military secrets, disclosure of which could seriously compromise national security. Of lesser importance is information, which, if disclosed, would reveal negligence of particular officials. Executive privilege is less clearly defined and is not as absolute as military and state secrets. A court might properly refuse to call the President or even the secretary of defense or state, but demand answers from lesser officials. The privilege is not absolute and is based on such factors as the status of the witness, the subject matter of the inquiry, the potential harm to be suffered by the government and the People, and the necessity of the information sought.

It is clear that the courts will not permit the calling of high officials simply to dramatize a cause or to add sensationalism to a trial. Even when considerations of due process mandate the questioning of a high official, it is appropriate to order the taking of a deposition—at the White House, State Department, or Pentagon—to avoid inconvenience to the official and overdramatization of the event.

(6.17) Privilege of the News Media

In the absence of a statute or court rule, a news reporter cannot refuse to disclose the sources of his information. The preservation of confidential sources is, however, in many cases, beneficial to the public, as in the case of police informants. There are also a number of reasons why news sources should remain confidential. First, the information learned serves the public interest. Second, informants would be reluctant to disclose information to reporters if their identities were later made public. Third, informants would be subject to harassment, embarrassment, or, in some cases, physical harm.

California has, therefore, passed a law that protects a journalist from a citation for contempt if he refuses to identify his sources in open court or before a grand jury. The privilege is limited in that it does not assist a reporter in a civil suit for libel. In a recent case in that state a newsman was put in the county jail for contempt of court because he had refused to obey an order of a state court trial judge to divulge the source of certain information. He sought a writ of habeas corpus from the federal courts; it was denied, and he pleaded. A U.S. court of appeals found that the state's interest in protecting the right of due process of the accused outweighed the interest of the newsman in protecting his sources of information. A balancing test was applied.

The results showed that the needs of the accused were "more important and compelling," and, in any event, the incarceration did not
violate any federally protected constitutional right. Thus, the writ was
properly denied.

(6.18) Summary

The original common-law rule forbade any pretrial discovery in
criminal cases. It is now generally agreed that courts do have the
power to allow such discovery, and so the modern trend in all courts
is to be increasingly liberal in this area.

The accused does not have an absolute right to discovery, and
it is still within the court's discretion. Informants for the prosecution,
victims of criminal acts, and witnesses who are subject to possible
criminal pressures are still protected from defense discovery.

Most evidence in the prosecution's files will be made available
to the defense if it can show good cause. Thus, the accused will be
given pretrial access to confessions, statements by witnesses, criminal
records, laboratory and experts' reports, and similar material.

The defense usually asks for much of the material in police
files. Police reports, interviews, and records of internal affairs may be
requested. Though courts allow some of this type of material to be
used at the trial for cross-examination of an individual police witness,
they are generally reluctant to allow pretrial access to it.

The prosecution is gradually being allowed some discovery from
defense files. Alibi claims with the names of supportive witnesses,
handwriting samples, medical reports, and physical specimens are
examples of material that the court will generally order the defense
to reveal to the prosecution before trial.

Refusal to grant discovery can result in contempt, dismissal of
charges, and other court sanctions.

Communications between certain people are legally privileged
and cannot be used in court without consent.

Communications between husband and wife are protected by
many state statutes. Oral and written communications, as well as
one spouse's observations of the other, may be covered. Offenses by
one spouse against the other spouse or against a family member are
not protected.

Doctor-patient communications, when concerned with treatment, are privileged by statute in various states. Hospital and medical records usually are included.

Confidential communications between a client and his attorney are protected from forced revelation in court. The privilege applies whenever the client seeks his lawyer's legal advice, but ordinary observations by the lawyer, or actual evidence connected with a crime, are not protected.

A communication by an individual to a clergyman is generally protected by statute if the rules of the minister's church forbid its disclosure.

Some miscellaneous privileges are granted by statute to reporters, nurses, and other paraprofessionals. Any of these privileges can be waived, however, and the testimony can be allowed by consent.

Police informants are entitled to maintain their anonymity, and officers can resist demands to identify them on the grounds of privilege. If the informant has contributed information bearing on the identity of the accused or on his guilt or innocence, it may be in the interests of justice to refuse the claim of privilege. Where, however, the informant has merely furnished information constituting probable cause to conduct a search, and the guilt of the accused can be shown by direct testimony, the privilege is respected by the courts.

The government has a privilege not to disclose confidential matters of state, particularly military secrets. This privilege also applies to continuing investigations of a criminal nature.

Statutes written for the express purpose of protecting news sources may grant a journalist limited privilege.

Discussion Questions

1. Who is the holder of a privilege?
2. Discuss the underlying social considerations for privileges.
3. What kinds of communications are protected by the attorney-client privilege?
4. What is the basis generally given for recognizing the marital privilege?
5. Why is the husband-wife privilege not recognized in criminal cases between spouses?

7
Prosecution and Defense

As to lawyers, their profession is supported by
indiscriminate defense of right and wrong.

—Junius

(7.1) Adversary System

Involvement of prosecutors and defense attorneys comes shortly after police make an arrest, particularly in some serious offenses, and a strange ritual known as adversary proceedings commences. Hundreds of years ago, in the Anglo-Saxon period, citizens were allowed to engage the services of champions to represent them in settling disputes in trials by combat. This heritage produced the present-day system of lawyers representing the state and the accused utilizing rhetoric and legal rules instead of swords and shields for the same purpose. The court is the modern-day descendant of the battlefield, and, however old-fashioned the scheme may appear, it provides a unique device for protecting priceless personal freedoms. To the detached observer, adversariness may appear a strange principle of justice; however, no totalitarian state can afford unencumbered representation of criminal defendants. That is central to such a peculiar scheme, but it is essential to our law and basic to our heritage of freedom.

The principal rationale for adversary proceedings is that they permit independent triers of law and fact, judges and juries, to benefit from hearing both sides of a controversy. The state prosecutor and the defense counsel have an opportunity to explain the maximum strengths of the arguments and to penetrate the weaknesses of the opposition. From the resulting controversy, the virtues and vices of each side may be determined and evaluated. Another benefit of adversary practice comes from the isolation of those who must ultimately determine guilt and set penalties. In the traditional legal system, the judge not only makes decisions but also develops, examines, and evaluates evidence. In common law jurisdictions, these latter functions become the responsibility of the opposing lawyers, thus allowing the court to remain detached, separate, and independent of the state's efforts to prosecute.

It is easy for a lawyer to become concerned more with victory than with justice and fairness. Adversary practice can place such an undue emphasis on success that ethics are put aside, and even collusion or deceit can become involved. Thus the ultimate purpose of criminal law—protection of both the state and the individual—may be put second in importance, behind "victory."

Adversary practice significantly affects rules of criminal procedure and evidence. For example, the order of trial depends on opportunities for both sides to contradict and compensate both argument and proof. These aspects may have significant impact upon the eventual outcome of the case. One unspectacular but important area of advocacy involves the acquisition of prior knowledge about the opposition's case. This may occur during a procedure known as discovery or pretrial disclosure of information. Such a process can bear significantly upon proceedings while helping to eliminate the pretense and surprise of advocacy. Discovery is widely used in civil suits but has some limitations in criminal matters. Statutory interpretation, local custom, and the personal relationship of opposing attorneys determine the extent to which details of evidence and argument will actually be revealed. Discovery can save time and effort for all concerned and is now becoming more widely accepted.

Hundreds of thousands of attorneys are licensed to practice law in the United States, but many do not practice at all, and fewer still become involved in criminal matters. Private claims, property, and technical advice make up the overwhelming majority of legal activity. Only a small part of lawyers' time is closely connected with criminal justice. Many private attorneys shun criminal practice because of its oftentimes unpleasant nature and its lower scale of fees.

(7.2) Prosecutor

Across the United States, hundreds of separate and independent agencies handle serious offenses, while thousands of municipal officials exercise control over minor local infractions. Shortly after a typical criminal case is initiated by arrest, the police take the matter to the prosecutor.

In our system of justice, the prosecutor occupies a prominent position fully comparable to those of police and judges. Because he exercises broad discretion in determining which charges are to be prosecuted and what plea bargains and sentences are to be recommended, he plays a most prominent part in our criminal justice system.

Prosecutorial responsibility rests in various government lawyers, proportioned according to jurisdiction. Federal law violations proceed directly to attorneys working for the federal government and grouped into offices in accordance with the number of U.S. district courts. These U.S. attorneys are appointed by the president subject to Senate confirmation. These well-paid positions ordinarily are a means of political patronage and change hands with changes in power. The actual work of federal attorneys, however, is generally accomplished by thousands of civil service employees. Their activities are necessarily limited to federal law violations, although this tends to expand rather steadily.

At the opposite end of the prosecutorial spectrum, attorneys, often employed part-time by municipalities, present charges growing from violations of strictly local ordinances. The majority of such cases reaching the courts falls within their authority. But these prosecutions are generally routine infractions of traffic or licensing laws.

Most serious offenses go directly to the district attorneys. These prosecutors and their thousands of assistants and staff members handle the bulk of major cases. Most district attorneys (also called state's attorneys, county attorneys, or commonwealth attorneys) are elected to office. The type of office maintained under these officials varies significantly in size and structure. In rural areas the prosecutor's office is quite small and may consist of only one prosecutor who works part-time and also maintains a separate civil law practice.

Prosecutors in large urban areas may employ hundreds of lawyers, secretaries, and investigators. Employment in such agencies frequently includes attractive salaries and the power of considerable political patronage.

Generally, lawyers employed by prosecutors are not paid as well as private practitioners and have little job security. Many are young lawyers seeking courtroom experience. Total prosecutorial expense nationwide makes up approximately 5 percent of all criminal justice costs. This fact may contribute to a combination of limited professional opportunity and occasionally rather gross maneuvering for public attention.

The rural district attorney may personally deal with almost every type of crime, from theft to murder. By contrast, in an urban area, the chief prosecutor serves primarily as an administrator who makes decisions about specific cases and appears in court only in unusual circumstances. His office is highly specialized, with separate units for felonies, bad checks, domestic problems, or other similar designations. This, of course, is not to imply that size is associated with efficiency. On the contrary, to a great degree, the benefits of individual attention are lost in large organizations.

In many jurisdictions, district attorneys and their investigators are statutorily given the same legal authority as police officers. Ordinarily, they depend on regular law enforcement agencies to provide charges in common street crimes. However, they frequently receive complaints from citizens to investigate certain business offenses and offenses against the family. Some district attorneys also direct activities against organized crime, vice activities, and official corruption. The precise relationship between police and the district attorney varies widely in different localities. In some communities, especially small towns, they may work in close cooperation. In other areas, however, there may be competition, contradiction, and hostility. Sometimes police and prosecutor, because of their differing roles, operate separately and totally without understanding each other's problems and responsibilities.

Because of decentralization in larger jurisdictions and because authority must be delegated, agents of the district attorney possess far-reaching and arbitrary discretion. They are responsible for conducting preliminary investigations to determine if charges are justified, for deciding when to pursue prosecution either directly or through the grand jury, and for preparing and presenting the resulting case. Conversely, these same officials can determine when not to proceed with an accusation. In the earliest stages, they exercise virtually absolute unlimited authority to release a suspect, and, even after formal grand jury indictment, it is possible for them to withdraw charges by simply entering a *nolle prosequi* declaration of no further intent to prosecute.

District attorneys have a great deal of discretion, largely without court supervision, in their day-to-day work. This tremendous power may, of course, be used for good or evil. It can be a vigorous element in mitigating the harsh realities of modern criminal justice or a serious threat to individual liberty. Examples of both sides exist across the country. Prosecutors dismiss or reduce charges in about half the serious cases involving adults. Many times these actions are commendable, as are occasional efforts of independent special prosecutors to expose malfeasance and crime. However, discretionary justice always opens the door for favoritism and corruption.

The key to understanding the prosecutorial system is in its politics. Elected district attorneys with widely ranging control over personal freedom create a dangerous formula. It sometimes surfaces in personal feuds, crusades for publicity, or improper announcements concerning unproven guilt. Prosecutors should be above imposing either personal concepts of morality or more obvious forms of political manipulation. Unfortunately, both varieties of misconduct exist in the United States. Our scheme of popularly chosen prosecutors and broad discretion does maintain the valuable benefit of ultimate community control, but it also poses serious problems of public and personal justice.

(7.3) Defense Attorney

Prosecutors' counterparts are the defense attorneys. Relatively few privately practicing attorneys take significant numbers of criminal cases. Compared to total expenditure for criminal justice, government money spent on criminal defense is negligible.

Every defendant, whether rich or poor, is entitled to a lawyer regardless of the evidence against him. He can retain private defense counsel if he is financially able to do so. Otherwise, the state will furnish him with an attorney at no cost, either a public defender or a court-assigned lawyer from the area bar. Criminal defense work is a specialty that many private attorneys avoid, except for minor cases. Those who become active criminal defense lawyers become expert in the field and many are both well regarded in the profession and financially successful. There are others whose reputation suffers because of the nature of their work and the type of clients they represent.

Criminal defense lawyers are often accused of abusing the system by using delaying tactics and by making numerous pretrial motions, excessive appeals, sleazy plea-bargain attempts, and other legal moves that pervert justice. This is often true. On the other hand, the highest ethics in the legal profession have been shown by courageous attorneys who have defended suspects supposedly involved in heinous crimes that have caused a public outcry.

This happens because in our system the accused is initially presumed innocent. So, in the trial itself, he needs to prove nothing. The state must produce all the evidence necessary to prove his guilt beyond a reasonable doubt. The duty of the defense lawyer is to see that the state does prove its case by bringing forth legal evidence in a fair trial.

A criminal lawyer may ethically defend even the most guilty of clients, since the defense does not have to prove anything, but must defend the accused by making sure that the state legally proves its case beyond a reasonable doubt.

Lawyers for indigent defendants are provided using methods that vary in design throughout the country. Most jurisdictions use a system whereby courts appoint attorneys to part-time defense assignments. Refusal to serve is considered highly improper, and limited compensation may be authorized based upon duties performed. The appointed counsel system has several significant defects. For example, lawyers assigned such obligations may manifest a lack of experience, interest, or concern with criminal matters. Occasionally, there is a tendency either to plead a client guilty to save time or to extend a case for lengthy periods to increase fees. Most assigned counsel, however, do neither of these and sincerely attempt to perform their undesired tasks adequately despite limited enthusiasm for such cases.

A second way of furnishing counsel to indigent defendants is through an office of public defenders. These regular government employees have as their full-time task the provision of legal assistance to the poor. This system exists in hundreds of jurisdictions nationwide. In some respects, the public defender is opposite to the prosecutor; yet similarities exist. This system also tends to utilize less than prominent attorneys mainly because of limited compensation and opportunity. Moreover, these practitioners are also able to develop respectable capability and effectiveness through continued practice in criminal matters.

Unlike appointed counsel, experienced defense attorneys, public or private, may develop good working relations with their legal opponents. This can significantly facilitate the workings of the justice system.

A third and final strategy for affording counsel for the poor is through voluntary defenders. This system exists in only a few areas, often in the form of extended legal aid, which is usually limited to civil cases. Voluntary defenders are normally organized in agencies, often privately sponsored with public support. Such a system benefits in some degree from the absence of government control; however, it is generally restricted in resources, personnel, and facilities.

Generalizations about criminal defense in the United States are virtually impossible because of the tremendous variations. The different systems of providing counsel for indigents and the diverse capabilities of practitioners combine to extend over a spectrum from splendid to dreadful. However, there is no question that money is the primary determinant of a vigorous defense. The American system operates to the disadvantage of the poor because they must confront the organized and structured office of the prosecutor without comparable assistance of counsel. As long as it is necessary to depend on part-time defenders, a balance could possibly accrue from using assigned or appointed prosecutors as well. Such a practice, in essence, has been used very successfully in England for many years.

(7.4) Counsel's Actions Affecting Speedy Trials

The Sixth Amendment to the U.S. Constitution provides that "In all criminal prosecutions, the accused shall enjoy the right to a speedy and public trial , by an impartial jury of the State and district wherein the crime shall have been committed...." In 1972 the Supreme Court held in *Baker* v. *Wingo* (407U.S. 514 [1972]) that determinations of whether or not the Sixth Amendment right to a speedy trial for defendants in criminal cases has been denied must be made on a case-by-case basis. Factors used to determine whether or not a defendant was denied a speedy trial include (1) the length of the delay, (2) the reason for the delay, (3) the defendant's assertion of his or her right, and (4) prejudice to the defendant.

Vermont v. *Brillon* (555. U.S. ___ [2009]) was argued before the U.S. Supreme Court on January 13, 2009, and decided on March 9, 2009. In July 2001, respondent Brillon was arrested on felony domestic assault and habitual offender charges. Nearly three years later, in June 2004, he was tried by jury, found guilty as charged, and sentenced to 12 to 20 years in prison. During the time between his arrest and his trial, at least six different attorneys were appointed to represent him. Brillon "fired" his first attorney, who served from July 2001 until June 2002. His third lawyer, who served from March 2002 until June 2002, was allowed to withdraw when he reported that Brillon had threatened his life. Brillon's fourth lawyer served from June 2002 until November 2002, when the trial court released him from the case. His fifth lawyer, assigned two months later, withdrew in April 2003. Four months thereafter, his sixth lawyer was assigned, and she took the case to trial in June 2004.

The trial court denied Brillon's motion to dismiss for want of a speedy trial. The Vermont Supreme Court, however, reversed, holding that Brillon's conviction must be vacated, and the charges against him dismissed, because the State did not accord him the speedy trial required by the Sixth Amendment. Citing the balancing test, the Vermont Supreme Court stated that four criteria listed in the *Baker* v. *Wingo* case weighed against the State. Weighing heavily in Brillon's favor, the Vermont court said that the three-year delay in bringing him to trial was "extreme." In assessing the reasons for the delay, the court separately considered the period of each counsel's representation. It acknowledged that the first year, when Brillon was represented by his first and third lawyers, should not count against the State. But the court counted much of the remaining two years against the State in which counsel failed "to move the case forward."

On writ of certiorari, the State of Vermont appealed to the U.S. Supreme Court. The Court held that the Vermont Supreme Court erred in ranking assigned counsel essentially as state actors in the criminal justice system. Assigned counsel, just as retained counsel, act on behalf of their clients, and delays sought by counsel are ordinarily attributed to the defendants they represent. The Court examined the primary issues for the delay in Brillon's trial. In applying *Baker,* the Court asked "whether the government or the criminal defendant is more to blame for the delay" (*Doggett* v. *United States* 505 U.S. 647, 651 [1992]). In *Baker,* the court reasoned that delay "to hamper the defense" weight heavily against the prosecution, while delay caused by the defense weight against the defendant. Because "the attorney is the defendant's agent when acting, or failing to act, in furtherance of the litigation," delay caused by the defendant's counsel is charged against the defendant (*Coleman* v. *Thompson* 501 U.S. 722, 753). The same principle applies whether counsel is privately retained or publicly assigned, for "once a lawyer has undertaken the representation of an accused, the duties and obligations are the same whether the lawyer is privately retained, appointed, or serving in a legal aid or defender program" (*Polk County* v. *Dodson,* 454 U.S. 312, 318 [1981]). Unlike a prosecutor or the court, assigned counsel ordinarily is not considered a state actor.

The U.S. Supreme Court stated that although the balance arrived at in close cases ordinarily would not prompt review by the high court, the Vermont Supreme Court made a fundamental error in its application of *Baker* that called for correction by the U.S. Supreme Court. The Vermont court erred in attributing the State delays caused by the failure of several assigned counsel to move Brillon's case forward and in failing adequately to take into account the role of Brillon's disruptive behavior in the overall balance. An assigned counsel's failure to move the case forward does not warrant attribution of delay to the State. Most of the delay the Vermont court attributed to the State must therefore be attributed to Brillon as delays caused by his counsel, each of whom requested time extensions. Their inability or unwillingness to move the case forward may not be attributed to the State simply because they are assigned counsel. A contrary conclusion could encourage appointed counsel to delay proceedings by seeking unreasonable continuances, hoping thereby to obtain a dismissal of the indictment on speedy-trial grounds. The U.S. Supreme Court reversed and remanded the case.

(7.5) Plea Bargaining

Most criminal cases are actually settled out of court. More than half of all criminal defendants arrive at this phase of the justice process through plea bargaining. Generally, this consists of negotiations between the district attorney and the defense counsel, and most cases are settled before they reach a judge.

Although it may seem improbable that a prosecutor would ever consider entering into an agreement with a criminal suspect, such thinking fails to take into account the realities of our somewhat outdated system. Actually, the present complex framework would simply collapse without extensive plea bargaining. If defendants demanded their full legal rights, prosecutors and courts would rapidly become so entangled and overloaded that the system would simply collapse under the tremendous weight of the resulting burden. Therefore, negotiations occur in the interest of expedience.

District attorneys are continually pressured to maximize convictions and minimize acquittals, and a variety of useful alternatives lies between these two extremes. Work can be simplified and time saved when an accused admits responsibility, thereby making the guilty plea the prosecutor's greatest asset.

About 90 percent of all cases, including two-thirds of all felony cases brought to court, are handled through negotiations. In many instances, prosecutors dismiss entirely the weakest charges, thus allowing them to focus attention on those cases having stronger evidence.

Many guilty pleas are the direct result of bargaining. Heavy pressure may be exerted by overcharging a suspect (that is, increasing the degree of the offense connected with a particular act). Other tactics may involve alarming family and friends or threatening to urge the severest possible penalties. Regrettably, these tactics are the rule and not the exception.

Plea negotiations occur for diverse reasons. Most often they result from the simple desire to expedite the case and reduce a backlog. Prosecutors may also gamble on a conviction, of any kind, when evidence is weak and might not withstand a court contest. Occasionally, the district attorney may wish to individualize a sentence, thus evading minimum penalties prescribed by law or perhaps providing for disposition beyond that available through the formal scheme of justice. Finally, he might be willing to bargain lenience for information about other offenses and offenders.

Naturally, the prosecutor, to strike a bargain, must offer something in exchange for guilty pleas, testimony, or something he wants from a defendant. He may, for example, withdraw prosecution of friends, accomplices, or relatives; however, the usual consideration accrues directly to the defendant. The most common benefit is the sentencing recommendation to the judge. In return for a guilty plea, the prosecutor agrees to request less than the maximum possible penalty. Second, he may press for acceptance of a reduced charge. Often, a prosecutor will exchange a lesser offense for a major one in return for sufficient cooperation from a suspect. Finally, he may completely dismiss the case, regardless of apparent guilt.

These generous gestures are frequently consolidated. Suppose, for example, the police arrest an offender committing an aggravated assault. Investigation shows that he is wanted for a similar offense. In return for an agreement to plead guilty in one case, the district attorney may offer to reduce the charge to simple assault instead of aggravated assault, recommend probation to the judge, and dismiss the second matter entirely. Everyone directly involved in the process benefits. The police have cleared two cases by arrest, the district attorney gets a conviction without a court contest, the judge saves time and trouble, and the criminal gets a probated sentence for two serious offenses.

Negotiated pleas are not binding on the court, and judges occasionally disregard recommendations in passing sentence. Ordinarily, however, they play a more delicate role in the process of bargained justice.

Modern practice requires a satisfactory basis for a plea, understanding on the defendant's part, and that the proposed plea be .appropriate. To this end there is an increasing tendency for judges to routinely schedule pretrial joint conferences with prosecutors and defense counsel in which the court acts as a moderator in seeking a fair plea agreement, thus eliminating the need for a trial.

Although some judges may, at times, opt to ignore the typical bargaining process, they sometimes must get involved to ensure a basic level of fairness. Otherwise prosecutors might obtain admissions of guilt through outright deceit. In cases of unfulfilled promises, the courts intervene, and pleas may be withdrawn. Without this safeguard, a criminal suspect could be at the mercy of an overzealous or unscrupulous district attorney. Still, once a defendant makes a voluntary and knowing plea, and a prosecutor fulfills his agreement, full admission of guilt will generally be accepted as conclusive.

Numerous problems arise for American justice from the widespread use of plea bargaining. The most obvious, of course, is the definite possibility that innocent persons may be compelled to plead guilty. Unfortunately, when conventional methods of fixing responsibility and imposing penalty become secondary to bureaucratic or judicial expediency, the entire system's reliability becomes suspect. Theoretically, the court's role is fundamental to the determination of guilt. In actual practice, however, it has become subordinate to administrative procedure.

Some lawyers and scholars argue that plea bargaining undermines confidence and integrity in the administration of justice and advocate that this abuse of the constitutional rights of defendants be abolished. Others maintain that when properly supervised by the court, the plea bargain not only expedites justice but can ensure its fairness.

(7.6) Summary

The adversary system of justice presumes that the best way to arrive at the truth is to have a contest between two sides, with the prosecutor on one side and the defense attorney on the other. Unfortunately, criminal law is not attractive to most leading attorneys. Prosecutors, most often called district attorneys, possess great power and broad discretion. This situation becomes more pronounced by political considerations on the part of many district attorneys.

By comparison, defense lawyers operate relatively independently. Because most people accused of serious crimes are indigent, the government is responsible for providing legal counsel. Defenders may be appointed, publicly employed, or volunteers.

Most criminal cases are decided out of court through plea bargaining. Negotiations between prosecutors and defense attorneys provide flexibility, speed, and simplicity, but they also pose continuing threats to the system of justice.

Discussion Questions

1. Discuss the advantages and disadvantages of electing judges.
2. Discuss whether prosecutors should be selected on a statewide basis rather than on a local basis.
3. Discuss the ways a defendant may be provided a lawyer.
4. Discuss plea bargaining.
5. Discuss the concept of a defense attorney representing a defendant he or she knows is guilty.

8
The Trial

Justice, sir, is the great interest of man on earth.

—Daniel Webster
Speech, September 12, 1845

The United States Constitution guarantees a defendant's right to trial before an impartial jury. Unless a defendant waives this right, the trial in a felony case and in many serious misdemeanors is held before a jury.

Some states require defendants to file a request for a jury trial when they enter a plea or at some time specified before the beginning of the court term in which a jury will be empaneled. Failure to file such a request constitutes a waiver of the right. In other states, an explicit waiver of jury trial is required.

(8.1) The Jury

The jury in a criminal trial is selected by a complex and often time-consuming process. Because the prosecution and the defense both rely upon the jurors for a favorable decision, factors involved in jury selection are of very great concern to both parties in the proceedings.

Eligible voters or taxpayers make up the list from which a group of potential jurors, called the jury panel, or venire, is selected. The group qualifies for jury duty as established by law in the jurisdiction of the court. In federal cases, the members of the jury are drawn from the entire jurisdiction of the district court trying the case. State laws may exempt certain categories of individuals from jury duty, including people with defective hearing or vision, those over sixty-five, and members of particular occupations or professions. Physicians, members of the clergy, and women with infants or small children may also be excluded at their own request.

A group is summoned from the panel of potential jurors to appear in a particular case and questioned in open court to determine their general qualifications for jury service. Questions are asked concerning their understanding of the English language, citizenship, and problems involving health or personal hardship that could possibly interfere with their performance as jurors. Felony convictions, in some jurisdictions, will disqualify a person for jury service. The trial judge hears requests for exemptions and dismisses those with legitimate cause.

Names of prospective jurors are randomly selected from the veniremen remaining after the initial questioning. One method of making such choices is to place into a large drum the names of those eligible and to have the court clerk draw the names one at a time. As a juror's name is drawn and read, that person takes his or her place in the jury box. Then, in the process known as *voir dire*, both counsel question the prospective jurors. *Voir dire* is a procedure by which potential jurors are questioned as a group and individually regarding their eligibility as jurors. They are questioned about any topic that might affect their judgment, such as prior knowledge about the case, any relationship to the trial participants, and any opinions they may have formed. An affirmative answer to any of these questions may cause the potential juror to be "excused for cause." Counsel have unlimited challenges for cause. Both lawyers and the judge may question potential jurors.

During this stage, each side is allowed a specified number of peremptory challenges—requests to the court to exclude a prospective juror without specific reason. For example, the prosecutor may not want a female of a specific age or a male over a certain age. The defense attorney may be uncomfortable about a potential juror's facial expression, appearance, or conduct. These reasons, whatever they are, need not be justified or even stated to the court.

The reason for peremptorily excusing a juror need not be stated. However, prosecutors particularly have used peremptory challenges to keep blacks and other minorities from a jury when any racial question is involved or the defendant is a member of a racial minority. Black defendants have successfully litigated against this method of ensuring an "all-white jury." Our courts now hold that such a racial exclusion policy violates a minority defendant's right to equal treatment under the Fourteenth Amendment. Now, when a racial-minority juror is excused from the panel by a peremptory challenge, opposing counsel may object and the party exercising the challenge must convince the court that there are valid reasons other than race for the exclusion. Otherwise, the potential juror is allowed to remain (*Griffith v. Kentucky,* 479 U.S. 314 [1987]).

The U.S. Supreme Court examined a preemptory challenge case in *Rivera* v. *Illinois* (555. U.S. ___ 2009) that was decided March 31, 2009. During jury selection in petitioner Rivera's state-court first-degree murder trial, his counsel sought to use a preemptory challenge to excuse venire member Deloris Gomez. Rivera had already exercised two preemptory challenges against women, one of whom was African-American. The court conceded that there was no basis to challenge Gomez for cause, stating that she met the requirements for jury service, and that Rivera did not contend that she was biased against him. The trial court rejected the preemptory challenge out of concern that it was discriminatory. The court looked at *Batson* v. *Kentucky* 476 U.S. 79 (1986) in which it was found that the prosecutor's use of preemptory challenges to exclude four blacks from the jury violated Baston's Sixth and Fourteenth Amendment rights to a fair jury trial and his Fourteenth Amendment right to equal protection under the law.

In the *Rivera* case, the court found that the *Batson* ruling stated that parties are constitutionally prohibited from exercising preemptory challenge to exclude jurors based on race, ethnicity, or sex. The jury, with Gomez as it foreperson, found Rivera guilty of first-degree murder. The Illinois Supreme Court subsequently affirmed the conviction, holding that the preemptory challenge should have been allowed, but rejecting Rivera's argument that the improper seating of Gomez was a reversible error. Observing that the Constitution does not mandate preemptory challenges and that they are not necessary for a fair trial, the court held that denial of Rivera's preemptory challenge was not a structural error requiring automatic reversal. Nor, the court found, was the error harmless beyond a reasonable doubt. In affirming the Illinois Supreme Court's decision, the U.S. Supreme Court found that Rivera received precisely what due process required: a fair trial before an impartial and properly instructed jury, which found him guilty of every element of the charged offense. The Court held that all jurors seated in a criminal case are qualified and unbiased, the due process clause does not require automatic reversal of conviction because of the trial court's good-faith error in denying the defendant's preemptory challenge to a juror.

A few states have altered the right of a person charged with a felony to demand a trial by a twelve-member jury. Some have amended their constitutions to allow variations in civil cases and in misdemeanor criminal cases. Six-member juries were introduced into the federal court system in 1971. The previous year, in *Williams* v. *Florida,* 399 U.S. 78 (1970), the United States Supreme Court sanctioned the right of state courts to use six-member juries in trials of serious felony offenses. The Court stated that the principal purposes of a jury were to function as fact finders, to exercise commonsense judgments, and to ensure community participation and shared responsibility in determining guilt or innocence. It expressed the belief that fulfillment of these purposes does not depend on a particular number of people who make up a jury and has since extended the six-member prerogative to civil suits in federal courts. The United States Constitution does not specifically state that a jury must have twelve members. The significance of the number twelve has been lost in antiquity.

(8.2) Opening Statements

Once the jury is empaneled, the trial opens with a reading of the indictment or information. The prosecution presents its opening remarks first. The order in which the prosecution and defense present their cases varies from jurisdiction to jurisdiction, but each follows a legally established procedure. Generally, however, the prosecution begins and, in the opening address to the jury, explains the charge, describes the alleged offense, and presents a general picture of what the state intends to prove "beyond a reasonable doubt." Opening comments are to provide the members of the jury—who are unfamiliar with legal procedures—with an overview of the major objectives of the prosecution's case, the evidence it plans to offer, the witnesses it intends to call, and the facts it will attempt to prove through their testimony. Of course, the idea is to make it easier for jurors to grasp the meaning and significance of evidence and testimony and to keep them from becoming confused by the complexities of the case.

The prosecution, however, must avoid promising evidence it is unable to produce. Once the prosecution has concluded its opening statements, the defense has the option of making an opening statement or deferring such presentation until later in the case. Common practice is for the defense to describe its plans to expose weaknesses or inadequacies of the prosecution's case and to demonstrate to the jury the defendant"'s innocence. No state requires the defense to make an opening statement.

Following opening remarks, the prosecution calls its first witness, who takes an oath or affirms to tell the truth, and questioning begins. The question and answer procedure is designed to elicit information from the witnesses about the case.

Normally only the lawyers and the judge can question witnesses. Now, several courts are experimenting and allow jurors to submit questions to a witness. The juror gives the written question to the court, who will then ask it of the witness if the query is proper. This has the advantage of bringing out some fact of the case that neither the judge nor either counsel has touched on. Jurors' questioning of witnesses is under debate by those involved in the court system.

Once the initial witness, usually the arresting officer, is sworn and introduced, he or she describes the details of the investigation as it has been conducted. Physical evidence is introduced by a witness under oath. Evidence must be validated by a witness who can explain to the court how the evidence was obtained and that it is what the prosecution (or defense counsel) claims it to be.

When the prosecution concludes the questioning of a witness, the defense attorney has the option to cross-examine. Cross-examination is designed to test a witness' powers of observation, recollection, veracity, and possible bias against the cross-examiner's side. On cross-examination, the witness can be questioned only about things to which he or she testified on direct examination; however, the cross-examiner is permitted to ask leading questions (i.e., questions that imply or suggest the desired answers). The right to impeach a witness is, with few exceptions, restricted to the opposing side in cross-examination. Thus, except in rare circumstances, an attorney may not attempt to impeach his or her own witness.

The cross-examiner may ask any question to test the truth or accuracy of the witness' testimony. He may also seek additional information not brought out on direct examination. The cross-examiner may try to impeach the witness by bringing out anything unfavorable in his background. Once the cross-examination is completed, the attorneys may be allowed some additional direct and cross-examination. This questioning is restricted to matters covered in the immediately preceding examination.

The prosecution presents all of its evidence first. When the prosecution rests, the defense routinely moves for a dismissal, claiming prosecution lacks proof beyond a reasonable doubt, or making any other claim for a dismissal or directed verdict of "not guilty."

Ordinarily, the dismissal motion is denied and the defense puts on its case just as the prosecution did. Sometimes, the defense will produce no evidence at all, relying on the presumption of innocence. In our system, the defendant is not required to testify, and his failure to do so cannot be held against him. Once the defense is completed, the defendant rests his case.

(8.3) Rebuttal and Surrebuttal

At the conclusion of the defense's case, the prosecution is given an opportunity for rebuttal. That is, it may summon additional witnesses to bolster its case, which may have been weakened by evidence and testimony presented by the defense. Testimony offered in rebuttal must be limited to matters covered in the defense's case. Additionally, if the prosecution chooses to conduct rebuttal, the defense may call surrebuttal witnesses to support its case.

(8.4) Closing Arguments

Closing arguments, or summations, provide the defense counsel and the prosecutor with an opportunity to summarize evidence and testimony and persuade the jury to accept their interpretations of the case. In summing up, counsel may make any fair comment on the evidence or lack of evidence but are forbidden to state any personal opinion on the case, giving facts not in evidence, or making inflammatory suggestions.

(8.5) Charging the Jury

When all the evidence has been presented and both sides have rested their cases, the judge has the responsibility to instruct the jury. The jury has the prerogative to decide the facts, but the court must instruct it on matters of law that apply to the case. For example, if the defense is based on insanity, the judge must explain to the jurors how insanity is determined in that particular state.

Both prosecutor and defense have the opportunity to submit instructions for the jurors. These instructions incorporate the respective attorneys' theories concerning interpretation of the facts of the case. The judge selects from the instructions suggested by the attorneys or prepares his or her own instructions. In the absence of specific instructions, the judge may use a standard set that applies to cases of a similar nature. After the instructions are prepared, the judge reviews them with both attorneys. The lawyers may enter in the record any objections they have to the proposed jury instructions, thereby preserving the right to have this considered on any appeal.

The final instructions read to the jury in open court cite specific issues of evidence or testimony in the case and traditionally cover the following areas: (1) the definition of the alleged crime, (2) the presumption of the defendant's innocence, (3) the fact that the burden of proof is upon the prosecution, (4) the fact that if, after consideration of all the evidence, there remains reasonable doubt as to the defendant's guilt, he or she must be acquitted, and (5) the procedures for electing a foreman and returning a verdict.

In many jurisdictions, jurors are given written instructions to take with them into the jury room during deliberations.

Instructions as to possible verdicts are given to the jury. Guilty or not guilty are the usual alternatives in a criminal case; however, the jury may also be given the choice of deciding on the degree of the offense in a particular case (e.g., murder in the first degree, murder in the second degree). Many courts provide a written form for each verdict, together with instructions that the appropriate form be returned to the court as soon as a decision is reached.

The case of *Waddington, Superintendent, Washington Corrections Center* v. *Sarausad* (555 U.S.____2009) was argued before the U.S. Supreme Court on October 15, 2009, and decided on January 21, 2009. Respondent Sarausad alleged that in his guilty conviction, the jury instructions were improper. Sarausad drove the car in a drive-by shooting at a high school, which was the culmination of a gang dispute. En route to school, Ronquillo, the front-seat passenger, covered his lower face and readied a handgun. Sarausad abruptly slowed down upon reaching the school; Ronquillo fired at a group of students, killing one and wounding another. After the shooting was over, Sarausad sped away from the scene. Sarausad, Ronquillo, and Reyes (another passenger) were tried on murder and related charges. Sarausad and Reyes were tried as accomplices; they argued that they were not accomplices to murder because they had not known Ronquillo's plan and had expected at most another fistfight. In her closing argument, the prosecutor stressed Sarausad's knowledge of a shooting, noting how he drove at the scene, that he knew that fighting alone would not regain respect for his gang, and that he was "in for a dime, in for a dollar." The jury received two instructions that directly quoted Washington state's accomplice-liability law. When it failed to reach a verdict as to Reyes, the judge declared a mistrial for Reyes. However, the jury convicted Ronquillo on all counts and convicted Sarausad of second-degree murder and related crimes.

In affirming Sarausad's conviction, the state court of appeals, among other things, referred to an "in for a dime, in for a dollar" accomplice-liability theory. The state supreme court denied review, but in a subsequent case the court clarified that "in for a dime, in for a dollar" was not the best descriptor of accomplice liability because an accomplice must have knowledge of the crime that occurred. The court also explicitly reaffirmed its precedent that the type of jury instructions used at Sarausad's trial comport with Washington law. Sarausad sought review under 28 U.S.C. Article 2254, which *inter alia,* permits a federal court to grant habeas relief on a claim "adjudicated on the merits" in state court only if the decision "was contrary to, or involved an unreasonable application of, clearly established Federal law, as determined by" this Court. The district court granted the petition, and the Ninth Circuit Court affirmed, finding it unreasonable for the state court to affirm Sarausad's conviction because the jury instruction on accomplice liability was ambiguous and there was a reasonable likelihood that the jury misinterpreted the instruction in a way that relieved the State of its burden or proving Sarausad's knowledge of a shooting beyond a reasonable doubt.

On writ of certiorari, the state asked the U.S. Supreme Court to reverse the state supreme court. The U.S. Supreme Court held that the state court's decision did not result in an "unreasonable application of clearly established Federal law and that the Ninth Circuit erred in granting habeas relief to Sarausad." The high court found that even if the instructions were ambiguous, the Ninth Circuit still erred in finding it so ambiguous as to cause a federal constitutional violation requiring reversal. The Washington courts reasonably applied the Court's precedent when they found no "reasonable likelihood" that the prosecutor's closing argument caused the jury to apply the instruction in a way that relieved the State of its burden to prove every element of the crime beyond a reasonable doubt. The case was reversed and remanded.

(8.6) Jury Deliberations

After receiving their instructions, the jury retire to the jury room to deliberate. They choose one of their number to act as foreman. The foreman presides over their deliberations and speaks for them in court, but has no more power or authority than any other juror. No one except the bailiff is allowed to communicate with the jury during deliberations. In serious cases, the jury may be sequestered and housed overnight each night until a verdict is reached.

Early in deliberations, the jury foreman may call for a vote. On rare occasions, the first vote may result in a unanimous verdict. Generally, however, the vote reveals a three-way split among jurors, with some voting guilty, some voting not guilty, and some undecided. The jury then discusses the case, with the foreman as moderator. Occasionally, a jury asks to review a particular piece of evidence or line of testimony or requests further instructions from the court on a point of law.

A unanimous verdict in criminal cases has been a basic requirement of common law since the fourteenth century. The United States Supreme Court upheld this requirement in both the nineteenth and twentieth centuries, and most states have endorsed this position in their provisions for jury trials. However, in *Johnson* v. *Louisiana*, 409 U.S. 1085 (1972), the Court held that Louisiana's use of nine to three verdicts in major criminal cases was constitutional. A similar decision was made in *Apodaca* v. *Oregon*, 406 U.S. 404 (1972), regarding Oregon's ten to two vote verdicts in serious criminal cases. More recently, the Court dealt with the question of less-than-unanimous verdicts in cases involving fewer than twelve members. In *Burch* v. *Louisiana*, 441 U.S. 130 (1979), the Court held that a five to one vote for conviction was unconstitutional, leaving a vote of six as the minimum requirement in criminal jury cases.

A hopelessly deadlocked jury, after prolonged deliberations, may inform the court, at which time the judge may instruct the members to return to the jury room for a final effort at reaching a verdict. The judge usually sets a specific time period for this to be done. If all reasonable methods are exhausted without reaching unanimity—resulting in a hung jury—the judge dismisses the jury, declares a mistrial, and schedules a retrial of the case with a new jury.

When a jury does return a verdict, the defense counsel may

request that the jurors be polled. The court clerk or the judge then asks each juror individually if the verdict announced is his or her verdict. The purpose of this is to determine if each juror has voted freely for the announced verdict. Occasionally a less-than-unanimous verdict will be uncovered or a reluctant juror may change his mind on being polled.

Should polling disclose a less-than-unanimous verdict where one is required by law, the jury may be instructed to return to the jury room and continue its deliberations, or it may be dismissed and a mistrial declared. A mistrial places the defendant in the same position as if no trial had occurred, and proceedings may be reinstated against him or her. If the verdict is not guilty, the defendant is discharged. Figure 8-1 summarizes this entire process.

(8.7) Sentencing and Appeal

Prior to the sentencing stage of the criminal justice process, the defendant has either pled guilty to or been found guilty of a criminal offense. The court must then decide an appropriate disposition for the individual. Often, this is a complex and difficult decision for the judge. In earlier times, specific punishments for specific offenses were laid down by the law, and once a verdict of guilty was returned, the judge merely ordered the appropriate sentence to be carried out. The main thrust of the court's sentence was the offense and not the offender. However, as a consequence of societal reaction to crime and criminals, sentencing today involves a broad range of alternatives for the offender. Many of these involve rehabilitation and require the assistance of professionals in psychology, sociology, education, and social welfare.

Sentencing is regarded as one of the most significant stages in the administration of justice. It determines how criminal offenders will spend a portion of their future or—in the case of capital punishment—if they will face death.

For years, disparity of sentences for similar crimes has been a major concern to both inmates and penologists. Federal courts now operate under a system of sentencing guidelines designed to bring some consistency to sentences (1984 Sentencing Reform Act, 18

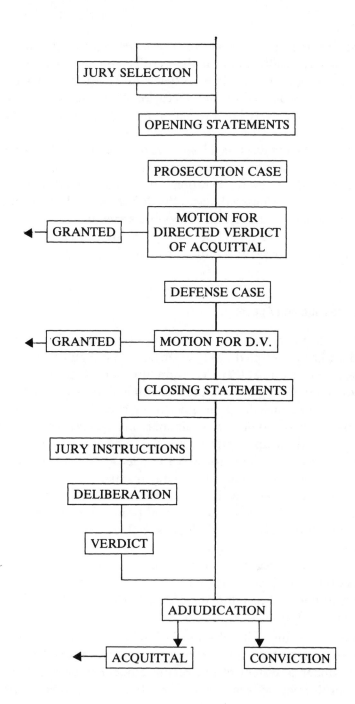

JURY SELECTION

OPENING STATEMENTS

PROSECUTION CASE

GRANTED ◄— MOTION FOR DIRECTED VERDICT OF ACQUITTAL

DEFENSE CASE

GRANTED ◄— MOTION FOR D.V.

CLOSING STATEMENTS

JURY INSTRUCTIONS

DELIBERATION

VERDICT

ADJUDICATION

ACQUITTAL ◄—   CONVICTION

Figure 8.1. Trial flow chart.

U.S.C.S. 3551), and the Supreme Court has upheld the constitutionality of the system (*Mistretta* v. *U.S.* 102 L.Ed.2d 714 [1989]). Many states have adopted similar guidelines for sentencing. (See Figure 15.1 for a sample of a state criminal sentencing guideline system; and Section 15.3 explains how it is applied.)

A basic doctrine of the American criminal justice process holds that every accused person is presumed innocent until proven guilty by legally obtained evidence. Appellate review acts as a safeguard for an individual caught up in the processes of criminal trial, incarceration, or supervision in the community. The state has great power, and citizens must be protected against the capricious and arbitrary use of such power. The right to appeal the verdict in a criminal trial is one of the most important aspects of due process, although it is not spelled out in the Bill of Rights.

(8.8) Postconviction Remedies

The public gives little attention to criminal cases once the defendant has been found guilty and sentenced. The trial may be over, but the defendant's actions are far from over. In some respects, his or her work has just begun.

The convicted defendant has two powerful postconviction remedies: appeal and habeas corpus. The current use of both of these has caused what may justly be labeled the most serious defect in the entire American criminal justice system.

a. Appeals

In both state and federal courts, every convicted defendant is entitled as a matter of right to one appeal. The state is not permitted to appeal from a verdict of acquittal. If the prosecution could appeal and get a new trial, this would be double jeopardy, a legal situation prohibited by both federal and state constitutions.

The state's only right of appeal is in some procedural matters, such as a court-ordered dismissal of charges or suppression of evidence. A recent Supreme Court decision approved a federal law that allowed the government, in some situations, to appeal a sentence that was claimed to be too lenient. Nevertheless, a not guilty verdict still ends a trial—permanently.

Of course, for the defendant, this is not so. Appeal is not a constitutional right; rather, it is a statutory right. A defendant needs only to file a notice of appeal with the clerk of the court within the time permitted. If he or she cannot afford an attorney, the court will appoint one at public expense to handle the appeal. Records of the trial and all other necessary information will be provided at taxpayer expense. Even if the appeal is useless, it can still be filed, and no screening process exists to prevent frivolous appeals.

An appellate court, made up of several judges, is one that hears felony appeals. Their decision centers on the trial record, legal briefs, and counsel's argument. The appeals court will affirm the conviction, dismiss the charge, or send it back for a new trial because of some error in the lower court. Unless the case is dismissed on appeal because of insufficient evidence, it can be tried a second time after a defendant succeeds in getting a reversal. This is not double jeopardy because the defendant is the one who seeks the new trial.

If conviction is affirmed on appeal, the defendant may, in many cases, have the appeal moved to the state's highest appellate court. Usually, this can be done only with court permission. Appeal is often pursued by means of a petition called *certiorari*, which can be denied or granted at the highest court's discretion. *Certiorari* is itself an alternative to appeal, especially where a complaint of complete illegality exists, such as lack of jurisdiction in the lower court.

Once the appeal process is over, the defendant still has options. There may be an additional state remedy, the writ of *coram nobis*, which, whether in common law or statutory form, is a petition to the original trial court seeking a review of the case on the claim that there was some factor unknown to the court at the time of the trial that made the conviction improper. In some jurisdictions, the defendant can even appeal all over again if the *coram nobis* petition is denied.

The criminal appeals procedure is a major weakness in the American justice system. First, there is delay. The first appeal alone, even under ideal conditions, may take months, and the entire process may take years. Second, the multiplicity of criminal appeals clogs appellate courts beyond reason. Third, bail is often allowed pending an appeal, and the convicted defendant can sometimes remain free for years until the final appeal is decided.

James Morgan confessed to the brutal murder of Gertrude Trbovich. Her skull was smashed with a wrench, her face beaten with a glass vase, and her fingers ripped with a knife. Her wedding ring was crushed. She was sexually assaulted. Morgan's defense was insanity. He was tried and convicted four times, the case being reversed three different times on appeals. His last conviction was in 1989. Over twelve years were consumed in four trials for one murder. More appeals and writs are still to come.

The valid premise that "justice delayed is justice denied" cannot be argued. The very number of criminal appeals, often completely through two court systems, assures delay after delay. However, the right to appeal is not a constitutional guarantee. So the matter could be corrected by new restrictive appeal statutes if the authorities would only adopt them.

The indigent convicted defendant is jailed pending appeal. Regardless of the amount of the bail, the defendant is unable to raise any money. However, the convicted person with funds remains free. In addition, when the defendant is free on bail pending appeal, counsel exhausts every possible means of delaying the appeal process. Defense counsel may file papers at the last possible moment, seek extensions of time to file appellate briefs, and then seek to postpone the time for oral arguments.

Busy appellate courts are often lax in requiring promptness. Delay is always on the side of the defendant. A witness may die or lose interest, or the evidence may be lost before a new trial can be held. New court decisions may open new legal loopholes. United States courts have all inherited a slow-motion background, and delay has been accepted as part of the system. Only in recent years have speedy trial rules come into being. However, speedy appellate rules are generally not being used.

Eventually, even the most active inmate "prison lawyer" will finally exhaust all his or her state remedies. Is the case finally finished? Not at all. Having used all the state's legal options, the convicted defendant begins in the federal court system. The weapon? Habeas corpus.

The appeal process related to the capital murder conviction of Dorsie Lee Johnson Jr. will likely take from three to five years to complete, court officials say.

Johnson, 19, was sentenced by a district court jury here Nov. 14 to death by lethal injection. He was found guilty of killing an Allsup's convenience store clerk during a robbery of that store March 23.

According to District Attorney Ernie Armstrong, who successfully prosecuted the state's case, the local sentence is just the first step of a three to five year journey through state and federal courts.

Included in this, he noted, could be as many as three to four execution dates set and overturned.

The sentence cannot be executed until all legal avenues of appeal have been exhausted, and Armstrong said this could take up to five years "if every ruling is in the state's favor."

The appeal process begins now with the transferring of trial records to the Texas Court of Criminal Appeals in Austin for review.

The first appeal is mandatory under the capital murder statute and no execution date can be set until the conviction and sentence is affirmed by that court.

Armstrong said the first appeal would likely take a year to a year and a half.

Once the case is affirmed in Austin, Johnson will be brought back to Snyder where he would appear before 132nd District Court officials for the setting of the first execution date.

According to Armstrong, nothing is guaranteed or automatic after the first appeal.

Technically, the defendant could at that time petition the United States Supreme Court for a hearing conditional on that court accepting the case for review.

Armstrong said, however, that Johnson would not likely choose that route due to the fact that if the Supreme Court heard the case and ruled in favor of the state, the appeal process would be over and the execution could be carried out.

He said the more standard procedure for defense attorney's in these cases is to come back from the mandatory appeal and "attack the conviction" via legal action filed in state district court.

Assuming that the appeal was overturned here, they could then appeal the ruling on that writ back to the state court of criminal appeals.

If the application for the writ was overturned in Austin a second time, the defendant would most likely carry the appeal to the federal courts.

At that point, according to Armstrong, a number of federal district courts could become involved in the case including those in Lubbock—having jurisdiction over Snyder where the crime occurred and the case tried—and the court having jurisdiction over Huntsville—where Johnson will be held.

Rulings in the state's favor in the federal district courts would then be appealed to the U.S. 5th Circuit Court of Appeals in New Orleans.

Once in the federal courts, the case could, in Armstrong's words, "bounce around (between district courts and the 5th circuit) two or three times" before a final ruling is issued.

Once a final ruling is issued in New Orleans, Johnson would still have a right to petition to the U.S. Supreme Court for a hearing as the court of last resort.

In Armstrong's evaluation, it is unlikely that the Supreme Court would accept this particular case for review.

The multiple execution dates would result from the multiple rulings expected on the appeals.

Each time the conviction is affirmed by an appellate court, Johnson would be given a new execution date.

Each time the conviction is appealed to a new court, any previously set execution date would be wiped out pending a ruling on the new appeal.

Source: Noble B. Young, "Murder Appeal to Be Lengthy." *Snyder* (Texas) *Daily News*, November 23, 1986, p. 1.

b. Habeas Corpus

Habeas corpus is one of an American's most precious rights. Once a prisoner files a habeas corpus petition, the receiving judge must inquire into the legality of the case without delay. The judge must either dismiss a groundless petition or issue the writ to cause a prompt court review. If the judge finds that the conviction was illegal, the defendant is to be ordered discharged.

Habeas corpus can be filed in both state and federal courts. In the United States, its use, particularly in federal courts, has been so expanded that it is often abused. A defendant convicted in a state court can initially file habeas corpus, thereby claiming a legal defect in the conviction. If denied, the defendant can appeal the habeas corpus case itself in many jurisdictions.

Once finished with the first habeas corpus petition, defendants can file another if they can think up a new legal claim. The process can go on indefinitely. In one state, the volume of habeas corpus petitions from inmates necessitated a computer system to discourage duplication. If no relief comes in the state court, the inmate may file habeas corpus in federal court. The only requirement is to discern a federal constitutional question that can be raised about the conduct of the trial. No trial is perfect, and new court decisions defining various legal technicalities amounting to a denial of due process are issued daily.

Federal courts are empowered to release state prisoners on habeas corpus in the same way that federal prisoners are released. This permits federal judges to review state trials completely, sometimes years after the defendant was convicted, as long as a federal constitutional question is raised. A single federal district, under this system, has the power to overrule the entire state court system that has previously reviewed the case and affirmed the conviction.

Even if habeas corpus is originally denied by the federal district court in which it was filed, defendants may be able to appeal and work the case all the way to the Supreme Court for a decision. Even if denied there, they can continue to file new habeas corpus petitions as long as they claim new grounds of constitutional procedure in the case.

By contrast, in England, there are no postconviction remedies other than the restricted right to an appeal. When the original court process is completed in England, the case is finished. Finality of judgment in criminal cases in the United States under the present system is virtually unknown. Without finality of judgment, there is no justice.

(8.9) Variations in Juvenile Procedures

Under the common law of England, a child under the age of seven was incapable of committing a crime. Child criminals above this age were harshly treated. In fact, by 1800, thirty-three offenses called for capital punishment for children.

Public reaction against such severe treatment of child offenders grew, and, in 1817, the Society for the Prevention of Pauperism in New York City was one of the early groups concerning itself with the treatment of juveniles.

The House of Refuge in New York City was created in 1825; here, at last, children were confined separately from adults. Work projects and a system of rewards and deprivations characterized the program, but it still had punishment such as whippings and solitary confinement. Boston and Philadelphia developed similar systems for child offenders; however, black children were excluded. By the mid nineteenth century, Massachusetts had built the first reform school and accepted boys under sixteen. Later, it was the first state to build a girls' reformatory. Some of these institutions were located in rural areas to remove the children from the "evils of the city."

During the same period, the New York Children's Aid Society was placing children in country homes instead of jails. Many of these children were sent to homes in the West. By the time of the Civil War, ship schools, where boys under sixteen could study aboard ship and be exposed to military life, were being tried. The ship schools had a short life, however, because they were expensive and displaced adult, able-bodied seamen from their jobs. These conditions and circumstances brought forth the idea of a separate court for youths—a juvenile court. Illinois organized the world's first juvenile court in 1899. Denver and Rhode Island followed later that same year.

Denver's juvenile court, under the leadership of Judge Ben Lindsey, is perhaps the best known. Other states modeled their juvenile courts after his. The thrust of the juvenile court was that the child should be removed from the regular criminal court system and should be the court's primary concern. Protection as well as reform were the goals. Judges were to be specialists in their field; court hearings were to be informal, without rigid legal proceedings or technicalities. Perhaps even more revolutionary were the secret court proceedings set up to protect the child from the stigma of crime.

The names of juveniles were not published, and court files were to be sealed. Children found guilty were labeled "juvenile delinquent" rather than criminal. Technically, then, they did not have criminal records. With few modifications, these are the principles followed by today's juvenile courts.

All juvenile courts, or family courts, as they are sometimes called, handle more than the juvenile criminals. Many of their efforts are directed toward so-called status offenders: the truant, the runaway, or the incorrigible child. Such status offenders have hearings on their errant behavior and are declared to be "persons in need of supervision." Status offenders can be imprisoned the same way as juvenile delinquents, although they are in no sense criminals.

Juvenile courts also deal with abused, neglected, or abandoned children. The old common law doctrine was that of *parens patriae*—the crown was regarded as the parent of every child with the right to protect the property rights of children and orphans. From this came the modern juvenile court philosophy that the court should be the protector of the problem and the neglected child.

In the past forty years, both the state and federal governments have become heavily involved in child welfare and deliquency prevention. Counseling, mental health facilities, and professional and psychiatric care have been made available to treat the young offender. Treatment for some youths has sometimes proved to be as elusive as that for adults, and the "professional" advice offered to the court is sometimes far from being such.

Juvenile courts, like the rest of the system, are fragmented. An analysis of California's system showed that at one time it had 450 police agencies, 391 courts, and 60 probation departments and state correctional agencies, all dealing with juveniles.

Although there is no one uniform juvenile court system, the general pattern is similar from state to state. The top age ranges from sixteen to twenty-one, and some have no minimum age. Others take children at the age of seven. The usual court process involves the following:

1. formal charges in the form of a petition
2. arraignment, with counsel and a plea at a "detention hearing" to decide if the juvenile should be released or temporarily detained in a juvenile shelter
3. a formal two-part hearing (adjudicatory and dispositional) by a judge in chambers (except for a few states that allow a jury)
4. dispositional options ranging from foster home care to a private or public institution, or probation

Hearing secrecy and the goal of informality contributed to abuses that crept into the juvenile court system. Judges were often more autocratic than sympathetic. Status offenders, "children in need of supervision," found themselves convicted of noncriminal offenses and jailed, sometimes for years.

Modern day complaints of lack of due process procedures in juvenile courts became general, citing such practices as the use of detention as punishment, youths not represented by counsel, and no records of testimony. This led to a series of changes mandated by the Supreme Court, which ruled that the same Fourteenth Amendment due process required for adults also applied to juvenile court adjudications. The *Winship* case in 1970 established the standard proof in juvenile cases to be "beyond a reasonable doubt," the same as adults. The most notable juvenile case, *In re Gault*, 387 U.S. 1 (1967), decreed that a youth in juvenile court was entitled to (1) notice of charges, (2) the right to counsel, (3) the right to confront and cross-examine witnesses, and (4) the right to remain silent.

Finally, in *McKeiver* v. *Pennsylvania*, 403 U.S. 528 (1971), the Court decided to agree with a hundred-year-old California decision that a jury was not required at a juvenile delinquency proceeding. In spite of these procedural changes, our juvenile courts continue to be criticized by the public. Police with a juvenile complaint see the young defendant released back to the street before the officer can even complete the paperwork. The public sees too many young offenders summarily processed and then released. The young, streetwise offender regards juvenile court as a joke. Recent statistics reflect a marked increase in juvenile crime and juvenile arrests doubling over a ten-year period, which is twenty-three times faster than the increase in adult arrests for the same period. Other studies indicate a 75 percent recidivism rate among juveniles released after processing.

Critics find little comfort in being told that youthful crime is society's problem, not the court's, and that, under present conditions, the juvenile courts simply are unable to cope with the problem. But at least we now better understand some of the causes of juvenile crime. Dyslexia, or minor brain damage, undiscovered and untreated early in childhood, gives the child reversals or jumbled perceptions so that he cannot read, understand, or express himself. (Dyslexia is almost always a male affliction.) This and other learning disabilities lead to school failures. Unfortunately, juvenile offenders commonly are misfits in schools. Defective family life, the unwed mother, delinquent parents, gang behavior, drugs—all lead to deliquency. Today's declining morality and deteriorating family life breed juvenile delinquency like a mathematical progression.

One symptom of the general public attitude toward juvenile courts' "leniency" is new legislation in many states that allows the transfer of certain juvenile cases from juvenile court to adult criminal court. Ideally, this will at least keep young murderers from being "treated" in juvenile court, where they can be jailed for only a short time.

This transfer legislation, however, can lead to ridiculous legal situations; yet some things can be done. Most juvenile courts are too busy, overworked, and understaffed. They are poorly funded, being an unpopular cause with governments. Who wants to divert badly needed tax dollars to the problems of dealing with young toughs? More diagnostic and treatment centers would help courts do their best for the child.

The old reformatories, admitted failures in treating today's youth, have largely been abolished. New types of institutions and community treatment centers are being tried. However, putting children in the best institution will not correct the problem at home, where they will return. Real attention outside the court system must be paid to the kind of family situation that produces delinquency.

Cross-training between police and correctional staff can help. Defense counsel needs to be motivated to concentrate on what is best for the child rather than winning a legal victory in juvenile court. Steps can be taken to foster closer cooperation among courts, youth correctional institutions, and aftercare facilities.

A hard-line attitude on the part of all juvenile court personnel, the elimination of mandatory secrecy requirements, improved court procedures, and a gradual change in institutional treatment offer additional hope.

(8.10) The Youthful Offender

In some court systems, the youthful offender is a legal hybrid, standing in age between the juvenile delinquent and the adult criminal. Usually, the youthful offender is between eighteen and twenty-one. Based on the idea of rehabilitation and the aim of "protecting" youths, many states adopted special youthful offender statutes.

Most youthful offender treatment is available only to youths in the age bracket who have no prior felonies. Such treatment often is made discretionary with the sentencing judge. Some states seal youthful offender conviction records, and, like the juvenile delinquent, the youth does not have a criminal record. All these acts provide for a sentence of imprisonment, normally to special youth-oriented institutions, but the term of confinement may be less than that for an adult.

Some states provide for secrecy of the youthful offender's name. There, the press is excluded from the court proceedings, and the offender's name cannot be published. There is growing agitation to remove the secrecy from youthful offender proceedings because of the feeling that persons of this age are responsible for their actions, and the community should know about them.

Youthful offender proceedings generally follow normal due process procedure, except that some states give the youths the option of requesting youthful offender treatment. In turn, however, they must waive their right to a jury trial.

Youthful offender statutes have received little criticism other than of the secrecy and the sealing of records. This may change, but there seems to be no reason for eliminating youthful offender programs.

(8.11) Summary

A convicted defendant has two remedies: appeal and habeas corpus. All defendants are, at present, entitled to one appeal at state expense if they are indigent. The state cannot appeal a not guilty verdict because any new trial ordered would be double jeopardy. If the defendant's conviction is affirmed on the first appeal, then he or she may go one court higher to the state's supreme court, if the court consents. In some instances, the defendant may go back to the original trial court on a *coram nobis* petition of error. Our appellate system is unduly lengthy, allows too many appeals, and, in many cases, allows the convicted defendant to remain free on bail for years until the appeal is decided.

Once the appeal process is over, a defendant can still litigate the case by filing a habeas corpus petition in a state court, claiming a legal defect in the conviction. If he or she can show any type of due process or other constitutional error in the case, the defendant can file a habeas corpus petition in federal courts. Federal courts have the power to release state prisoners. The convicted defendant may be able to take his or her case review all the way to the United States Supreme Court.

The delay and lack of finality in this country due to these postponement remedies are two of the justice system's most serious defects.

Child offenders in the past were often harshly treated and confined with adult offenders. Some progress toward reform of these conditions was made in the nineteenth century. The idea of a separate court for children resulted in America's first juvenile court in 1899.

The major thrust of the juvenile court is to remove children from the regular court system and consider them as the court's main interest. The purpose is to protect as well as to reform errant children. Procedure is informal, nonjury, and run by juvenile court judges. Proceedings are not public, and the child's name is not made public. The court handles not only delinquent children, but noncriminal "status offenders," such as truants, runaways, and incorrigibles. These status offenders are often imprisoned like delinquents, and this has brought criticism. The abandoned or neglected child is also a juvenile court concern. Counseling, mental health, and other community facilities are available for juvenile courts.

Juvenile court proceedings begin with the filing of a petition, an arraignment, and a detention hearing. Any trial has two parts: an adjudicatory hearing to determine guilt or innocence and a dispositional hearing for sentencing. Supreme Court decisions mandate counsel for the juvenile and a general following of due process requirements in juvenile court. In certain special cases, a juvenile can be transferred to the jurisdiction of adult criminal court for trial and disposition.

A youthful offender, from eighteen to twenty-one, may be treated under special statutes. In most cases, these have to be felony first offenders. Youthful offender treatment may be discretionary with the judge, and it may involve the youth waiving jury trial. Youthful offenders may be imprisoned, but the term is usually less than that of an adult. Time is usually served in special institutions. Some states seal the youthful offender's files, and that person is not considered to have a criminal conviction.

Discussion Questions

1. Discuss the role and function of the trial jury.
2. What is *voir dire?*
3. What is the significance of *Williams v. Florida*, 399 U.S. 78 (1970)?
4. Discuss the process of "charging the jury."
5. What is the usual outcome of a hung jury?

9
Rules of Evidence

All presumptive evidence of felony should be
admitted cautiously: for the law holds, that it is
better that ten guilty persons escape, than that
one innocent suffer.
—Blackstone, Vol. IV, Ch. 27, p. 3

(9.1) Development of the Rules of Evidence

Every society evolves its own court system to resolve individual
disputes or to settle the claim that one of the rules of the group has
been broken. We classify the first (disputes between individuals) as a
civil action. This type of suit usually concerns property or money.
The second (violating the rules of the group) is a criminal case.

Our trial system has its origins in medieval England. Crimes
were originally considered private wrongs, and the offender was required to pay a fine to the injured party. At the close of the Middle
Ages, crimes were no longer regarded as individual matters but were
considered offenses against the crown.

The church became involved in English criminal cases and
received considerable revenue from convicted offenders. Trial by
ordeal was the process by which guilt or innocence was established,
with the ritual itself taking place on church grounds. The idea was
that God would preserve the innocent and uncover the guilty. While
the ordeal was in process, two rows of spectators on either side of the
church would pray that "God would make the whole truth clear."

Trial by ordeal might require the accused to plunge his ban-
daged hand into a caldron of boiling water to retrieve a stone. Three

days later, the bandage was removed, and if the arm was scalded, he was guilty. However, if unharmed, God had confirmed his innocence by protecting him. Another ordeal was walking barefoot on red-hot iron. If the suspect was not burned, he was innocent. Finally, however, the Pope, in 1215, removed the church from any further involvement with or endorsements of trial by ordeal.

Another form of determining guilt or innocence was trial by compurgation. Although less barbaric, it was no more scientific. A group of compurgators would swear to the innocence of the accused and thereby establish guilt or innocence. The number of compurgators was determined by the seriousness of the offense and the social position of the accused. Perjury was commonplace, but the oaths, if sufficient in number, were accepted as proof of innocence; if lacking in number, they were considered proof of guilt.

In 1066, the Norman Conquest of England brought with it the trial by combat, which became the usual method of trial, replacing the ordeal. The theory here was that the God of battles would uphold the righteous and make him victorious in personal combat. Women, children, clergy, and physically handicapped individuals were exempted. Persons of means could employ professional champions to fight in their place. Champions were usually armed with clubs or swords; noblemen were allowed to fight on horseback.[1]

The jury trial became the final descendant of trials by ordeal and combat. Juries, in one form or another, had existed for many years, but the jury had its greatest development during the reign of Henry II (1115–1189).

The jury, an Anglo-American legal institution whose roots rest in the unwritten past, may have originated in England, or it may have been brought there by the Normans. Under Norman rule, jurors were summoned to render verdicts under oath, a practice that may, in fact, predate the Norman influence. We are certain, however, that the jury itself came into common use under the Normans in England.

Henry II, in a further effort to strengthen England's central government, planned a system of royal courts to administer a law common to all of the nation instead of the various legal rules that had grown up in the manorial courts. He offered an inducement to use his courts—the jury system. Only the king had authority to summon

---

1. *4 Blackstone's Commentaries on the Laws of England,* pp. 336–342.

juries. Henry did not grant this power to private courts and limited juries to those who sought justice in his royal courts.

At one time, English juries were character witnesses for the accused. They gradually became investigatory bodies assembled to determine guilt or innocence. Jurymen were not selected for impartiality; in fact, they were chosen from among those who would most likely already know the facts of the case. Jurymen questioned witnesses and visited the crime scene. Under Henry II, a unanimous verdict by twelve men was required. Hung juries were not allowed. If twelve men could not agree, more jurors were added until twelve did agree.

If a judge disagreed with a verdict, the jury itself could be tried by a panel of twenty-four knights and the jurymen fined or even jailed. By the fifteenth century, trials by ordeal and combat were replaced by the English jury. The principle of the jury system descending from the days of Henry II is that law flows from the people, not from the monarch.[2]

We have come a long way from settling matters by trial by combat or trial by ordeal. Neither have the English-speaking peoples adopted trial by inquisition, in which the accused himself must supply much of the proof by answering questions. In the United States we employ the adversary trial system. This system is based on the idea that the truth will more nearly come out if it is tested by the giving of testimony in open court under the questioning and cross-questioning of opposing lawyers.

In order that everyone who is accused of a crime might receive the same treatment, the courts of England, on which our system is based, gradually developed rules defining what matters would be allowed as proof in criminal cases and how trials should proceed. Without such rules, one person's case might be tried in one way and another person's in another way. That is, without such court-approved consistency, we could never hope to approach a system of equal justice.

The gradual development of our law of evidence traces back to early English court decisions. Even today judges will occasionally use an old English case as a guide in deciding a question of evidence. Through the years they have had to decide what proof would be received in individual court cases and what would be rejected. Many

2. W. L. Warren, *Henry II*, (Berkeley: University of California Press, 1973), pp. 320–322.

of these judicial decisions are written down and then collectively printed in book-form court reports. The federal government and every state publish their own court reports throughout the year. These reports are available to bench, bar, and public as guides to past judicial rulings.

The law ever seeks stability. Thus each court tries to follow the precedent of earlier cases within its jurisdiction that have been decided on the same issue. This adherence to legal precedent is known by the Latin phrase "stare decisis."

Another basis for legal stability is the fact that the lower courts are bound by the decisions of the higher, appellate courts in their state. If, for example, the highest court in California rules that book-maker slips can be used as evidence in a gambling case, then every lower court in that state must do the same thing.

The body of law found in court decisions is generally referred to as being part of the "common law," as opposed to the statutes enacted by legislatures. Legislative bodies do pass laws concerning evidence, and we must often consult both sources to determine what is legal evidence in our area.

Thus, the rules of evidence, whether common law or statutory, are not the same in every state; nor are they identical with those in the federal courts. The similarities, though, are much greater than the differences. In general, all American courts follow the same basic rules of criminal evidence. A detective from Chicago testifying in a murder case in Ohio would find himself very much at home.

Though we depend heavily on legal precedent, our law is not stagnant. With the passage of time, the courts themselves gradually modify, change, and sometimes overrule prior decisions. In the past fifteen years, for example, largely because of federal court decisions, there have been more changes in the American law of criminal evidence than in twice the number of years preceding. Times change, and so do the courts. For example, rules governing the use of letters and documents as evidence in court have evolved to include the use of tape recordings, moving pictures, and closed-circuit television. Currently, court decisions are split regarding the use of lie detectors and voice prints.

We are protected by the law's slowness, but nurtured as well by its change. To know the law of evidence requires the learning of its rules of yesterday, but prudence dictates that we also anticipate its changes of tomorrow.

(9.2) Enactment of Evidentiary Codes

Some foreign countries are code states and do not have a common-law system. From the time of Hammurabi to that of Napoleon, governments have attempted to put all their law into statute form. The strength of the system of legal codes is that all the law is in one place, the statutes. The weakness of it is its rigidity because human affairs are never constant.

As has been said, the United States combines the two systems, mixing the rigidity of the statutes with the flexibility of the common-law court decisions.

All states and the national government have statutes on the law of evidence. Some states, among them California (California Evidence Code), have complete evidentiary codes. The Congress of the United States by Public Law 93-595 (Federal Rules of Evidence, effective July 1, 1975) has also enacted a complete evidentiary code. It covers a broad spectrum, from defining what evidence is relevant to the use of documents and expert testimony and the method of hearing witnesses.

Laws affecting the use of evidence are also often found in many individual state statutes that are not included in an evidentiary code as such. They may range from a motor vehicle statute governing the use of blood alcohol tests in traffic arrests to the use of official laboratory reports before grand juries and the use of police and business records in criminal trials.

All of the above brings us back to the same point. In order to be certain of any specific rule of criminal evidence, you must consult your area's evidentiary code, if there is one, its statutes, and its court decisions on the subject.

(9.3) Burden of Proof in General

There is a common saying among prosecutors that it is easy to indict but hard to convict. This is true. Before the indictment and arrest of a suspect the advantage is with the state, with its paid professional staff of investigators, its laboratory technicians, and its police and prosecutors—all supported by public funds. Once the suspect is arrested, he becomes the defendant, and the advantage is with him. His greatest advantage is that the prosecution has the entire burden of proving his guilt. The prosecution must, in fact, not only prove the defendant's guilt, but must prove it beyond a reasonable doubt. It is not necessary for the defendant to prove a thing. Unless he chooses to do so, he need not even take the stand to testify and to answer the accusation against him.

Many thoughtful people question the wisdom of this system because it so favors the defendant, but the majority feel that it is preferable to have a guilty person go free than to have an innocent person convicted.

The roots of the idea that the prosecutor must prove everything go back to the days of the king's hangmen, the rack, and the torture chamber. Confessions were extorted by literally stretching men's bones, and the axman's block was almost a relief. Hence, the Fifth Amendment to the Constitution, which manifests our suspicion of tyrannical oppression, provides that no man may be compelled to testify against himself. Thus, the People must not only prove guilt beyond a reasonable doubt, but they must do it without taking any testimony from the defendant. In fact, the right against self-incrimination is so carefully guarded that it "forbids either comment by the prosecution on the accused's silence or instructions by the court that such silence is evidence of guilt," as was stated in *Griffin* v. *California*, 380 U.S. 609 (1965).

Certain information may, however, be obtained from a non-testifying defendant: a handwriting sample, a mental examination, or observation of the defendant in court.

An additional factor, adding still more to the prosecution's burden of proof, is the presumption of the defendant's innocence. From the moment he steps into the courtroom, the jury must presume he is innocent. This presumption stays with him throughout the entire trial until, and if, it is overcome by the People's proof of guilt beyond a reasonable doubt. The presumption of innocence applies to every element of the crime with which the defendant is charged. It is not intended to shield the guilty but to prevent the conviction of the innocent.

The presumption of innocence is predicated not upon any express provision of the federal constitution, but upon ancient concepts antedating the development of the common law. Legal historians trace the idea to Deuteronomy and the laws of Sparta and Athens. It is not so much a rule of law as a substantial right of a citizen.

And so, in summary, the burden of criminal proof is completely on the People, the defendant is protected by the Fifth Amendment, and the trial commences with the presumption that he is innocent. The prosecution's burden, and, by extension, law enforcement's, is a heavy burden of proof indeed, and this burden never shifts.

(9.4) Prima Facie Case

When the prosecution rests, having presented all of its proof, the defense counsel usually asks the judge to dismiss the charge on the ground that the People have failed to prove a "prima facie" case. Sometimes the motion is granted.

Prima facie literally means "first view." Prima facie proof in a criminal case is evidence that on its surface is sufficient to prove the charge. It is not necessary that the evidence be conclusive. The defense may always rebut it by contradictory or explanatory evidence, if it has any.

The prosecutor has the burden of producing enough evidence that, at first view, standing alone, is sufficient beyond a reasonable doubt. For example, the prosecution proves the identity of an accused rapist by the testimony of a passerby who saw the suspect leave the building in which the rape took place or by the victim's hair sample on the defendant's clothing. The victim herself can only give a general description. Though the defendant may have an alibi or other defense, the state at this point has proved a prima facie case.

(9.5) Corpus Delicti

The prosecution must always prove the "corpus delicti," the fact that a crime has been committed. A jury cannot deliberate as to who committed it, unless the state first proves that there has been a criminal act. The jimmied store door and the blown safe inside is the corpus delicti of a burglary, that is, proof that there was a criminal act of breaking in to steal. The half-burned house with evidence of the gasoline used by the arsonist to start the fire would be the corpus delicti of arson.

Because the phrase "corpus delicti" literally means "body of the crime," people often mistakenly think it only refers to the body in a homicide. A popular misconception has grown up that the police cannot prove a murder unless they find the body. This is not so. Producing the corpse only proves a death, not a crime. Murder has been proven many times by circumstantial evidence of the crime even though the body was lost forever.

In the days of sailing ships an English murder case (*Rex* v. *Hindmarsh*, 2 Leach C.C. 569) established a rule that is still followed today. There was an indictment for two counts of murder, one for killing by beating and the other for killing by drowning. The alleged crime occurred at sea. A witness testified that he was awakened at midnight by a violent noise, that on reaching the deck he saw the accused murderer pick the captain up and throw him overboard, and that the captain was not heard from again. Another witness stated that he had earlier heard the prisoner threaten to kill the captain. Near where the captain had been seen a large piece of wood was found, and the deck and part of the accused's clothing were stained with blood. The defense counsel called for an acquittal because the body was never found, arguing that the captain might have been picked up at sea by a passing ship. The court found sufficient proof of corpus delicti, however, and sent the case to the jury. The jury found the defendant guilty, and he was executed.

The problem of corpus delicti in a murder case still exists today, and the courts often disagree as to the required measure of proof.

Years ago an English judge, in discussing the proof required for the corpus delicti, supposed a situation in which a man was seen to enter the London docks quite sober, only to come out later quite drunk, staggering from the door of a wine cellar where millions of gallons of wine were stored. "I think," said the judge, "that this would be reasonable evidence that the man had stolen some of the wine, though no proof be given that any particular vat had been broached."

Larceny can be proved without recovering the stolen jewels,

kidnapping without finding the victim, England's great train robbery without the million pounds—just as long as the prosecution can prove by other evidence that a crime was committed, that is, the corpus delicti.

And so, today as yesterday, evidence proving the corpus delicti is always a part of the prosecution's burden of proof.

(9.6) Shifting of the Burden of Proof

Appellate courts everywhere have wrestled with the legal theory of whether or not the burden of proof ever shifts from the prosecution to the defense. What happens when the defendant offers to explain the crime in some way, such as presenting an alibi? Does the defendant also have to give proof beyond a reasonable doubt and assume all the other responsibilities that are normally those of the prosecution? Though the legal theory of shifting the burden of proof is mainly a problem to be discussed by court and counsel, men's necks have, nonetheless, often been stretched over legal points finer than this one.

The generally accepted answer to the question above is that the accused is not required to explain anything, although he may do so if he wishes. After the state has made a prima facie case of guilt, the task of showing any contrary evidence is up to the defendant. The accused must come forward with any defense he may have. Thus it is said that he has the "burden of explanation."

Evidence offered to explain or excuse the charge that is peculiar to the defendant's own knowledge or that is more readily available to him is always his responsibility to initiate. From that point on, courts have split on who has the burden of proof. Some authorities have ruled that when a positive defense such as alibi is raised by the defendant, the burden immediately shifts to the People, who are then required to prove the negative beyond a reasonable doubt.

The Supreme Court (*Martin* v. *Ohio*, 480 J.S. 228 [1987]) has approved a variation of this generally accepted rule by approving an Ohio statute that requires a defendant to prove self-defense by a "preponderance of the evidence."

The most generally accepted rule is that once the defendant introduces this type of explanatory evidence, the burden of proof rests with the prosecution, but the jury must consider all the evidence and find guilt only if it is convinced beyond a reasonable doubt.

Another problem of burden of proof arises when the criminal charge rests on a negative. Some examples of this are a charge of operating a business without a permit or a criminal charge of carrying a pistol without a license. The state does not have to prove an absence of a permit or a license in these cases because knowledge concerning the charges rests solely within the defendant. If the defendant has such a permit or license, he can easily offer it in evidence. The state is required to prove a negative matter only if it is something not peculiarly known to the accused.

(9.7) Affirmative Defenses

In criminal cases there are a variety of explanatory defenses that the law labels "affirmative defenses." When one of these is used, the defense in effect may be saying "Yes, I do not deny the crime occurred, but I am not guilty because . . . ." The burden of proving such matters and the way they affect the state's case may vary with the nature of the defense.

a. Alibi

The dictionary defines "alibi" as a plea of having been elsewhere "at the time of the commission of an act." Since the law uses the same definition, an alibi goes farther than a denial that the defendant was at the scene of the crime. An alibi is evidence that the defendant was at another place at the time the crime was committed, thus making it impossible for him to have been guilty. It is a complete, legitimate defense.

Legal authorities have quibbled over whether or not an alibi is technically an affirmative defense, which could result in a shifting of the burden of proof to the defendant. Many jurisdictions now make the defense give the state pretrial notice of any alibi defense and require the production of the names of alibi witnesses and revelation of the names of any counteralibi witnesses on the other side.

The settled rule is that the accused must take the initiative to prove the alibi, but he is not held to any definite measure of proof. The ultimate burden of proving guilt still stays with the prosecution.

b. Capacity and Insanity

The law assumes that everyone has ordinary intelligence and is, therefore, capable of committing criminal acts. Though there was an old common-law provision that infants under seven were incapable of committing crime and that those between seven and fourteen were presumed to be incapable, this has largely become obsolete as each state has enacted its own laws defining juvenile delinquents.

Since normality is presumed, the state does not have to prove it and, therefore, does not have to prove criminal capacity in general. This is simply a practical matter. If the prosecution had to prove every defendant was normal, conviction would be impossible. Hence, this is the basis for the assumption that every person has ordinary intelligence and the capacity to commit criminal acts, with the exception of certain matters involving infants that have been referred to previously.

By the same reasoning, the law also presumes that everyone is sane. In most jurisdictions insanity is considered an affirmative defense to be proven by the accused. Federal law requires that in a federal criminal trial the defendant raising an insanity defense has the burden of proving insanity by "clear and convincing evidence" (18 U.S.C. 17 [1986]). The measure of proof required of the defendant to prove insanity can be set by statute. Requiring the defense to prove insanity by measurable proof is constitutional because it does not actually shift the burden of proving one of the elements of the crime, there being a presumption of sanity.

c. Statute of Limitations

In the absence of a law setting a time limit on bringing criminal charges, prosecution could be started at any time. Most jurisdictions, however, have statutes of limitations listing the time when various criminal prosecutions must begin. In general, all misdemeanors and most felonies have time limits; murder usually does not.

The prosecution has the burden of showing that the crime was committed within the proper time. Some statutes state that the time limit is suspended when the defendant is out of the state. If so, the defendant must prove he was not absent all of the time, as this would be something that would be peculiarly within his knowledge.

d. Duress

Sometimes the accused claims that he was coerced or forced to commit a crime. This is the affirmative defense of duress. Suppose, for example, a banker was taken at gunpoint from his home, with his wife held there as a hostage, was driven to his bank, and was directed to remove $200,000.00 from the vault. He would have a good defense of duress were he charged with grand larceny.

Since the affirmative defense of duress does not remove any element of proof from the prosecution, the defendant has the burden of proving it. As with the proof of insanity, the measure of the defendant's proof of duress may also be set by the jurisdiction.

e. Entrapment

Entrapment is inducing a person to commit a crime that he would not otherwise have committed. It is recognized everywhere as an affirmative defense. Entrapment, like duress, does not negate any essential element of the state's proof. It is an affirmative defense, and the statutes may define the amount of proof required.

People v. *Laietta*, 30 N.Y. 2d 68 (1972), cert. den. 407 U.S. 923, illustrates the burden of proof required in an entrapment case. Laietta was charged with attempting to extort money from a businessman named Friedman. Police "wired" Friedman and tape recorded Laietta threatening him by saying, "We're not threatening you but look, you're going to get hurt if you don't pay. This idiot called some ginzo in. Italian families are closely knit." Laietta claimed entrapment saying that Friedman was an agent of the police and had induced him to commit the crime.

A New York statute made entrapment a defense to be proven by a preponderance of the evidence. The trial was held on this theory, and Laietta was convicted, holding that entrapment was an affirmative defense, and the defendant could be required to prove it since this did not in any way lessen the People's burden of proving its own case beyond a reasonable doubt.

The well-known FBI Abscam bribery investigation of various congressmen involved undercover FBI agents whose bribe offers to these officials were recorded on videotape and resulted in bribery prosecutions. The defendants claimed entrapment. There were differing rulings on this question in the various trials and appeals.

f. Miscellaneous Defenses

There are other affirmative defenses that the defendant must raise and prove if he is going to use them. Among them are a claim of double jeopardy (being tried more than once for the same crime); immunity from prosecution granted by a prior court in return for testimony incriminating another defendant; consent of the victim; and self-defense.

In many cases statutes define other affirmative defenses, such as the claim in an arson case that a fire was set for a legal purpose; in the defense in a bad check case that the loss was paid back in a specified time; or in a larceny case that the property was appropriated under a good faith claim of right. This type of defense also does not shift the burden of proof in any way, and the People must still prove a prima facie case beyond a reasonable doubt.

(9.8) The Burden of Going Forward

When courts are concerned with the technical problems involved in the burden of proof, they are careful to distinguish between the burden of going forward—introducing the proof of the explanatory defense—and the burden of proving such a defense.

In all cases of positive defense, where the crime is not denied but the defendant offers proof to explain or justify himself, the courts are unanimous in saying that such a defendant has "the burden of going forward." That is, the defendant, not the state, first has to introduce the evidence of avoidance of guilt. If it is an accepted affirmative defense, the defendant may be required to prove it by a preponderance of the evidence. The courts insist, however, that, in the end, the real burden of the proof of guilt, regardless of the type of positive defense, never shifts from the state. And the state must still prove guilt beyond a reasonable doubt.

(9.9) Proof Beyond a Reasonable Doubt

In a civil case, such as a suit for money or property, all that is required of the plaintiff is that he prove his case by a "fair preponderance of the evidence," enough simply to tip the scales of justice. But in a criminal trial, as we have emphasized, much more evidence is needed, since proof of guilt must be beyond a reasonable doubt.

This ancient precept of English justice, which applies to everyone accused of a criminal act, means exactly what it says: a doubt based on reason and arising out of all the evidence or the lack of it. A reasonable doubt is not just any doubt that a person might have. It is a doubt to which one can assign a reason. The prosecution is not, of course, required to prove guilt to a mathematical certainty. If that were so, it would be useless to prosecute anyone. It is possible, however, to prove guilt to a reasonable certainty, and the People are held to that standard only. This, then, is the measure of evidence that law enforcement personnel must gather and produce in legal form in order to convict a suspect—proof beyond a reasonable doubt.

(9.10) Stipulations

An entirely different way of admitting proof is by stipulation, that is, agreement of the attorneys. Opposing lawyers sometimes agree to let certain evidence be used. Evidentiary matters can then be settled by a stipulation in open court by both the prosecution and the defense. They may stipulate, for example, that a certain state of facts exists or that if a named witness were called he would testify in a certain manner. A counsel will occasionally stipulate that something be introduced as evidence that the court would ordinarily reject; polygraph test results are sometimes used in this way. Usually, however, stipulations as to evidence are employed by counsel for noncontroversial matters, and they are made to expedite the trial of cases.

(9.11) Admissibility of Evidence

No evidence has any practical value unless the judge allows it to be used in court, that is, admits it as evidence. To be legally usable, the proof offered must first pass a series of tests. And, of course, any evidence to which an objection is made must properly pass the test of legality.

Initially the evidence must be "relevant." A stock objection the opposing counsel may use is that evidence is "incompetent, irrelevant, and immaterial." This broad attempt to block the admissibility of evidence covers all possibilities, but will normally be rejected as not being specific enough. Yet there are occasions when the evidence is so obviously inappropriate that just the word "objection" will be sufficient to have it excluded.

(9.12) Relevance and Materiality

Many a legal hair has been split by judges, attorneys, and writers of textbooks in an attempt to decide whether an evidentiary item was relevant or material. For all practical purposes, any theoretical difference between the two terms may be disregarded. Strictly speaking, evidence is relevant if it tends to prove a fact in issue before the court. But relevant evidence must also be material; that is, it must be important. If immaterial evidence were admissible, trials could drag on for months. Evidence that is only remotely connected to the crime is said to be immaterial. If, on the other hand, the evidence proves something, but what it proves is not in issue in a particular trial, it is said to be irrelevant.

The problem of relevancy of evidence is the same for both the law enforcement officer and the judge. Does the item of evidence tend to prove the guilt or innocence of the accused? Does it have a bearing on the issue? If it does, is it a direct or remote bearing?

Relevance is really not susceptible to a legal definition, but rests on common sense. As one authority put it, "The only test of relevancy is logic. With this simple statement we must be content. Nothing could be gained in a code of rules making it a thesis on the subject . . . ."

When evidence is offered and an objection is raised, the trial judge must decide whether the item really tends to prove or disprove the issue before the court. If it does, it is relevant and thus passes the first test of legal usefulness.

(9.13) Exclusion of Relevant Evidence

Evidence may be considered relevant, and yet it may not be admitted for some other reason. That is, another rule may exclude it. This means that the law of evidence is largely a study of the rules of exclusion.

A relevant matter may be excluded, for example, simply at the discretion of the judge. He may exercise this discretion if he feels that the evidence to be presented, though otherwise material, might lead to undue hostility, sympathy, or prejudice on the part of a jury. Uncommonly gory police photographs are often not admitted as evidence because they might influence the jury excessively.

Another reason for exclusion is the possibility that the proof might unfairly surprise an opponent. Sometimes relevant evidence is excluded because it could confuse the jury or cause them to argue about a matter that is not part of the issue in question. Relevant evidence may also be rejected simply because it is cumulative. Thus, if a matter has been proven once, it need not be proven a second, a third, or a fourth time.

It is the general rule that evidence will not be excluded unless one of the sides states an objection. Though the judge may reject it on his own motion, he is not likely to do so. The opponent must take the initiative in excluding evidence. If he makes no objection to what the other side introduces, he waives the rule, and any evidence can be used.

(9.14) Evidence of Other Crimes

At this point we are not dealing with the use of evidence of other crimes to discredit a witness or as rebuttal evidence. What happens when the prosecution offers proof of other crimes committed by the defendant as direct proof of guilt in the present situation? Great caution must be exercised when this type of evidence is allowed, since the commission of one crime is not proof that an individual would commit a second. Thus, evidence of other crimes is objectionable, not because it has no probative value, but because it has too much. "The natural tendency of the tribunal . . . is to give excessive weight to the vicious record of crime thus exhibited and either to allow it to bear too strongly on the present charge or to take the proof of it as justifying a condemnation, irrespective of the guilt of the present charge." Even a habitual criminal may well be innocent of the crime with which he is charged.

In non-English-speaking countries the entire past criminal record of the accused is an important part of the prosecutor's case. So it was in England before 1680. Eventually the English changed this and barred the use of such proof by the crown. In 1692 there was an English murder case known as Harrison's Trial, *12 How. St. Tr.* 833, in which a witness for the crown was asked about a felony committed by the accused three years before. The judge stopped the testimony, saying: "Hold, hold. What are you doing now? Are you going to arraign his whole life? How can he defense himself against charges of which he has no notice? And how many issues are to be raised to perplex me and the jury? Away! Away! That ought not to be: that is nothing to the matter."

Like so much of the law of evidence, this rule of exclusion is subject to several exceptions. Three hundred years after the judge's cry of "Away! Away!" in Harrison's trial, New York's highest court had to deal with the same problem. In so doing, it enumerated and explained the exceptions that do allow the state to include additional crimes as part of its case.

The case in New York was concerned with a society murder that was a sensation in its day. On December 24, 1898, Henry Cornish received a package in the mail containing a blue bottle labeled "Bromo Seltzer®." Thinking it a Christmas gift, he passed it on to one of the women of the household. A day or two later he saw another one of the women (Mrs. Adams) in the kitchen with her head resting on her hands, suffering from a headache. At his suggestion she took some of the medicine from the blue bottle to alleviate the pain. When she complained about the taste, Cornish took some of the medicine, saying "Why that stuff is all right." Mrs. Adams started for the kitchen and collapsed. Her face turned blue, and she was dead before the doctor arrived. Meanwhile, Cornish had become ill and, after visiting the police, left for the Knickerbocker Athletic Club, "the journey being marked by frequent interruptions necessitated by the condition of his stomach and bowels."

The "Bromo Seltzer" was found to contain cyanide of mercury. Molineaux, an athletic director of the Knickerbocker Athletic Club, had had a dispute with Cornish, had sent him the bottle of poison, and was thus tried for Mrs. Adams's murder. The prosecutor was not content simply to prove the murder at hand, although he had ample evidence, including proof of Molineaux's handwriting on the package. The state proved, in addition, all the details of a prior murder, claiming that Molineaux had once poisoned a man named Barnet by mailing him a packet of "Kutnow" powder containing cyanide of mercury. It seems that Molineaux was jealous of Barnet's attentions to the woman with whom the defendant was in love.

The court explained the rule on this type of additional criminal proof: "Evidence of other crimes is competent to prove this specific crime charged when it tends to establish (1) motive (2) intent (3) the absence of mistake or accident (4) a common scheme or plan . . . (5) the identity [of the accused] . . . ." The court thus reversed Molineaux's first-degree murder conviction, pointing out that proof of the Barnet murder did not come within any of the exceptions that would allow evidence of one crime to prove another (*People* v. *Molineaux*, 168 N.Y. 264 [1901]).

Though the Molineaux trial occurred many years ago, its rule still applies today. The five exceptions allowing evidence of additional crimes as proof of the crime charged are detailed below.

a. Motive

When motive is an issue, evidence of other of the defendant's acts is admissible, if the acts are not too remote. Proof that a police officer charged with bribery had previously received hush money from other houses of prostitution has been allowed. In cases of adultery, statutory rape, or incest, sexual acts subsequent to the act charged are relevant to show a lascivious disposition on the part of the accused. In cases involving assault, previous similar acts of the defendant against the victim are allowed as proof of motive. In cases concerned with gambling, previous possession of betting slips or proof of prior gambling convictions is allowable.

A less obvious illustration than the above involved the robbery-murder of a sixty-six-year-old upstate New York chicken farmer named Charles Bower. The victim was found shot dead, lying in front of his garage. The evidence showed that he customarily carried money in a wallet in his left shirtfront pocket. When the body was found, the wallet was missing, the shirt pocket was torn, and the button from his overalls' strap was discovered nearby. One, Delorio, was accused of the murder. At his trial the judge allowed the state to prove that Delorio had only three cents in his pocket when he was released from jail on another charge three days before the killing. The jury found him guilty, and he appealed the conviction. The appellate court approved of the use of this evidence as showing that Delorio had a motive to steal, even though it involved proof of another crime (*People* v. *Delorio*, 33 A.D. 2d 350 [1970]).

b. Intent

Motive and intent are often thought of as being the same, but there is a clear legal distinction between them. Motive is the moving power, the reason for doing something. Intent is the mental purpose to do a specific thing to bring about such a result. The jealous husband may well have had a good reason (motive) to kill his wife's lover, but probably did not have the intent to kill him, since he stated: "I only meant to scare him away. The gun went off by accident."

Sometimes guilty knowledge as bearing on intent may be proven separately, often by evidence of other crimes. For example, in a homicide case the state would be allowed to prove that the defendant stole a pistol the day before the killing and used it in the crime. Other illustrations might include proof of previous occasions of passing counterfeit money to show this was an intentional act in the present case; earlier receipt of stolen property as evidence of a similar present offense; prior offenses of forgery as proof of possessing forged checks; former fraudulent thefts to demonstrate larceny by false pretenses.

c. Absence of Mistake

Where guilty knowledge is an issue, evidence of other offenses by the accused can properly be used to show that his act was not done by mistake. Illustrations used previously allowing evidence of other crimes to prove intent apply equally here.

d. Common Scheme or Plan

Evidence of other crimes is admissible when it is closely connected with the crime charged and tends to prove a common scheme. It is relevant, however, only if it is offered as circumstantial proof of the present charge. Often one crime may be closely connected with another so that proof of crimes A and B can be introduced as good evidence of crime C. Proof of a series of treatments might be offered to show one event of practicing medicine without a license. Mail fraud or embezzlement cases might involve evidence of a series of these acts to establish the one being charged.

e. Identity

Frequently evidence of other crimes is used to prove the defendant's identity. This can only be done, however, where identity is an issue in the case. There must be a connection between the two offenses to show that whoever committed the first crime also committed the second. This connection can usually be made where an unusual method (modus operandi) was used. If the same method was employed in both crimes, proof of the earlier one would be allowed as tending to identify the accused as the guilty party in the present offense.

In a federal fraud case one Fernandez was charged with defrauding a bank with a supposed timber sale that was part of a swindle. The bank received telephone calls about the timber deal from a man calling himself Belcher and from a timber cruiser supposedly named Rotschy. The government claimed that Fernandez made all these calls. A bookkeeper who had formerly worked for Fernandez was allowed to testify that on various occasions, not connected with this case, Fernandez made other telephone calls in which he misrepresented himself. One of the counts of the indictment in the crime being charged against Fernandez involved a forged deed. The bookkeeper told how Fernandez had used the duplicating machine and cellophane tape to add unauthorized signatures to other papers.

The court approved the use of all of this testimony as showing a particular modus operandi. It ruled that this was circumstantial proof that Fernandez was the guilty person in this case, even though the testimony involved proof of other crimes (*Fernandez* v. *U.S.*, 329 F. 2d 899 [1964], cert. den. 379 U.S. 832).

f. Use of Confessions Involving Other Crimes

An entirely different problem arises when the accused makes a confession in which he also admits to other crimes. The police are not going to stop his recital since it could be very useful. But what happens at the trial when the prosecutor attempts to offer this confession in evidence?

The defense counsel will, of course, object to the use of a confession that mentions crimes other than that for which the defendant is being tried. As we have seen, this is normally a valid objection. If possible, the confession will be redacted (which is the legal term for edited), and any mention of other crimes will be removed. Should the confession containing references to other crimes be allowed as evidence, the conviction will probably be set aside on appeal.

A murder case in Washington, D.C., involved just such a situation. Davis was found murdered in the hallway of a tourist home, having been shot in the chest. A witness had seen a man wearing dark trousers and a blue jacket with gold buttons near the premises. A detective noticed the similarity of dress on a man named Wiggins, who had been arrested later on another charge. He interrogated Wiggins at the station house, later in an unmarked police car, and in various locations around the city, asking him about the Davis murder. When they were riding in the police car, Wiggins began to talk. At the murder trial the officer testified about this conversation:

> "I don't know what you are going to think, but I killed Frank, and I don't know what you are going to think, but I killed Davis." He continued to talk and he told me there was a contract out for Davis' life and that he took it . . . that killing Davis didn't bother him but the fact that . . . he was looking at Davis face to face when he shot him bothered him . . . the contract was worth fifteen hundred dollars. He got five hundred dollars and was supposed to get the other one thousand. He mentioned that this wasn't the first time he had killed someone. He had killed three other people. He looked at me and said "You want to know their names don't you?" and I said "No." Then he stated "Well I'm not crazy. I kill only on contract."

The appeals court, noting the prejudicial effect of allowing proof of the other killings, pointed out that this material could have been excised without impairing the confession. Wiggins's murder conviction was reversed, and the case was sent back for retrial (*U.S.* v. *Wiggins*, 509 F. 2d 454 [1975]).

The law enforcement officer should always keep the Wiggins case in mind. If a suspect's confession includes references to other crimes he has committed, be sure that if the confession is put in writing, the additional crimes are included in one paragraph. That portion can then be omitted when the defendant comes to trial.

g. Confessions of Codefendants

There is an additional problem involving the use of confessions. When there are codefendants, the confession of one may implicate the other. But confessions can only be used to incriminate the person who has made the confession and not his accomplice.

If A and B are tried jointly, and the prosecution uses A's confession, which implicates both, B has no chance to defend himself against the accusation unless A testifies. If A does take the stand, then B's lawyer can cross-examine him concerning the matter that was in the confession. There is, however, no guarantee in most cases that A will testify in his own behalf. Therefore, unless the references to B can be omitted from A's confession, there will have to be separate trials for each defendant in order that the court can be certain that A's confession will be used only against A. At B's trial A's confession could not, of course, be used.

Recently several courts have met this co-defendant confession problem not by holding two separate trials but by ordering a joint trial with two juries, one for each defendant. When proof is offered concerning defendant A only, B's jury is temporarily excused from the courtroom. This temporary jury removal is done for both defendants. Separate verdicts are rendered, and the extra trial eliminated completely (*People* v. *Harris*, 255 Cal. Rptr. 352 [1989]).

(9.15) Weight of Evidence

During the course of a trial an objection may be made regarding the "weight of evidence," as opposed to its admissibility. For example, in a case of drunk driving the defense might object to the acceptability of the blood alcohol test as evidence because the blood sample was kept in the arresting officer's home overnight. The defense might claim that the sample was contaminated. A judge could well admit the test results in evidence for whatever they might be worth, holding that the irregular custody did not preclude the legal admissibility, but could only affect the "weight of the evidence," that is, its accuracy and believability.

Though courts and attorneys sometimes confuse the two terms, as long as evidence is legally admissible, it should be allowed for whatever value or weight the jury might assign to it.

(9.16) Circumstantial Evidence

Circumstantial evidence is indirect proof of a fact, that is, proof from which one can logically infer that a fact exists. The defendant's fingerprints from a burglarized store, bloodstains from the trunk of a murder suspect's car, and the sudden wealth of a bank teller suspected of theft are all examples of circumstantial evidence. None is direct proof of the crime, but each provides strong circumstantial evidence of guilt.

There is a popular misconception that circumstantial evidence should not be believed. All courts, in fact, carefully circumscribe its use. First of all, it cannot be too remote, and it must be logical and not mere conjecture. Circumstantial evidence cannot be used to draw "an inference from an inference," and it must be "clear and convincing." Accepted with these limitations, circumstantial evidence is often the most convincing type of proof there is.

We commonly use circumstantial evidence in our daily lives. Suppose, for example, Mother goes into the kitchen and finds Junior with crumbs on his face and the lid off the cookie jar. Junior, perceiving the danger, says, "I didn't do anything!" Whom is she going to believe—Junior or the circumstantial evidence? The evidence in our cookie case can be classified like that of any crime. If the mother were called on to testify, her recitation about the cookie crumbs would be direct evidence that her son had a dirty face, but it would be circumstantial evidence that he had taken the cookies from the jar and had eaten them.

Usually the only way to demonstrate a state of mind, intent, motive, or malice is by circumstantial evidence. Intoxication normally falls into this category since the proof may largely be a description of the individual's unsteady walk, slurred speech, or erratic driving.

A typical example of a crime proved entirely by circumstantial evidence was the conviction of one Wachowicz for attempted burglary. A tavern manager locked his doors and left the premises at 3:30 a.m. Sometime later a prowl car observed Wachowicz and another man near the tavern. As the police got out of the car, the defendant "made three or four quick steps" while his companion stuck something in his shirt that proved to be a pinch bar. Examination of the tavern showed one door partly pried open with the inside hooks pulled loose. There were jimmy marks on all the doors, and the pinch bar fitted the marks on the wood. Upon being questioned, neither man would admit a thing. Thus circumstantial evidence constituted the entire case against Wachowicz.

The defendant was convicted and appealed the decision. The appellate courts upheld the conviction, saying that the only reasonable conclusion that could be drawn from the evidence was that when the police arrived the defendant had just attempted to break into the tavern (*People* v. *Wachowicz*, 22 N.Y. 2d 369 [1968]).

The lesson a police officer should learn from this type of case is never give up just because your proof is entirely circumstantial. If logic is on your side, the jury and the court usually will be also.

It is plain, then, that both kinds of evidence—direct and circumstantial—are acceptable in court. There is no reason for anyone to refuse to accept circumstantial evidence in a criminal case as long as there are proper instructions from the court concerning its use.

(9.17) General Presumptions

What if the prosecutor had to prove that the judge was qualified and was legally elected or appointed, that the criminal statute involved had been properly passed by the legislature and signed by the governor, and that every defendant was sane? If the state were required to do all this, it might never get around to proving the crime itself. But all this and much more are eliminated by a variety of presumptions applicable to criminal cases. Some are presumptions of law and others of fact, but both materially affect the burden of proof.

Legal scholars argue whether something from which a jury can draw a conclusion is a "presumption" or an "inference." Though the modern trend is to use the latter term, the legal result is largely the same regardless of which is used.

Some presumptions are said to be "conclusive" and others "rebuttable." Strictly speaking, there cannot be a "conclusive presumption" in the sense that an opponent is precluded from showing any evidence to rebut it. A conclusive presumption is usually a rule of law. Examples might include the presumption that a child under a stated age cannot commit a felony or that a boy under fourteen is incapable of rape. It must be remembered that in the jurisdictions that have these rules they are actually laws. They are not rebuttable and must be accepted.

Several classes of genuine presumptions are recognized everywhere. They are discussed below.

a. Presumptions of Fact and Law

These presumptions generally are regarded as being the same as an inference. To be legally valid, however, there must be a reasonable connection between the fact proven and the ultimate conclusion inferred from it. The inference must flow naturally and logically from it. Otherwise the presumption will be ruled unconstitutional because it lacks due process of law. There have been a number of court decisions on this precise point.

One of the earliest landmark cases in the U.S. was *Yee Hem* v. *U.S.*, 268 U.S. 178 (1925). The federal law stated that illegal possession of opium gave rise to the presumption that it had been unlawfully imported. The court held that the statutory presumption was logical and therefore valid, on the ground that it was highly improbable that there could be a legitimate possession of opium outside the medical field. Thus, any possessor must know that the opium was illegally imported.

In 1969 the same court had to deal with a federal marijuana charge against Timothy Leary (*Timothy Leary* v. *U.S.*, 395 U.S. 6 [1969]). Customs agents found marijuana in Leary's car when he tried to cross from Mexico on the international bridge. The drug was on the person of his teenage daughter. A federal statute authorized a jury to infer from a defendant's possession of marijuana that it was illegally imported. The courts struck down this statute as unconstitutional, saying that since marijuana is grown in this country, there is no logical basis for stating that because a person has it he must "know" that it was imported.

The Supreme Court met the problem again in a case involving heroin and cocaine (*Turner* v. *U.S.*, 396 U.S. 398 [1970]). Turner and two other men were stopped by federal agents in New Jersey just as their car emerged from the Lincoln Tunnel. The agents saw Turner throw a package on top of a wall. It proved to be a foil-wrapped package of 1.468 grams mixture of cocaine. Under the car seat they discovered a tinfoil package of heroin. At the trial the government introduced both packages in evidence, but gave no other proof of where they came from.

A similar federal statute was involved. It stated that the possession of heroin and cocaine created a presumption that the possessor knew that the drugs were illegally imported. The court upheld the presumption concerning heroin, since it is not produced in this country, but struck down the law making the same presumption regarding cocaine. Because cocaine is manufactured here, a possessor cannot "know" that the drug was illegally imported.

The courts must deal with problems concerning presumption in areas other than drugs. An example was a federal statute involving the possession of a gun or ammunition by any person who had been convicted of a crime of violence or who was a fugitive from justice. It stated that if such an individual was found in possession of a gun or ammunition he could be presumed to have transported it in violation of the federal law governing interstate shipment of firearms. The decision was that there was no reasonable inference between such possession and illegal interstate transportation of guns. The statutory presumption was thus held to be unconstitutional.

A New Jersey statute at one time provided that if a person could not give a good account of himself, this was prima facie evidence that he was in New Jersey for an unlawful purpose. Further, anyone in the state for an unlawful purpose was guilty of disorderly conduct. The federal courts also struck down this law as being an illogical presumption. The fact that a person cannot give a good account of himself might conceivably mean that he is up to no particular good, but it is not reasonable to say that what he is up to must be "unlawful."

The state of Washington passed what might be considered a very convenient statute. It stated that if a defendant charged with a violent crime is armed with an unlicensed weapon, it is prima facie proof of his intent to commit such a crime of violence. A defendant named Odom left the state employment office, returned with a .44 caliber magnum (unlicensed), and shot the supervisor twice, leaving him permanently paralyzed. The appellate court, in reversing Odom's conviction, pointed out that a presumption created by statute must follow beyond a reasonable doubt from the first fact. You cannot· conclude that because a man has an unlicensed weapon he intends to do violence with it. The statute therefore lacked constitutional due process of law.

A teacher's oath case from Oklahoma involved a different type of presumption that was found to be unconstitutional. The statute required teachers to take an oath that they had never belonged to any organization listed by the U.S. attorney general as being subversive. The court ruled that under this statute the mere fact of membership would be a conclusive presumption of disloyalty. This, the court said, would be a violation of due process as set forth in the Fourteenth Amendment since membership in a Communist front organization might be innocent.

b. Presumption of Innocence

The presumption of innocence is perhaps the best-known presumption in English criminal law. Here, the jury must assume that the accused is innocent from the moment he enters the courtroom. This presumption stays with him through the entire trial and remains until, and only if, the prosecution overcomes the presumption by proof of guilt beyond a reasonable doubt. This presumption is surely the strongest we have that favors the defendant.

c. Presumption of Intent

Intent is a material element that the prosecution must prove in the majority of criminal cases. Did the youth really intend to steal the car, or did he simply take a joyride? When the janitor picked up the wallet from the washstand shelf in the airport men's room, did he intend to steal it, or are we to believe his story that he was going to turn it in at the airline desk? Intent is a mental operation. One cannot open a person's head, look inside, and determine his intentions. To meet this problem, the law has had a long-standing presumption that a person is presumed to intend the natural consequences of his voluntary acts. However, this rule can no longer be used in criminal trials. In *Sandstrom* v. *Montana*, 442 U.S. 501 (1979), the Supreme Court held that such a presumption would be unconstitutional in criminal cases as it would deprive the defendant of due process of law. (See also, *People* v. *Hester*, 544 N.E. 2d 797 [Ill. 1989].)

d. Knowledge of the Law

A general belief exists that everyone "is presumed to know the law." A more accurate way of putting it is that an accused may not claim ignorance of the law as a defense in order to escape punishment.

A common illustration of this concerns possession of a gun. A man from a state where a license is not required may drive into one where it is. He has a pistol on the seat of his car, which is perfectly legal in his home state but which is a serious crime in the new state. Even though he was completely ignorant of the requirement of a special license, this is no defense.

e. Failure to Testify

There is no presumption against an accused who fails to take the stand in his own defense. He is protected by the Fifth Amendment, and the Constitution "forbids either comment by the prosecution on the accused's silence or instructions by the court that such silence is evidence of guilt" (*Griffin* v. *California*, 380 U.S. 609 [1965]). On the contrary, where the defendant does take the stand (except in some limited situations such as pretrial hearings), he waives this constitutional privilege and may be completely cross-examined on any pertinent matter, the same as any other witness.

f. Nonproduction of Evidence

It may be inferred from the unexplained failure of a defendant to call an available witness who has a particular knowledge or to produce evidence within his control that the evidence would be unfavorable to the accused. There are, however, at least three conditions under which this inference will not be made: if the witness is equally available to both sides; if the witness has been subpoenaed, but fails to appear; or if the witness is hostile.

Even when the above conditions are met, the courts are cautious in allowing the inference and may give a narrow interpretation as to whether the witness is "available" or "under the control" of the party or whether he actually has a "particular knowledge" of the facts.

g. Character or Reputation

In criminal cases "character evidence" is a recognized and often effective defense. The most widely accepted view, however, is that there is no presumption one way or another as to whether the accused is of good or bad character.

Some jurisdictions do maintain that there is a presumption of good character. Whether the court rules that there is or is not such a presumption, the practical result at the trial is the same. First of all, the term character evidence is a misnomer. The prosecution cannot prove that the accused is a nasty character by demonstrating that he pulled wings off butterflies when he was a child and now runs nefarious errands for the Mafia. Neither can the defense show what a good character he is by having his minister testify that he goes to church every Sunday, gives generously to the United Fund, and is fond of dogs and little children.

Character evidence is, actually, the rankest kind of hearsay.

It reflects the reputation one has in his community, and it depends on the reputation for truthfulness of the person who is testifying.

Should the defense offer evidence of good character, the state may, in rebuttal, offer evidence of bad character if it has any.

(9.18) Official Presumptions

There are many official presumptions. They presume that official acts were performed properly, and they are rebuttable.

a. Legality of Proceedings

It is presumed that all past legal proceedings have been legally and properly carried out. The rule applies to courts, commissions, and all other legal bodies.

The state commonly uses this rule in prosecutions where the offense or punishment is more severe because of a prior conviction for a felony. The prosecution simply introduces the certificate of prior criminal conviction, and it is presumed to be legal. If the accused claims that the old conviction was improper, he has the burden to come forward and prove it.

A court hearing a criminal case is presumed to have been regularly constituted and to have jurisdiction over the defendant concerning the crime for which he is being tried. It is also presumed that the court's records and its warrants are correct.

An even wider application is involved where the accused claims a conviction or court judgment was unconstitutional under either the state or federal Constitution. Here, too, it is presumed that the judicial proceeding was constitutional. The objector has the burden of overcoming this presumption.

b. Acts of Officers and Officials

Similarly the acts of officers and officials in the performance of their duties are presumed to have been done legally and within the realm of their authority. Unless there is proof to the contrary, the acts of officers making court-authorized searches and seizures or in executing warrants are presumably legal. The same is true of arrests.

It is presumed that information on which an arrest and indictment are based has been legally secured by the officials involved.

This presumption of official legality applies to all officers and agents of the government. Included among them are the governor who forwards extradition papers, the postman who mails the requisition, the sheriff who serves the governor's warrant, the district attorney who conducts the hearing, and the officers who return the wanted man to the state demanding him.

There is also a presumption of the regularity of a judicial record, which includes the fact that the signature is genuine on a document having an official seal.

Even the posting of signs in municipal speed zones has been done regularly.

c. Legislative Acts

All laws, ordinances, and other legislative acts are presumed to have been validly adopted. Were this not so, the prosecution would have the ridiculous burden of proving the validity of every law involved in every criminal case, from the murder statute down to the evidentiary code. Thus, all federal, state, and local laws are presumed to be valid and binding.

d. Foreign Laws

In some criminal cases the law of a sister state or a foreign nation is involved. Proof can always be presented by testimony from a legal expert knowledgeable in the field or by the introduction of reference material. If such proof is absent, the court may presume that the foreign law involved is the same as that of the local jurisdiction. In some situations, however, the court may take official notice of what the foreign law may be.

(9.19) Presumptions Concerning Particular Acts

A variety of acts, which are discussed below, do not require special proof.

a. Use of the Mails

In the ordinary course of postal service any letter that has been properly addressed and mailed is presumed to have been received. This practical rule is universally adopted, not because the courts have some unwarranted confidence in the U.S. mail, but because the sender is not in a position to prove that the letter was received. The recipient must overcome the presumption of delivery, if he can.

b. Identity

Identity will ordinarily be presumed from the same name. The more unusual the name, the stronger the inference of identity. Thus, a record of conviction in the same name will be sufficient in some jurisdictions to establish the defendant's criminal history. In other courts it is taken as prima facie proof, but not enough standing alone to establish the record.

c. Continuing Fact or Condition

It is often difficult to prove the exact conditions that existed at the time of the crime. This is, for example, a common problem in cases of drunk driving. Witnesses may describe the individual's condition an hour before the arrest. A blood test may be taken a half hour after the accident, but what was the driver's actual condition at the time of the crash?

The victim of a rape or an assault may not be examined until the day following the crime. A sanity test may take place a week or many months after the offense occurred. Mental or physical condition at the time of the crime can be a vital issue.

The same is true of many other facts related to physical conditions. Police photographs may show road signs, highways, bridges, or buildings months or days before or after the event.

Medical testimony will often help to relate physical or mental conditions back to the time of the crime. Sometimes, however, there will only be evidence of a condition before or after the crime. In this situation the law of evidence comes up with a presumption: once a fact has been proven, the condition continues until proven otherwise.

A few states restrict the use of the rule when it is applied to criminal cases. As a general rule, however, evidence of a condition before or after the event is accepted on the common-sense ground that it was the same at the time of the crime. Once a thing has been proven, its existence is presumed to continue where that would normally happen in human experience.

The use of such evidence is largely left to the discretion of the trial judge. Its admissibility, and, of course, its weight, will be affected by how closely it is connected in time with the crime itself.

d. Sobriety, Normality, and Sanity

As has been said, the law assumes that everyone is sober, competent, and sane, unless, of course, there is evidence to the contrary.

To begin with, it is presumed that every accused is sober, since that is the normal course of human events. The presumption is refuted by evidence of intoxication.

The law further generalizes by presuming that individuals are normal, both physically and mentally. If a sex offender claims that he is mentally retarded, he must produce evidence of low intelligence.

Finally, the law presumes sanity. The definition of criminal insanity varies somewhat from state to state as modern psychiatry seeks to modify the law's relatively narrow view. The usual rule has been that if the accused was aware of his act and knew it was wrong, he was criminally responsible, regardless of any label of mental illness that the medical profession might attach to him. If insanity is a defense, the accused must offer proof of his insanity and thereby overcome the presumption that he is sane. In actual practice the presumption usually leads to a battle between opposing psychiatrists. This simply means that the psychiatrists for the defense testify first, they are contradicted by the prosecution's mental experts, and the jury makes up its own mind.

These factors relating to the defendant's mental and physical condition are peculiarly within his own knowledge. Thus it is only fair that he be the one required initially to offer proof of any abnormal condition where it is pertinent.

e. Suicide

Suicide is a most abnormal event, and so there is a legal presumption against it. Should suicide be a defense in a murder case, for example, the defendant, to overcome this presumption against suicide, must do so by offering what evidence he can to show that the victim did in fact kill himself.

f. Legitimacy

This is one of the strongest presumptions known to the law. The husband is presumed to be the father of any child born in wedlock. It occasionally is involved in criminal matters where the relationship is material. Family offenses or incest are examples that come to mind.

This presumption of legitimacy sometimes produces harsh results, but it is necessary. Otherwise, a husband could escape responsibility for his children simply by denying his parentage.

(9.20) Presumptions Indicating Guilt

If the evidence plausibly points toward guilt, it may be accepted. Such proof is, strictly speaking, not a presumption. It is circumstantial evidence from which an inference of guilt may be drawn.

a. Flight or Concealment

Suppose, for example, there is a bank robbery, and the police catch a suspect running down the street away from the bank. One might consider his flight as strong evidence of guilt. Or suppose the the police find a man hiding in a closet in an apartment where drugs have recently been purchased. Again, one could assume from the suspect's concealment that at least an inference could be made concerning evidence of guilt.

Though all courts desire to protect the accused from false charges, they differ somewhat on the value to be given evidence of flight or concealment before an arrest. Most courts, however, hold that neither raises a presumption or inference of guilt.

Courts will accept proof of flight or concealment, such as that of a suspect fleeing the city soon after a crime has been committed and then hiding out. These actions will be taken as some proof of guilt, although other reasons may be introduced to explain them

If you, as a police officer, ever become involved in prosecuting a charge with this type of circumstantial evidence, you should remember one rule. Proof of flight or concealment may be shown, but it is up to the jury to determine what value it has, without benefit of any presumption or inference. Juries have more common sense than they are often given credit for, and they are quite likely to take either of these actions as a strong indication of guilt.

b. False Statements

The prosecution can prove occasionally that the accused gave false statements, either in oral or written form. They may have evidence at other times that the defendant obtained false statements from third parties to support his defense. In either case an inference of guilt results.

c. Malice

In some cases actual malice is an element. The only possible way to prove this is by evidence of the facts and circumstances. The very nature of the crime itself may create a presumption that it was done maliciously, that is, with a deliberate attempt to harm or destroy. Assault with a deadly weapon is often cited as an example of this.

d. Possession of Fruits of Crime

The possession of the fruits of crime is by itself proof from which an inference of guilt may be drawn. Though the possession of stolen goods soon after a crime has been committed is not conclusive proof, that fact alone gives rise to a strong inference of guilt. Once the crime has been proven, the unexplained or falsely explained possession of stolen property, such as from burglary, robbery, or larceny, is generally said to give rise to a presumption of guilt.

When this type of proof is offered, defense counsel may argue that such a presumption has the effect of violating the defendant's rights under the Fifth Amendment. By giving this legal result to his possession, one is, in effect, making the defendant testify against himself. The defense made this claim in a recent case where one, Barnes, was accused of forging government checks. The government also offered evidence that he was found to possess recently stolen government checks payable to third persons. The court held that such evidence was proper. It ruled that one could presume from the unexplained possession of these checks that the defendant knew they were stolen. This was proven and was thus offered as circumstantial evidence of the forgery. The court said, furthermore, that this did not violate his Fifth Amendment right not to testify.

e. Possession and Ownership

Some presumptions regarding possession and ownership are widely accepted in civil law and occasionally come into play in some criminal cases. The general rule is that whatever is found in a person's possession is presumed to be his. Also, if a person exercises acts of ownership over property, there is a similar presumption that it is his.

f. Statutory Presumptions

The state and federal governments all have various statutes containing presumptions that arise from certain situations. Illustrations of this type were discussed in the cases listed earlier under "General Presumptions." Some other examples are statutes that presume that a pawnbroker has knowingly accepted stolen goods if he has made no reasonable inquiry as to the legal ownership; that presume that the presence of a weapon in an automobile is the possession of everyone in the car; and that presume that the presence of illegal drugs in a car or in a room in clear view is evidence of possession by all the occupants.

(9.21) Judicial Notice

There are some things that a court will accept as true without any proof. The judge does this by taking "judicial notice" of them without any introduction of evidence. Though this is an inherent power in all courts, in some jurisdictions its use may be somewhat restricted by statute (for example, California Evidence Code, Sec. 453). In addition, different judges have different ideas on the subject. Thus the wise police officer will find out in advance what the judge's attitude is on taking judicial notice. He will then know, for example, whether the court will take judicial notice that La Salle Street runs into Green Street or whether he will be required to testify to this fact.

It must be remembered that a judge can take judicial notice of matters of general knowledge, not of something that he may be acquainted with. He may, for instance, be personally aware of the fact that there is a stoplight in front of a certain station house, but cannot, without proof, take judicial notice of it at a trial.

a. Judicial Notice of Facts

Facts that are so universally known that they cannot reasonably be the subject of dispute will generally be recognized by judicial notice. When this is the case, it is not necessary to introduce an almanac or an encyclopedia in evidence. Matters of common knowledge, natural phenomena, history, language, and geography fall into this category. No one, for example, has to offer proof that water freezes or objects fall.

Scientific phenomena are often recognized by judicial notice. In recent years, for instance, courts have taken judicial notice of the validity and accuracy of radar. It is only necessary to prove the accuracy of the particular apparatus used in the case.

Matters of geography are commonly accepted in this way. As an illustration, one court took judicial notice the tide affects the San Joaquin River past the port of Stockton.

In the realm of language even "street talk" has been judicially noticed. Thus, in a drug case in California the court took judicial notice that the term "reds" means capsules of Seconal®.

One judge aptly stated the rule concerning the judicial notice of facts in *AhKow* v. *Nunan*, 5 Sawy. 552: "We cannot shut our eyes to matters of public notoriety and general cognizance. When we take our seats on the bench, we are not struck with blindness and forbidden to know as judges what we all see as men."

b. Judicial Notice of Laws

Without exception, every court takes judicial notice of treaties between the United States and foreign countries, including official interpretation of these treaties. Courts even take judicial notice of the absence of treaties such as those concerned with extradition.

They also take judicial notice of the laws within their jurisdiction, even if the attorneys forget to mention one. Courts above the municipal level are sometimes fussy about taking judicial notice of municipal ordinances. They may require proof of their existence, but will allow the presumption that they were validly enacted. In addition, official regulations, such as sanitary codes and rules governing the income tax, are judicially recognized since they have the force of law.

Courts generally do not take judicial notice of foreign laws since they are beyond their field of knowledge. A number of states, however, judicially recognize the laws of sister states.

In regard to judicial records, a court always takes judicial notice of its proceedings, but not those of other courts. Official records of the latter must be introduced in evidence.

(9.22) Summary

Much that the police gather as "evidence" cannot legally be used in court. It is necessary, therefore, that every law enforcement officer have a basic knowledge of the law of criminal evidence.

Evidence is any matter offered in court to prove the truth or falsity of a fact in issue. There are two general classes of evidence— direct and circumstantial. Direct evidence is proof from a witness's five senses that in itself is proof of the fact in issue. Circumstantial evidence is indirect proof from which one can logically infer the ultimate facts in issue.

There are two sources of the law of evidence. One is the common law, which is based on past court decisions. The other is found in individual statutes or in evidentiary codes. Both must be consulted in order to learn the laws in any one jurisdiction. Though the law of evidence varies from state to state, the basic rules are the same in all of our courts.

The defendant in every criminal case is presumed to be innocent. Because the accused is protected by the Fifth Amendment, he cannot be made to testify. And he is not required to prove anything. The prosecution must overcome this presumption of innocence by proving the guilt of the defendant beyond a reasonable doubt.

The state attempts to prove initially a prima facie case, that is, proof of guilt "at first view." It has the burden in every criminal trial of proving the corpus delicti—the fact that a crime was committed. If some affirmative defense is to be used, such as insanity, alibi, or duress, the accused must introduce this proof. Even if the accused employs an affirmative defense, however, it is generally accepted that the state must still prove guilt beyond a reasonable doubt. This burden, in fact, never shifts.

Evidence is of no value unless it can be used in court. To be admissible it must be relevant, and even then it must pass a variety of other tests.

Evidence of other crimes committed by the accused may be offered by the prosecution. Courts restrict its use, however, because of possible undue prejudice toward the defendant. Such proof is limited to proving motive, intent, identity, absence of mistake, or a common scheme or plan.

Motive and intent are terms that are easily confused. Motive is the reason for the crime. Intent is the conscious purpose to commit the criminal act.

Confessions containing reference to other crimes raise difficulties in the trial. Often the only way such a confession can be admitted in evidence is if the recitals of other crimes can be removed.

There are a number of legal presumptions or inferences. Some of the well-recognized ones are the presumption of innocence; the presumption that a person intends the normal consequences of his actions; and the negative presumption against a litigant resulting from the nonproduction of evidence that is within his control.

In order for a presumption to be constitutionally valid, there must be a logical connection between the initial fact proven and the conclusion drawn therefrom.

There exist several official presumptions: that past legal proceedings are valid; that officials have acted legally in performing their duties; that laws were properly adopted.

Some presumptions apply to particular situations—that mail has been received; that a proven fact has continued to exist; that persons with the same name are the same. Sanity, normality, and sobriety are presumed. There is a strong presumption against suicide. Finally, the husband is the presumed father of children born in wedlock.

There are presumptions of guilt. The giving of false statements or possession of the fruits of crime are examples. Flight or concealment, while not labeled a presumption of guilt by many courts, is accepted as circumstantial evidence against the accused.

Courts will often take judicial notice of generally known facts of geography, history, or science, thus bypassing the necessity of proof. Judicial notice will also be taken of the laws of the forum or of a court's own proceedings.

Discussion Questions

1. Discuss the evolution of evidence rules.
2. Distinguish between "preponderance of evidence" and "beyond a reasonable doubt."
3. How is relevancy different from admissibility?
4. Discuss the rationale behind the judicial notice doctrine.
5. Discuss "burden of proof."

10

Examination of Witnesses

There is nothing so powerful as truth and often nothing so strange.

—Daniel Webster
from trial argument, April 6, 1830

A. GENERAL EXAMINATION OF WITNESSES

(10.1) In General

Witnesses testify first by being questioned by the attorney who called them and then by being cross-examined by opposing counsel. This is often followed by a further brief redirect examination by the first attorney and then a recross-examination by the second.

This order is sometimes varied by allowing opposing counsel a preliminary cross-examination on some evidentiary point before the direct questioning is completed. There are rare occasions when a witness, hostile to both parties, is needed. Under these peculiar and infrequent circumstances, the court may call such a witness, who is subject to cross-examination by both lawyers.

Testimony is thus produced by questions asked by attorneys and answers produced by witnesses. Sometimes, in the interest of justice or for the sake of clarity, the court may intervene and question the witness. This is quite proper as long as the judge does not indicate his own opinion, does not take the examination out of counsel's hands, and does not himself ask improper questions over the objections of counsel. A juror may wish to question a witness, but the courts are divided on its propriety. The danger is that an improper question may be asked. Trial courts that permit the practice are most cautious in its use.

All testimony is ordinarily given under oath. Rules on the method of administering the oath are not uniform, but, where a witness has scruples against taking the oath because of its religious connotations, he will normally be allowed to "affirm" to tell the truth without using a Bible. Some courts allow children or incompetents to testify without taking an oath because they do not understand its meaning.

In an administrative disciplinary hearing, the witnesses involved were two inmates of a mental hospital who had IQ's of 43 and 50. A psychologist testified that both knew the difference between the truth and lying. The hearing examiner determined that an oath would be meaningless to them and let them testify unsworn. The appellate court approved of their testifying without an oath, saying that a proper foundation had been laid for it.

A subpoenaed witness receives a small fee allowed by law. Expert witnesses, such as engineers, doctors, and the like are normally paid for their services by the party calling them. It is against public policy for any other witness to be reimbursed in any way.

(10.2) Attendance

Some witnesses appear voluntarily. This would be the usual case with police officers. Others are summoned by subpoena, which is, in effect, a court order issued by the judge, court clerk, or attorney, directing the witness to appear in court at a specified time and place. A subpoena in a state court has no legal effect outside the court's jurisdiction, which usually means within the state. There is a uniform act that provides a way of subpoenaing in criminal cases material witnesses from another state. Federal court subpoenas are not barred by state boundaries. Material witnesses in criminal matters can, in some circumstances, be confined by court order pending trial, thus assuring their appearance when needed.

One can attempt to obtain relief against an improper subpoena by a motion to quash, and this motion will sometimes be granted. Anyone who has material evidence can, however, be compelled to testify, regardless of the inconvenience to the person subpoenaed.

a. Subpoena Duces Tecum

A subpoena duces tecum requires that an individual produce such evidence as documents, books, and so forth. The person who is so subpoenaed must comply by presenting the material in court or sending an employee or other representative who can identify the material. Privileged matter such as doctor-patient records or attorney-client communications cannot, however, be obtained in this way. The protection of privileged material is thus maintained.

A public official cannot be forced to bring a document into court when counsel or the court can easily obtain an official copy.

A problem often arises when incriminating documents are subpoenaed. A defendant cannot be forced to produce incriminating evidence in his possession since this would clearly violate his protection against self-incrimination.

But how about a *witness* who is subpoenaed to bring in incriminating material? A case in point is the following. A grand jury was investigating a criminal charge, and a witness, Ballmann, was subpoenaed to bring in his cashbook, wherein his name apparently was listed with some money transactions. He refused to honor the subpoena, claiming that he could be incriminated in a "bucket shop" gambling charge. The lower court held him in contempt. The U.S. Supreme Court reversed the decision, stating that Ballmann was constitutionally protected and could not be made to produce incriminating evidence by means of a subpoena duces tecum even though it was necessary for the grand jury's investigation.

The situation differs if the incriminating material is in the hands of a third party who is not involved in any possible criminal activity. In the case of *Couch* v. *U.S.*, 409 U.S. 322 (1973), the Internal Revenue Service subpoenaed the taxpayer's income tax records that he had given to an accountant. When the accountant was subpoenaed, he gave the records to the taxpayer's attorney. A possible crime in relation to income tax was involved. Thus, the claim of possible self-incrimination was made. A federal court found that the accountant was not the taxpayer's employee, refused to honor the last-minute transfer of the records to the attorney, and ruled that the claim of self-incrimination was personal to the accused and held that the accountant could not, therefore, raise it.

Once a subpoena duces tecum is issued, the witness may resort to one of two tactics. He can ask for a protection order, or he can move in court to have the subpoena quashed. The court must then decide if there is any valid reason why the evidence should not be produced. This was the point in question concerning the Nixon tapes, and the courts decided against the President. He made no move to claim the constitutional protection against self-incrimination, and thus his resignation followed.

b. Duty to Testify

It is every person's duty to respond to either kind of subpoena, no matter how inconvenient that might be. Once the subpoena is served, and the witness receives the fee prescribed by law, it is his legal duty to testify. One can only escape by getting court relief in the manner described above. Failure to testify is contempt of court and can result in a fine or imprisonment in some cases. Even the advice of counsel is no excuse for failing to answer the subpoena.

(10.3) Competency of Witnesses

Not every person is legally competent to testify. Age, mental capacity, or other factors may be reasons for disqualification.

a. Children

The trial judge usually makes the decision as to whether children can testify. Some states have statutes that stipulate at what age a child must testify under oath, with younger ones being allowed to testify unsworn if they do not understand the meaning of the oath. If a possible child witness does not understand an oath, it is legal to instruct him about this before he enters the courtroom or in the court itself.

No general rule defines a particular age at which a child is legally capable of testifying. A four-year-old child has, for example, been allowed to testify in a murder case.

In addition to the usual problems that may be involved in using a child as a witness, there is a particular one when a child is connected with a sex crime. Appellate courts are, for some reason, skeptical of the testimony of children concerning sex offenses and will often require corroborating testimony before sustaining a charge of rape or perversion. Because such offenses invariably occur in private, the criminal investigator has real difficulty in obtaining corroboration of the child victim's story. For this reason, many child molesters go unpunished. It is ironic, however, that practicing attorneys, police, and experienced court personnel will believe a child witness rather than an adult avoiding the truth. This practical evidentiary problem in child sex cases is found in all areas where appellate courts take this negative attitude toward the testimony of children involved in sex crimes.

b. Mental Incapacity

Often the only witness may be ignorant, illiterate, mentally retarded, or insane. Such a witness is not barred absolutely from testifying. If he understands an oath and can present a reasonable account, the court will normally allow him to testify. As has been discussed, this has even occurred when the mental ability of the witness was so low that he could not understand the oath. Unless there is a statutory bar against it, even a lunatic may be allowed to testify if he can give an account of events.

A seventeen-year-old boy was found shot to death in the basement of an ice cream parlor. The store manager confessed that he and Krombholz killed the boy because he had been stealing from the till, and the owner of the store told them to do so. Krombholz was a witness for the prosecution. Both defendants were convicted of murder, and the store manager was sentenced to death. After the trial, a mental examination revealed that Krombholz had a long history of mental illness, and he was committed to a hospital for the insane. The court pointed out that even though the witness was mentally ill, that condition did not "per se disqualify him from testifying. He may give evidence provided only that he has sufficient intelligence to understand . . . an oath and give a reasonable accurate account of the subject." A new trial was ordered, however, because his mental condition was not revealed to the judge and jury at the first trial.

A trial in 1845 illustrates the lengths to which courts can go to allow the handicapped to testify. The defendant was convicted of a rape committed upon the person of Mary Marshall. She was then an inmate of the county poorhouse, "about thirty years of age and of imbecile understanding. One witness considered her an idiot." The act occurred in a woods near the highway. Triskett, the poorhouse keeper, found her shortly after the crime. He testified that, although Mary could not talk, "she communicates her ideas by signs" and that he had no difficulty communicating with her. Triskett stated that "her face was bloody and her clothes soiled." When he asked her what had happened, she told him by signs "that she had been violated." The court, in reviewing the trial, found that it was improper for Triskett to have testified for her and said that there was no reason why Mary herself should not have testified "to give evidence through the medium of this witness as an interpreter by signs."

The trend today is to let incapacitated witnesses testify for whatever their testimony may be worth. Even a witness who is under the influence of drugs or alcohol is not incompetent to testify. Whether he testifies is determined by the court. The jury's function is to weigh such testimony.

c. Convicts

In early English common law a person convicted of a serious crime was thereafter completely barred from being a witness. The theory was that such a person was so depraved as to be unworthy of belief. The modern rule is different. Under it, a criminal conviction does not make a witness incompetent to testify. It is up to the jury to judge his truthfulness and accuracy, taking this factor into consideration along with all others. A few areas, however, retain the rule barring testimony by convicts, and some jurisdictions forbid testimony by individuals convicted of specific crimes, such as perjury.

d. Relationships

The relationship of the witness to the individual involved in a crime does not bar his testimony. An exception to this rule is the marital privilege, by which one spouse can prevent the other from testifying in court against him. A blood relative, close associate, or friend may be a witness. The owner of the stolen goods that are involved in the case may testify in a larceny prosecution. A witness who will receive a reward should a defendant be convicted is even allowed to testify. None of these relationships to the crime or the suspect disqualify the witness. It is his believability, not the legality of what he says, that is important.

e. Unsworn Testimony

As has been mentioned, children or witnesses unable to understand an oath may be allowed in some cases to testify without being sworn. The proposed witness may occasionally be an atheist and therefore object to taking an oath. In addition, some religious sects reject the idea of oaths. The court allows these individuals to "affirm to tell the truth" without using a Bible.

f. Miscellaneous

A particular set of circumstances can disqualify a witness or nullify his testimony. An example follows.

Chicago police entered Albea's apartment and found a girl, Lee Vaughn, buying heroin from him. The subsequent search, and seizure of the drugs, was declared illegal by the court. At Albea's trial, the prosecution had the girl testify only in regard to the events in the apartment before the entry of the police. She stated that she was an addict and had gone to Albea's apartment because she wanted "ten things" (heroin capsules). She paid Albea $12.50, and as he handed her three capsules there was a knock on the door accompanied by a voice that said "Western Union." At that point, Albea swallowed the other seven capsules. Though he was convicted of selling drugs, his conviction was overturned. The court ruled that the discovery of the girl witness was the product of an illegal search and that she was incompetent to testify to anything, even events preceding the entry.

A second unusual situation excluding a witness, which is popularly known as the "dead man's statute," exists in many states. These statutes bar a witness who is interested in the outcome from testifying against the estate of a deceased person concerning a personal transaction the witness had with the deceased. The reasoning behind these statutes is simple. Because the dead man cannot deny the transaction, an interested party should not be allowed to give testimony in regard to it. This situation frequently disqualifies a witness in civil suits, though it is highly unlikely that the rule could ever be involved in a criminal trial.

(10.4) Adversary System versus Inquisitorial System

In this country the adversary criminal trial system is used. This system calls for evidence to be produced by two opposing sides, with all witnesses subject to cross-questioning by opposing counsel. The inquisitorial system, which is used in other parts of the world, is quite different. There, the prosecution proves its case by asking questions of the accused, as well as by producing any other witnesses it can find. The defendant is thus forced to defend himself in court by answering the state's questions. The adversary system completely rejects this idea. Here, we have gone so far in the other direction that we protect the accused from having to testify at all.

(10.5) Form of Questions and Duty to Object

All testimony is given in the form of questions and answers. The witness is not allowed to testify in a block by giving a general narrative of events. He presents his story piecemeal in answer to questions. In terms of brevity and clarity this is a handicap, but it is necessary so that no evidence will come out unless it is valid.

Questions should seek testimony based on the facts known by the witness. The answers sought should be factual, not based on the witness' "understanding" of what happened. Questions should be clear. A compound question containing more than one part is improper. A question may not be so general as to include illegal evidence, and it must not be misleading, ambiguous, or indefinite. Any question that does not fit this description is legally objectionable.

In the adversary system, opposing counsel has the opportunity to make legal objection to the question being asked or to the answer being sought. This method thus prevents the introduction of improper evidence. If, however, opposing counsel does not object, any evidence may be used, even though it may be completely irrelevant or invalid.

(10.6) Leading Questions

This type of question suggests the answer, often leaving the witness simply to reply "Yes" or "No." In theory at least, lawyers are not supposed to put answers in the mouths of their own witnesses. Though leading questions will be allowed in preliminary testimony, opposing counsel may properly object to them when the material part of the testimony is reached.

Counsel may ask such preliminary leading questions as "You are Mary Jones?" "You live at 51 Main Street?" "You were home at 10:00 p.m.?" The objection to counsel's asking a leading question would arise if he then queried: "Did the defendant break down your kitchen door and attack you?" Proper questioning would proceed along the following lines. Counsel would call the witness' attention to the critical time and place. He might then ask: "What happened first?" "Then what happened?" "What finally happened?"

Cross-examination introduces an entirely different situation. Counsel is here seeking to test an adversary witness for truth and accuracy. Leading questions are quite proper, and the witness may be led in any direction and to any degree. As a matter of fact, should counsel's own witness prove hostile, he is allowed to ask him leading questions. Counsel can also ask his own witness leading questions when he is in the realm of delicate matters in sex cases, when he is dealing with an immature or incapacitated witness, or when he is attempting to refresh the witness' memory. Leading questions are also generally permissible when counsel is asking about matters that have already been testified to.

(10.7) Assumption of Facts

A question may not assume facts that have not been introduced in evidence. The reason for this is readily apparent. If unproven assumptions are used in questions, both the witness and the jury may be misled. This tactic may, however, be allowed at the court's discretion. Thus, neither on direct examination nor on cross-examination may the questioner misstate the facts or assume something in his question that is not a part of the evidence. Opposing counsel can object to any such question.

(10.8) Argumentative Questions

Lawyers are supposed to question witnesses, not argue with them, although that frequently happens. More leeway is allowed in this area in cross-examination than in direct examination, but it is technically incorrect in both types of examination. Where the question really amounts to arguing with the witness, it is properly objectionable.

(10.9) Asking for Conclusions or Opinions

With a few exceptions, the witness is supposed to confine his testimony to facts, to things that he has personally observed. He is not supposed to give his opinion or conclusion about the case. If this were not so, a trial could be decided by a parade of witnesses on both sides saying what they thought about the defendant's guilt or innocence.

There are, however, several areas involving matters of common observation where lay witnesses are allowed to make estimates or to state an opinion.

In a robbery trial, the defendant claimed that there was no forceful taking of money, but that he had swindled the complainant. His counsel called a defense witness who testified that the complainant told her: "Your friend [the defendant] beat me." The witness then offered to explain that in street talk the term "beat" meant to steal or to defraud rather than physical assault. The trial court refused to accept the explanation, saying it was opinion. The reviewing court disagreed, reversed the conviction, and held that a lay witness can give his opinion as to the meaning of a statement when the words have a doubtful or ambiguous meaning.

Often it is not readily apparent that a question is really calling for a conclusion. For example, an assault victim may be asked: "Did the defendant threaten you?" The question can be properly objected to as calling for a conclusion. To avoid the objection the examiner should draw the witness' attention to the relevant time and place and then ask a series of questions. "What did the defendant do?" "Then what did he do next?" "What did he finally do?" In this way he gets a detailed description of all the actions.

The jury—not the witness—draws a conclusion as to what actually happened. They must decide if the actions of the accused amounted to a threat. When opinion evidence is allowed in any case, either from laymen or experts, the jury is not bound by it. They may reject it or accept it as they wish.

Experts are, of course, allowed to state their opinions. As a matter of fact, the purpose of calling an expert is to get his professional or scientific judgment on a matter outside the realm of common experience. Physicians, engineers, and laboratory technicians are common examples of expert witnesses.

(10.10) Improper Foundation

In a courtroom one may hear an objection to a question on the basis of "improper foundation," and the objection is often sustained, much to the surprise of the uninformed. What usually happens is that a question is asked prematurely or facts are included that have not yet been proven. For example, a question may be asked regarding an exhibit, such as a confession or a photograph, before the exhibit has been admitted in evidence; thus the question lacks a proper foundation. In order to make the question proper, counsel must have the exhibit introduced in evidence or bring out the needed basic facts before he asks it again.

In fact, the physical exhibit itself cannot be introduced without "laying a proper foundation," that is, without proving its relevance, authenticity, and sameness of condition.

(10.11) Parol Evidence Rule

"Parol" is a short way of saying "word of mouth." The parol evidence rule is one saying that, with few exceptions, a written document is what it says it is. For example, ambiguities in documents, such as technical or trade terms, may be explained by verbal evidence. The law will not normally allow oral proof to take precedence over written proof, however, for the spoken word vanishes with the wind, while the written word remains.

Because this rule has little application in criminal trials, it need not be discussed in detail here. It is mentioned only because of its general application in all court proceedings.

(10.12) Self-Serving Declarations

The counsel for the defense is not allowed to introduce in evidence his client's statements demonstrating his innocence. The defendant could write letters in which he declares his innocence to his congressman, the governor, the President, and the newspapers and publicly proclaim his innocence on television. But none of these things has evidentiary value.

Only if a person admits something against his interest can any validity be attached to it. People usually do not make derogatory statements about themselves unless they are true. For this reason, a voluntary confession of a crime is considered the strongest type of evidence against an accused. On the other hand, personal protestations of innocence are regarded simply as manifestations of self-preservation, and so are not admissible as evidence in one's own defense.

Some textbook writers and judges have criticized this blanket ban against the use of self-serving statements as being too broad. It is possible, therefore, to find court rulings in which a defendant has been allowed to show that he made statements indicating lack of motive or interest, demonstrating goodwill toward the victim, or proving that there was a plan not to perform an act.

(10.13) Facts Not in Issue

Except for introductory questions to show the background of a witness, all questioning should be material to the issue at hand. If it does not relate to a fact at issue, it is subject to the objection of being immaterial. The trial judge usually determines whether the facts are indeed material.

A line of questioning that seems irrelevant will sometimes be allowed "subject to being connected up." Should the later testimony actually tie the earlier testimony to the case, the latter will be allowed to stand. If not, the court will order the prior testimony stricken from the record and will instruct the jury to disregard it.

As has been said, there is no set of rules to define what is material for the facts at issue. It is actually a matter of common sense, and so the same standards do apply in judging whether a question involves a fact at issue in any particular case.

B. ANSWERS OF WITNESSES

(10.14) In General

A witness' answers should be exactly that—answers. If he digresses, he runs the risk of introducing illegal evidence that could result in a mistrial. He may, however, feel that he should say something that is not a direct answer to the query. In this case, the proper procedure is for the witness to ask the court if he may say something or to ask to step down and confer briefly with counsel before answering.

(10.15) Unresponsive or Improper Answers

The question may be perfectly legal, but the answer may not be. An objection can, therefore, be made to the latter. The witness may, for example, argue, give an unsolicited opinion, or volunteer added information. Opposing counsel can object even after such an answer is given and ask that it be stricken from the record. The court will then order the answer to be expunged and instruct the jury to ignore it.

An example of an improper answer occurred in a larceny trial where the witness committing the legal sin was, of all things, an attorney-accountant appearing on the stand for the prosecution. It was claimed that the accused had defrauded Mrs. Bates of her stock and its proceeds. The above-mentioned witness was asked: "Did you examine the books . . . with reference to Wanita B. Bates' account?" To this the witness replied: "That was one of the various larcenies discovered." The defense attorney promptly called for a mistrial, but the trial judge denied the motion. The appellate court, however, held that the answer was unresponsive and highly prejudicial and therefore ordered a new trial.

Answers of this kind are as improper as questions of the same type and are always subject to being stricken from the record.

(10.16) Revival of Memory

Witnesses forget, just as the rest of us do. This is especially true in criminal matters where the normal procedure delays considerably the time of the trial from the original date of the crime. The most effective way of solving this problem is for the attorneys to ask leading questions. For example, a witness who cannot recall a date might be asked: "Wasn't it in the winter?" "Do you remember telling me that it was shortly before the end of the school vacation?" Though these questions are leading, they are an acceptable way of refreshing a witness' memory. Another way of jogging a person's memory is to refer to prior statements, testimony, or written memorandums.

(10.17) Past Recollections Recorded

There are times when leading questions, statements, or memorandums do not revive a lost memory. In that case there may still be a valid evidentiary method to produce the needed evidence. If the witness has a written record of the facts that he made shortly after the event, that record may be introduced in evidence as a "past recollection recorded." The witness is shown his own written memorandum, and if, after reading it, he still has no independent recollection of the event, the memorandum may be used as evidence. Though this may sound implausible, it does sometimes happen.

(10.18) Witness's Use of Memorandum or Record

Doctors, businessmen, police officers, and many others in this xerographic age keep a wide variety of written records and memorandums. We are not concerned at this point with how such records can be used against a witness, but with the way the individual who is testifying can use his written records to strengthen his testimony.

He cannot, of course, offer his prior written record to support what he is now saying. As we have seen, this would be self-serving testimony. Neither can he present a diary entry or police reports that say: "Here is what happened. It's all in my record." It is not possible for opposing counsel to cross-examine a piece of paper.

A witness can legitimately use his memorandums to refresh

his memory. Doctors, laboratory technicians, and other expert witnesses could not be expected to recall independently detailed information in individual cases. Such witnesses repeatedly jog their memories by looking at their notes. They are not ordinarily allowed to read directly from these memorandums, but use them only as an aid to memory. It is even more common for the witness to review his memorandums, statements, and records outside the courtroom just before testifying. This is, as a matter of fact, a legitimate and proper way to prepare for giving testimony.

(10.19) Inspection

When a witness uses a written record to aid his testimony, opposing counsel is entitled to inspect that record. The modern trend is to carry this rule further. Even when the witness testifies without using his earlier written records, his counsel is expected to make them available to opposing counsel. The following is typical of this rule.

Rosario and two others were involved in a robbery-murder of a restaurant proprietor. At Rosario's murder trial, one witness testified that Rosario, with his gun in hand, ordered him "into the lavatory." Another witness stated that she was later given the gun. A third witness told how Rosario admitted "shooting" and said, "We all had guns and shot together." As each witness finished his direct testimony, the defense counsel demanded copies of the statements each had given to the prosecutors prior to the trial so that he could use them in cross-examination. The trial judge allowed defense counsel to use only that part of the witnesses' statements that varied from their direct testimony. The appellate court reversed the judge's decision, asserting that defense counsel should be given copies of the complete pretrial statements of any witness even though they were not used as such in the trial.

Police officers or private investigators should be particularly careful about written reports. A faulty one can lose a case. The example of Officer Dwyer is a case in point. This officer monitored telephone taps during an investigation of ticket scalping. He made shorthand notes of the messages, transcribed them into longhand, and then dictated the material to a court clerk who put it all into a criminal complaint.

Officer Dwyer had previously appeared in court and had been subjected to a long, detailed cross-examination concerning his notes. Because of that, he deliberately destroyed all of his original records in the case of ticket scalping. At the trial, Dwyer stated that he had no memory of these calls and admitted destroying his original notes, but said he could testify by using the complaint he had dictated to the clerk. The appellate courts ruled against this, holding that, where the destruction of records was deliberate, the witness could not use any other record as an aid to his memory. Thus, the case was lost.

And so, any witness in modern criminal trials can expect that opposing counsel will see any personal records he uses in testifying. Further, it is likely that the court will allow inspection of any memorandum or records a witness has made prior to his actual testimony.

C. IMPEACHMENT OF WITNESSES

(10.20) Purpose

The purpose of impeaching (discrediting) an adverse witness is to weaken the case of the opposing side, and it is always proper for opposing counsel to use this tactic. He may do so by showing that the witness was inaccurate, untruthful, or unworthy of belief. The most common method of demonstrating the weakness of the witness is to cross-examine him. In some situations, counsel may even be allowed to present affirmative proof that tends to throw doubt on the witness' credibility.

(10.21) Complainants and Defendants

It is obvious that both the complainant and the accused are interested in the outcome of the trial. A complainant in a rape case or the victim of a mugging naturally wants to see the defendant convicted, and every defendant is interested in acquittal.

Because both parties are concerned with the outcome, the jury may consider this as one of the factors affecting their credibility as witnesses. It is legal for the attorneys to bring out such self-interest. This may be done by questioning the witness and by presenting legal arguments to the jury. Both methods are intended to impeach the witness. Such witnesses are also subject to the methods of impeachment discussed below.

(10.22) Competency

Evidence of the witness' lack of normal mental capacity may always be shown by way of impeachment. If a child testifies, for example, his age, his progress in school, and his intelligence as demonstrated by test scores can be scrutinized. Proof of mental retardation, senility, or insanity may also be presented in order to discredit a witness.

(10.23) Bias and Prejudice

Evidence tending to show bias or prejudice on the part of a witness is always relevant and can be introduced, even where the witness has denied it. A number of factors may indicate bias. The opposing attorney may show, for example, that the witness was an accomplice, a friend, or an enemy of either the defendant or complainant. He could also be related by blood or marriage. Any financial or business relationship is relevant. Immoral relations between the witness and one of the parties have a bearing on impeachment. The fact that a witness is a private detective hired by one party could easily bring about a charge of bias.

(10.24) Accuracy of Direct Testimony

The most common method of impeachment is to demonstrate any inaccuracies in a witness' direct testimony. A cross-examiner invariably questions the witness on the minute details of his story. He might ask what time the witness heard a shot. If his answer varies from what he stated in direct testimony, the attorney will forcefully point this out, thus discrediting the witness. It is safe to say, however, that no witness remembers the past exactly, and all observers see things in different ways. But, regardless of the problems involved, bringing out inaccuracies and misstatements is a fair way to attempt to discredit a witness. Juries are affected by the tactic, which is, after all, the reason why trial lawyers use it.

(10.25) Conviction of a Crime

It has been the general rule that a witness could be impeached by asking him about any criminal act of his past life. He could be cross-examined concerning the details of such criminal activity as rape, robbery, or burglary as well as the fact of his conviction for that offense. The universal limit on such questioning for purposes of impeachment is that counsel must have a fair basis for doing so. Every witness automatically presents himself as being worthy of belief. This is the justification for the general rule that any immoral or vicious act in his past life should be allowed to be shown as affecting his credibility.

In some states the field of impeachment is narrowed considerably. California law, for example, restricts cross-examination to the details of offenses that were mentioned on direct testimony. A few states limit impeachment questioning to felony convictions and will not allow inquiries into juvenile adjudications or misdemeanors. All courts bar questions regarding arrests or indictments since they do not involve convictions.

If a defendant takes the stand in his own behalf, he is subject to cross-examination just as any other witness. He can usually be asked about prior criminal convictions within the limitations established by the state in which he is being tried. Should he deny the past conviction, the prosecutor may offer a certificate of that conviction as impeachment evidence.

The attitude of the court toward the use of criminal records as impeachment testimony is currently undergoing change. The new Federal Rules of Evidence (Rule 609) restrict the use of criminal records to impeach any witness, including a defendant. Barred are the use of convictions over ten years old, juvenile adjudications, misdemeanors, and felony convictions that have been pardoned or granted certificates of rehabilitation. Even felony convictions that are not barred can be excluded as impeachment evidence against the defendant under the federal code. This occurs if the court feels that damage to the accused is greater than the value it might have for the case.

Various court decisions have approved of a procedure whereby defense counsel asks for a ruling in advance of the trial as to which prior criminal conviction can be introduced in evidence. The judge weighs the theoretical prejudice against the defendant the and "probative value" of such evidence and decides which record of convictions, if any, can be used. On the basis of this decision, the defendant with a criminal record can determine in advance of the trial whether or not he wants to take the stand.

In all likelihood this trend toward eliminating criminal records for the purpose of impeachment will continue. It is imperative, therefore, that anyone involved in law enforcement keep informed of statutes and current judicial decisions in this field.

(10.26) Drug Use

With the widespread use of drugs, all the way from tranquilizers to heroin, there is an increasing problem with witnesses. Evidence of drug addiction usually impeaches a witness. Some older decisions refuse to allow this evidence to discredit a witness, but the current majority rule is that it may do so. There is, in fact, general agreement that the effect of drugs on a participant at the time of trial can and should be shown, even though it may not be done for the purpose of impeachment.

Gary Pray was tried in Vermont for the murder of his brother-in-law. His defense was insanity. At a pretrial hearing, the defendant turned over a table and tried to attack a psychiatrist who was testifying. The state therefore put him on medication, which made him appear quiet, well oriented, and cooperative throughout the trial. Because the jury was never told that Pray was sedated, they found him guilty. The decision was appealed, and the appellate court held that the state had a duty to reveal the defendant's true condition. It stated: "The jury never looked upon an unaltered, undrugged Gary Pray . . . yet . . . his deportment . . . was a part of the basis of their judgment . . . of his defense of insanity . . . . In fact, it may have been necessary to expose the jury to the undrugged, unsedated Gary Pray in so far . . . as safety might permit." Pray's conviction and life sentence were, therefore, overturned.

While drug addiction itself may be used to impeach a witness, there are limits to which one can use this type of evidence. A defendant was convicted of selling heroin, largely on the basis of testimony by Giles, who witnessed the sale. Giles was a mainliner with a five-year habit, but he was not under the influence of drugs at the time he testified. In order to impeach the witness, the defense called a doctor to testify on the veracity of addicts. The doctor was asked whether, in his opinion, "a person addicted to [drugs] . . . as a mainliner . . . can testify in a normal manner." The counsel for the prosecution objected to the question. The defense then asked the doctor if, in his opinion, Giles was telling the truth. There was a further objection. The court sustained the exclusion of this evidence. It felt that, while the fact of addiction itself was pertinent, Giles's credibility was entirely up to the jury and that the court would not accept expert testimony that addicts are unworthy of belief.

(10.27) Immoral Acts

A witness may be cross-examined about any immoral acts in his past, as long as the examiner has a fair basis for asking about them. This is based on the assumption that honesty is associated with morality and good character. Thus, inquiry concerning behavior that demonstrates lack of morality and good character is allowed by way of impeachment.

This presents a real problem in the prosecution of a rape case. The victim must, of course, testify regarding the circumstances of the rape. Defense counsel, in the guise of impeaching her credibility, may cross-examine her regarding her complete moral history, in both major and minor aspects. Even though the victim's answers give no indication of immorality, counsel suggests past indiscretions simply by asking the questions. He is not actually trying to impeach her credibility, but is suggesting that she consented to intercourse. In response to public pressure, some states are enacting laws that limit such cross-examination of complainants in rape cases. Many people have come to feel that this type of question has produced unfair results. These new statutes, therefore, forbid cross-examining the rape victim about her past moral history.

(10.28) Character and Reputation

There is a major exception to the rule barring self-serving evidence. In criminal cases the defendant may offer evidence demonstrating good character. This is usually in the form of testimony by third parties concerning the defendant's reputation in the community. However, some states follow the federal rule and allow the witness to give his opinion as character evidence. If the defense offers evidence of good character, then the prosecution, in rebuttal, can show impeaching evidence by giving similar proof of poor character.

Also, when any witness, including the defendant, has taken the stand, the adversary party may offer evidence of poor reputation for truth and veracity by way of impeachment. This is done by asking the witness who knows of the reputation if he would believe the prior witness when he is under oath. The other side may then introduce rebuttal evidence to the contrary.

(10.29) Prior Inconsistent Statements

A prior inconsistent statement can always be used to discredit a witness. The examiner must always lay a foundation for using this tactic. First he calls the witness' attention to his prior testimony or statement. Once the witness admits that he made it, or outside proof is submitted showing that he did so, the witness may be queried about the discrepancies. Any variations may then be introduced in evidence.

A witness in a criminal trial can expect that his prior testimony before a grand jury or at a preliminary hearing, as well as any of his earlier written statements, will be used against him in this fashion.

(10.30) Use of Collateral Matters in Impeachment

Questions used in cross-examination by way of impeachment inquiring into past improper acts of a witness are, of course, concerned with side issues that are not involved in the trial before the court. The scope of these impeachment factors must be limited. If it were not, a trial could degenerate into a series of trials within a trial in which opposing counsel would attempt to prove or disprove the alleged indiscretions of the witness. For this reason, a universal rule has been adopted. Except for past criminal convictions, if the witness on cross-examination denies the existence of any alleged disgraceful or vicious act on his part, that ends the matter, and the questioner is bound by the answers.

A case involving stolen property is illustrative of this rule. The defendant testified in his own defense. The prosecutor, on cross-examination, asked the defendant if he had bought and passed counterfeit money at one time. The defendant denied that he had. He was then asked if he had not confessed to doing so at one time. Again he denied the accusation. Though the defendant was shown his signed confession, he continued to deny it was true. At this point the prosecutor read the entire confession to the jury. The defendant was found guilty of the present crime. A higher court set aside the conviction. It was pointed out that, though inquiry into the forgery was a collateral matter allowed by way of impeachment, "the cross-examiner . . . is bound by the answers to his questions on collateral matters" and that "inquiry as to immoral or criminal acts . . . for the purpose of impeaching his credibility is purely collateral."

D. CROSS-EXAMINATION OF WITNESSES

(10.31) Purpose and Character

In contrast to what is portrayed on television, in real courtrooms during cross-examination, witnesses do not break down on the stand and tearfully confess that they committed the crime. One of the general purposes of cross-examination, as has been discussed, is to point out inaccuracies, falsehoods, or collateral matters tending to weaken the believability of the witness. Another general aim of the cross-examiner is to pry out all the favorable information possible from the opposing witness. Police and prosecutors often neglect this area in preparing for trial, forgetting that the defense will attempt to elicit helpful information by cross-examining the People's witnesses.

These two aims, impeachment and the obtaining of favorable information, are the general purposes of most cross-examination.

(10.32) Right to Confront and Examine Witnesses

Cross-examination of witnesses is basic to our adversary trial system. The defendant has a constitutional right to confront the witnesses against him and to cross-examine them.

This presents a problem when there are co-defendants who have confessed and the prosecution wants to use both statements. If A's confession also implicates B, and A does not testify in person, B is damaged by his co-defendant's statement. In effect, A has been a witness and B's lawyer has no way to cross-examine him. B therefore has lost his right of confrontation. B then is entitled to a separate trial where A's confession would not be in evidence. (See Sec. 5.15, g.)

The increasing number of alleged child abuse cases has raised new problems in how to protect the young child from the stress and emotional damage that the child could incur from testifying in open court and yet preserve the accused's right to confront the witness against him. Shall the child be forced to testify and be cross-examined in open court, all in the presence of the accused molester?

Many jurisdictions are experimenting with new procedures to try to meet this problem. For example, Illinois passed a statute allowing the use of pretrial videotapes in child sex abuse cases in which the defendant was not allowed to cross-examine the child. The Illinois Supreme Court invalidated the statute, holding that it violated the defendant's constitutional right to confront the witnesses against him (*People* v. *Basten*, Ill. Sup. Ct. 45 CrL 2242 [1989]). Pennsylvania courts have made similar rulings.

Iowa tried a variation of this, allowing the child sex abuse victim to testify on closed-circuit television or behind a screen. In *Coy* v. *Iowa*, 43 CrL 3226 (1988), a screen was used in court that allowed the defendant to dimly see the child witness, but the testifying child could not see him. The Supreme Court found that this violated the accused's right of confrontation.

The Supreme Court has now approved a method of avoiding the confrontation problem in child abuse cases (*Maryland* v. *Craig*, 58 LW 5045 [1990]). Maryland's procedure required, first, that the trial court make a finding that the child would suffer serious emotional distress from courtroom testimony. Then, the child is examined and cross-examined in a separate room with only the child witness and both counsel present. The judge, jury, and defendant remain in the regular courtroom and watch the questioning on one-way television. The defendant can talk to his lawyer by means of electronic communication. The Supreme Court ruled that the confrontation clause does not guarantee an absolute right to a face-to-face meeting with a witness and that the state's interest in protecting the child justifies the use of this procedure.

(10.33) Scope of Cross-Examination

Every witness who testifies, including the defendant, is subject to cross-examination. Though there are limits as to what may be asked, in general the examiner may question any matter testified to on direct examination. Included within these limits are the usual questions testing credibility. Thus, a cross-examiner is not allowed to question the witness on any unrelated matter. Neither can he badger the witness nor otherwise treat him unfairly. It is up to the trial court to limit such questioning, which means that the judge largely determines the area that is to be allowed.

(10.34) Relevancy to Issues

While there is much latitude in cross-examination, it still must be relevant to the issue. The opponent must object, however, if he wants to keep the examination within bounds.

Anything concerning the accuracy or credibility of the witness is relevant. Questioning based on his direct testimony must relate to material matters recited by the witness. If the direct testimony included immaterial elements, the cross-examiner is not allowed to pursue these further. It stands to reason that facts that were irrelevant in direct testimony are just as irrelevant in cross-examination.

(10.35) Particular Subjects

Illegal evidence, such as privileged communications, cannot be inquired about in cross-examination any more than it can be done in direct questioning. Neither may counsel cross-examine the witness on matters about which he can have no knowledge. In addition, the Fifth Amendment forbids questions by which the witness could incriminate himself.

Should the defendant testify, he does so at some risk since the prosecutor may cross-examine him regarding any fact that may convict him of the crime of which he was accused. The defendant can, however, still claim his privilege against self-incrimination with respect to any other crime, and the cross-examiner will be prevented from inquiring further into such areas.

Another general area of testimony may be forbidden to the cross-examiner. It arises if he brings out new relevant facts on cross-examination that the witness had not mentioned in his direct testimony. When this occurs, the generally accepted rule is that the examiner has "made the witness his own." In effect, he has adopted this witness as if the examiner had called him. In this event, he can no longer contradict or impeach the witness. Most courts are reluctant to apply this rule rigidly, however, and so some leeway may be allowed in impeachment or contradiction of a witness that one has made his own.

(10.36) Refusal to Answer

On occasion the witness refuses to answer. Though this would normally occur during cross-examination, from time to time a hostile witness might refuse to respond on direct questioning. Before the witness can be held in contempt of court, there must be a genuine refusal to answer. Evasion is not contempt unless the court directs the witness to be more specific and he does not comply. Refusal to answer an incriminating question is not contempt. Failure to reply to a degrading question does not constitute contempt unless the answer is material. Another exception involves a prosecution witness. He can refuse to name an informant unless the court directs him to do so.

Any contempt of court that comes about because of refusal to answer can result in fine or imprisonment. As a matter of fact, in many jurisdictions the recalcitrant witness can be jailed until he does answer.

(10.37) Law Enforcement Courtroom Demeanor and Testimony

In a very real sense, the law enforcement officer is an officer of the court. In most jurisdictions, officers must fulfill certain court responsibilities. For example, they may serve subpoenas or act as bailiffs. Or officers may be directed by the court to make certain inspections or investigations. The duty with which the officer is most concerned is the duty to act as a witness in any criminal case.

In all cases, professional law enforcement work requires the best conduct on the part of the officer and the highest regard for the court and the principles of criminal justice. Your attitude, appearance, and conduct in the courtroom are essential to the profession. The way you testify, the knowledge of the law you show and the impression you make on the judge and jury are equally important in convicting the guilty and acquitting the innocent.

Most evidence presented in the courts is spoken. Often, there is no physical evidence, and verbal testimony is the only way to tell the court what facts relate to the case being prosecuted. Also, much of this testimony must be given by a law enforcement officer, who may have investigated a traffic accident and issued a citation, or who may have seen or heard something connected with a crime. Even when there is physical evidence, spoken testimony is needed to identify it, to explain what it is and where it was found, and to show its relevance to the case. So, all your work in investigating the offense, catching the defendants, and bringing those people to trial may be useless if you fail to convince the judge or the jury that your statements are true.

(10.38) Preparation for Court

A law enforcement officer's preparation for court begins with the first step in a police action. Almost everything done in carrying out your duty can be described and discussed during a trial. Crime scene duties—such as preserving, collecting, and marking evidence, and recording data and witnesses' statements—may become the basis for your later courtroom testimony. This is clearly one of the major reasons for making prompt, accurate, and detailed notes in your field notebook. Also, complete all other forms and reports as soon as possible. Defendants have been acquitted because the lack of such records made a jury doubt an officer's statements. In other cases, officers who had not made detailed records did not seem confident enough of the facts to give good explanations and answers.

Once a law enforcement officer is told that he or she is to appear as a witness, he or she should review all field notes and any other records. You may generally refer to these notes when you testify. In any case, you should review these records before the trial, because a long time may have passed between the crime and the trial.

A law enforcement officer often gets a notice from the state attorney's office requesting a pretrial conference. Such talks help the prosecutor decide how much the officer knows about the facts of the case and also help the prosecutor ask useful questions in the court. Such discussions are proper, and it is correct to confirm on the witness stand that you discussed the case in this way. Be careful never to change your recitation of the facts to provide what you may think the prosecutor wants.

In some jurisdictions, it is a good idea for the law enforcement officer to speak to the prosecutor the day before the trial. If the defendant has changed his or her plea, the prosecutor may need more information.

(10.39) Appearance in Court

Be sure your personal appearance is the best possible when you appear in court. You represent the whole law enforcement organization in such cases. So the way you look can affect what the jury thinks about what you say. A judge or jury member who sees you slouching down in a chair may decide that your observation is also sloppy. A well-groomed officer looks accurate and certain.

Agencies have different dress requirements for courts. Sometimes, you must wear your uniform if you are a uniformed officer and if the case is being heard during your normal duty hours. You may be allowed to wear civilian clothes if you are a plainclothes officer or would normally be off duty at the time. Other jurisdictions require the arresting officer wear what he or she wore at the time of the arrest. Others require uniforms in the lower courts and civilian clothes in the higher courts.

Make a good impression on others by wearing appropriate clothing. Your clothes are clearly visible and make the first impression. When wearing civilian clothes in court, always be well-scrubbed and exceptionally clean; your hair must be trimmed and groomed. Clothing should be fresh and clean, and shoes should be shined and in good repair. There should be nothing on the coat or jacket besides what is needed. No pens or pencils should stick out of visible pockets, and don't wear emblems or loud, fancy, or distracting jewelry. *Never* wear dark glasses, chew gum or tobacco, or smoke.

Make sure that you can be in court at the appointed time. Often, testimony must be presented in a certain order. Testimony of some witnesses, for example, may not be admissible unless prior testimony—perhaps yours—has established certain facts. Also, courts have dismissed cases because a prosecution witness did not show up.

Your appearance in court as a witness is generally in response to a subpoena. Not complying with a subpoena is serious; a subpoena is a court order and must be obeyed. If you really cannot get to court on time, you must contact the prosecutor or the court and explain. Also, if you must leave the court before being excused, you must tell the prosecuting attorney and the bailiff.

A subpoena is a court order requiring attendance in court or some other specified location for a specific purpose. Failure to appear may result in either civil or criminal contempt proceedings. A *subpoena duces tecum* requires the person "bring with you" items specifically listed when appearing. The clerk of the court may issue a subpoena upon request of a judge, a district attorney, or a defense attorney. A subpoena may also be issued by administrative, civil, or regulatory agencies. Only certain individuals can serve subpoenas. These include the sheriff or his or her deputies, the district attorney's investigator, state law enforcement officers, or process servers.

(10.40) Officer's Testimony—Direct Testimony

First impressions are very important when a law enforcement officer is called to testify. Your conduct and attitude can go a long way toward getting a favorable reception for your testimony. While you are taking the oath, look at the person administering the oath. Your right hand should be at left shoulder level with fingers extended until the oath is completed. Then, sit down comfortably on the witness stand. Be natural on the witness stand, speaking as though talking to friends. Stay calm. Never show arrogance or an attitude of self-importance. And, do not show fear or timidity to the point of being unsure of the facts. Do not act nervous or irritable. Never make signs; that is, do not shake your head for yes or no answers, because the court reporter cannot record such signs well.

Your manner in testifying is even more important. Sit straight, with both feet on the floor and with your hands on your lap or on the arms of the chair. Sit still, and do not play with keys or change or other items. Consider each question carefully before responding. Give the answer in a direct, honest, confident, dignified, and unemotional manner. Answers should be as short as possible. Use the words "yes, sir" and "no, sir" ("yes, ma'am" or "no, ma'am") when appropriate. The way you speak should show your competence as well as the full facts of the investigation. Do not lose the work done on the case by speaking poorly. The effectiveness of testimony depends on being clearly understood in the entire courtroom and on the good impression your voice makes.

Speak loudly enough and distinctly. Answer questions promptly, without rushing. Jurors and the court reporter must be able to hear your testimony. Use the microphone if there is one; speak in a natural voice, using steady, conversational, calm, and pleasant tones.

Choose words carefully for meaning. Do not use slang or profanity except when you must repeat someone's exact words. When you think the language you must repeat may offend someone, you may say so. You must then do what the judge tells you to do.

Never editorialize, volunteer information, or answer questions that are not asked. If you feel that important facts have not been brought out in your testimony, you can tell the prosecutor after you have been excused from the witness stand. A note is better for this purpose than other means that may distract the court or other witnesses and may look unprofessional. Then the prosecutor, if he or she wants to, can bring you back to the stand.

Do not guess at the answers to questions. It is correct to say, "I don't know," or "I don't remember," if that is true. Guesses that are later shown to be wrong will discredit your statements that were based on actual knowledge. Except when asked to express an opinion, do not say "I think" or "In my opinion." Such remarks may cast doubts on your impartiality and lack of prejudice.

The prosecutor questions the law enforcement officer first. He or she qualifies you as a witness, asking your name, rank, position, assignment, connection with the case, and other related information. The prosecutor then asks questions about your knowledge of the case until he or she has all the information that he or she feels the judge or jury needs.

(10.41) Officer's Testimony—Cross-Examination

The defense attorney may then cross-examine you to bring out more facts and to discredit or raise doubts about the testimony. During the cross-examination, center your attention on the question. Think before you reply. Briefly delay answering, to give the prosecution a chance to object if the question is out of order. Respond clearly and concisely. Control and suppress any personal feelings you have about the case, the defendant, or the defense attorney.

The defense attorney must make the best possible case for the client. He or she often tries to do this by showing the witness to be ignorant, corrupt, or biased. This does not make him or her your enemy. He or she is simply seeking the truth.

Part of the defense attorney's job is to look for loopholes and contradictions in your testimony and for ways to embarrass you. So you must stay polite and self-controlled during cross-examination, to avoid traps. Treat all attorneys alike, do not get irritated or angry, do not be led into an argument, and do not be either clever or timid.

Before trial, become familiar with all aspects of the case, including dates, places, times, addresses, and so forth. Study the case thoroughly. If necessary, get help from the prosecutor and other officers who are involved in the case. During the trial, do not discuss the case with any witness who has testified before you. Accurate answers are a very important part of testifying well.

The choice of words is also very important. The truth is the best defense against getting tripped up during cross-examination. A witness shown to have lied at any stage of the trial is clearly untrustworthy.

State only facts and do not color or exaggerate; tell only what you know, and never guess at answers or what an attorney may want for an answer. If the answer warrants it, ask if you may explain a "yes" or "no" answer. When giving an opinion, use descriptive words. For example, if a man was nervous, you might say, "His hand shook," "His speech was slurred," or "His forehead was covered with sweat." You are not expected to recall exact spoken words, but you are expected to remember the content of a conversation. From time to time, you may need to refer to notes you prepared on the case. Make sure there are no embarrassing comments in the notebook, because the defense has a right to examine the notebook and may read something aloud. If you must use notes, do so only after asking the judge for permission.

(10.42) Officer's "Do's and Don'ts"

A person is considered innocent until proven guilty beyond a reasonable doubt. Never let your personal bias or prejudice enter into your testimony. And do not be influenced by the testimony of other witnesses. Do not let the prosecutor or the defense attorney put words into your mouth.

Never refer to the defendant in a derogatory way. Always be polite to the defense counsel. Also, even though some of the facts may put the defendant in a favorable light, answer questions truthfully. The facts speak for themselves. Include all points, major and minor, because this will show that a thorough investigation was made.

An officer may be asked to give an opinion about some fact such as speed, distance, size, or emotions. The rule is that a *lay* (or ordinary) *witness* may give an opinion only if it is based on the witness's own observation of the facts and helps provide a clear understanding of the witness's testimony. Sometimes an officer may qualify as an *expert witness* and be asked to give an opinion as an expert on a particular subject. An officer is qualified to give an expert opinion if the subject is beyond common experience, and expert opinion would be helpful, and if the officer has special knowledge of the subject.

The judge decides who is qualified as an expert witness. Unless the attorneys agree that the officer is an expert, the prosecution may ask the officer about the training and experience that would qualify the officer as an expert. The officer may then be cross-examined by the defense lawyer and the judge. Whenever an officer is asked to give an opinion, he or she must tell the court the facts on which the opinion is based. Take extra care to keep fact and opinion separate.

One way to qualify someone as an expert is for an officer-witness to state that he or she is an expert. When classifying yourself as an expert, clearly describe your experience and training. Give your opinion only when asked, and then stand by the opinion. Give the facts on which your opinion is based and the reasoning that led you to form the opinion.

Confessions do not have to be in writing or recorded, but when the defendant signs a written document that says he or she actually committed a crime, the court has a powerful weapon. You must know how to handle this weapon to bring about a conviction.

If the actual writing of the confession was not done by the suspect, the officer can testify to the circumstances under which the suspect read, corrected, and signed the confession. You can testify to the signing of the statement and report the witnesses who were present. You can also testify that the confession was made in your presence, and you can show the signatures of the witnesses.

The confession is valid only when it was voluntary. Proof that the defendant confessed voluntarily may rest on statements made at the time of the confession. You can testify (1) that the confession was made of the defendant's own free will, (2) that the *Miranda* warnings were properly read before the confession was made, and (3) that you made no promises. If the confession was given voluntarily and either (1) while *not* in custody or (2) not as the result of an interrogation, then *Miranda* warnings are not needed.

Both the confession itself and the notes on the case are important physical evidence. The documents are handled by carefully prescribed procedures.

The defendant is called the "subject" or "defendant" in a criminal complaint. The term "suspect" is used if his or her identity is unknown. It is better (clearer) to frequently name the defendant. When the defendant was arrested with one or more other people, and the others are not parties to the proceeding, call all others by name. Avoid special terms and jargon. If the court orders witnesses out of the courtroom, all witnesses subpoenaed to testify should leave but remain available to be called. This procedure is called "invoking the rule." Not leaving when told to do so may be grounds for the witness/ officer to be held in contempt of court.

On cross-examination, defense counsel concentrates on winning the case for the defendant. Regardless of the defendant's apparent guilt, the defense attorney will work to assure that the client receives every opportunity allowed by law. Sometimes it can seem that no holds are barred in the tactics and techniques the defense uses to achieve its ends. For example, the defense may be soft-spoken and flattering one minute and in the next become a harsh browbeating type whose only goal is apparently to impeach the officer's testimony.

When defense is praising or flattering, the officer can tend to ramble, possibly giving more information than a question requires. The officer susceptible to flattery will often make many mistakes and express inconsistencies in the course of testifying. The most effective way to deal with this strategy is to carefully think about each question asked and then answer as clearly, concisely, and accurately as possible; then stop.

A heavy-handed type of counsel may try to arouse your anger as an officer-witness to make you lose your poise, reducing the effectiveness of your testimony by creating an impression with the jury that you are overly concerned with seeking a conviction. You can effectively counter this tactic by maintaining self-control, thinking before speaking, and answering truthfully. An effective rebuff to this type of attack is to avoid looking at the attorney, even when being questioned. The officer-witness, in such cases, should address responses to the jury or judge and never argue with the attorney.

Questions the court considers improper, after counsel objects, are usually disallowed and have to be rephrased. The court will not, however, permit an excessive number of objections, and the officer will eventually be required to reply. There is a good rule for the testifying officer to follow in answering all queries: Do not answer a question that is not clear. If you do not understand the question, ask to have it repeated or rephrased, providing of course there has been no objection. Do not be misled by questions that, after objection, have only been slightly altered by adding new words or substituting words that mean the same thing. For example, "Officer, haven't you discussed this case with other people?" after objection can be rephrased to, "Isn't it true, Officer, that you talked about this case with other persons?" Both questions imply that the officer has talked promiscuously and thoughtlessly about the case. Of course, the officer has reviewed the case with the prosecutor or other investigators, and until the question is put in this context, the officer cannot give a proper answer.

As a professional officer, you must not allow yourself to be badgered. Remain calm and polite regardless of the tactics the defense uses and relate the facts as you know them, remembering that the best testimony is frank, honest, and impersonal. As an officer-witness you may recognize that it is difficult to work hard for a long time and not have feelings about a case. You also know, though, that allowing personal feelings or prejudices to affect your testimony is both improper and potentially damaging.

Finally, the professional officer always strives to be a better witness, a goal that requires practice and self-evaluation. Each time you testify, you should critically evaluate your own method of testifying. If possible, discuss your responses and technique with the prosecutor or other officers present in court. Above all, however, evaluate and improve your testimony.

(10.43) Summary

Our adversary trial system depends on the questioning and cross-questioning of witnesses. Anyone having material information can be subpoenaed to testify and can be made to produce evidence in his possession. The criminal defendant cannot be forced to give testimony.

In direct examination, questions must be relevant, avoid general conclusions, seek facts; they must not be leading or argumentative. In cross-examination much more leeway is allowed in all these areas. Answers must be responsive and produce valid evidence. Opposing counsel must object to any improper question or answer. If he does not do so, even illegal evidence may be used.

Witnesses are not disqualified solely because of age, incompetency, past criminal history, or even insanity. If the court is satisfied that such a witness is able to give a reasonable account of events, his testimony can be taken. These conditions actually affect credibility, not admissibility, of such testimony. Even unsworn testimony is allowed under certain conditions.

A witness may, if necessary, use a personal memorandum or record to aid his memory, but ordinarily he will not be allowed to read this directly to the jury. Opposing counsel may see the record and use it in cross-examination.

Every witness is subject to possible impeachment by any legitimate means. His competency, accuracy, and truthfulness are all subject to question. The witness's interest in the outcome, his relationship to the parties involved, and his bias or prejudice may be shown as bearing on credibility. Cross-examiners commonly inquire into past criminal history, drug addiction, and immoral acts. A witness may decline to answer incriminating questions, as may a testifying defendant, except in relation to the crime for which he is presently being charged.

Any prior inconsistent statement made by the witness may be used for impeachment. The same is true if he has a poor reputation for honesty. A defendant may use evidence of good character as a defense. If, however, he introduces such evidence, the prosecution may show the opposite.

Every defendant has the constitutional right to confront the witnesses against him and to cross-examine them. Though cross-examiners generally must stay within the limits of the direct examination, they may seek out information favorable to their side and can inquire into any legitimate matter of impeachment.

Discussion Questions

1. Discuss the rules concerning children as witnesses.
2. What are the general qualifications of a witness?
3. Define competency as it relates to witnesses.
4. What is the fundamental purpose of cross-examination?
5. What does "scope of cross-examination" mean?

11
Articles and Exhibits of Evidence

Some circumstantial evidence is very strong, as
when you find a trout in the mill .
—Henry David Thoreau
Journal, November 11, 1854

(11.1) Documentary Evidence in General

Legal evidence is not, of course, limited to the oral testimony
of witnesses. Tangible objects that can express a fact or that tend to
clarify the truth or untruth of the issues in question are admissible
and fall under the classification of documentary evidence. This broad
category includes private writings, documents, official records, newspapers, maps, or any other object on which symbols have been placed
with the intention of preserving a record of events or impressions.

Documentary evidence is subject to the same rules that govern
oral testimony. It must, therefore, satisfy the threefold test of materiality, relevance, and competence. The issues of the case determine
the materiality and relevance of the document; such determinations
are within the bounds of discretion granted to trial judges. The
competence or reliability of documentary evidence presents problems
that do not exist in the context of oral testimony. Thus, the basic
question is whether or not the document offered as evidence has a
sufficient guarantee of reliability. As a result, the judge is often
called upon to make a judgment on the inherent reliability of the
type of document offered. One important, if somewhat overly flexible, standard states that documentary evidence satisfies the test of

competence if the document was made and preserved in such a way as to appear to state directly, accurately, and truthfully a fact relevant and material to the legal issue in question.

Once the tests of materiality, relevance, and competence are met, the category of admissible documents becomes very broad. The document may be in the form of letters, numbers, marks, or symbols upon any type of surface or substance.

In deciding the admissibility of writings, the type is not important. The test is the content of the document and the purpose for which it is offered. Many types of documentary evidence are admissible, such as private writings, memorandums, letters, church and family records, tables, charts, graphs, and commercial paper of all types, plus reports and records of officials and agencies.

(11.2) Authentication of Documents

Before a writing can be admitted as documentary evidence it must be authenticated. Authentication is a legal process of proof that is designed to establish the genuineness of the writing and may be accomplished in a number of ways. The document may, for example, be supported by an authenticating witness, whose function is to establish that the writing is what it purports to be and that it was made by the party to whom it has been attributed. In some cases the authenticating witness is not necessary. The opposing party may concede the genuineness of the document, or it may fall within one of the limited exceptions to the authentication requirement. The party offering the document as evidence should, nevertheless, always be prepared to establish its authenticity. In all cases the genuineness of the writing must be demonstrated to the satisfaction of the trial judge before it will be formally admitted into evidence. If he is not persuaded that the writing is authentic, the writing will not be allowed to be read or shown to the jury or to be considered by the judge in a nonjury trial.

It is important to remember that the authentication process should never be confused with the necessity to establish proof of the writing's contents after the documentary evidence has been received at trial. After the judge is convinced that the writing is what it purports to be, the party introducing the evidence must still convince the jury that the content of the document is truthful.

Though there are many ways to authenticate a document, the final determination of its authenticity and reliability remains a matter firmly within the discretion of the trial judge. The easiest way to authenticate a document is, of course, to obtain the stipulation of the opposing party that the document is genuine. It is more common, however, to do so by locating the author of the document or one who observed the making of the document and placing him on the stand as an authenticating witness. Such persons are regarded as persuasive guarantors of the document's source and genuineness.

In some cases such formal authentication is not required because the nature of the writing is such that its authenticity can be presumed as a matter of law. The most prominent example of self-authentication are ancient documents and official records.

A former ironclad rule of authentication required that, whenever a writing offered as evidence carried the signature or mark of an attesting witness, the witness should be called to prove the fact of execution, unless, of course, he was incompetent or incapable of testifying. Failure to produce such a witness had to be explained to the judge's satisfaction. If it was not, the evidence would become inadmissible. The apparent reasoning behind this rule was that the subscribing witness was considered by the writer of the document to be an appropriate person to establish the fact of execution; thus, he probably had a greater knowledge of the document's authenticity than any party other than the writer.

Many states have modified this rule by statute. Such statutes generally make attested writings provable without the testimony of the attesting witnesses. This does not affect the duty of the party offering the document to establish its authenticity; it merely relieves him of the obligation to account for the whereabouts of the attesting witnesses.

When the attesting witness is used to authenticate a document, whether or not he is required by law to do so, he need not be able to recall the transaction or to have an independent recollection of the contents of the document. It is sufficient for the attesting witness to be able to identify his signature or mark on the document; he can thereby establish that the document was executed in his presence. This satisfies the requirement of authentication since the objective is only to establish the genuineness of the writing, not the truth of its contents.

If the attesting witness or author of the writing is unavailable or unable to authenticate the writing, it is possible to prove the document's authenticity through the use of circumstantial proof. In the case of a handwritten document, there are three ways to establish authenticity. First, a person who is familiar with the alleged writer's handwriting can identify the document. Second, courts have allowed the testimony of handwriting experts to establish authenticity. The expert compares the questionable document to an authentic example of the writer's handwriting and is thus able to express an expert opinion on whether or not the two documents were written by the same person. Though the expert is not required to explain the reason for his judgment, the value of his opinion will be greatly enhanced if the judge or jury is made to understand the basis for his decision. As in all cases of expert testimony, the court is free to give little weight to the opinion or even to reach an opposite conclusion. Most courts, however, consider handwriting expertise a valuable tool in the authentication process. Third, one may present the sample and the questioned handwriting to the jury itself. This can be done only after the comparisons have been entered in evidence and will usually serve to evaluate the judgment of a handwriting expert.

Another means of authenticating a questioned document through the use of circumstantial evidence arises when a reply is requested to a letter. By referring to the content of the return letter, the courts have held that it is possible to authenticate the identity of the writer of the reply. This ruling is based on the theory that only the party who had received the original letter would be familiar with the subject matter contained in the reply.

The ancient document rule is an exception to both the rule excluding hearsay evidence and that requiring authentication of documents. The traditional rule was that a writing that was thirty or more years old, if relevant to the inquiry and free from suspicion, was admissible in evidence without the ordinary requirements of proof of execution. The Federal Rules of Evidence (Secs. 803 [16] and 901 [b] [8]) reduced the definition of "ancient" to twenty years and also indicated that if a document is ancient, the proof of its age suffices as authentication.

(11.3) Specific Kinds of Records

If the litigants are the two parties to a transaction, a receipt, or notation of payment, will generally be admissible in evidence. A receipt of full payment is proof of a settlement and is not merely evidence of the sums specified in the note. On the other hand, a receipt for the payment of an account is not evidence that the account was due if the existence of an account is the question in issue. A receipt will not be competent evidence against a person who was not a party to that transaction, for such evidence is hearsay, as concerns the parties to the case. Many states have adopted provisions concerning business records that exclude from the hearsay rule written records made in the regular course of business. The rule under the Federal Rules of Evidence (Sec. 803 [6]) is slightly broader as it refers to "regularly conducted activity." If the receipt can be fitted into one of these exceptions, it will be admissible in evidence against third parties as well.

a. Church Records

Church records and baptismal, marriage, and other certificates are admissible as evidence if made by the clergyman, official, or other person authorized to make such records. Because these records are private, they do not fit within the range of public reports for which authentication is unnecessary. If the clergyman who made the record is still living at the time of the lawsuit, he will be required by some courts to authenticate the reliability of his records. Such records can only serve the limited purpose for which they were intended they cannot be used for extraneous purposes. For example, a priest was not allowed to testify concerning the age of a party when his information was based on the age he had been told to place on the party's baptismal certificate.

It is well established that entries in a family Bible or similar record can be entered in evidence when offered to prove the birth, death, marriage, or other fact of history there recorded. The entry must be duly authenticated and is subject to the best evidence rule that would prefer public or official documents if they are available. It is not necessary to prove the identity of the individual who made the entry, but it should be shown that the Bible had been taken from the custody of the family in question, that there was some guarantee that the date was recorded at the approximate date of the occurrence, and that the family generally accepted the record as accurate. The timing and purpose of the entries may have considerable significance in the effort to establish the competence of the entry as it relates to the issue on trial.

b. Letters

Letters are a frequent form of documentary evidence and are admissible if they are communications between the parties and are properly authenticated. To be documentary evidence, letters must be relevant and material to an issue of the lawsuit, but they need not have been written after legal action was commenced. Previous letters written between the defendant and victim may be relevant to the case if they are informative concerning the writer's state of mind, motives, or plans. A letter written by a defendant after his arrest usually meets the requirements of relevance and materiality, but is inherently suspect as self-serving. It will, therefore, probably be given little weight by a jury.

Authentication is a vital element of a letter offered as documentary evidence. The fact that the letter purports by its signature to have been written by a particular party on a particular date is inconclusive in a determination of authenticity. When it is impossible to obtain authenticating evidence from the alleged author or from a witness, and handwriting comparisons fail to settle the issue, courts have allowed circumstantial or secondary evidence to complete the authentication. This type of evidence may include the style or tone of the letter if it is in any way distinctive or proof that only the alleged author could have had the knowledge required to write the particular letter.

Facsimile (fax) messages, once authenticated, are admissible in evidence in the same way as letters.

Letters written between third persons are generally excluded from evidence on the basis of their being outside the scope of the trial (irrelevant) or violative of the hearsay evidence rule (incompetent). They may be admitted, however, if it can be shown that the person against whom the evidence is presented was in some way aware of the communications or if they are used to prove a collateral issue such as the person's state of mind or location at a particular time.

c. Telegraph Messages

These messages are subject to the same rules of evidence as all other types of documentary evidence but with an additional twist. A telegram may be accidentally or intentionally altered by telegraph operators at either end of the line. This means that telegrams are subject to the rule that prefers the original written message as evidence if it is still available. Should it not be available, the sender is faced with a major problem of authentication; he must prove that a telegram was sent in his name and that he authorized or caused the telegram to be sent in his name on a particular date.

d. Books

Books or other publications will not usually be received as documentary evidence, despite their usefulness as sources of information. This is in keeping with the general rule barring hearsay evidence, which specifies that such publications are thought to be written records of information on which persons could be called to provide oral testimony. There are several recognized exceptions to this general rule. If, for example, a particular book is the work of a deceased author who is unquestionably reliable, and if the book concerns general facts of history, the work will be admitted. In cases where the author of the work is still living or where the facts are of such recent interest that many persons would be able to give oral testimony concerning these facts, however, these persons should be called as witnesses, and the book will be inadmissible.

e. Newspaper and Magazine Articles

Newspaper articles or magazine accounts usually will not be admissible. The statements made in these publications were not made by a party under oath, and there is no opportunity to cross-examine the author. A newspaper account may be admissible if it concerns historical events of obscure or ancient origins that cannot appropriately be the subject of oral testimony. A newspaper account can also be accepted as evidence if it qualifies as an ancient document.

In all cases, printed material, whether a newspaper, a magazine, or a book, must be adequately authenticated to the satisfaction of the trial judge. In a case involving a newspaper account of a fire in a clock tower, an issue relevant to the trial, the court admitted the account as evidence, not because it was fifty-eight years old and was an ancient document, but because it felt that the requirements of materiality, relevance, and reliability were all satisfied, and there was no other means of obtaining the information contained in the article.

f. Learned Treatise

The use of a learned treatise as documentary evidence has recently been redefined by the Federal Rules of Evidence. Most jurisdictions had refused to admit medical and scientific treatises as evidence of the theories and opinions they stated. Rule 803 (18) allows such evidence once its authoritativeness has been established before the trial judge. For the first time it may be used as substantive evidence in federal courts rather than merely as a means of impeaching the expert testimony offered by the opposing side. If, in the past, an expert accepted a treatise as authoritative, and the treatise contained information that contradicted his testimony, the opposing attorney could use these contradictions to impeach the witness. He could not, however, enter the treatise as substantive evidence.

In those states that still exclude treatises from being offered as substantive evidence, the hearsay rule is the basis for the exclusion. That is, there is no way to evaluate the validity of the opinions contained in the book since there is no opportunity to challenge or cross-examine the author, and the opinions were not made while under oath. This rule may be relaxed when the treatise is used to impeach the oral testimony of an expert witness. In that case the evidence is not being offered as the truth, but is introduced to challenge the oral testimony given under oath.

g. Commercial and Scientific Publications

The rule against hearsay evidence is further relaxed regarding the use of commercial or scientific publications, which include market quotations, scientific treatises, histories, atlases, and similar reference publications. In the case of the exception for commercial publications, the rationale parallels that for business records, which constitutes a major exception to the hearsay rule. It is expected that the information in commercial publications, such as catalogues, price lists, and indexes, will be relied upon. If it is established that the commercial world does indeed rely on these figures, the document will be admitted as evidence. The rationale for allowing scientific publications and histories is not as strong since it is more difficult to establish their authoritativeness or reliability. There is, however, a basis for their exception in that such works are the products of expert authority and can usually be checked against corroborative evidence and research data.

h. Official Records

Official records and other official writings are significant exceptions to the hearsay rule. When a document sets forth the record, report, statement, or data compilation of a public agency or official, and when it is the duty of that agency or official to make such a report, the records are public in nature and will usually be admissible in evidence without requiring proof by the person who actually made the entries. There must, however, be some indication that the official making the report had firsthand knowledge of its contents; otherwise the evidence would be no more than hearsay on the part of the reporting officer. Many states have statutes dealing with official reports or certified copies of those reports. They provide that reports concerned with a matter within the officer's statutorily defined duty should be admitted as evidence of the facts contained in those reports. The Federal Rules of Evidence (Sec. 803 [8]) go beyond the state rules and allow the receipt in civil cases and against the government in criminal cases of findings from investigations made pursuant to a legally granted authority.

i. Records Concerning Death

Death certificates and autopsy reports are special types of documentary evidence, combining an investigating and a recording function. Either the original certificate or certified copies are admissible evidence of the facts contained in those reports. In addition, the records of the coroner and his staff or copies of those records are accepted as evidence. These reports are not conclusive evidence, however, and are subject to impeachment and contradiction.

(11.4) Tables

Most charts, graphs, and tables constitute another form of documentary evidence that is subject to the same requirements of relevance, materiality, and competence as are all forms of written evidence. They must also be authenticated before they are received as competent evidence. Some tables, however, are used so frequently and unquestioningly that they have generally become admissible without further proof of authenticity. As an example, life insurance companies prepare mortality or life expectancy tables to establish the probable remaining life expectancy for a person at any given age. Since these tables are compiled by disinterested parties and come as close as is humanly possible to statistical exactitude, courts will usually admit them without question when a determination of life expectancy is relevant to the issue on trial. In all cases involving tables, of course, the trial judge must be satisfied that the tables are authentic and accurate. If the court is not satisfied, it will be necessary to establish the authenticity of the table through the presentation of competent evidence.

(11.5) Vital Statistics

Data relating to birth, marriage, death, or other vital statistics that are collected by a public official pursuant to a requirement of the law are admissible as evidence on judicial notice, and there is no requirement of authenticating such documents. A distinction should be made here between a public official responsible for compiling such statistics and the clergyman or family member who may keep a parallel record. Because the official is under a duty to maintain accurate records, certified copies of these records are admissible without further authentication. On the other hand, persons who are not public officials are under no obligation to record such matters, and the accuracy of their reports cannot be presumed. Thus, these records must be authenticated.

(11.6) Business Records

The business records exception to the hearsay rule grants an important concession to the modern business world. If the hearsay rule were strictly applied, evidence arising in the course of business operations would only be admissible when the individual who made the specific business entry or wrote the particular check could be placed on the stand. With the advancing complexity of most business operations, it became necessary to find a compromise between the rigid requirement of the hearsay rule and the desirability of receiving evidence where there is a sufficient guarantee of reliability.

The result is, of course, the business records exception. Thus, courts usually admit business records without the authenticating proof of the person who made the entry. There are two reasons for this exception. First, business records could only rarely be accepted since it is virtually impossible to trace the activities and duties of each employee in a modern business operation. Second, courts accord business records a high presumption of reliability because they are the main source of information on which business decisions are made, and, thus, they can be expected to be carefully prepared and preserved.

Five basic requirements must be met if a writing is to be brought within the business records exception to the hearsay rule:

1. The record must be a writing of some type, which has been interpreted to include all kinds of commercial paper, journal entries, and even computer printouts. Oral business records have not, however, been incorporated into this exception.

2. The entry must be made in the regular course of business. This is a most flexible standard, but it excludes writings incidental to the business made by individuals who could, under the general rule, be able to claim the protection of the exception. The theory is that only matters arising in the regular course of business have the inherent qualities of reliability that underlie the exception.

3. The party offering the evidence must be able to show that the custom of the business was to record the particular type of transaction at the same time the record was made or within a reasonable period of time thereafter. For two reasons this is a further guarantee of reliability. First, it establishes that the entry was probably recorded soon after the transaction. Second, there is little danger that the person who made the entry has a faulty memory of the event.

4. If the party offering the information was not connected with the business, the entry will not be admissible. This is because

information supplied by an outsider lacks assurance of reliability.

5. The record must be authenticated as being what is purports to be. This does not mean that every business entry must be authenticated, for this is what the exception was designed to eliminate. Instead, the offering party is merely required to prove that the entry was made in the usual place for such entries and that the book in which it was recorded be the actual record kept by the business.

The usual procedure is for the custodian of the records to bring the account book, checkbook, or whatever document is sought as evidence. He must then prove to the court's satisfaction that what he brought is the authentic record of business activities. If the court is so convinced, the business record is entered into evidence although no one has authenticated the making of the actual entry sought as evidence.

(11.7) Demonstrations in General

Demonstrative evidence can be classified as two basic types. The first, selected demonstrative evidence, also known as preexisting evidence, is used to give a jury a better concept of an item of evidence. In a murder trial, for example, a woman raises as a defense that she was incapable of wielding the alleged murder weapon, a baseball bat. The prosecution may introduce a baseball bat as evidence to impeach that claim, even though the bat is not the actual murder weapon, but is only a preexisting sample of a typical bat.

The second type of demonstrative evidence, prepared or reproduced, includes, among other things, photographs, scale models, drawings, and casts. Such evidence is prepared and offered in court to aid the jury in understanding the issues and testimony of the trial. If these representations can be shown to be accurate and correct, courts will usually admit them as evidence on the theory that they constitute a tangible form of testimony from a qualified witness that he may use instead of more detailed and possibly less graphic oral testimony.

The newest form of demonstrative evidence is computer-generated reproductions of scenes or illustrations of an expert's findings. Prepared in advance of trial, this kind of evidence is now being offered in civil cases, and will be used increasingly in the field of criminal evidence.

It is necessary to establish the authenticity of all demonstrative evidence offered for admission. If, for example, the diagram or exhibit is not made in the presence of the court, evidence must be offered to establish the accuracy of the representation. In this respect, the requirements of authentication do not differ from those required of all evidence offered by an out-of-court party. In order to satisfy the tests of the hearsay rule, it is necessary to establish the reliability of the evidence to the satisfaction of the trial judge: If the evidence consists of a drawing or diagram made in court by a witness, its admission is not likely to be challenged since the evidence was produced in court while the witness was under oath. It is thus sufficient to satisfy the requirements of the hearsay rule.

a. Photographs and Recordings in General

If counsel lays a proper foundation of accuracy and reliability, photographs and sound recordings may be accepted as evidence if they are relevant and material to the issues and if they are not unduly prejudicial. Photographs are probably the most commonly used form of demonstrative evidence. The reliability of their reproduction is generally accepted, they are a relatively inexpensive means of representing the actual physical evidence, and they are very convenient.

As with all other evidence, a photograph must be shown to have some relevance to the matter in controversy at the trial in order to be admitted. The trial judge determines the relevance, which is based on the relevance of the photograph itself, not that of the fact the offering party is attempting to establish. If it is determined that the photograph is not relevant to the purposes of the trial, the fact may be established through the use of some other evidence.

b. Accuracy of Representation and Authentication

A photograph cannot be submitted anonymously and be accepted as evidence. Without a sponsoring or authenticating witness, a photograph has no value as evidence because it is impossible to establish what the photograph shows. Thus, a competent witness must provide the court with evidence that the photograph is a fair and accurate depiction of persons, objects, or scenes. It is not necessary for the photographer to establish the accuracy of his work, although in some cases that may be the best way to establish authentication. Any witness who is competent to speak from personal experience on the accuracy of the scene depicted is suitable as an authenticating witness. If the witness is someone other than the photographer, he need not have been present when the photograph was taken. His presence would, however, add weight to his testimony.

The trial judge has considerable discretion in ruling whether the photograph was substantially accurate. He may even allow its admission when there are contentions that the photograph is inaccurate. In those cases, however, the jury must weigh the evidence in order to determine the accuracy of the photograph.

c. Time and Changes of Conditions

One of the basic questions that must be clarified before the court will allow a photograph in evidence is that of change or the possibility of change in the contents of the photograph. There is, in addition, basically a question of relevance. For example, even if the depiction is an absolutely accurate portrayal of the present condition of a railroad crossing, it may have no relevance to a trial concerning the way the crossing appeared twenty years ago. Thus it is necessary to establish two separate and distinct proofs. First, the photograph must be an accurate depiction of the subject that it appears or purports to represent. Second, the scene must be shown to have some relevance to the issue at trial. This can only be established by showing through competent proof that the photograph aids in understanding the conditions of the subject as it appeared at the time with which the trial is concerned.

The fact that there was a lapse of time between the incident in question and the making of the photograph need not result in a ruling of inadmissibility. If the party offering the photograph as evidence can produce witnesses to testify that the photograph fairly depicts the subject as it appeared at the time in question, the photograph should be admitted. If, on the other hand, a photograph was made immediately after the incident, but conditions had materially changed before the picture was taken, the photograph has little relevance and will probably be excluded. Every effort should be made, of course, to see that conditions in the photograph closely approximate those existing at the time of the incident. Thus, if the issue is visibility along a train track, the photograph should be taken with the approximate amount of daylight as was present at the time of the incident. A photograph that does not coincide in every detail with conditions at the time of the incident may be admitted. The jury must, however, be instructed to consider it only for a certain limited purpose. For example, in a case of battery the victim was pushed over a bannister. A photograph taken after the bannister was removed might be admissible for the limited purpose of showing where the battery took place. That is, as long as the changed conditions in the photograph do not unduly influence the jury, a trial judge may be persuaded to admit the photograph as evidence.

d. Prejudicial Use of Gruesome or Nude Photographs

Since the judge must approve all photographs before he admits them into evidence, there is a natural obstacle to the submission of photographs that are unduly prejudicial. If a photograph is inflammatory, horrifying, or gruesome, it will be admissible only if the judge feels it would be helpful to the jury in understanding a case. If, on the other hand, the value of these photographs is outweighed by the danger they pose in prejudicing the interests of either party, they are properly excluded. Thus, judges usually apply a balancing test between the probative value of the evidence and its prejudicial effect.

e. Colored Photographs and Motion Pictures

Colored photographs and slides are admissible as demonstrative evidence and are subject to the same limitations placed on black-and-white photographs. Though color photographs provide a more accurate depiction of appearances and conditions than do those in black and white, there is a greater danger that they might be unduly prejudicial and inflammatory. Colored photographs may, in fact, be excluded in their entirety when an inaccurate portrayal of colors raises the possibility of misleading a jury.

Motion pictures are also admissible as evidence when properly authenticated. The authentication procedure may be more complex than that for a still photograph because of the possibilities of inaccuracy. A motion picture consists of a series of still photographs exhibited in sequence. It is, therefore, possible for a motion picture of an actual event to be tampered with in such a way as to be imperceptible to the untrained viewer. Lens settings, interruptions of the photographic process, elimination of unfavorable frames, and tampering with the sound track are only the most obvious examples of abuse.

Because of these factors, courts have placed a heavier burden on counsel seeking the admission of moving pictures in evidence than they have for the admission of a still photograph. Evidence must be provided of the circumstances in which the pictures were taken, with particular attention paid to technical aspects. The manner and circumstances in which the film was processed and developed must be established, and the court may require evidence of the accuracy of the speed at which the movie is shown and the size of the depiction on the screen. It is also necessary to have available a person who was present at the making of the film in order that he might testify that the movie is an accurate portrayal of the events filmed.

The fact that a motion picture film has been edited will not render it inadmissible if the court is satisfied that the accuracy of the representation is established. In some cases, a court may even direct the party offering the film in evidence to edit it in order to remove irrelevant materials. There is, of course, always an inherent danger of deception whenever motion pictures are offered in evidence. If, however, they are properly authenticated and clearly relevant to an issue at trial, they are acceptable forms of demonstrative evidence.

f. Videotapes and Sound Recordings

The increased use of videotapes in recording events has led to suggestions that they be introduced as evidence in legal proceedings. At this point it appears that they will be subject to the same rules that apply to the admission of motion pictures. Once again there is a danger of tampering, but, if the foundation of accuracy and relevancy is adequately established, there is no reason why these tapes should not be an acceptable form of demonstrative evidence.

It is generally accepted that sound recordings are admissible if they are appropriately authenticated. The process of authentication includes a demonstration that the recording device was capable of making an accurate recording, that the operator of the device was authentic and accurate, that there were no additions to or deletions from the recording, that the recording was properly preserved, and that voices or other sounds on the recording were properly identified by the offering party. At the preliminary hearing concerning admissibility, the judge may instruct the offering party to erase irrelevant or incompetent materials, which do not, of course, affect an otherwise admissible sound recording.

In spite of the general acceptance of sound recordings as demonstrative evidence, they may be held inadmissible if they violate a rule of competency. If the recording was made through the use of an illegal wiretap, it is incompetent and hence inadmissible in a federal court. Recorded admissions and confessions are inadmissible if they were obtained by unconstitutional means. Tape recordings do, however, present a potentially valuable tool to police in establishing that a confession was voluntarily given with full knowledge of the party's *Miranda* rights. If used properly and authenticated to the judge's satisfaction, such recordings should be admissible as evidence.

g. Models and Casts

A trial judge has the discretionary power to admit any model into evidence if he is satisfied that it is relevant to the issues in a trial and is an accurate replica or representation of the object in issue. If it is likely that a model will mislead or confuse a jury, it may be excluded from evidence. If, however, the discrepancy between the model and the actual object can be explained to the jury, the model should be admitted.

Models often help the jury to understand complex physical conditions or such things as the layout of a building or any other structure with which they could not be familiar but which they must understand in order to render a verdict in the case. Perhaps the most common type of model are reproductions of the human body, its skeleton, and organs, which are used to illustrate the expert testimony of a medical authority.

Another common type of demonstrative evidence is the plaster cast, which reproduces an impression made in mud, sand, or a similar substance. As an effective substitute for photography, the cast is often used by police to present a three-dimensional reproduction for the purpose of recreating a mark left at the scene of the crime. If a proper foundation of relevancy and accuracy is laid, judges generally admit casts in evidence.

h. Experiments

To the extent that experiments conducted by police are relevant to the issues of a trial, they should be admissible as evidence. When these experiments are performed outside the courtroom, the party offering the evidence should show that the tests were made under circumstances similar to those existing at the time of the incident or crime. Among the experiments that are accepted by the courts are use of sniffer dogs to locate drugs or explosives, ballistics tests, tests of motor vehicle parts such as brakes and headlights, tests of the sensory powers of a witness, and chemical tests for intoxication. This type of evidence can be very persuasive as well as being an important source of factual information. Since accuracy is the single most important test of admissibility, these experiments should be conducted by qualified experts whenever possible. Courts do not generally favor proposals for the jury's participation in experiments that take place in the courtroom. And, where test results are inconclusive or might be confusing to the jury, the trial judge should properly exclude them from evidence.

i. Diagrams, Drawings, and Graphs

While photographs are often an important aid in recreating the scene of the incident at issue, they do not always tell the whole story. It may be necessary to provide additional drawings and diagrams in order to describe a particular locale thoroughly. For example, photographs of a murder scene may inadequately portray the overall appearance of a room, and a photograph taken at a distance necessarily sacrifices specific details. The solution to this problem is often a diagram, either drawn by a third party and corroborated by the witness or drawn by the witness himself.

The fact that these diagrams or drawings are not made strictly to scale does not automatically render them inadmissible. It may, however, have a considerable impact on the judge who must determine whether they will aid or hinder the jury in its consideration of the case. A certain amount of latitude for minor inaccuracies is allowed where the exhibit is intended only to act as a guide to the testimony of the witness. If, on the other hand, the diagram is to be used as substantive evidence, such as to prove the location of boundary lines or a topographical feature of a landscape, great care should be taken to establish the accuracy of the exhibit.

The use of maps and graphs as an aid to comprehending testimony is also common. In many cases, under the rules of documentary evidence, it is unnecessary to establish the factual basis for the exhibits such as the process of gathering data on which the graph is based or, in the case of a map, the accuracy of the surveyor. Even if these documents fit within the applicable hearsay exception, it is still necessary to establish that the particular graph or table offered is the one it purports to be. Should it be necessary to enlarge the original graph, the enlarging process must be authenticated.

(11.8) Best and Secondary Evidence Rule

The *best evidence rule* is actually an expression of the legal system's preference for the strongest or most authentic evidence available. Although the rule generally applies only to documents in writing, the Federal Rules of Evidence (Sec. 1001) also make the rule applicable to recordings, photographs, X rays, and films.

The rule requires that the contents of any writing be proven by the contents of the writing itself or that failure to do so be adequately explained. If the trial court finds the explanation satisfactory, the judge has the discretionary power to admit secondary evidence of the writing, usually in the form of a carbon copy or other copy. When there are no secondary sources, oral testimony concerning the contents of the writing is admitted so long as the court is satisfied that no superior (that is, written) evidence is available.

The best evidence rule does not involve a judgment on the persuasiveness or conclusiveness of evidence. Indeed, that entails a strategic decision that must be made by the attorneys for each side. The primary purpose of the best evidence rule is to prevent fraud. The most effective way to prove the contents of a written document is, of course, to introduce the document itself. When an unexecuted copy of a document is offered to prove the contents of the original, the possibility always exists that the copy is not an accurate representation of the parties' intentions at the time the document was signed.

In order to have secondary evidence of a writing admitted, the offering party must go through a three-part proof. Thus, he must prove:

1. that the original existed at one time;
2. that the original was genuine and represented the intent of the parties;
3. that there was an adequate explanation for the failure to produce the original.

There are many acceptable reasons for not producing the original document. The purpose of the best evidence rule is not to ban the use of nonoriginal writings, but to be certain that the original is no longer available. Two of the most common reasons are that the original was destroyed by the offering party without fraudulent intent or that the original was lost and a diligent search has failed to produce it.

a. Legal Documents and Public Records

If the evidence sought concerns a legal proceeding, the best available evidence is always the official record of the proceeding. It thus becomes necessary to produce the official transcript or record to establish any evidence made public at a trial. A witness is not allowed to give oral testimony concerning the outcome of a trial or testimony given at trial if an objection is made under the best evidence rule. Secondary evidence of legal proceedings is admissible only where the judicial records are no longer available or where the trial record is incomplete with respect to the issue at trial.

The best evidence rule also applies to records kept by public officials or agencies and to the proceedings of public bodies. Secondary evidence is only admissible when there is no available official record.

b. Photographic Copies, Duplicates, and Carbon Copies

The traditional application of the best evidence rule barred photographic duplicates of an original where the failure to produce the original was not adequately explained. These copies are not regarded as duplicate originals of the documents since they were not executed at a point simultaneous to the execution of the original; thus, the possibility of fraudulent alterations still exists. Increased sophistication of and reliance on photoduplication equipment have, however, seriously undercut the application of the best evidence rule in this area. A number of states have passed statutes that allow qualified photographic reproductions to be admissible as evidence and with the same status as the original writing. This parallels developments concerning documentary evidence that admit a certified copy of a public record with the same authentication process required of an original.

The courts have generally held that photostatic copies of public records are admissible. Because the courts seem to have taken judicial notice of the accuracy of photographic reproduction, it is not necessary to include a scientific explanation of the camera's accuracy as a part of the authentication process. Issues in which the courts assume accuracy of reproduction are sometimes termed "self-authenticating."

If the original document cannot be located, but the offering party is able to offer a duplicate original, the best evidence rule will not exclude the duplicate original. The clearest example of a duplicate original is a legal document, which is normally executed in tripli-cate. Because of the nature of the execution and the identity of the documents themselves, there is no basis for distinguishing the original from the duplicates.

There is a division of opinion concerning the application of the best evidence rule to carbon copies of the original document. Some jurisdictions treat carbon copies as the equivalent of duplicate origi-nals even when there has been no formal execution of the copies. In such cases, the carbon copy must still be authenticated in some way as having been made at the same time as the original.

Where either the original document or the copy of the original has not been accounted for, the rule operates to exclude a copy made from a copy, unless it is the best evidence available.

(11.9) Form of Proof, Adverse Production, and Complex Documents

The objective of the party seeking to have secondary evidence introduced is to convince the trial judge that he has exhausted all reasonable avenues of discovery and has been unable to locate the original writing. Any competent proof may be used to establish that the original has been lost, destroyed, or otherwise made unavailable. It is not necessary to offer positive proof of a writing's destruction. If the trial judge has any suspicion that the document is being improp-erly withheld, however, he may deny the admission of secondary evidence by invoking the best evidence rule.

It is not sufficient for the party seeking to produce secondary evidence of a document to indicate that the adverse party is in possession of the original. In order to fulfill the requirements of the best evidence rule, he must be able to show that he has given the opponent a request for production (notice), and there has been a failure to comply. The requirements of notice vary among juris-dictions, but generally include a written request for production of the document and allowance of a reasonable period in which to produce it. If the document is clearly unavailable by reason of its remoteness, it is within the court's discretion to order admission of the secondary evidence. In addition, most jurisdictions do not require a defendant to produce a document that incriminates him.

When the best evidence rule is made inapplicable by the vast number of documents or when the complexity outweighs their value as evidence, the court has discretion to authorize or to order an approximate summary. This occurs most frequently in complex commercial cases where it is impractical to require the production of thousands of canceled checks or a complete accounting of a firm's financial status. In such cases, the original documents must be submitted to the adverse party so that the accuracy of the summary can be tested on cross-examination.

A. ROUTINE PHYSICAL EVIDENCE

(11.10) In General

Any physical evidence that tends to prove or disprove the crime charged may be offered. If it is relevant, and the proper foundation laid, it will be admitted as part of the proof. The range of objects and materials that may be offered in evidence is limitless. Relevancy is the key word.

(11.11) Admissible Objects

No rule excludes any particular object as evidence. As long as the evidence tends to prove the issue, it should be usable.

If, however, the exhibit is too gruesome or inflammatory, the court will exclude it on these grounds. In a homicide case arising out of an illegal abortion, for example, the dead fetus may have been preserved and offered in evidence. It would be excluded on that ground, no matter how relevant it might be to the proof. If the exhibit can be misleading, such as an unfair or slanted photograph, it will be rejected if there is an objection.

(11.12) Fruits of the Crime

"Fruits of the crime," such as loot from a robbery or a burglary, are relevant and admissible in evidence. If it is impracticable to bring the actual objects into court, photographs of them can be used in evidence. A stolen car or truck, for example, would be returned to the owner and would be described by witnesses with the aid of photographs.

(11.13) Instrumentalities

Anything used to commit crime is relevant evidence. A murder weapon, a gun employed in a robbery, a burglar's tools, an acetylene torch used to open a safe, a gasoline can from an arson scene—all such objects may properly be offered in evidence in each particular case.

(11.14) Masks and Clothing

Any type of mask used during the commission of a crime would be admitted in evidence. Police sometimes overlook clothing as evidence of a crime. If, however, the clothing is some type of disguise, it would be strong evidence. More frequently the suspect's or victim's clothing may yield stains, foreign substances, powder burns, or wound marks that make the clothing very useful as evidence.

At one time a medical examiner in Maryland issued a death certificate stating that a man had died from natural causes. The deceased, a middle-aged man with a history of heart trouble, was found dead, lying across the bed in his motel room, clad in his underwear. The cause of death was determined to be heart disease. Because of an anonymous telephone tip suggesting murder, the medical examiner reopened the case. The examiner found a tiny hole in the front of the man's undershirt with a bloodstain on it. The autopsy revealed that he had been stabbed to death with one blow of an ice pick, which was apparently delivered by the other occupant of the room, his paramour. Thus, the overlooked undershirt was a prime bit of evidence in the prosecution's murder case.

(11.15) Changes in Objects

If an exhibit is to be admitted in evidence, it must reasonably be in the same condition at the time of the trial as it was at the time of the crime. In the event it has been altered because of laboratory or scientific testing, expert witnesses can describe the changes, and the evidence will still be admitted, even though it is in a different condition. Though some types of evidence deteriorate naturally, they still may be allowed in evidence if they remain usable and if the change in condition is not prejudicial in some way.

If, however, the evidence has been carelessly handled or damaged so that it has been changed materially, the defense has valid grounds to object to its use, and court may exclude it.

(11.16) Exhibition of Persons

As has been mentioned in Chapter 4, the defendant can be ordered to present himself in a lineup. He can also be made to rise in court or otherwise exhibit himself or any part of his body, if this is relevant to the proof. He may have, for example, been described as strong and husky. The court may thus allow him to remove his shirt and show that he really is of slight physique or that he has a physical impairment, such as a crippled arm.

Exhibiting the body or any part thereof is also left to the discretion of the judge. He will allow nothing of this nature if it is indecent or inflammatory in the court's judgment.

B. SCIENTIFIC EVIDENCE

(11.17) In General

With the advance of science, scientific evidence allowed in court has changed. Pictures of bank robbers taken by hidden cameras or closed-circuit television, for example, are now used in evidence. Such proof was unknown years ago. Acceptance by the courts of new types of scientific evidence is slow, however, and does not keep pace with the latest advances in science. Whenever a new type of scientific evidence is offered, considerable expert testimony must support it.

In addition, a time of successful use must first be shown before the courts will allow the new method in evidence.

Whenever a new type of scientific evidence is offered, considerable expert testimony must support it. The general rule on scientific evidence has always been that it will not be received until it has "general scientific acceptance."

There is a modern tendency to relax this, following the lead of the Federal Rules of Evidence, Sec. 702, and admit any scientific proof that will help the jury "understand the evidence or determine a fact

(11.18) Firearms and Ballistics

Much valuable evidence can be obtained by firearms and ballistics tests, but they are not completely perfect as popularly imagined.

In case of close-range firing, reliable tests exist to measure burning, powder marks, and other residues. Tissue may be burned or fabrics scorched. Carbon or powder particles may penetrate or adhere to the surface of the wound. Such proof is often crucial in determining whether a shooting was suicide, accidental, or homicide.

Firearms themselves may be identified through restoring obliterated serial numbers. Gun barrels leave distinguishing marks on bullets. Shell casings also receive individual markings that can often identify the weapon from which the shell was fired. Bullet or shell comparisons, however, are not always completely conclusive, depending on the fragment recovered at the time of the crime. Experts can often state only that the bullet could have come from the weapon in question. The evidence is still acceptable, although it is not conclusive proof of the connection between the projectile and the weapon.

Gunshot residue tests from a suspect's hands—the so-called paraffin tests—have been known for many years. Many experts now doubt their value, largely because similar residues may be found on an innocent person's skin.

(11.19) Tool Marks and Micrography

Photographs taken through a microscope and then enlarged often provide strong circumstantial evidence for use in court. Pry marks from a forced entry may show identical markings with a tool when they are compared microscopically. Other examples include broken tools compared with a piece recovered at the scene of the crime, knife marks on bone, cut marks on wires, and crimp marks on detonators.

Microscopic examination of such evidence is often successful. The term "comparative micrography" is used to describe such examinations where a hard object is applied against a softer one. Tool marks, as has been said, can be examined in this way. The mark itself, or a cast impression, is microscopically compared with the mark made by the suspected tool on a soft substance such as lead. A photograph of the mark is termed "photomicrography." Matching striations, a piece of the blade from a suspect's knife, or a portion from a broken tool can often be successfully demonstrated by photomicrography. Because the photographs often contain areas of apparent differences that the expert must interpret and explain, however, it is not unusual for him to testify without using photomicrography.

(11.20) Forensic Pathology

The trained medical examiner can often supply the best evidence of the details of a suspected crime. In all suspicious or violent deaths an autopsy is required. The pathologist determines the cause and the approximate time of death. Was it a drowning, or did death occur outside the water? The postmortem tells.

Bruises and wounds can be measured and photographed. Hairs, blood, bodily fluids, stomach and blood contents, and condition of the body and wounds—all reveal a story to the trained examiner. In the case of sexual offenses, seminal and other stains may be analyzed. Blood alcohol is commonly tested where intoxication is involved. Evidence concerning poisons, drugs, and many other physical conditions is often given by pathologists.

(11.21) Toxicology and Chemistry

When poisoning is suspected, the pathologist performing the autopsy removes the bodily material such as blood, urine, stomach contents, or tissue from vital organs. He then turns the material over to a toxicologist (a specialist on poisons and their effect) for his examination. The toxicologist presents his findings in a report.

Laboratory Detective

The nude body dumped behind Frank's Nursery in Davie was Deborah Lynn Herdmann's. She was twenty-three, single, an aerobics instructor. She had a roommate, an apartment in Sunrise, a boyfriend who was seeing another woman, and no known enemies. At least, no one who would want her dead, police thought. Not tortured to death.

But there she was, sprawled alongside a cement mixer, hands bound behind her with duct tape, screams silenced with a silver piece stuck across her lips. That was what killed her. She slowly suffocated.

The homicide detectives took inventory of clues. It wasn't a long list. No guns with fingerprints. No tire tracks in the dirt. Rings were still on her fingers, so robbery was out.

Just a naked body and a white blouse dumped behind potted palms.

Everything added up to zip. Everything that is except what Bruce Ayola, a police scientist, found later in the lab: a few almost invisible threads stuck to the duct tape, threads so small you could not make out their color even under a microscope. Peering through a microspectrophotometer, Ayola saw that the fibers were gray and blue. A sliced section under a polarized light microscope showed shape and thickness. A spectrometer showed that the threads were nylon. Ayola deduced that these were coarse fibers, the kind found in automobile carpeting.

Detectives already had learned that the girl had been dating a two-timing limousine driver. They found his car. It had blue carpet and grey mats. The fibers matched. Faced with the evidence the boyfriend, Vincent A. Walsh, and his buddy, Michael John Bedford, confessed.

Walsh got life.

Bedford got the electric chair.

Reprinted with permission of *The Miami Herald*,
Tracie Cone, staff reporter.

A chemical expert may be called in for laboratory tests in cases concerned with drug abuse or situations involving intoxication. These tests include the use of chemical reagents, crystalline comparisons, chromatography, and other methods of chemical testing. All methods have strengths and weaknesses, and an investigator or attorney should be aware of them as they relate to evidence involved in a criminal prosecution.

Alcohol tests are the most frequently encountered by the officer in the field. Blood, breath, urine, or saliva can all be checked for the presence of alcohol. A police investigator must, however, take certain precautions. The breath test may be defective if the machine has not been aerated to remove moisture. Sterilizing the skin with any kind of alcohol may contaminate a blood sample that is taken for alcohol testing. A blood sample taken at a postmortem to determine the amount of alcohol is useless if the body has been embalmed.

Various factors weaken the effectiveness in court of a blood test for alcohol where intoxication is involved in the criminal charge. After the blood sample is taken, the chemist will actually be unable to state exactly what the alcoholic content of the blood was at the time of the event. It is obvious that the sample had to be taken at some point after the alleged crime. Heavy drinking just before the crime would produce a high percentage of alcohol in the blood at the time of the test. Because of the time necessary for alcohol to be absorbed in the bloodstream, a laboratory expert would have to admit that the blood-alcohol level at the time of the crime would have to have been lower. Experienced defense attorneys are aware of such test deficiencies where alcohol is involved, and they can often convince juries of the weaknesses in such proof.

(11.22) Serology

A serologist is used to analyze bodily fluids such as blood, semen, saliva, and the like. Analysis of blood is the most common.

Several tests are conducted first to classify the specimen as blood. Lipstick, catsup, even iodine are some of the substances that resemble blood. Further tests indicate whether it is animal or human blood. Once it is found to be human, blood is divided into types, either A, B, AB, or O. The types can be readily determined. Approximately 40 percent of Americans are type A, 43 percent are type O, 14 percent are type B, and 3 percent are type AB. There are other systems as well for classifying human blood. Unlike fingerprints, blood samples cannot specifically identify any one individual. An expert can only testify that the blood samples are of the same group, not that they are from the same person. He can, however, eliminate a possible source if the two samples are of different classes.

Until recently, blood samples could not be identified with any particular person but could only show that the sample was of the same or different blood group as that of the individual involved. A new blood testing technique is now being developed. The test, called electrophoresis, came to us from Scotland Yard. It involves a method of sorting out enzymes in the blood and can come much closer to identifying the individual from whom the sample came.

In a Florida murder case, Priscilla Bradford was accused of beating her husband to death. She claimed that the blood stain on her blouse came from herself and not from her murdered husband. Electrophoresis showed that she and her husband had three similar enzymes in their blood but that they differed in two. The difference in the enzymes showed that the blood on the blouse was his. The court accepted these test results. She was convicted and sentenced to thirty-six years in prison.

The Kansas Court of Appeals approved the use of the Multi-System blood analysis test in which three enzyme systems are tested from one blood sample at one time. A chemist was allowed to testify from these test results in a murder case, the court finding that this test now had general scientific approval.

Those people who have type A, type B, or type AB secrete the antigens characteristic of these blood groups in such bodily fluids as saliva, tears, semen, and perspiration. Blood grouping tests from these bodily secretions can, therefore, be made for about 80 percent of the population.

In cases involving rape or perversion, serology tests are often made to determine the presence of semen and sperm cells. Seminal fluid is secreted by the glands along the seminal tract to which sperm is supplied from the testes. Sperm will not be present if the suspect has had a vasectomy or if too much time has elapsed between the crime and the taking of the sample. The specimen may be tested for acid phosphatase to reveal if it is human seminal fluid. Swabs may be taken from the vaginal or cervical area of the female. In cases of perversion anal or oral swabs are used. Stains may be found on the clothing of the victim or suspect or at the scene of the crime.

The HLA (Human Leukocyte Antigen) test has been developed as a more scientific method of proving paternity than the use of blood types. Florida now admits the test results as evidence and can order the putative father to submit it. This test may have application in some criminal cases.

Science has now developed DNA (deoxyribonocleic acid) testing, which is the newest identification tool. DNA, the genetic material that makes up chromosomes, is unique to each individual except identical twins. Experts have testified that the possibility of two individuals' DNA matching is one in sixteen billion. DNA can be extracted from any sample that has cells. Using enzymes that snip DNA at precise points, scientists divide the DNA itself into pieces and organize them by size. When the DNA is sorted into a pattern, it produces a bar code that can be "read" electronically and matched with other DNA samples. The result can then be computerized and stored as a permanent record.

The DNA, for example, can be extracted from a suspect's blood, semen, or hair and matched with that found at the crime scene. It readily convicts the guilty or exonerates the innocent. Courts in many jurisdictions are accepting DNA evidence, and convictions have followed in many major criminal trials.

The Texas Court of Appeals, in 1990, first considered the reliability of DNA evidence (*Glover* v. *State*, 787 S.W. 2d, 544 [1990]). Citing decisions of several other state courts, including Florida, Minnesota, Maryland, New York, and Virginia, the court concluded:

> DNA fingerprinting—its underlying principles, procedures, and technology— is a scientific test that is reliable and has gained general acceptance in the scientific community in the particular field in which it belongs.

Presently, the majority of the states have accepted DNA evidence in criminal trials and judicial proceedings, the first being in a 1987 rape case. Some federal appellate courts have held that DNA test results are acceptable evidence in federal criminal trials; however, the U.S. Supreme Court has yet to address the issue.

This technique is so effective that police agencies across the country are establishing their own DNA laboratories. Prison authorities wanting to take advantage of this new science have proposed taking samples from all inmates for DNA identification. Other law enforcement agencies want to take samples from all arrestees for DNA identification. Police want to build DNA files and have these computerized like today's massive fingerprint files.

Just over the scientific horizon is an added identification tool for the criminal justice system—retinal identification. Each person, including identical twins, has a unique pattern of blood vessels in the retina of the eye. Read by a scanner when a beam of low-intensity light is sent through the pupil of the eye, the pattern of retinal blood vessels can be digitized and stored in a computer. A new ultra-rapid computer can search a data base of eyeprints in seconds, whereas using computers to match fingerprints can take hours. This identification system is now being used by the Pentagon and some national laboratories.

Laboratories may also use an Immunobead Assay test to detect antisperm antibodies that are found in less than 5 percent of males; this test also gives further proof of identification.

Saliva stains are not often thought of, and yet they may be found on cigarette butts, cigars, pipes, or other objects. As has been said, they can often be used to classify blood types. Similar results can also be obtained from perspiration stains, which normally remain on coats, hats, shirts, and dresses. Even fecal matter and vomitus yield test results to the serologist.

(11.23) Narcotics and Drugs

Because the use of narcotics and various drugs has become so widespread, law enforcement personnel continuously find themselves deeply involved in drug control.

It has even been a legal problem to devise a definition of "narcotic" that is scientifically correct. Those who draft statutes have avoided the problem by simply listing a series of drugs that must be labeled "controlled substances." Some jurisdictions have statutes that attempt not only to regulate narcotics traffic but to make it a crime to be a user. California attempted this with a possession statute making it a crime to "use or be under the influence, or be addicted to the use of narcotics."

In *Robinson* v. *California*, 370 U.S. 660 (1962), a suspect arrested under this law had needle marks and scabs on his inner arms. He confessed to the use of narcotics. A police narcotics officer testified that, in his opinion, the marks on the defendant, Robinson, resulted from the use of a nonsterile hypodermic needle. When Robinson took the stand, he repudiated his confession and said that the marks came from an allergy contracted in the military service. Robinson was, nevertheless, convicted. The U.S. Supreme Court finally overturned his conviction. It pointed out that, while the state can legally regulate narcotics traffic, here they were making a crime of addiction, even if the drugs were used outside the state of California. The court reasoned that this would be similar to considering mental illness or venereal disease a crime. In the opinion of the court, this amounted to cruel and unusual punishment and violated the Eighth and Fourteenth Amendments.

a. Types of Drugs

Opiates are one of the general classes of drugs. Derived from the opium poppy, they include opium, codeine, morphine, heroin, and synthetics such as methadone and meperidine. All opiates are addictive and are labeled narcotics.

Marijuana, often listed as a narcotic, is correctly classified as a hallucinogen, as are mescaline and LSD. As the term indicates, users of hallucinogens perceive sights, sounds, and colors that are not real. Though none of these drugs are considered addictive, many are dangerous.

Cocaine is an alkaloid derived from cocoa leaves. A stimulant, it reduces inhibitions. Extended use may produce hallucinations. It is normally taken by sniffing or by injection.

Barbiturates are used as sedatives, hypnotics, and antispasmodics. Overuse produces symptoms similar to intoxication and can result in physical dependence.

Amphetamines are stimulants. Their use does not cause physical dependence.

b. Tests for Drugs

The police chemist is frequently called on to identify unknown materials in order to determine if they are drugs or narcotics. In cases of deaths and of traffic violations, tests of blood or urine are used to provide information concerning the use of drugs. These range from relatively simple physical and chemical tests to nuclear activation analysis.

Tests to determine addiction to narcotics are among those generally employed by police laboratories. Urinary analysis is the best-known method. Laboratory findings based on urinalysis are accepted as legal evidence. One problem with urinalysis is that police are often careless in obtaining and preserving the sample.

In the 1950's, the nalline test was developed to discover narcotic addiction or recent use by individuals. The test involves injecting a drug, nalorphine, into a subject and measuring the reaction of the pupil of his eye.

An early California case ruled on the admissibility of nalline test results for narcotics use (*People* v. *Williams*, 164 Cal. App. 2d

858 [1959]). Two suspects had been arrested as being drug users. Each admitted to having used drugs previous to that time, but denied recent use. Both of them had old and new needle marks on their arms. The doctor who administered the test testified in court that the subjects were injected with nalline after having their pupils measured with a test card that contained a series of dots. Thirty minutes later their pupils were measured again. A comparison of the measurements showed that each one had dilated pupils. The appellate court approved the use of the test results in conjunction with the expert's opinion that both defendants were then under the influence of narcotics. While the nalline test itself has limitations, such as the possibility of inaccurate readings of the pupillometer, it is now generally received in court.

Courts now routinely allow witnesses to testify concerning needle marks ("tracks") on a suspect's arm and to give an opinion as to whether they are recent or old. Such evidence has been received as proof in possession of heroin.

A wide variety of scientific tests for narcotics and drugs are accepted by modern courts, providing there is proper identification of the sample, its custody, and the qualification of the expert witness.

The public pressure for more widespread drug testing will end up pitted against court rulings resulting from appeals by objectors who claim that drug testing violates their "right to privacy." The United States Constitution does not contain a right to privacy, but some courts have recognized it in civil litigation that seeks to bar various testing. Courts have used the First, Third, Fourth, and Fourteenth Amendments as the bases for their rulings that individuals have some sort of constitutional right to privacy. In general, the government's invasion of privacy may be justified by a compelling governmental interest. Because of a popular resentment against testing, some states (Alabama, Montana, California, Florida, and New Jersey) have adopted in their state constitutions provisions that protect an individual's "right to privacy."

In criminal cases the rules have been much broader in approving blood testing and the like as not being "searches" or not being a violation of the Fifth Amendment protection against self-incriminating testimony. Such testing has been generally approved wherever the state has had probable cause to do such testing.

It remains to be seen whether the civil case "right to privacy" litigation will spill over into the field of criminal evidence.

(11.24) Fingerprints

The skin of a person's fingers, palms, toes, and feet contains a series of friction ridges, which is nature's method of giving man traction. These ridges form patterns that remain the same from birth to death. All friction skin has perspiration pores, and body oils leave a pattern wherever the skin ridges touch a smooth surface. Impressions accidentally left on such a surface are called latent prints. Though they are normally invisible, they can be made visible by means of powders, vapors, or chemicals. They can be lifted by the use of a transparent adhesive tape or other means and kept as a permanent record. The latent prints once brought to life can be photographed and then compared with known fingerprints.

The newest development in the detection of fingerprints is the use of lasers. Widely used in Canada, it has growing acceptance in the United States. The FBI used laser fingerprinting in the Tylenol poisoning cases. Lasers, focusing on the natural fluorescence of human secretions in fingerprints, cause a bright glow that can be photographed. Permanent laser units are used in laboratories, while portable ones taken to a crime scene can rapidly scan an entire room and all its contents for prints.

All fingerprints can be classified under an accepted formula, which makes it possible for them to be filed and retrieved. Identifying the unknown latent print with the known one is entirely different from classifying it. There can be an untold number of prints in the same general class, but only one print of a particular individual.

To identify the particular print, the expert looks for four elements. The standard rule is that there must be at least eight identical ridge comparisons; generally, more concordances are desired. The latent print at the scene of the crime is usually used to identify the defendant and to place him at the scene.

Thus, fingerprint evidence has two uses: to prove the identity of the accused or of the victim or to provide evidence that the defendant committed the crime.

Testimony regarding fingerprints must come from an expert trained and experienced in the science of classifying and identifying them. This type of evidence is so widely accepted that the defense now has little room for attacking the technician's testimony. There are, in fact, a number of cases in which a conviction has been won and sustained even though it is based mainly on fingerprints.

People v. *Rodis,* 145 Cal. App. 2d 44 (1956), concerned the burglary of a drugstore in California. The burglar entered the store through a rear window that was nine feet from the ground. A screen was removed, and the defendant's fingerprint was found on the outside of the window. At the trial the only evidence against the defendant was this fingerprint. Contrary evidence was provided by his family who testified that he was at home the night of the burglary. The defendant himself took the stand and denied ever having been in the store. In spite of the evidence provided by the defense, the defendant was convicted on the strength of the fingerprint evidence. The appellate court affirmed the conviction, pointing out that the fingerprint was found on the outside of the window, nine feet from the ground. Thus, it would have been necessary for a person to use a ladder or a platform to remove the screen. All of these facts militated against any innocent placement of the fingerprint. There is, however, a more generally accepted rule regarding fingerprint evidence. It holds that, in cases where the only evidence of guilt consists of fingerprints found at the scene, the evidence, to be legally sufficient, must be coupled with proof of other circumstances tending reasonably to exclude the idea that the fingerprint was left at a different time. Unless these circumstances are present, the courts will not sustain a conviction based only on fingerprint evidence.

Often it is important to know when a latent print was made, but it is doubtful if such proof can be obtained from fingerprint evidence. The courts sometimes make unusual decisions on this point, as illustrated by the two *Barum* cases cited above. In one of these, Barum was convicted of stealing from a private home a valuable coin collection contained in two empty jars. His fingerprints were found on the jars, but the government's witness admitted that the prints could have been on the jars "for a period of . . . years." The appellate court reversed the conviction. It held that there was insufficient evidence to convict and said that the prosecution should have produced evidence to show that the prints "were placed on the jars at the time of the crime." Barum's other burglary conviction resulted from fingerprints found on three objects in a house, a tea canister, a metal cash box, and a glass table top. The appellate court upheld this conviction on the theory that Barum could have had no previous access to these articles.

In presenting fingerprint evidence, the prosecution must demonstrate the qualifications of its expert and his method of gathering the evidence and its custody, the means of expert examination, and his opinion. The defense may counterattack by attempting to show errors made by the technician and irregularities owing to dirt, variations in finger pressure, scars, and excess use of ink. If the fingerprints were incident to an unlawful arrest, the defense can have them excluded from evidence.

As has been illustrated previously, if the defendant can show that he had innocent access to the scene of the crime, the fingerprint evidence will lack value. The defense may also be allowed to offer evidence that there were no fingerprints at the scene. In this situation the state may rebut the defense by offering proof to show why no fingerprints were found. The fact that other fingerprints may have been present at the scene of the crime may not be relevant evidence and will thus be excluded by the trial court. In a bank robbery case, the defense was an alibi. The prosecution introduced evidence that the defendant's fingerprint was on the bank window. Farley offered to introduce evidence that other fingerprints were on the window besides his. The court properly denied his offer of proof. It stated that the presence of his prints was shown to disprove his alibi defense. If fingerprints belonging to someone else were there also, it was immaterial.

(11.25) Questioned Documents

The modern specialist who examines documents has come a long way from the so-called "handwriting expert" of previous years. Aided by present-day scientific developments, he is able to do many more things than analyze handwriting. It is true that a questioned document often involves handwriting comparisons, and the expert is called in solely to perform this function. He might, for example, identify the author of a written extortion or ransom note, a forgery, or a letter. He is often asked to do more than this. Has the original document been changed? Were words inserted? Have pages been added? Is the entire paper a fake? These and many similar questions are often submitted to the examiner of questioned documents for his analysis and for his subsequent court testimony.

During the last hundred years, the science of document examination has grown and become more sophisticated. There were initially many so-called experts whose court testimony was based more on self-confidence than on expertise. While there is no recognized professional course of study for a document examiner, the individual must have a technical background and much experience in his field. Those prerequisites will qualify him as an "expert." Though document examiners sometimes vary in their opinions, this does not occur often. When they do disagree, it is usually because they did not have the same materials or they worked under different conditions.

What is a questioned document? It may be a letter, a check, a contract, or a will. It may, in fact, be any material that contains a mark or signature. Criminal cases often involve a variety of things, from the psychopath's scrawled message in lipstick on a mirror to hotel registers, drivers' licenses, and passports. Whenever a document or any part of it is questioned or its authorship is in doubt, the examiner is called in to analyze it and to give his opinion.

The document itself must be treated with great care by the field investigator. Handling is avoided whenever possible so that fingerprints will not be added or minute changes made. The document will usually be picked up with tweezers, placed in a plastic envelope, and sealed. The investigator's mark will then be put on the outside of the container, not on the item itself.

If handwriting is involved, the examiner must have as many genuine exemplars as possible. The defendant can be ordered to furnish these specimens. The expert prefers examples of the suspect's handwriting that use the same words as those appearing in the questioned document. Similarities as well as differences are important in arriving at an opinion on handwriting.

A typewritten document can often be traced to a particular machine. The document examiner keeps a file of samples of the type from various kinds of typewriters. This often allows him to determine immediately the make or model of the typewriter involved. Because each machine develops its own particular characteristics, such as type wear and varying impressions, the expert can go on to make a precise identification of the typewriter used. It is even possible to identify typewriters with revolving elements, although this type of machine does cause added problems for the expert examiner. The trial of Alger Hiss was one of the most widely publicized cases in which the conviction was largely based on typewriter evidence. Some expert findings are now questioning the reliability of typewriter evidence.

In the field of altered documents the skilled examiner can often show the most dramatic results. By using infrared or ultraviolet light and other methods, he may be able photographically to reproduce charred documents, disclose words previously removed by chemicals, or even reproduce the original writing from indentations transferred to paper that lay underneath.

The document examiner may use demonstrative evidence for the jury to illustrate his testimony. Some courts criticize him when he uses this device, and others criticize him when he does not. In *People* v. *White*, 365 Ill. 499 (1937), the defendant was accused of forging a signature on a promissory note. The state claimed that a genuine signature was first traced on the note with carbon paper and then written over in ink. The expert for the prosecution claimed that this left flecks of carbon on the paper. A microscope was set up in the courtroom, and each juror was allowed to look through it. The expert asked each in turn if he saw the flecks, and every answer was "Yes." The appellate court very properly criticized these actions and said that such a demonstration and interrogation of the jurors was improper.

It is interesting to contrast this with a federal case involving income tax fraud. The IRS received a forged letter that was allegedly signed before May 1967. The government expert testified that the signature was made with an ink that was not manufactured until after that time. To prove his contention concerning the ink, he performed a demonstration in the courtroom. He punched holes about the size of a hypodermic needle from the questioned signature and dissolved these small pieces of paper containing the ink in a solution that was then placed on a coded plate. The ink separated into its component dyes, and the expert compared this unknown ink with chromatograms. He testified that the original comparison chromatograms were made on glass plates that fade quickly. The court criticized the expert for not taking colored photographs of the plates and offering photographs in evidence. The court pointed out that the actual demonstration provided no way for the jury to see what the basis for his comparison was. Had they been shown colored photographs or slides, they could have assigned proper weight to this testimony.

Thus, when materials are properly handled in the field and when the modern qualified document examiner is provided adequate handwriting exemplars, he can often be the strongest witness the state can produce.

(11.26) Microanalysis

The term microanalysis refers generally to analysis of minute particles of evidence and not just to evidentiary testing by microscope. Microscopes of various kinds are used by technicians in this process.

Examination of small particles of hair, paint, fibers, soil, and glass frequently yields significant results. Paint smears from burglaries or chips from an automobile accident, for example, can often be analyzed and classified by such testing. Paint may be many layers, and the number and kinds of layers can reveal matching characteristics.

Glass fragments from car headlights, broken windows, eyeglasses, and the like may be important evidence. Particles may be found in a suspect's clothing or matched with those in a suspected vehicle. Various techniques of microanalysis can also reveal the chemical or physical characteristics of glass for scientific comparison.

One can test hair to discover whether it is human or animal. It is possible to identify hair from different areas of the body. Racial differences and sometimes sex can be determined by the examination of human hair.

Fibers are of varied types, from synthetic to animal, and the examiner can usually classify them and make accurate comparisons. Even in very small quantities, fibers yield information that can be useful. Those obtained from clothing, for example, may match those from insulation where burglars forced an entry through a wall or ceiling. Tools, clothing, and fired bullets may have fibers connected to them. Threads found on a murder or rape victim may help identify the suspect.

Soil may either be left or removed from the location where the crime occurred. Proper preservation by the investigator enables laboratory technicians to obtain useful evidence from soil, but comparisons are very difficult.

(11.27) Neutron Activation Analysis

One by-product of atomic science, which has been employed since 1964, is neutron activation analysis of evidence in criminal cases. This process involves bombarding the evidence with a stream of nuclear particles from a nuclear reactor that is used for research. This produces radioactivity in the bombarded material. The radioactive material "decays," and in so doing it gives off gamma rays. The rays are counted and their intensity measured. This information is then compared with known data to give an analysis of the quantity of the elements present in the evidentiary sample. Gunshot residue, soils, paint, grease, drugs, and a variety of other substances can be tested by this method. It is obvious, of course, that the facilities for this type of testing are limited.

U.S. v. *Stifel*, 401 U.S. 994 (1970), is the leading case supporting evidence obtained by neutron activation analysis. Orville Stifel was convicted of murdering Dan Ronec, in his parents' home, by sending a bomb through the mail. The package was in the form of a mailing tube that exploded when Ronec unscrewed the top. The evidence against Stifel was circumstantial, the alleged motive being jealousy over a woman. Stifel had worked for a large soap company and had access to its mailing tubes and labels. The government used neutron activation analysis on these, and its expert testified that the mailing label and tube fragments were the same "elemental composition" as those of the company. The metal cap and the tape "were the same manufacture" and were produced on the same day as the ones made for the company. The court admitted the evidence resulting from the neutron activation analysis, pointing out that no appeals court had refused it and that its scientific basis had been widely accepted by a variety of state decisions.

More recently, in 1974, the Minnesota Supreme Court approved the use of this type of scientific evidence, with a slight warning. In the case involved in this decision, *State* v. *Spencer*, 216 N.W. 2d 131 (Minn., 1974), the defendant had been convicted of aggravated assault and of shooting an off-duty policeman. When the suspect was arrested, his hands were swabbed with nitric acid solution, and the swabs were sent to the Treasury Department laboratory in Washington for neutron analysis. At the trial, the expert testified that the test results showed the presence of barium and antimony on the defendant's right hand and that this meant that the defendant had fired a gun. On cross-examination the expert admitted that there were about a hundred other ways that these chemicals could have contacted the defendant's hands. The court approved the use of the the neutron activation analysis evidence. It pointed out, however, that the expert should only have been allowed to state his opinion that the chemicals came from firing a gun. He should not have been allowed to state this as a positive conclusion.

There appears to be no serious court opposition to the use of

this new method. While its access to the police is necessarily somewhat limited, the results can be spectacular.

(11.28) Polygraph

This is a widely used device for testing a person's truthfulness.
Developed a number of years ago, it operates on the theory that
lying produces tension even in the hardened criminal. This in turn
affects bodily reactions such as blood pressure and respiration. These
are measured by the machine as the subject is being questioned, and
they are recorded on a continuous graph. By reading the graph, a
well-trained operator can determine the speaker's truthfulness with
great accuracy.

Police forces everywhere have used the polygraph for a number
of years in criminal investigations. Was the woman raped, or did she
consent? Did the witness see the shooting, or is he purposely accusing
an innocent man? Prosecutors and police need to know the truthfulness of witnesses and complainants, and the polygraph has been a
useful aid in determining this.

An accused sometimes submits to a test voluntarily. If the
machine indicates his protestations of innocence are true, the prosecution is ordinarily dropped. If it shows that he is lying, a confession
may follow. Even where there is no confession, and the machine
points to guilt, the police at least know that they are on firm ground
in making the charge against him.

If a suspect refuses to be tested, the prosecution usually feels
that he is guilty. An innocent person has nothing to fear, and the
device should show his innocence.

It occasionally happens that both the defense and the prosecution stipulate that a polygraph test be given and the test results used
in evidence. Without such a stipulation, most courts will refuse to
admit polygraph evidence. They feel that the machine is being used
as a substitute for the court's and the jury's determination of
truthfulness.

New York's highest court excluded polygraph evidence in *People
v. Leone*, 25 N.Y. 2d 511 (1969). Oklahoma also refused to admit it
in *Fulton v. State*, 541 P. 2d 871 (Okla. Cr App. 1975), even though
both sides had agreed by stipulation that the results could be used.

Ballard v. Supreme Court, 64 Cal. 2d 159 (1966), illustrates
the narrow view that courts can take regarding polygraph tests.
Walter Ballard, a physician, was charged with raping a woman patient.

He was alleged to have given her a drug to prevent her resistance and then to have had sexual intercourse with her. The police physician examined her and found semen on her clothing. Later the police put a microphone in her purse and had her see the doctor in his office while they recorded their conversation outside. They also did the same thing by having her call the doctor on the telephone. The police subsequently gave her a polygraph test. When the doctor was arrested, he demanded the results of the test in order to prepare for trial. The court refused his request, saying that polygraph test results could not be used in court, and, therefore, the evidence was inadmissible. It did, however, allow him to be given the questions asked and her replies to them.

As has been said, most courts have consistently refused to allow such test results to be used. At present, however, there are a few indications that polygraph test results will be allowed under prescribed restrictions. One such indication came in *State* v. *Dorsey*, 532 P. 2d 912 (N.M. App. 1975), aff'd 539 P. 2d 204 (N.M., 1975). In that case the defendant was accused of attacking another person with a knife. He claimed self-defense, saying that he did not pull his knife before leaving his car and that the alleged victim struck the first blow. A polygraph test indicated that the defendant was telling the truth. He offered the test result to support his statement. The prosecution objected, and the trial court excluded the evidence. The appeals court held that this was in error. It ruled that, even though there had been an objection, the use of the polygraph was now a scientifically approved test, and, within the reasoning of *Chambers* v. *Mississippi*, supra, it should have been admitted.

(11.29) Voiceprints

Another scientific device now coming into wider use is the voiceprint, which reproduces a person's voice spectrographically. The test is based on the fact that no two people have the same voice characteristics. This is because the vocal cavities and organs of articulation—lips, tongue, teeth, and the like—all vary from individual to individual.

The voice spectrograph electronically analyzes the complex speech sounds, disburses them into their various parts, and reproduces them on current-sensitive paper. This visual result is the voiceprint. When certain cue words are compared with previously recorded voiceprints of the same words, identification of the voice becomes possible. The prints lend themselves to computerized classification so that a central file can be compiled. This file makes it possible, for example, to compare a kidnapper's or a blackmailer's telephone call with voiceprints of known criminals with similar backgrounds.

Scientific opinion regarding voiceprints is presently divided, despite their very high degree of accuracy. Both federal and state courts are also divided. At this point, however, courts in Massachusetts, California, and Minnesota have accepted voice spectrograms as evidence of identification in criminal cases, as have a few federal courts. *Commonwealth* v. *Lykus*, 327 N.E. 2d 671 (Mass., 1975), involved the kidnapping and murder of a young boy. The police taped the kidnapper's ransom calls. A specified amount of money was dropped, and, after three attempts, the suspect collected it. When it was traced to him, he admitted that he had picked up the money. He stated, however, that he had been hired to do it for $500 by a man who was involved in drug traffic, and he claimed that he had left the money where this person had instructed him to do so. The boy was found shot to death in a wooded area. At the trial, six witnesses identified the defendant's voice, but one could not. A voiceprint expert testified that the defendant was the one who made the calls. He based his statement on the tapes and voice exemplars. The defendant was found guilty and appealed. The appellate court approved the use of the voiceprint evidence and upheld the conviction.

The latest device designed to evaluate the voice electronically is the psychological stress evaluator. The theory behind this machine is similar to that of the polygraph in that it measures certain stress-related parts of speech. Involuntary indications of stress made by the voice are traced on a graph, and the results are interpreted. Unlike a polygraph, the machine does not have to be attached to the subject. It is necessary only to make a recording of the questions and answers. The recording of the interview is later fed through the evaluator, and the voice reactions are charted. The psychological stress evaluator is presently being used as an investigative tool in law enforcement agencies and in the business world, but it has not yet received court approval.

(11.30) Narcoanalysis and Hypnosis

Scopolamine, sodium pentothal, and the like, often labeled truth serums, are, at times, used as an interrogation or diagnostic tool. The technique is known as narcoanalysis and is based on the theory that this type of drug will break down the subject's mental resistance so that he will respond truthfully to questioning. Suspects may consent to such a test in order to clear themselves, or both counsel may stipulate that the test be given.

Courts consistently reject the introduction of any statement, by either a defendant or a witness, made under the influence of these drugs. They hold that the validity of the test has not been scientifically proven.

Statements made while the subject is under hypnosis are viewed by the courts in the same way as those made while an individual is undergoing narcoanalysis. A hypnotized person is, of course, powerfully subject to suggestion. Stage performers for many years have used posthypnotic suggestions to induce subjects to perform actions after the hypnotic trance is over. And yet, in spite of the court's rejection of these tests and of the widespread nonprofessional use of hypnosis, both hypnosis and narcoanalysis have legitimate investigative and diagnostic applications.

The human mind is a strange and largely unknown mechanism. Even the process of memory is not fully understood. People remember by different means. Some remember consciously less than others. Also, many tend to erase unpleasant or horrible experiences from their minds. What of the rape victim who cannot recall the events of the assault? Narcoanalysis or hypnotism may actually allow her to remember.

Narcoanalysis is, however, a recognized method used by psychiatrists to diagnose mental illness. But the information the patient gives the psychiatrist when drugs are administered for the purpose of diagnosis cannot be admitted as proof of the truth of what was said. An example of this occurred in a murder case in New York. In response to the defendant's request for a sanity test, one examining psychiatrist used a drug injection as a method of diagnosis to determine whether the defendant was insane or malingering. The trial judge allowed the doctor to describe this method of testing and to give his resulting opinion on the sanity of the subject. The physician was not, however, allowed to relate any admissions or drug-induced statement that the defendant may have made. The appellate court approved this decision and affirmed the conviction.

A more difficult problem exists when a statement is given after the truth serum treatment is completed. A similar situation can occur where the defendant is an addict and he has been given medication to ease his withdrawal symptoms, and then confesses. At the time of trial, he may claim that his confession was drug induced and thus involuntary.

In *People* v. *Townsend*, 11 Ill. 2d 30 (1957), the defendant, Townsend, was convicted of a mugging murder in which $4.80 was involved. While he was being interrogated, at the time of his arrest, he complained of stomach pains. A doctor was called in and found that the suspect was an addict suffering withdrawal symptoms. He administered phenobarbital and other drugs to relieve him. The defendant later gave a detailed statement confessing to the murder. He was subsequently sentenced to death. On appeal, Townsend claimed that his confession was drug induced and thus involuntary. The Illinois court affirmed his conviction, saying that the fact that he was given beneficial drugs to ease his pain was not proof that he was drugged for the purpose of securing a confession.

Six years later Townsend took his case to the U.S. Supreme Court via habeas corpus (*Townsend* v. *Sain*, 372 U.S. 293 [1963]). It found that one of the drugs given Townsend for treatment of his pains was hyocine, which is the same as scopolamine—a truth serum. For this reason, the court found that there was a real possibility that Townsend's later confession was drug induced, not voluntary. Thus, they remanded the case to the district court for a complete hearing on the subject.

Posthypnotic statements have, on occasion, received less harsh treatment from reviewing courts. In cases of amnesia, for example, posthypnotic suggestion is a legitimate means and a recognized method of restoring memory. If hypnosis is carefully used, with no suggestion made to the subject other than that he will be able to remember when his trance is ended, his later statement might possibly be allowed in evidence. The court would have to be assured that the test was so administered, however, because any posthypnotic statement is highly suspicious.

People v. *Leyra*, 302 N.Y. 353 (1951), was a case in which a son was convicted of the hammer slaying of his aged parents. When he was interrogated, he gave partial and conflicting statements. The police called in a doctor who questioned Leyra at length, using suggestion and other psychological tools. The defendant subsequently confessed orally to a police captain, to his business partner, and to the district attorney. During Leyra's first trial, at which he was found guilty, the taped interview with the doctor was heard by the jury. When the decision was appealed, the defendant claimed that he had been hypnotized and that none of his statements had been voluntary. The appellate court reversed the conviction and ordered a new trial. It stated that the recorded interview should not have been heard on the question of his guilt and that its only relevance could have been on the question of voluntariness.

Leyra was retried, and this time the doctor's interview was not used, only the subsequent confession. He was convicted again. His case was finally taken to the U.S. Supreme Court via habeas corpus. There his conviction was reversed a second time, the court holding that his statements to the doctor were coerced psychologically and that the other confessions followed so closely that they were one continuous process and were all involuntary.

In at least one reported incident—in a murder trial in Ohio— hypnosis was allowed in the courtroom. The jury was excused, and, by agreement of attorneys, the defendant was hypnotized in the presence of the judge. The prosecution then questioned him. As a result of the questioning, the prosecutor reduced the charge to manslaughter.

There are now several different approaches to the use of hypnosis in the criminal justice system. Some court decisions and state statutes completely bar the testimony of witnesses who have had their memory refreshed by hypnosis. Other jurisdictions allow such a witness to testify only as to the facts he could recall before hypnosis (*Bundy* v. *State*, 471 So. 2d 9 [1985]) rather than disqualify the witness entirely. A few decisions allow the entire testimony of a witness who had previously been properly hypnotized, if the jury is cautioned to weigh the testimony in the light of the procedure.

(11.31) Miscellaneous

Fluorescein powders have long been in use. Though invisible to the naked eye, they produce a fluorescent glow when excited by an ultraviolet lamp. They are frequently used to catch sneak thieves, such as dishonest employees.

In a highly publicized case in suburban Chicago, police suspected a dentist of performing indecent acts upon his female patients after administering gas. One woman volunteered for "dental treatment" and was gassed. Her private parts had been lightly covered with gynecological jelly mixed with fluorescein paste. When the dentist was later confronted, his face and sexual organs fluoresced.

At least one case has held that the use of ultraviolet lamps on a suspect's outer clothing or hands is not a search within the meaning of the Fourth Amendment. Thus, a search warrant is unnecessary.

A variety of other things provide scientific proof in criminal cases. Dentistry, for example, is increasingly used. Bite mark evidence is generally accepted. Unknown bodies may be reliably identified by dental records. This method is highly reliable because it is unlikely that any two people exist with the same dental history. Anthropologists and others may, in much the same way, be able to supply information on sex, race, and other characteristics from human remains found many years after death.

As science progresses, new fields of scientific evidence continue to expand. Instruments have been developed that can find a single grain of cocaine in a kilogram of flour. Lasers can reveal otherwise invisible semen, saliva, and blood stains.

A laboratory worker by chance discovered that Krazy Glue fumes will expose oils in fingerprints, making them appear where none could otherwise be seen. Krazy Glue helped catch California's Night Stalker by locating a fingerprint on the rear-view mirror in the killer's stolen car. Science continues to produce criminal evidence that juries increasingly rely on; such evidence is far superior to possible contradictory evidence from oral testimony.

It is necessary to insert a word of caution concerning scientific proof that depends on scientific measuring instruments. There are no American court decisions holding that evidence of measurements by mechanical means or scientific instruments are presumed to be correct. Seldom does the defense raise the objection that there has been no proof of the accuracy of the scientific measuring device used by the expert witness. The legal question is open, however, and anyone offering scientific proof should be aware that the problem exists.

C. PRESERVATION AND CUSTODY OF EVIDENCE

(11.32) In General

Evidence is of no value to the prosecutor unless it can be used in court. The police must, therefore, exercise care in collecting, identifying, and preserving any physical evidence connected with the crime. Unless properly connected with the crime and sufficiently authenticated at the trial, the evidence cannot be used.

(11.33) Collection

Evidence at the scene of the crime cannot be collected too carefully. Photographing the weapon at the scene of a murder or the tool marks of forced entry where a burglary occurred should, for example, be routinely done. The evidence itself must be kept free of contamination, fingerprints, or damage so that its original condition remains unchanged. If the item is numbered, the numbers should be written down for the police records. Exhibits should be carefully placed in separate evidence envelopes, preferably of clear plastic, and should be tagged immediately.

(11.34) Marking

Where possible, evidence should be marked by the officer who first recovers it. His initials may be put on the exhibit. The butt plate from a rifle, for example, can be removed and the initials scratched on the stock before replacing the plate. If the object itself cannot be marked, the envelope or other containers should be labeled with the investigator's initials. Where glass or tube containers are used, it is a sound practice to seal them with tape and then sealing wax, with the officer's fingerprint placed on the warm wax.

(11.35) Preservation

All evidence should be placed in a locked cabinet. Valuable and dangerous items should be kept in a fireproof, locked vault or safe. Laboratory technicians ought to preserve by chemical or other methods anything that might decompose, such as bodily tissue. Any article taken into custody or removed should be logged in and out in in an evidence register. The 3M Company markets a specially developed tape that is transparent except for the word "Evidence," which is in red letters. The tape is designed to be affixed over initials or a signature. It destroys itself in a noticeable manner whenever it is tampered with.

(11.36) Testing

Testing, whether done by the laboratory or by a firearms expert, may consume part or all of an exhibit. This is acceptable, and the expert witness can easily explain it in court. Any material remaining after the tests are made must be returned to police custody for later use at the trial.

(11.37) Chain of Custody

The general rule of "chain of custody" (which is more accurately termed "chain of identification") applies to evidence that has undergone expert analysis, such as a blood sample or material from bodily specimens. The side offering the evidence must show that the technician received the same sample that was originally taken from the person involved or from the place in question. It must also lay a foundation by testimony from every person who had the object in his custody, beginning with the officer who originally took it through the technician who examined it. If one person who had it in his custody cannot be found to testify to this, the court will usually rule that the chain has been broken and that the object will not be admitted into evidence. It is obviously impossible to follow the chain of custody rule exactly. If, for example, a specimen is mailed to a laboratory, every postman and clerk who handled it cannot be produced in court. Proof of mailing and the laboratory receipt of the package will suffice. What is required is proof that the exhibit now in court is the same one that was tested. It is extremely important for police authorities to keep the chain of custody unbroken and to maintain an exact record of everyone who had any object in his possession.

This rule usually applies only to exhibits that are part of an expert's testimony. If the knife found at the scene of a murder is proved by a witness to be in the same condition as when found, it generally is admissible in evidence without the various police evidence custodians having to testify that it was in their possession.

(11.38) Courtroom Authentication

There is a standard way of introducing an exhibit. First, it is marked for identification. Next counsel says: "I show you Exhibit 2 for identification. What is it?" The witness identifies the object and describes finding it. He is then asked: "Is it in the same condition now as when you originally found it?" If he answers in the affirmative, the exhibit is sufficiently authenticated to be offered in evidence.

(11.39) Destruction of Evidence

Evidence must be preserved during the time of trial and any appeals, including postconviction attacks through habeas corpus. Once the process has ended, the evidence can be safely returned to its rightful owner. In some cases, the defendant, through his attorney, will acknowledge the existence of an item, its value, and the description of it. This enables the owner to obtain his property much sooner, and thus prevent a hardship. Police often receive a court order allowing the destruction of evidence from closed cases some time before they actually dispose of it. Because of growing police corruption arising from narcotics, some jurisdictions provide for analysis of the evidence and a court-ordered destruction of the drugs even before the trial.

Destruction of evidence can create problems. In one investigation the police secretly videotaped a jailhouse visit two people made to an accused murderer. The district attorney viewed the tape to see if it contained anything that would be helpful to the defense. Finding nothing, he erased the tape. One of the visitors was later a prosecution witness at the trial. The defendant was found guilty and appealed. During the second trial he argued that the destruction of the tape violated his right to impeach the witness. Though the court affirmed the conviction, it warned that if the police destroy evidence as being nonmaterial without first notifying the defendant, the burden will be on the prosecution to show that this destruction did not prejudice the defense.

In the past, police in California encountered a problem concerning destruction of evidence because they routinely destroyed breathalizer ampules that had been used to detect the presence of alcohol in those accused of driving while intoxicated. Thus, a defendant contesting the result could not retest the ampule. The court ruled, therefore, that they should not be destroyed.

A safe rule to follow before destroying evidence is this, notify the defendant and seek court approval where it is appropriate.

(11.40) Summary

Most of the underlying rules governing admissibility of documentary evidence do not differ in principle from those regulating testimonial evidence. Like hearsay, there are well-recognized rules governing particular types of documents, such as church records, letters, books, and other publications.

Official records are usually admissible if made by a public servant who had firsthand knowledge of the information recorded. Photographs, motion pictures, and videotapes are also admissible if there are sufficient indicia of reliability. Like models, casts, and diagrams, they assist in the fact-finding process.

The best evidence rule serves to ensure that the most original record or copy will be the one received in evidence. Duplicates and copies of copies will not be excluded if originals are not available, but the rule requires parties to make an effort to locate documents that are more likely to be trustworthy.

Physical evidence relevant to the crime can be used if properly taken and preserved. Fruits of the crime, burglar's tools, clothing, even the defendant's person, may be relevant evidence.

Much scientific proof, such as fingerprints, ballistics tests, and chemical analysis, is available. Tests for narcotics are now commonplace. Document examiners using modern methods can give detached proof of forgeries, handwriting comparisons, and even individual typewriter identification.

Microanalysis of soil samples, paint chips, or fibers often can supply dramatic evidence against a defendant. Neutron activation analysis is a more recent method of identifying the elements present in evidentiary samples. It has been used to identify the place and even the date of manufacture of items. Courts are now recognizing the validity of neutron activation analysis.

Polygraph and voiceprint analysis are both widely used investigative tools. Courts still reject polygraph results, but are beginning to allow voiceprint evidence in court.

Narcoanalysis and hypnosis are medically approved diagnostic tools, but any courtroom use is narrowly circumscribed.

Proper care must always be taken in the collection and custody of both physical and scientific evidence. Evidence collected at the scene must be properly labeled and preserved. The chain of custody of any bodily sample used in a laboratory test must be carefully recorded and then testified to in court.

Any after trial destruction of evidence should normally be done under court order.

Discussion Questions

1. What is the "best evidence rule?"
2. Describe "chain of custody" as applied to evidence.
3. Discuss the polygraph as evidence.
4. Discuss the role of the forensic pathologist.
5. Describe the evidence rules governing documentary evidence.

12

Opinion Evidence

Human emotions and human passions are not
themselves physical entities, susceptible of
proof, as such. Like the atmosphere, the wind,
and some acknowledged forces in nature, they
are seen only in the effects they produce. . . .
—*Daniel* v. *State*, 73 So. 2d 370 (1954)

(12.1) In General

Witnesses on the stand frequently find their testimony blocked
because they have stated an opinion rather than an actual observation. All witnesses have opinions as to what happened, but are
generally not allowed to state them. They must confine themselves
to facts. This brings to mind Sergeant Friday of the television program "Dragnet." When he was interviewing a witness he frequently
cut off her story by saying, "Just give me the facts, Ma'am." This is
still a good expression of the rule regarding opinion evidence in court.

This is not to say that a person's opinion is not relevant evidence. There are many situations where an opinion may be received
in court. On the question of one's bias or prejudice, for example,
the individual's opinion could be most material, no matter how it is
shown. In some cases, a type of opinion evidence is allowed where
the witness cannot remember clearly or is not quite sure of a fact.
When opinions are accepted, however, they are not allowed to be so
broad as to invade the jury's prerogative of deciding guilt or innocence. Nevertheless, opinions from both laymen and experts are
received in many situations where the courts have found this to be
practical.

Because the rules concerning opinion are not ironclad, the exceptions barring this type of evidence must be learned.

(12.2) Lay Witnesses

A lay witness is any witness who has not been qualified as an "expert witness" or as a "skilled witness."

a. Common Experiences

There are actually large areas where a witness is allowed to state his opinion, mainly in matters of common experience. A layman can say whether it was light or dark and give his estimate of the size, shape, or color of an object. How far away was the defendant? How old was he? How tall? All of these are proper questions, and the opinion answers are allowed as being common observations. In addition, the witness may estimate speed or measurements without being an engineer.

One reason for allowing opinion evidence in matters of common observation such as size, distance, and time is that it is most difficult to get exact data on such matters. Illustrative of this was the evidence in a civil suit over an insurance claim (*Stout* v. *Pacific Mutual*, 130 Cal. 471 [1900]). A man fell from a boat, struck his head, and died. The insurance company questioned the accidental death claim. A witness was the man's young son, who was asked if the blows his father received to the head were light, heavy, or medium. The court allowed his opinion because it felt the testimony was a matter of common observation.

Often the answer by a witness will be part fact and part conclusion. Many times this will pass undetected, but, where an objection is raised, the court must decide on its admissibility. In this situation the court customarily rules that the answer given is the only adequate way the witness can describe an incident and will admit it as a type of "shorthand rendering of the facts."

In a case involving a charge of assault to commit rape, the complainant testified she was at a party when the defendant suggested they go into the bedroom. When she refused, he grabbed her by the wrist, pulled her down the hall into a darkened bedroom, and pushed her onto the bed. When she continued to protest and tried to get up, he threw his left leg across hers and "would pull my dress up." The prosecutor then asked if she knew what the defendant was trying to do, and she answered, "Yes." The defense immediately objected, saying she was being asked to give a conclusion. The objection was overruled, and she was allowed to answer further. She said: "He was trying to have sexual intercourse with me." The evidence was sustained on appeal. It was held that, however justified the opinion rule was, the answer was based on facts previously testified to and "was a compound of fact and conclusion—a 'shorthand rendering of the facts'—and was properly received."

b. Intoxication

Any witness may testify on the question of intoxication. An individual who has observed drunken people—a common sight in everyday life—can testify directly concerning his opinion on the person's drunkenness or sobriety. A better practice, however, is to have the witness in a case of drunken driving describe the erratic behavior of the car and then give details regarding the defendant's personal appearance, such as slurred speech, staggered walk, and odor of alcohol. Then he should be asked directly: "In your opinion, was the defendant drunk or sober?" This is allowable, even though there is no precise measurement of intoxication and other conditions, such as diabetes or medication, that can produce symptoms similar to drunkenness. In the opinion of *People* v. *Eastwood*, 14 N.Y. 563 (1856), "A child . . . may answer whether a man (whom it has seen) was drunk or sober: it does not require science or opinion to answer the question, but observation, merely."

c. Identity

Witnesses commonly are allowed to testify as to identity, naming the accused as being the one involved in the crime. Identity is a conclusion about which people often differ, but, regardless of how unreliable it is, such evidence is accepted by the court.

Many years ago in the *Tichborne* case, an English judge, Lord Cockburn, charged the jury in this way:

Frequently a man is sworn to, who has been seen only for a moment. A man stops you on the road, puts a pistol to your head and robs you of your

watch and purse; a man seizes you by the throat and while you are half
strangled his confederate rifles your pockets; a burglar invades your house by
night and you have only a rapid glance to enable you to know his features.
In all these cases, the opportunity for observing is so brief that a mistake is
possible and yet the lives and safety of people would not be secure unless you
acted on the recollection of features so acquired and so retained and it is done
every day.

d. Mental Capacity

Because everyone observes "normal" behavior in others every
day, any lay witness is allowed to describe "abnormal" behavior in
an individual and to give his opinion as to that person's mental
condition. He can state whether he thinks the person is sane or
insane or had the mental capacity to understand what he was doing.

The layman's opinion must be based on his personal observations and not on an abstract situation. In two cases (*McKenzie* v.
U.S., 266 F. 2d 524 [1959]; *Hixon* v. *State* [Fla. App.], 165 So.2d
436 [1964]) laymen testified on the question of sanity, and the
appellate court explained the rules saying that a nonexpert in a
criminal case "may be permitted to give an opinion regarding sanity,
but it cannot be a general opinion independent of circumstances
within his own knowledge." The witness must lay a foundation for
his opinion by first testifying as to the "appearances, actions, and
conduct . . . of personal knowledge and observation."

It is necessary at this point to introduce a word of caution.
While the above is the generally accepted rule of opinion evidence
concerning mental condition, some states have statutes limiting this
type of evidence in criminal cases. These laws must, therefore, always
be consulted.

e. Voices

Testimony on voices is similar to that on identity: a layman
may express his view in regard to a person's voice. As long as he
has some basis for recognizing the voice, he may give his opinion,
even though he never heard the voice before the time of the crime.

f. Handwriting

Anyone who knows another person's handwriting may give his
opinion as to whether the writing in question was made by that

person. Because this is also an area of common observation, all courts agree that a layman who is familiar with a particular handwriting may state his opinion concerning its identity even though he is not a handwriting expert.

In the case of *Criner* v. *State*, 236 Ark. 220 (1963), the manager of a soybean company was convicted of forgery. He would "buy" grain from a fictitious seller, make out a company check to him, forge the seller's name on the back of the check, and pocket the money. The company's secretary, testifying for the prosecution, said that the defendant had a distinctive handwriting and that he was familiar with it. When he was shown a number of questionable checks, he said that, in his opinion, the person who wrote the face of the checks also endorsed them. This testimony by a nonexpert witness was allowed because he stated the facts on which his opinion was based.

Some court decisions hold that a layman can testify on handwriting as long as he has become familiar with the handwriting, even though he has never actually seen the person write.

g. Demeanor or Appearance

Although some courts take a narrower view, many hold that a witness may describe another's demeanor or appearance by conclusory words, such as "agitated," "nervous," "angry," or "disturbed." Clothing can be described as "messed up" or "disheveled." This testimony showing a person's emotions or appearance may be very important as proof of motive or intent. The reason for allowing this type of conclusion is that it is difficult for the average witness to put such descriptions into words, and this is the most helpful way for him to describe such conditions to the jury.

h. Miscellaneous

In some areas commonly thought of as requiring expert, scientific evidence laymen have been allowed to give their opinions, and these opinions have been considered facts of common observation. Courts have, for example, let nonexperts present their opinions on blood, powder burns, the similarity of footprints, tire marks, and the like.

i. Qualified Answers

A witness often qualifies his answer by saying "To the best of my knowledge," "I believe," or even "I think." Does this make it simply his opinion, rather than a fact, and thus disqualify the answer? Such language will not ordinarily result in eliminating his testimony as long as he was only explaining a faulty memory or admitting his uncertainty. The court generally allows this type of answer to stand on the ground that it is fully admissible. Its weight, however, is then up to the jury.

(12.3) Skilled Witnesses

There is a class of witness between laymen and technical experts, often referred to as a skilled witness, who may be allowed to give his opinion in court in his particular field. A cutlery worker, for example, might testify that the stone and mineral oil found in an accused convict's cell could have been used to grind down a mess hall table knife into the murder weapon used in assaulting another convict.

In a trial in Georgia Clif Byrd was convicted of the shotgun slaying of John Mandeville (*Byrd* v. *State*, 142 Ga. 633 [1914]). A lay witness testified that he examined the gunshot wound inflicted on Mandeville and that, in his opinion, it was done with a "cut shell." The latter, he said, was a shotgun shell with the paper almost completely cut off between the powder and the shot (now often referred to by police as a "wad cutter" shell); thus, when the shot was fired, it stayed together in a lump instead of scattering. He explained that he had fired such shells at objects other than humans and had observed the effects. The court approved the use of his testimony. While not an expert, he was, said the court, a witness experienced in such matters with knowledge on the subject, and he could, therefore, state his opinion.

(12.4) The Scope of Expert Witnesses

The area where opinion evidence is accepted most widely is that of the expert witness. An individual who has special knowledge, education, skill, or experience is qualified to be such a witness. Doctors, engineers, and chemists are among those routinely used as expert witnesses. Under proper limitations, the expert is allowed to state his opinion, which is intended to aid the jury in making its decision.

a. General Limitations

The expert may, of course, give opinion evidence only within the area of his special knowledge. If, however, the matter involved is one on which jurors of ordinary experience can make a decision, an expert will not be allowed to give his opinion. There is no reason, for example, to call a minister or professor to testify that something is obscene. The jury can decide that as a matter of common experience. Neither can a psychologist give his expert opinion that a witness is lying, because this is also a matter of common knowledge for the jury's determination.

In a prosecution for receiving stolen property, the assistant post quartermaster was a government witness. On cross-examination he was handed two pairs of socks, admittedly not stolen, and asked if they did not have the same appearance as the stolen articles. The court properly disallowed the question since this was a matter of common experience that the jury was well qualified to decide.

Many years ago in *Ferguson* v. *Hubbell,* 97 N.Y. 507 (1884), an appellate court stated what is still a correct rule:

> It is not sufficient to warrant the introduction of expert evidence that the witness may know more of the subject than the juries; . . . the jurors may have less skill and experience than the witness and yet have enough to draw their own conclusions . . . where the facts . . . are of such nature that jurors generally are just as competent to form opinions . . . there is no occasion to resort to expert or opinion evidence.

Even where expert opinion is properly used, it is still just that, an opinion. The jurors may accept or reject it. They still are the sole judges of the facts, not the experts.

b. Province of the Jury

An expert cannot give his opinion on the ultimate question to be decided by the jury. Even the most experienced criminologist or investigator is not allowed to testify that the defendant is, in his opinion, innocent or guilty.

In an interstate case involving a stolen automobile, the charge was that a car had been taken in Georgia and sold in Alabama. An F.B.I. witness was asked: "Do you know whether he stole the automobile or how he got it?" He answered: "I believe he did." The appellate court, in reversing the conviction, held that this questioning invaded the jury's province, since the witness was being asked to give his opinion on the defendant's guilt or innocence.

While questions of this scope still will not be allowed, there is a growing tendency for courts to widen the area of expert testimony. In many cases the testimony is allowed in evidence for what it may be worth, even though technically the expert's opinion invades an area in which the jury must make a decision.

The current federal rule (Federal Rules of Evidence 704) allows great leeway for experts to state an opinion on "an ultimate issue to be decided by the trier of fact; except when it comes to the mental condition of the accused."

Formerly, when there was an insanity defense, the expert, usually a psychiatrist, would examine the defendant and then testify, giving his expert medical opinion as to the defendant's mental condition. Now, ultimate issues upon which experts are not allowed to testify in federal court include insanity, capacity to distinguish right from wrong, and capacity to conform behavior to the requirement of law (*U.S.* v. *Gold*, D.D.C. 1987, 661 F. Supp. 1127).

When President Reagan was shot and seriously wounded and Secretary Brady permanently disabled by the same attacker, the assassin pled insanity, and was never sent to jail. Instead, he ended up in a rather plush mental hospital, subject to the control of medical personnel rather than the criminal courts. The actual shooting was seen on television and by millions of viewers. Members of Congress and the general public were shocked by the fact that the armed attacker was not convicted of a crime.

As a result, the federal law on the insanity defense was tightened (Rule 704). Meanwhile, other jurisdictions have become disturbed by the fact that even violent offenders could escape a criminal conviction by pleading insanity and be placed in a civil mental hospital to be later released whenever the medical authorities felt he was "cured." The criminal courts had no say on whether or not he should then be released to society. So, in criminal cases involving a defense of insanity these states have adopted a new jury verdict: "guilty but mentally ill." Such an accused then has a criminal conviction and can be confined in a hospital for the criminally insane; any ultimate release is controlled by the criminal court.

(12.5) Qualifications of Experts

Before an expert witness can give his opinion, the foundation for it must be laid by showing his qualifications, education, experience, and training. This is ordinarily accomplished by having the witness recite the facts of his experience and his background. At this point, opposing counsel is often allowed a preliminary cross-examination to question the expert's qualifications. It can happen, however, that counsel will state that the witness is an expert and that his qualifications need not be questioned. This commonly occurs when doctors are testifying.

The court must always be satisfied that the witness is a qualified expert before it will allow him to testify.

Expert witnesses are normally paid a fee for testifying, and in some cases the fee is very substantial. This is a proper procedure and provides no grounds for disqualifying them from testifying.

(12.6) Hypothetical Questions

A common method of obtaining the opinion of an expert witness is to ask a hypothetical question. This is done by requesting that he assume certain facts about which other witnesses have testified and then ask for his opinion based on the assumed facts. Doctors testifying in homicide cases are routinely questioned in this way. Previous testimony may have shown that the deceased had a split skull and that a bloody ax was found at the scene. Questioning of the doctor might proceed thus:

Q. Assume Doctor, that the deceased was found with a wound at the top of the skull approximately four inches long, a half inch wide, and extending into the brain and that this ax, Exhibit 1, was found near the body. Can you state with reasonable medical certainty whether or not Exhibit 1 could have caused such a wound?

A. I can.

Q. You may state your opinion.

A. In my opinion Exhibit 1 could have produced the wound you have described.

In the past, hypothetical questions were universally used to solicit the opinions of experts. They do, however, cause problems. In the first place, the question itself must be precise, and one can only assume the exact facts already in evidence. If anything beyond these facts is assumed, both the question and the answer are improper. In the second place, doctors and other expert witnesses have resisted the use of the hypothetical question because they consider it unduly restrictive and a handicap to the presentation of their findings.

Modern decisions and some procedural statutes avoid the hypothetical question on direct examination and simply let the doctor or other expert tell what his examination revealed and what his conclusions are. The hypothetical question is still widely used on cross-examination, however, to test the expert's findings and to try to impeach his conclusions. Opposing counsel may assume only part of the evidence in his question and base his hypothetical questions on his own view of the facts.

A hypothetical question may be used only with expert witnesses. The nonexpert who is allowed to state an opinion must base it on his own observations and nothing else. Thus, theoretical or hypothetical questioning of a lay witness is improper.

(12.7) Basis for Opinion

The expert may give his opinion from personal observations. When a psychiatrist has made a mental examination, he may base his opinion regarding sanity entirely on this examination. A pathologist who has performed a postmortem examination may give his opinion on the cause of death on the basis of that examination. The lay witness, as has been said, can base his opinion solely on his personal observations.

The expert may base his opinion on past medical history and hospital records as well as on personal observations. He can also draw his conclusion entirely from the hypothetical question that assumes the facts and then asks for his opinion.

(12.8) Scientific Books

Scientific books cannot be used on direct examination to back up the expert's findings. Otherwise each side would present titles of learned tomes to prove the view of each witness, and the jury would be left to read all of the books cited in order to reach a decision. Even if a single book were introduced to prove a point, it would not be allowed because opposing counsel would be denied the right of cross-examination. Only mathematical or mortality tables can be quoted.

The expert can say that his opinion may have been formed in part by his study of scientific books, even though he cannot read from them in testifying. The expert must give his own opinion, not that of someone else.

Material from scientific works can be effectively used in cross-examination. Counsel can ask his opponent's expert if he recognizes certain authorities and then point out conclusions in these books that differ from his opinion. The court has discretion in this matter and will not let books be used in cross-examination merely as an excuse to put contrary opinions before the jury. The Federal Rules of Evidence (Rule 803, 18) have relaxed the general ban against using books as evidence and do allow scientific treatises to be used as evidence under some conditions.

(12.9) Subject Matter of Expert Opinions

A number of considerations govern this area. A discussion of each follows.

a. Legal Opinions

Legal opinions ordinarily are not a proper subject for an expert witness. The expert may give his opinion of facts, not of the law. A lawyer cannot be called in to give his opinion as to the meaning of a local law applying to the case. That would be a conclusion of law for the trial judge, not for the witness. There is, however, at least one exception to this rule. If foreign laws are involved in the case, a legal expert might be allowed to give his opinion concerning these laws.

b. Estimates

Opinion regarding value must frequently be given by an expert. Stolen property or buildings destroyed by arson do not have a definite market value, and therefore, estimates of value by experts must be used. Because there was no actual sale between a willing buyer and seller to fix the market price, estimated value cannot be exact. Estimated value by an expert in the field is the best possible measure.

c. Time, Speed, Weight, Duration, and Number

Time of death, speed of vehicles, direction, and similar measurements can seldom be determined with mathematical certainty. As stated, lay witnesses can estimate such things on the basis of their observations. The fact that laymen may give such opinion evidence does not mean that experts are not allowed to do the same. The expert may give similar estimates on the basis of both the evidence in the case and his technical background. An accurate estimate of speed may be obtained from such information as the weight and size of the vehicle and skid marks. A contractor or engineer might estimate the number of cubic yards of fill placed on a land area. The direction from which a blow is struck and shots were fired would also be proper subjects for expert opinion.

d. Mechanical and Agricultural Matters

An endless variety of mechanical and agricultural matters can involve expert testimony. Problems involved with the safety of machinery and with construction, such as the strength of structures, all involve expert testimony. Examples of agricultural items calling for expert evidence include value of a crop loss, whether or not milk has been adulterated, and whether stolen timber came from the complainant's woodlot.

(12.10) Physicians and Psychologists

Medical witnesses are the most common of all expert witnesses; their usefulness is discussed here.

a. Injuries

Almost all criminal cases involving injuries call for expert testimony from physicians. Is there tissue injury indicating force in a rape case? Was "serious physical injury" inflicted? A doctor's opinion is obviously necessary in this kind of situation. Physicians can give opinion evidence as to type, extent, and cause of wounds and injuries. Some states even allow them to state whether they feel the wound was self-inflicted.

A defendant, charged with murdering a woman with whom he had been living, argued that her death from gunshot was suicide, not murder. The pathologist who performed the autopsy found that death came from a bullet that entered below the left armpit, traveled across the thorax, penetrated the heart and lungs, and struck the right arm three inches below the shoulder. He was asked if, in his opinion, the wound could have been self-inflicted. Over objection, the court permitted him to reply, and he said it "would be a very unusual pattern for a self-inflicted wound." The court allowed the answer to stand, even though this was the crucial fact in issue. It held that self-inflicted wounds were not such a matter of common experience as to exclude expert testimony.

b. Physical Condition

There are times when it is necessary to have expert opinion on an individual's physical condition. If, for example, the defense claims a forced confession was beaten from the accused, and the prosecutor says that the man beat his own head against the cell bars, the jail physician who examined the defendant is the most qualified expert witness to help resolve the question. Another example arises when there is a claim of self-defense. In this case the general physical condition of both the accused and the victim of an assault is pertinent. An extremely important contemporary example concerns the necessity of a physician's opinion when a defendant contends that medication was the cause of his condition, rather than intoxication or unauthorized drugs. There are, of course, countless other factual situations where expert medical testimony is required in criminal cases.

c. Mental Condition

Only in rare cases is an individual so obviously deranged that the testimony of a trained psychiatrist, physician, or psychologist is not needed. Though the court usually accepts the expert testimony of a general practitioner on sanity, a few jurisdictions require the opinion of a specialist.

d. X Rays

Laymen are not capable of interpreting X rays. If X rays are to be used in evidence, they must be introduced through expert testimony and interpreted for the jury by either a qualified physician or a radiologist.

(12.11) Cause of Death

Expert testimony is ordinarily required in statements regarding cause of death. While it is true that laymen often observe death and dead persons, they have no common knowledge as to its various causes.

The pathologist studies tissues and organs to determine the cause, while the medical examiner may discover that the cause was the result of wounds, drowning, burning, and the like.

Where special knowledge is necessary to find death's cause, the prerogative of the jury is not violated.

(12.12) Fingerprints and Documents

In cases where fingerprints have been found, a fingerprint expert must give testimony concerning them, as only he can explain the points on which he has based his opinions.

Determination of the authenticity of documents—faked stock certificates, wills, letters, and others—requires examination by an expert. Typewriters differ by make, model, and even by individual machine. Here, too, an expert, by careful examination and with the aid of enlarged photographs, can identify and authenticate the typewritten material in question. Laymen can give testimony concerning handwriting, but experts in the field are frequently needed for an examination and a professional opinion.

(12.13) Character and Reputation

So-called "character evidence" is often used by the defendant in criminal trials. This is done by having witnesses testify as to the defendant's good reputation in the community. The theory, which is not terribly sound, is that an individual's misdeeds are generally known by friends and acquaintances. Thus, a good reputation is evidence of one's innocence of the crime charged. Such evidence is generally accepted as sufficient to raise a reasonable doubt among members of the jury.

If the defendant offers character evidence, the prosecutor may introduce evidence of poor character in rebuttal. In addition, character witnesses can be cross-examined as to whether they have heard of specific improper acts on the part of the defendant.

In a related area, evidence of a poor reputation for truthfulness and accuracy can be presented as impeachment material against a witness.

No one can testify as an expert on an individual's character and reputation, since the basis for such testimony is public discussion by people in the community. Therefore, those who are qualified to give testimony are laymen, people familiar with the individual's reputation.

(12.14) Modern Developments in Opinion Evidence

The field of expert testimony that is accepted by the court expands as scientific knowledge increases. Those who examine questioned documents can now testify freely on typewriter comparisons. Evidence based on breathalizer tests is now allowed to prove intoxication when the test was administered by trained personnel, and the results are, in effect, conclusory. Expert testimony on voiceprints is now being offered and accepted in some courts. Polygraph investigations are routinely used and relied upon by police forces everywhere. Properly administered by trained and experienced experts, the polygraph has proved itself a reliable guide in the search for truth. And yet, with few exceptions, courts have refused to accept the results of polygraph tests. Only gradually are they being allowed as evidence.

In the area of narcotics, expert opinions on the effects of drugs and the way they are used and administered are increasingly being accepted. Even nonscientific personnel with experience in the drug field have been allowed to qualify as skilled witnesses and to give opinion testimony.

There is now wider acceptance of expert testimony on modus operandi, where actions that seem normal on the surface are actually methods of committing a crime. Gambling, bookmaking, lottery, and even burglaries are examples. For instance, in a trial in California the defendant was charged with a form of burglary known as "till tapping." Testimony indicated that the defendant stood by the store's checkout counter and asked for a number of grocery items that caused the clerk to turn his back. A customer saw the defendant's accomplice withdraw his closed hand from the cash drawer. Testifying as an expert in the area of "till tapping," a police officer stated that this was the usual method of committing such a crime. The court allowed this testimony because the defendant's conduct at the checkout counter appeared normal, and, for this reason, the jury might have found him to have been an innocent bystander.

The theory behind this loosening of the strict ban on opinion evidence was set forth in a federal case involving five thousand dollars in counterfeit money found in the defendant's dresser drawer. He told the F.B.I. agent that counterfeiting was not in his "line" and that a "rat" had left the bills there the night before. During the agent's testimony he was asked if the defendant had not given him the "impression" that he did not know the bills were in his room. The trial judge would not allow the question since it called for a conclusion. The appeals court, however, said that the question and answer should have been allowed. It stated that a blind following of the rule against conclusions "may . . . become a substantial obstacle to developing the truth . . . for our perceptions are always 'conclusions.' The rule should be held lightly and in many cases let the witness state his opinion and leave to cross-examination a searching inquisition to uncover its foundations."

(12.15) Summary

Though witnesses are supposed to recite facts, not opinions, there are wide areas in which opinion evidence is accepted.

Lay witnesses may estimate speed of vehicles, distances, time, and other measurements. They are also allowed, solely on the basis of their own observations, to state their opinions on another person's identity, handwriting, voice, sanity, and even his state of intoxication.

An expert witness is in a different class. He is called for the sole purpose of stating his expert opinion about some facet of the case. He cannot, of course, go so far as to decide the case for the jury. They are free to accept or reject his conclusion as they see fit.

Once having established his credentials in court, the expert can give his opinion, not only from his own observations, but from an assumed state of facts based on the evidence in the case. The expert may sometimes give opinions in the same areas as laymen, such as measurements, handwriting, and the authenticity of documents.

Many areas of opinion evidence, such as fingerprints and scientific, engineering, and mechanical matters, come only from experts.

Physicians are commonly needed for opinion evidence regarding physical condition, types and extent of injuries, and the cause of death.

Character evidence is a common defense in criminal trials. This is nonexpert testimony concerning the reputation one has in his community and is based on discussions of local people. If the defendant produces evidence of good character, the prosecution may offer proof of poor character. A witness may be attacked by evidence of poor reputation for truth. Though character evidence is pure opinion, it is, nonetheless, legal.

Discussion Questions

1. Who is an expert? On what may an expert give an opinion as an expert?
2. Discuss the major aspects of the opinion rule.
3. Define "lay witness."
4. Distinguish between character and reputation.
5. Discuss the concept that "reputation in a community" is hearsay evidence.

13

Hearsay Evidence

The hearsay evidence rule, with all its subtle-
ties, anomalies, and ramifications, will not be
read into the Fourth Amendment.
Stein v. *New York.* 3 45 U.S. 156 (1953)

(13.1) What Is Hearsay?

The subject of hearsay is widely misunderstood. This need not be. All that is needed is some initial analysis, followed by a two-step process, which is given below.

The ban against hearsay is of ancient origin. The general concept of hearsay is the idea that a witness is forbidden to mention what someone else has told him. This is not so. Many out-of-court statements must be allowed in evidence. The first thing to do is to understand exactly what hearsay is.

"Hearsay" is an out-of-court statement offered to prove the truth of the matter contained in the statement. It is only hearsay *if it is offered to prove that the statement itself is true.* If it is introduced for some other purpose, it is not hearsay. It may be objected to on other grounds, but not on the basis of hearsay.

This is the most important step in recognizing hearsay, and one that even many attorneys miss. The first question to be asked is "What purpose is the conversation being offered for?" If the offeror does not care whether the statement is true or false, then it is *not* hearsay.

For example, Davis is being tried for murder, and his defense is insanity. His lawyer offers to prove that shortly before the shooting Davis was seen standing on the corner of Main and Delaware, wearing a cocked hat, with his hand in his shirt front, shouting "I'm Napoleon." An objection is raised on the grounds that the statement is hearsay. No one was claiming that he was Napoleon. The statement was offered to prove Davis was insane. Therefore, it was *not* hearsay.

So whenever a question of hearsay arises, remember this Napoleon example. If the conversation is not offered to prove its truth, it is not hearsay.

Make your own analysis. Do any of the following situations involve hearsay?

1. A spectator offers to testify that just before the complainant was struck with a beer bottle, he shouted at the defendant, "Hit me and I'll kill you."

2. A bank customer, now a witness in an armed robbery trial, offers to testify that he heard the teller say to the defendant, "Don't shoot me. Don't shoot me. I'll give you the money."

3. The charge is blackmail. The prosecution offers a legally recorded telephone conversation in which the defendant said to the victim, "Pay me five bills or I'll tell your wife what went on in room 209 of the Paradise Motel last night."

4. The bank officer is accused of embezzling $100,000 from dormant bank accounts. The state produces a fellow employee who offers to testify that on several occasions during the period in question, he heard the defendant say, "A man can't live on the stingy salaries this outfit pays."

5. The charge is burglary of the Empire Warehouse. The first officer who arrived at the scene in his patrol car testified that just before this, he had received a radio message saying, "Go to the Empire Warehouse at the corner of Main and Elm."

None of these can be classed as hearsay. The offeror does not care whether or not any of the statements is true. The answers to the illustrations are as follows.

1. This was offered to show provocation or self-defense, and it matters not whether the victim would have killed his assailant or not.

2. The teller's "Don't shoot" statement is evidence that she was giving up the funds under fear of physical harm, which is an element in robbery. Even if the bank robber only had a water pistol and

could never have shot her, the statement is proper to show her state of mind.

3. The blackmailer's threat may well have been pure bluff and entirely untrue. True, or false, it is only offered to show the threat as part of the crime, and the truth of the threat is immaterial, and so it is not hearsay.

4. Whether or not he could live on his salary is immaterial. The statement was not offered to prove that the bank was penurious. Its purpose was to show the defendant's motive for stealing. Hearsay was not, therefore, involved in his testimony.

5. The radio call was not offered as proof that there was a burglary, but simply to show why the officer went there. It would not have mattered if the dispatcher had been giving him a false instruction. Since the truth of the message was not involved, it was not hearsay.

Statements that show motive, intent, or bias are not always hearsay but can easily be confused with it. Usually, such statements are offered, not to prove the content as being true, but to show a state of mind like the earlier example of Napoleon. For instance, a husband is accused of murdering his wife. The People offer evidence by a neighbor who overheard him calling her a whore, just before the fatal shot. The evidence is accepted, not to prove that she was immoral, but that he hated her enough to kill her. In addition, the prosecution might reveal that, before the murder, the defendant told a third person that he was going to marry a long-time woman friend. Whether or not he was going to marry her is beside the point; a statement is properly received in evidence to prove that he intended to and hence had a motive for murder. Courts normally accept this type of statement for the purpose of showing mental operations.

It is not just an oral statement that can be classified as hearsay. A "statement" can be oral, written, or even nonverbal conduct that conveys a message. The basic objection to hearsay is that, if it is used, the opponent is denied his right to confront and cross-examine the person who made the statement. It is not possible, of course, to cross-examine an out-of-court statement. This is the reason why an expert is not allowed to bolster his testimony by reading from a scientific book. The testimony would be offered to prove the *truth of the matter in the book*, and there is no way counsel can cross-examine a volume. Thus, such testimony is objectionable as hearsay.

For the same reason, a case cannot be proven by submitting a sworn affidavit, instead of having the live witness. Cross-examination and confrontation would be lost. If the affidavit would be offered to prove its truth, it would be objectionable as hearsay.

Gestures often are questioned as possibly being hearsay. In *People* v. *Plummer*, 36 N.Y. 2d 161 (1975), a defendant was convicted of armed robbery of a store clerk. The defendant and two others went into a store, held a knife to the clerk's throat, and the defendant said that if she did not cooperate, he "would slit [her] throat." They took her wallet and over two hundred dollars from the cash drawer. Three days later, she saw the defendant in front of the same store looking at her and crossing his throat with his finger. He did this several times later and also pointed to his head, imitating a pistol. The defendant's sister also made threatening gestures. Though objection was made to the evidence of these threats, the appeals court ruled that this evidence was all admissible.

The question of hearsay was not actually raised, but what if such an objection had been made? The gestures were a message. The defendant was telling her what was going to happen if she did not cooperate. This evidence would be acceptable, not as proof that they actually were going to kill her, but as evidence of the defendant's state of mind, his animosity, all of which was relevant to the charge of armed robbery.

(13.2) Exceptions to the Hearsay Rule

Whether the problem involves an out-of-court conversation, document, or message type of action, your analysis must always begin with the first step. Stop. Ask yourself, what purpose is it being offered for? If offered to prove the truth, then it is hearsay.

This does not end your hearsay inquiry. It only begins it. Practicality dictates that a great number of out-of-court statements such as those of child victims must be allowed in evidence. Contracts are made by word of mouth. Threats and promises may be made the same way. There are, then, a number of exceptions to the hearsay rule that are allowed in both civil and criminal litigation.

Having first determined if the evidence offered is basically hearsay, the next step to determine is: does it fall within any of the many exceptions to the hearsay rule?

(13.3) Confessions

The confession of an accused is probably the most commonly understood exception to the hearsay rule. Such an out-of-court statement is offered to prove the truth of its content, and as such it is hearsay. It is, however, allowed as an exception to the hearsay rule.

The reasoning behind this is that people do not ordinarily admit to a criminal act. If they do, it is likely that their statements are true. Thus, if the confession is voluntary and meets the necessary constitutional requirements, it will be allowed as an exception to the hearsay rule as evidence against the person who confesses.

a. Admissions

An admission is a kind of miniconfession. Though the accused might never have actually confessed, he might have made a partial admission regarding the crime. Perhaps he told a girl friend that he was at the scene of the crime or showed her a gun that he claimed was used in an armed robbery. If voluntarily made, such an admission can be used as evidence against an accused, as an exception to the hearsay rule.

b. Admission by Silence

On rare occasions there may be an admission or a complete confession simply by silence. There is a widely held misconception about this. Many practitioners think that if a defendant is present during a conversation then the words can be used as evidence against him. This is not true.

The mere presence of a defendant does not in itself make the conversation admissible. If a statement (not written) is made in the presence of the accused incriminating him *under circumstances calling for his denial*, only then is his silence deemed an admission. For example, if he is arrested, and the lieutenant says, "You stole this gun," the defendant's silence means nothing, for he has a constitutional right to remain silent. So, if the accusation is made in open court, or while the man is in custody, his silence is not an admission. If, on the other hand, there is a street fight, and the victim confronts a man saying "You cut me," the man's silence can be taken as an admission of guilt. The statement "You cut me" could be introduced in evidence by any witness who heard it.

In a case of murder on an Indian reservation, an Indian was convicted of killing his wife. The evidence showed that the husband had been on a drunken spree, came home, and shot his wife. His defense was that he was so drunk he did not know what happened.

After the shooting, the defendant ran to his parents' home. Another Indian testified as a prosecution witness that he went to the parents' house and questioned the people who were there. "In the defendant's presence" he asked the father what happened, and the father answered that the defendant had said, "I killed Jeanette." Because this was a third party, not the father testifying, it was not in the nature of a confession the witness had heard from the defendant. The trial court admitted the statement by a third party because it was "made in the defendant's presence."

The appellate court properly reversed the conviction. It noted that, according to the record, the investigating Indian first sat by the defendant, but when he spoke to the father, he moved to another part of the room. The defendant may never have heard the conversation, or, if he did, he was admittedly in shock and recovering from intoxication. There can be no admission by silence unless all the circumstances call naturally for a denial from the accused. Only if the circumstances are so strong that the defendant's silence amounts to an acquiescence, may the accusatory conversation of a third party be admitted as an exception to the hearsay rule.

c. Confessions of a Codefendant

As discussed earlier, a defendant's confession is admissible only against the defendant. It cannot be used against a codefendant because it is pure hearsay in regard to the other party. It is admitted only against the person who confesses, as an exception to the hearsay rule, on the common-sense premise that people do not ordinarily admit a crime of their own unless it is true. But there is no reason to be afraid to say that someone else committed a crime. It is only when an individual implicates himself that the statement has the ring of truth.

(13.4) Statements of Coconspirators

A conspiracy is an agreement between two or more people to commit a criminal act. The conspirators are then partners in crime. In civil law, one partner is bound by the actions of the other if they are performed in the course of their business partnership. Each is, therefore, the agent of the other. It is the same with a criminal conspiracy. The federal rule is generally applicable. It holds that the statement of a coconspirator is admissible in evidence against all conspirators under three conditions. First, the conspiracy must be established by independent evidence. Second, the statement must be made in furtherance of the conspiracy. Third, it must be made during the conspiracy.

In a federal vice case, the defendant was accused of conspiring with his wife to transport another woman from New York to Miami for prostitution. After the prostitute had been taken to Miami and the defendant arrested, she came back to New York. This ended the conspiracy. Then the prostitute and the defendant's wife had a conversation in New York. At his trial the prostitute was allowed to relate the conversation she had with the wife in New York as follows: "The wife said 'You didn't talk yet?' and I says 'No' and she says 'Well don't . . . until we get you a lawyer . . . . Be very careful what you say . . . . It would be better for us two girls to take the blame than Ray [defendant] . . . . He couldn't stand to take it.'" Partially on the basis of this testimony, the man was convicted. His conviction was eventually reversed by the Supreme Court because the conversation took place after the prostitution conspiracy ended. Thus, what the two women said was not binding on the husband and was inadmissible hearsay.

For the same reason a *confession* of one conspirator is not admissible against the others. Because the conspiracy was over by the time the man confessed, his confession, like that of any codefendant, was binding only against himself.

(13.5) Declaration against Interest

Declarations against interest are out-of-court statements by one who is not a party to the crime and can be used as evidence when a witness is not available.

Ordinarily, a person does not publicly admit things that are harmful to (that is, against) his own interest. If he does, it is a good indication that what he says is true. One example is a declaration against pecuniary interest, such as admitting a debt. More commonly involved in criminal trials is the declaration against penal interest, where an individual other than the defendant admits to a criminal act. As a matter of fact, these declarations, which are exceptions to the hearsay rule, always apply to people other than the defendant. If we were talking about a defendant's statement, this would be a confession admissible against him under that exception.

The declaration against penal interest ordinarily constitutes evidence that the defendant tries to use in his own behalf. He offers it to prove that *someone else has admitted committing* the crime he is accused of. In the past the declaration against penal interest was not usually considered an exception to the hearsay rule. The modern trend of court decisions, however, is to recognize this type of declaration as an exception to the hearsay rule and to admit it under certain circumstances.

The pioneer federal decision in this area is *Chambers* v. *Mississippi*, 410 U.S. 284 (1973). Chambers had been convicted of murdering a policeman during a demonstration in Mississippi. As the policeman fell, he turned and fired his gun, wounding Chambers. A man named McDonald left town shortly after the shooting, but later returned and confessed to Chambers' lawyer that he, not Chambers, had actually shot the policeman. When McDonald was called as a defense witness, however, he repudiated his confession. Chambers offered the testimony of three of McDonald's friends that McDonald had admitted to the shooting. The court refused to allow this. Chambers was convicted.

The Supreme Court, in reversing the conviction, recognized the reliability of a declaration against penal interest where the circumstances such as these indicated the truthfulness of the statement. The court avoided the usual requirement that a declaration against penal interest cannot be offered unless the declarant is unavailable, by pointing out that McDonald was there, and he could have been cross-examined. Various states are following this example and are now admitting the declaration against penal interest in evidence.

Another case involving the declaration against penal interest is

People v. *Brown*, 26 N.Y. 2d 88 (1970). Brown was convicted in New York of murder. He claimed self-defense, saying that the deceased had a pistol in his hand when Brown shot him. The fact that the police found no other pistol near the body seemed to negate his claim. At the time of Brown's trial, Seals was in jail for robbery. Seals told Brown's lawyer that he "picked up a gun" immediately after the shooting. When he was called as a witness at Brown's trial, Seals refused to testify on the basis of his rights under the Fifth Amendment. The trial court refused to allow testimony concerning Seal's conversation with Brown's lawyer. The appellate court, however, reversed the conviction. It recognized the validity of Seal's declaration as being against penal interest because his statement would constitute the admission of a crime on his own part. In the court's opinion, when the declarant is dead, when he is beyond the court's jurisdiction, or when he refuses to testify, his admission against penal interest should be received in evidence.

The state of Pennsylvania has accepted the declaration against penal interest as a recognized exception to the hearsay rule. The federal courts also recognize this exception, making it part of the Federal Rules of Evidence (Section 804). Some court decisions now approve the use of a declaration against penal interest whether or not the speaker is available to testify.

It is undoubtedly true that, with the limitations traditionally applied to the declaration against penal interest, third-party confessions to a crime will increasingly be allowed in evidence as part of the defendant's case.

A word of caution about relying on the use of a declaration against penal interest should be mentioned. It may not be used unless the speaker is actually faced with the possibility that he will be punished. If he cannot be punished for what he says, it is not an acceptable declaration against penal interest.

A man named Dovico and a codefendant were convicted on a drug charge. While the codefendant was in a federal penitentiary, he told a cellmate that he, not Dovico, was the one who had put the cocaine in the trash. The codefendant never testified at Dovico's original trial and died before the case was appealed. Because of the codefendant's death, Dovico sought to use the statement to the cellmate. The reviewing court determined, however, that the statement was not a declaration against penal interest. By assuming all the blame when he made the statement, the codefendant was not subjecting himself to any possible additional punishment. He had already been convicted of the crime, and, because he had never testified in court on the matter, he was not even opening himself to a possible charge of perjury. Since no additional criminal punishment was possible, this was not a genuine declaration against penal interest.

a. Homicide or Suicide?

Declarations of suicide are admitted as an exception to the hearsay rule. They are similar to other declarations against interest on the logical basis that threatening suicide is generally regarded as a disgraceful act that an individual ordinarily would not falsify. It is true that the declaration of suicide is offered to show a state of mind, but normally its purpose is also to prove the truth of the matter contained in the statement. It is unimportant whether the statement is made orally or is in the form of a suicide note. The result is the same. All such statements are hearsay, but are received as exceptions to the rule.

A defendant named Salcido was convicted of murder. He had been riding in the backseat of a car with his girl friend (*People* v. *Salcido*, 246 C.A. 2d 450 [1966]). They began to argue, and it appeared that he threatened her with his gun. A witness in the front seat heard a shot and saw that the girl was wounded and that the defendant was wiping his gun. The defense attempted to prove that, on the way to the hospital, the victim told the ambulance driver and the defendant that she had shot herself. The trial judge would not allow this testimony, and Salcido was convicted. The appellate court reversed the conviction. It stated that, though the suicide statement was offered to prove the truth of the matter in the statement, it was receivable as an exception to the hearsay rule.

(13.6) Dying Declarations

The dying declaration of a homicide victim has long been accepted as an exception to the hearsay rule. In order for the declaration to be considered an exception, however, certain conditions must be met. First, the victim must be "in extremis." Second, he must know that he is dying and that he has no hope of recovery. Third, if he were living he would be competent as a witness. Fourth, his statement must relate to the cause of his death. Courts have based this exception on the theory that if a person knows he is about to die, he is unlikely to lie about who injured him. What he says is thus guaranteed to be true as much as if it had been under oath in court.

People v. *Coniglio*, 79 Misc. 2d 808 (N.Y. 1974), demonstrates a dying declaration. A police officer called to the scene of a shooting found a woman lying on the floor bleeding from bullet wounds. As he bent over her, she said: "Benny shot me. Benny shot my husband and he's dead and I'm going to die too." The officer asked: "Benny who?" She answered: "Benny Coniglio." "Where is Benny?" he asked. She replied: "Around the corner on 11th Avenue." She was taken to surgery and died a few hours later.

The trial court found that her statement met all the conditions for a dying declaration in a homicide case. It ruled, however, that only those portions of the statements bearing on her own death, not on that of her husband, were admissible. Strictly speaking, the dying declaration can be used only in a criminal case arising out of the declarant's death.

In the absence of authority granted by statute, courts have refused to accept the following types of statements: the dying statement of a burglar that his codefendant was innocent; the dying victim's statement where the crime charged was assault with intent to kill rather than homicide; and the statement of a convicted murderer about to be executed that his codefendant was innocent. None of these statements are true dying declarations in homicide. Neither would they be received as declarations against penal interest, as the dying speaker could in no way be subjecting himself to any further punishment, knowing that his life was about to end.

In the past the classic restriction on the use of a dying declaration has been to apply it only to homicide cases. Some jurisdictions have now widened the rule to apply to matters other than homicide, but limit it to the declarant's description of the circumstances of his own death.

It is possible in a criminal prosecution involving death that the victim's statement can now be admitted in evidence as an "excited utterance" even though it does not meet all the requirements of the classic dying declaration.

(13.7) Res Gestae

The term "res gestae" (literally meaning "things done") is a general catchall used by courts for admitting various conversations that are connected in some way with a transaction.

One judge complained about the use of the term, saying, "Definitions of the term 'res gestae' are as numerous as the various cures for rheumatism and about as useful."

Courts continue to misuse the term, mistakenly admitting conversations as res gestae exceptions to the hearsay rule, when they really are not hearsay at all. The illustration used earlier—of a witness testifying that the bank teller said to the robber, "Don't shoot me. Don't shoot me. I'll give you the money."—would in most courts be admitted as part of the res gestae if there were a hearsay objection. As was previously pointed out, it is not hearsay in the first place and stands in its own right as a relevant proof that the teller was parting with money in fear, which is an essential element in robbery. It was not proof of a shooting.

The best way to handle the problem of res gestae is to realize that judges generally admit conversations, words, or acts that are incidental to and explanatory of the fact in controversy. This is, of course, an ill-defined and inexact way to rule on the admissibility of hearsay evidence. A much better way is to understand that there are three classes of genuine hearsay exceptions under the classification of res gestae: excited utterances; explanatory statements; and verbal acts. It is always preferable to use their correct names even if the judge terms them res gestae.

a. Excited Utterances

A speaker's spontaneous words made while he was under the stress of excitement caused by the event will be admitted *even as proof of the matter contained in the statement.* This type of statement, which is made under stress, is reliable because the speaker did not have time to fabricate. Thus, his words are spontaneous, generated by the circumstances themselves. The key to the admittance of an excited utterance is its spontaneity. In this way it differs from the dying declaration in a homicide case. The validity of the latter is based on the solemnity of the occasion and must meet all the requirements given previously. A murder victim's excited utterance made at the time of the crime is admitted because of the spontaneous nature, even though the victim is unaware of his imminent death.

A good example of this is *State* v. *McClain*, 25 N.W. 2d 764 (1964). The defendant, McClain, returned home at about 3:00 a.m. after a heavy drinking spree. He argued with his wife, hit her, and she fell across the bed. McClain then went into the kitchen and ate two sandwiches. He claimed that he came back to the bedroom, found the mattress on fire, threw it out the window, and went out looking for his wife.

The state's story was quite different. The prosecutor produced a neighbor who testified that he heard the McClain family argument and that the wife came to the neighbor's front porch afterward and asked him to "Call the law." The neighbor refused. The burned wife came out and sat on the steps, rocking back and forth and screaming. She accused her husband, saying: "Don't touch me under here, I'm burned up . . . Mac poured gas on me and burned me up." She died thirteen days later in the hospital. The court ruled that her statement was a spontaneous declaration made under stress, even though it was subsequent to the event, and was properly admitted in evidence as an exception to the hearsay rule. McClain was thus convicted.

The excited utterance is allowed in evidence even if made by a third party because the basis for its truth—spontaneity—is the same whether said by a participant or a spectator.

The admission of the excited utterance is gaining wider acceptance in court decisions. It is generally admitted as part of the evidence, whether or not the speaker is available as a witness. Many decisions, like the McClain case, also admit excited statements that are not strictly "contemporaneous" as long as they were made spontaneously under the stress of the event.

Even a statement made in response to police questioning can be classified as a "spontaneous utterance." A victim shot in the mouth and stomach managed to telephone the police and describe the shooting and his assailant. After the police arrived he answered their questions in the same way. The victim died at the hospital. The court found that the victim was distraught and in severe pain, the questions were not suggestive, and he had little time to deliberate. The court held that his statement qualified as an "excited utterance" worthy of belief without cross-examination (*People* v. *Farmer*, 47 Cal. 3rd 988, [1989]).

In a case in Colorado the victim, who was found in the street immediately after the defendant ran her down with his car, said that the driver was her husband. She stated: "That is my husband. He is drunk. He is trying to kill me." The court admitted her statement in evidence.

b. Explanatory Statements

Conversations accompanying the fact in issue will be admitted to explain ambiguous actions, even if they are offered to prove the truth of the statement itself. The conversation must actually "explain" the conduct. It must outline and give meaning to the act.

Much evidence of the explanatory type is not hearsay. Like the statement "I'm Napoleon," it is not offered for the truth, but to explain conduct or to show a mental condition.

Explanatory conversations occasionally are presented to explain, and the statement is also offered for its truth. This makes it a true hearsay exception. One such situation involved the defendant, Alexander, who was accused of murdering his partner, Stedman (*Alexander* v. *U.S.*, 138 U.S. 353 [1890]). Stedman had disappeared and was found ten days later shot through the head. Alexander maintained his innocence and argued that someone else had shot his partner. The defendant introduced evidence that, after Stedman had disappeared from town, a story circulated that he had run off with House's wife and that House and his friends armed themselves and went to look for the missing man. Alexander also offered proof that

House, during this time, threatened to kill Stedman, and the trial judge excluded this evidence. Alexander was subsequently convicted. The Supreme Court reversed the decision. It stated that, since evidence was allowed showing that House was looking for Stedman, his threats accompanying this search explained his actions and were admissible.

c. Verbal Acts

"Verbal act" is a term that is frequently used loosely. A contemporaneous type of statement is often admitted into evidence under the label "verbal act" because the statement accompanied the act. This use of the term is too broad. It is more accurate to confine the definition to a statement that is itself a fact and is an integral part of the action under investigation. A verbal act is actually what it says it is—an action by words.

If a pickpocket steals a man's wallet, he has committed a larceny with his hands. If he swindles him out of the same money by a dishonest investment scheme, he has committed larceny by word of mouth. Thus, his conversations on the latter subject would be admissible as a spoken form of larceny, that is, as a verbal criminal act. A criminal conspiracy is a similar example of a verbal act. In this case, every word of the criminal participants is admissible. The words of the conspirators thus amount to an act of crime—a verbal act.

In *Ward* v. *U.S.*, 296 F. 2d 898 (1962), the defendant, convicted of offering a bribe to a juror, appealed, claiming the trial court allowed some hearsay evidence. A witness, Staley, had testified that the defendant hired him to offer two hundred dollars to a prospective juror in order to obtain a hung jury. Staley offered the money to the juror, but the latter declined. Staley reported this to the defendant. The court allowed all of Staley's testimony. When the defendant appealed the decision, the appellate court affirmed the conviction, saying that Staley was the defendant's agent and that the conversation with the jury was a verbal act—the very crime of offering a bribe to a juror.

(13.8) Complaint of a Sex Victim

A complaint made by a victim of a sex crime will be admitted under certain conditions as an exception to the hearsay rule *as proof that the crime itself took place*. If the statement is made at the time of the attack, it is admissible as an excited utterance, but the type of exception being discussed here is a complaint made after the attack, when the stress of events may have passed.

If there has been a rape or an act of nonconsensual perversion, the victim usually complains about it at the first possible opportunity. Should the woman not complain, one might assume that she was not violated, but had consented to the act.

The person who heard the complaint can testify concerning it since the complaint is a natural, instinctive type of utterance and so bears a presumption of truthfulness. It is also allowed to overcome the negative reaction to silence on the part of the victim and to corroborate the victim's testimony if she is impeached as a witness. The victim's statement must not be too remote and must actually be a complaint.

In *Callahan* v. *U.S.*, 240 F. 683 (1917), there was a prosecution for statutory rape. An adult male was accused of having intercourse with a girl under the age of fourteen. Shortly after the intercourse took place she met her girl friend outside the house. The friend, called as a prosecution witness, testified that the girl had told her that she had gone to the house willingly, had intercourse with the defendant, and then showed the three dollars that he had paid her. The defendant was convicted and appealed. The reviewing court reversed the conviction, saying that the girl's statement was not a complaint or expression of outraged feeling nor even an excited utterance. It was merely interesting information passed on in a conversation with an intimate friend and was therefore hearsay.

Thus, in order for the sex victim's complaint to qualify for this hearsay exception, it must be recent, it must be given voluntarily at the first natural opportunity, and it must be an actual complaint.

Because of the great increase in the number of child sexual abuse cases coming before the courts, authorities are taking a more liberal view of the evidence required for conviction. Some state statutes and other rulings by court decisions are allowing a variety of out-of-court statements by child victims to be used in evidence as a further exception to the hearsay rule.

(13.9) Business Records

Over the years the courts have developed a set of rules for admitting business records in evidence. Sometimes known as the "Shop Book Rule," it is now usually referred to by a term such as "business records as evidence act."

This hearsay exception has evolved as a matter of practicality. For example, if a merchant suing a customer in regard to his charge account had to produce each clerk who made every sale, the employee who made the delivery, and the bookkeeper who made the account entry, it would clutter the courtroom endlessly and make proof extremely difficult. Thus, the rule has developed over the years allowing records regularly made in the course of business to be admitted in evidence as an exception to the rule against hearsay.

The rule has recently been expanded. It now includes records that are not strictly "business records" if they are made in the regular course of the "business," near the time of the event, and if, in the opinion of the court, the sources of information and the purpose of keeping the record were such as to justify its admission. Under this expanded interpretation, accident reports, police reports, and other regularly kept records not involved in any commercial business are often allowed in evidence in criminal cases. A police report can, however, normally be used only if the writer of the report was a witness to the facts or if the person giving the information to the writer was under any obligation to relate the facts.

In criminal trials the defense ordinarily asks for the production of police witnesses' notes, police records, and the like. As previously noted, the defense uses these in cross-examination. Occasionally, however, the defense may offer such a record in evidence under the business records exception as proof of the actual matter contained in the report.

(13.10) Computer Printouts

The computer world has now caught up with the courts. What to do with a computer printout made by a machine, not by human hands? A defendant convicted of making obscene telephone calls objected to the state's introduction of a printout that was automatically made by a telephone company computer that recorded all telephone numbers.

The court approved the use of the printout as an exception to the hearsay rule. They reasoned that the record was not a "statement" made by a person but was similar to the record of a scientific test or experiment and therefore admissible.

(13.11) Prior Statements of a Witness

Many types of earlier statements made by a witness may be allowed as evidence. If a witness has testified previously in the same case at an earlier trial, at a pretrial hearing, or in an examination before trial, when he could have been cross-examined, the record of his testimony can ordinarily be used in the later trial, should the witness be unavailable. His earlier testimony is then used as direct proof of its contents, just as though he were on the stand testifying in person.

In *California* v. *Green*, 399 U.S. 149 (1970), the Supreme Court announced an extension of the rule by allowing the use of earlier testimony in the situation even where the witness was available. In that case a sixteen-year-old boy was arrested on a drug charge, and he named Green as his supplier. He testified to this at Green's preliminary hearing. At the trial, however, the boy took the stand and said he had been taking LSD and could not remember. The prosecution then read from his testimony at the preliminary hearing and had an officer testify that the boy had orally named Green as his supplier. This was the state's only proof that directly linked Green to the drug sale. The Supreme Court approved this evidence, saying that the boy had testified at the trial and could have been cross-examined thoroughly in regard to his prior statements and his present testimony. The court further pointed out that it was not an unconstitutional deprivation of the right of cross-examination to use the prior statements as direct proof of the crime.

The use of a prior statement of a witness often becomes involved in cases of identity, where the witness identifies the defendant from the stand during the trial and has, of course, identified him earlier at the station house or in a police lineup. The general rule has been that prior identification is equivalent to a prior statement. If the witness had failed to identify the defendant earlier, that fact would be allowed as impeaching evidence to weaken the present testimony. If, on the other hand, it was a consistent identification whereby the witness had identified the same man twice, the prior identification would not be allowed in evidence unless the identity had been attacked and it was necessary in order to rehabilitate the witness.

A rule that is now evolving in court decisions is to admit the evidence of the earlier identification, even if it is consistent, on the theory that it was fresher and more reliable in the first instance than it is during the trial. Judges maintain that this situation is similar to that of *California* v. *Green*. Thus, when the identifying witness is on the stand, he can be thoroughly cross-examined, and, for this reason, the testimony of both identifications should be allowed. States still vary in this interpretation. Some, for example, will not allow testimony regarding prior identification simply to bolster the witness then on the stand. Some states also have statutes governing identity testimony.

(13.12) Miscellaneous Exceptions

A number of minor hearsay exceptions—official records, such as certificates of conviction, records of vital statistics, family records, and ancient documents—occur infrequently in criminal cases.

Some states now admit hearsay in general at administrative proceedings or preliminary hearings before indictment. Hearsay is also widely allowed as a basis for arrests and warrants. Some types of hearsay, such as official laboratory reports, may be introduced before a grand jury. A few jurisdictions have laws that permit the use of various declarations of persons since deceased. As previously mentioned, a written record of a "past recollection recorded" may sometimes be used where the witness has no present memory of the event.

(13.13) The Two-Step Rule for Determining Hearsay

There is a simple two-step rule that anyone can use to determine if evidence offered is hearsay. All you need to do is ask yourself two questions.

First, is the statement offered to prove the truth of its contents? If it is offered for some purpose other than to prove its truth, it is not hearsay. Remember the Napoleon illustration of the man on the street corner with his hand in his shirt, saying "I'm Napoleon." That statement was receivable, not to prove he was the Emperor, but to show that the speaker was insane.

Always do this *first*, and you will find that most conversations or writings offered are not hearsay, and the problem is eliminated. Many attorneys, and even some judges, miss this first step. In all fairness, it must be said that this is easy to do, unless in the first instance you stop and say to yourself, "Is this offered to prove it is true, or is it offered for another purpose?"

So—should hearsay arise, Napoleonize.

Next, if it is offered to prove its truth, the statement is hearsay, but it still may be usable.

A hearsay objection?
Try all the exceptions.

So, secondly, you must ask yourself, "Does the statement fall within any of the exceptions to the hearsay rule?" Number the exceptions off mentally. Is it a confession, an admission, an excited utterance, a dying declaration, an explanatory statement, or some other exception? Now, you have the final answer.

Follow the two-step rule and you will always find the answer to the hearsay question.

(13.14) Summary

Hearsay is an out-of-court statement offered to prove the truth of the matter contained in the statement. An oral or written statement offered for purposes other than its truth is not hearsay. Many written and oral statements are admitted as evidence, however, not to prove their truth, but to demonstrate motive, intent, bias, or other state of mind. They are not hearsay.

There is a two-step exercise in deciding hearsay. First, is the statement offered to prove its truth? If so, it is classed as hearsay. Second, if it is hearsay, does it fall within any of the exceptions?

Several recognized exceptions to the rule exist, even though they may actually be classified as hearsay. The best-known exception is a confession, which is an out-of-court statement received for its own truth. Admissions, even admissions by silence, fall in the same class. Statements of coconspirators made during and in furtherance of a conspiracy are usable against all conspirators as an exception to the hearsay ban.

Declarations made by a witness against his own pecuniary or penal interests are received in evidence as proof of the content of the statement itself. A dying declaration of a homicide victim is allowed, provided he knew that death was near and then subsequently died. By their very nature they are considered reliable and hence received in evidence, though they are plainly hearsay.

Many utterances accompanying or near in time to when the crime was committed are accepted, even though they are offered to prove their truth. Among these are excited or spontaneous utterances, explanatory statements delineating ambiguous conduct, and verbal acts that, in themselves, constitute a crime. Contemporaneous complaints by the victim of a sex crime are recognized as valid proof of the matter contained in the complaint even though they are properly classed as hearsay.

Records that are regularly kept in the course of any business are generally accepted. These include, among others, business and police records. Prior testimony and prior statements of a witness can be used in some circumstances as direct proof of the matter in the statement. Minor varieties of other hearsay exceptions include records of family lineage, official records, vital statistics, and records of criminal convictions.

Discussion Questions

1. Define hearsay and the hearsay rule.
2. Why have exceptions to the hearsay rule been developed?
3. Distinguish between confession and admission.
4. Discuss the origin of the current business records exception to the hearsay rule.
5. Under what circumstances may former testimony qualify as an exception to the hearsay rule?

14

The Jury

I consider trial by jury as the only anchor ever yet imagined by man, by which a government can be held to the principles of its constitution.
>   —Thomas Jefferson, in a letter to Thomas Paine, 1789.

It is not only his right, but his duty . . . to find the verdict according to his own best understanding, judgment, and conscience, though in direct opposition to the direction of the court.
>   —John Adams, who became the second U.S. President, in 1771; quoted in *Yale Law Journal* 74 (1964):173.

(14.1) Trial by Jury—A Brief History

Trial by jury originated in England in about 1066, replacing two other forms of trial—trial by battle and trial by ordeal. In trial by battle, two opponents faced each other in combat; the person who won the battle was considered "just," while the loser was found "guilty." The belief of the day was that God sided with the just and damned the criminal to defeat. Trial by ordeal meant that the accused was subjected to endurance tests such as being submerged under water or burned with hot irons. God was said to save only those who were innocent.[1]

In early Britain, juries were the "eyewitnesses" who decided on the guilt of the accused based on their observation of the crime. They were neighbors who investigated the incident in question and

---

1. James Levine, Michael Musheno, and Dennis James Palumbo, *Criminal Justice in America: Law In Action* (New York: John Wiley & Sons, 1986), pg.388.

judged the guilt or innocence of the accused. Later, juries were selected from people not connected with the incident who were considered to be unbiased. They would listen to the evidence and use their
common sense to determine what happened. In such cases, these "juries" would determine if the law fit the accused's actions, and thee
jury would enforce the law as they saw fit.

When the American colonists began to settle the land that would
become the United States of America, they were well versed in the
need to use juries to find facts and determine "guilt" or "non-guilt" of
a person accused of a crime. Following the Revolutionary War, the
use of jury trials continued when the United States Constitution replaced the Articles of Confederation. The framers of the Constitution
guaranteed the right to a trial by jury for defendants accused of federal
crimes. Article 3, Section 2, states:

The trial of all crimes, except in case of impeachment, shall be by jury; and such
trial shall be held in the State where the said crimes shall have been committed;
but when not committed within any State, the trial shall be at such place or places
as the Congress may by law have directed.

The initial constitutional guarantee to a jury applied only to persons accused of federal crimes. In the early states, the right to trial by
jury was defined by the constitution of an individual state. The federal
guarantee was reiterated in the Sixth Amendment to the U.S. Constitution:

In all criminal prosecutions, the accused shall enjoy the right to a speedy and
public trial, by an impartial jury of the State and district wherein the crime shall
have been committed, which district shall have been previously ascertained by
law, and to be informed of the nature and cause of the accusation; to be confronted with the witnesses against him; to have compulsory process for obtaining
witnesses in his favor, and to have the assistance of council for his defense.

The original framers of the Constitution feared a strong central
government and preferred to defer power to the individual states. The
legal theory was to leave the power in the hands of the people to de-

cide the way in which their respective state governments dealt with criminal law and procedure.[2]

Generally, most jurisdictions require that juries reach unanimous verdicts in criminal cases, although the U.S. Supreme Court has ruled that unanimous verdicts are not required in noncapital cases (*Johnson v. Louisiana,* 406 U.S. 356 [1972], and *Apodaca* v. *Oregon,* 406 U.S. 404 [1972]). Each state determines the standard used as outlined in the state's code of criminal procedures. In the event that a jury fails to unanimously agree to a verdict of either "guilty" or "not guilty," the jury is said to be *hung,* and a mistrial is declared. In such an instance, the state may decide to either commence a new trial or not. A new jury trial does not violate the Fifth Amendment prohibition against "double jeopardy" because *jeopardy* was never concluded in the previous trial.

(14.2) The Jury[3]

A *jury* is a sworn body of persons convened to render a rational, impartial verdict and a finding of fact on a legal question officially submitted to them, or to set a penalty or judgment in a jury trial of a court of law.

a Overview

In the criminal justice systems of most countries that require a jury, panels are initially selected at random from the adult population of the district served by the court concerned. A person who is serving on (that is, is a member of) a jury is known as a *juror.*

The requirements for a jury are fairly universal. The number of jurors must be a specified size (usually twelve or fifteen), and since there is always the possibility of jurors not completing the trial for health or other reasons, often some alternate jurors are nominated.

---

2. Jefferson L. Ingram, *Criminal Law: Theory and Practice* (New York: Pearson Education Inc./Prentice Hall, 2005). pg. 408.

3. This section is reprinted with permission from Wikipedia, the free encyclopedia. Students may see http://en.wikipedia.org /wiki/Wikipedia/Jury for complete text. This section is reprinted under Wikipedia:Copyrights Text of the GNU Free Documentation License, Sections 2 and 3.

An alternative juror follows the trial but does not take part in deciding the verdict unless he or she replaces an original juror part way through the trial.

Serving on a jury is normally compulsory if a citizen is chosen (exceptions and exclusions vary between jurisdictions and are discussed below). Since a jury is intended to be an impartial panel capable of reaching a verdict, there are often requirements for jurors—for instance, fluent understanding of the language. There are also procedures—for instance, the defense and prosecution lawyers may question potential jurors or otherwise exclude those who might be perceived as less than neutral or more partial to hearing one side or the other.

The jurors hear the case presented by both the defense and the prosecution, and in some jurisdictions a summing-up from the judge. Jurors then retire as a group to consider a verdict. The number of jurors constituting a majority required for a verdict varies. In some countries, a jury's decision-making process is private and may not be disclosed; in others, it may be discussed but only after the trial has ended.

In common-law countries such as the United Kingdom and the United States, the role of the jury is that of "finder of fact," while the judge has the sole responsibility of interpreting the appropriate law and instructing the jury accordingly. Occasionally, a jury may find the defendant "not guilty" even though he violated the law, if the jury thinks that the law is invalid or unjust. This is commonly referred to as jury nullification. When there is no jury (called a *bench trial*), the judge makes both factual and legal rulings. In most continental European jurisdictions, judges have more power in a trial, and the role and powers of a jury are often restricted. Actual jury law and trial procedures differ among countries.

The concept of a modern jury trial stems back to the Magna Carta, which gave English nobles and freemen the right to be tried by a panel of their peers, rather than by summary judgment of the king or other official who often had complete power to impose his own arbitrary judgment. The concept can also be traced to Normandy before 1066, when a jury of nobles was established to decide land disputes. In this manner, the Duke, being the largest landowner, could not act as a judge in his own case. Many ancient cultures had similar concepts, notably ancient Judea, whose panel of judges (called the *Sanhedrin)* served a similar purpose. By 505 B.C. the Athenians used the jury court, with votes cast by secret ballot. These courts were eventually granted the power to annul unconstitutional laws, thus introducing judicial review.

b. Selection

A common method for drafting jurors is to draw them at random from electoral rolls (this process is known as allotment or sortition). The most common exclusions are for people whose job in some way precludes them from serving (for instance, teachers, doctors, firefighters, and people who themselves work in the criminal justice system), are caring for young children, have an interest in the case, are under the age of 18 years, or have health problems or serious criminal records. In some jurisdictions in the United States, individuals with prior legal education or who are lawyers may also be exempted, under the theory they may overly influence other jurors. However, in recent years, many jurisdictions have eliminated these exemptions.

In the United States, potential jurors form the *jury in waiting* or *jury pool.* Jurors are picked by a selection process. If the jury in waiting is exhausted without the jury being completed, the clerk of the court is required to ask the jury assembly area to send more jurors.

Those chosen from the jury pool are generally subjected to a system of examination whereby both the prosecution (or plaintiff, in a civil case) and defense can object to a juror. In common-law countries, this is known as *voir dire.* The method and scope of the possible rejections varies among countries; for example:

- In England, these objections would have to be very well based, such as the defendant knowing a potential juror, to be allowed.
- Some jurisdictions, such as France, New Zealand, and the United States, give both the defense and prosecution a specific number of unconditional peremptory challenges. No justification has to be brought to exclude a specific juror. Generally, defense attorneys exclude jurors who have professions or backgrounds similar to that of the victim and who could thus feel an emotional link to

them, while prosecuting attorneys exclude jurors who might show
affinity to the defendant.

- Some systems allow argument over whether a juror's particular
  background or beliefs make them biased and therefore unsuitable
  for service on the jury. In the United States, and probably other
  nations, it is hardly unknown for citizens to try to deliberately get
  out of jury duty (for example by mentioning knowledge of legal
  concepts).

c. Verdicts

In general, there are no restrictions on how a jury may proceed to
reach a verdict, and no set time limit. Juries may deliberate for several
days, or they may reach a verdict in only a few hours.

Juries are traditionally expected to reach a unanimous verdict
through their deliberations. If this is not possible after an extended
period of deliberation, jurisdictions vary as to whether they will accept
a majority verdict or declare a mistrial.

Initially, a judge will usually instruct a jury not to contemplate a
majority verdict. After a time, if no verdict is forthcoming, the judge
may recall the jury and instruct them that he is prepared to consider
one. Some jurisdictions allow majority verdicts in criminal cases if a
juror becomes unfit to continue, or if a judge permits it when a jury is
deadlocked. Certain jurisdictions require a minimum number of jurors
to agree, but in others (notably Scotland) a simple majority is acceptable.

Sometimes a jury will take a wider view than the judge's summing up, and reach a verdict influenced by or based on its view of the
public interest—that is, whether the jury thinks it right, all things considered, for the defendant to be convicted of a crime. Verdicts that appear not to apply the law to the evidence are sometimes called "per-
verse" verdicts.

d. Secrecy and Independence

For juries to fulfill their role to analyze the facts of the case,
there are strict rules about their use of information during the trial.
They are not allowed to learn about the case from any source other
than the trial. Nobody involved in the trial is allowed to speak with a

member of the jury, and jurors are not allowed to read news or other accounts of the trial. In order to achieve this goal in high-profile cases, some juries are sequestered either for the deliberation phase or for the entire trial.

Conversely, jurors are generally required to keep their deliberations in strict confidence. Whether this nondisclosure requirement extends after the verdict has been rendered depends on the jurisdiction. In English law, the jury's deliberations must not be disclosed outside the jury, even after that case, and to repeat parts of them is contempt of court and can result in imprisonment. In the United States, this rule does not apply, and sometimes jurors have made remarks that called into question whether a verdict was properly arrived at.

Because of the desire to prevent undue influence on a jury, jury tampering is a serious crime, whether attempted through bribery, threat of violence, or other means.

e. Imposition of Penalties for Guilty Verdicts

In the United States, some juries are also empowered to consider some aspects of a defendant's sentence, if the defendant has been convicted. This is now a requirement in all death penalty cases. This is not the practice in most other legal systems based on the English tradition, in which judges retain sole responsibility for deciding sentences according to law. The exception is the award of damages in English law libel cases, although a judge is now obliged to make a recommendation to the jury as to the appropriate amount.

f. France (Napoleonic Code)

In France and similarly organized jurisdictions, the jury sits on an equal footing with three professionals judges. The jury and judges first consider the question of guilt. Then, if applicable, they consider the penalty to apply.

g. United States (Common Law)

In the United States, a jury cannot reach a verdict (a situation sometimes referred to as a *hung jury*), a mistrial is declared, and the case must be retried with a newly constituted jury. The practice generally was that the jury rules only on questions of facts on guilt; setting penalty was reserved to the judge. This has been changed by rulings of the U.S. Supreme Court such as *Ring* v. *Arizona, 536 U.S. 584* (2002), which found unconstitutional Arizona's practice of judges (in a trial by jury) deciding if the penalty in a capital case should be life or death, and reserved that decision for the jury. (The judge can, however, overrule the jury and reduce the penalty to life if he or she chooses, although this is unheard of.)

There is no set format for jury deliberations, and the jury will take a period of time to settle into discussing the evidence. In theory, electing a foreman is the first step, although for a short or straightforward case this may not happen until the delivery of the verdict.

If a foreman is elected at the beginning, he or she will chair the discussions, and it is his or her job to try and steer the jury toward a conclusion. The first step will typically be to find out the initial feeling or reaction to the case, which may be demonstrated by a show of hands. The jury will then attempt to arrive at a consensus verdict.

When people whose opinions differ from the emerging consensus present their views of the case, points will often arise about the trial that were not specifically discussed during it. The result of these discussions is likely that one interpretation is shown to be the most reasonable, and a verdict is thus reached.

In the United States, juries are used in both criminal law and civil law trials, though they are quire different. In criminal law, separate juries are convened: a *grand jury* decides if a suspect should be indicted (that is, formally charged with a crime) and a *petit jury* to decide if the suspect is guilty. In may areas, depending on the law, a third jury will determine what the penalty should be or recommend what the penalty should be in the penalty phase. When the word *jury* is used alone, it usually refers to a petit jury.

In each court district, a group of from sixteen to twenty-three citizens—a grand jury—holds an inquiry on criminal complaints brought by the prosecutor and decides if a trial is warranted, in which case an indictment is issued. In general, the size of juries tends to be larger if the crime alleged is more serious. A grand jury rejection of a proposed indictment is known as a "no bill"; an endorsement a proposed indictment is known as a "true bill."

The Sixth Amendment to the U.S. Constitution guarantees the

right to a jury trial in both state and federal criminal proceedings, although in practice most criminal actions in the United States are resolved by plea bargain. Juries are also used in many civil cases in the United States, and the Seventh Amendment to the Constitution explicitly protects the right to a jury trial in civil cases tried in the U.S. district courts.

As mentioned in previous section of this chapter, jury selection is a complicated process. A jury is made up from a list of citizens living in the jurisdiction of the court. When selected, being a juror is, in principle, compulsory. However, jurors can be dismissed for several reasons, and many people are released from serving on a jury. People can, for instance, claim hardship if they take care of their children, or claim to be biased. Many individuals are paid only the token amount issued by the court for jury duty, and must take time off from work to serve. Especially for high-profile trials, or long trials, it is unusual to compel one to serve because of the possibility that a juror would have other things on his or her mind, such as finances, during the trial or deliberations. Some commentators, exemplified by *The Simpsons* character Homer Simpson, have claimed that a jury is not a "jury of one's peers," but is instead "twelve people too stupid to get out of jury duty."

(14.3) Verdict

Depending on the trial, a jury verdict may be brief or last for days and sometimes weeks. Some juries will deliberate for only a short time and come to a decision. In the 1995 double-murder trial of O.J. Simpson, a Heisman Trophy winner and national football star who became a media personality, the jury found Mr. Simpson "not guilty" in a matter of hours, which is a relatively short time for such a complicated criminal charge. However, in 1997, a California jury found Mr. Simpson "liable" for the deaths of his ex-wife Nicole Simpson and an acquaintance Ronald Goldman; Mr. Simpson was ordered to pay $33.5 million in damages.

In April 2006, after nearly five hours of deliberations, a jury convicted auto mechanic Joseph Smith of the rape and murder of eleven-year old Carlie Brucia. In this shocking abduction case, the kidnapping was caught on tape at a carwash and broadcast worldwide.

In the death penalty phase of the trial, jurors weighed aggravating factors against mitigating factors and decided that Joseph Smith deserved to suffer death for his crime.

In May 2006, a federal jury of nine men and three women deliberated for seven days and decided that Al-Qaida conspirator Zacarias Moussaoui deserved life in prison instead of death for his role in the terrorist attacks of September 11, 2001, which killed nearly 3,000.

(14.4) Civil Juries

Rules for judgments in civil juries differ from rules in criminal juries. Criminal juries require a unanimous agreement for a verdict of "guilty" or "not guilty." Civil juries do not, in every jurisdiction, require a unanimous vote. For example, in Texas, a judgment can be reached in a civil case if ten of the twelve jurors concur in the finding. In Idaho, nine of the twelve jurors must agree to arrive at a verdict. Each state defines the number of jurors required for a civil verdict. The level of proof in civil proceedings is also different from criminal cases. Juries reach a verdict by a "preponderance of the evidence." This level of proof requires that the finders of fact (the jury) look at the amount of weight of evidence that is "most convincing"; another way of defining this level would be to say that the jury finds either the plaintiff or the defendant the more believable. The judgment in a civil case results in one party or the other being awarded money or property.

(14.5) Peace Officer Liability

In some instances, both a peace officer and his or her agency may be the defendant in a civil case. By its very nature, police work involves the necessary use of limited force to accomplish the law enforcement role. The U.S. Constitution requires that the use of force be "reasonable." Penal codes specifically outline that officers may use necessary force against someone when the officer reasonably believes it is immediately necessary to make an arrest or search, or to prevent escape after arrest.

The fact that the use of force may be justified under the penal code does not keep anyone from seeking any civil remedy for acts committed by peace officers in the line of duty. Generally, civil suits are directed at both the officer and his or her agency; the plaintiff expects to get a great sum of money from the city, county, or state rather than from the individual officer. Such suits usually contend that the officer's actions were an extension of the "policy or custom" of the agency, or that the agency failed to properly train the officer. Generally, the courts have held that a single act of misconduct by a peace officer is not sufficient to establish "policy or custom" for municipal liability purposes (*Oklahoma City* v. *Tuttle,* 105 S. Ct. 2427, 1985). However, in other limited situations courts have held that a single decision by "the appropriate official" may establish "policy," even though not every decision will do so (*Pembauer* v. *City of Cincinnati,* 106S. Ct. 1292, 1986). As a rule, most civil suits will be weighed in the officer's favor, provided that he or she follows generally accepted procedures and the guidelines of the agency. In contrast, however, officers who have gone beyond the limits of their authority have had to face the real fact of owing large sums of money to plaintiffs in civil actions.

Civil suits can happen in relation to almost any aspect of a peace officer's job. In one instance, the Supreme Court held that even while working under the authority of an arrest warrant, a peace officer does not have "absolute immunity" from liability for damages. (*Malley* v. *Briggs,* 106 S. Ct. 1092, 1986). Other Supreme Court cases held that peace officers have "qualified immunity" from liability for a prisoner's suicide (*Gagne* v. *City of Galveston,* 805 F.2d 558, 5th Cir. 1986).[4]

(14.6) Civil Actions—Police and Missing Persons

Prompt, courteous, and correct police action taken to locate missing person can generate positive community support. People seek law enforcement assistance because it is the most readily avail able and

---

4. Larry D Nichols, *Law Enforcement Patrol Operations: Police Systems and Practices,* 5th Edition (Richmond, Calif.: McCutchan Publishing, 2005), pgs. 25-29.

knowledgeable community resource (24 hours a day, 7 days a week) capable of locating missing persons. Correct handling of cases involving missing persons can also reduce possibility of civil liability. Inappropriate conduct or improper response, however, can result in both the agency and the involved officer defending themselves against suits in civil court. Consider the results of the following cases, in which the officer should have done no more than stand by and maintain the peace.

Anderson v. Roberts (C.D. Cal 1986 659 Sup 19—Enforcement of Child Custody Law)

A California peace officer was held liable to the father of a minor illegitimate child in the amount of $5,000 when the officer helped the child's mother take the child away from the father.

Shortly after his birth in November 1980, the child lived with the father, who permitted some visitation rights to the mother. In July 1983 the father allowed the mother a two-week visit. When the mother did not return the child after the visit, the father searched for them and found the mother and child in Phoenix, Arizona. After securing custody of the child, the father returned to California without consent or knowledge of the mother.

The mother filed a complaint with the Phoenix police department, which asked the California police department to verify the address where the father and the child were located. The police supervisor directed an officer to comply, and the officer interviewed the father at the police station, where facts of the case were documented.

On July 27, 1984, the mother appeared at the California police department and requested assistance in locating the child. The police supervisor issued instructions to have an officer company the mother to the father's residence and the keep the peace. An officer volunteered to take the assignment. At the scene the officer ordered the father to turn the child over to the mother.

> The officer told the father to come to the police station, where discussion about the custody of the child would continue. The officer drove the mother and child to the airport—rather than to the police station—after urging from the mother, according to the city attorney handling the case. Neither the mother nor child was ever located following their departure from the airport.
>
> In the subsequent civil trial, the city was not held liable because the father failed to name the city as a defendant. The police supervisor was not held liable because his order to "keep the peace" was proper. However, the officer was held personally liable for exceeding his authority and ordered to pay $5,000; the city attorney convinced a reluctant city to pay the judgment for the officer.

This case emphasizes the care investigators and law enforcement officer must take in handing child custody and visitation disputes. An officer must keep in mind that he or she is dealing with fundamental rights secured by the U.S. Constitution and enforceable through the federal and state courts; the officer can be held personally liable in such cases.

The first principle established by the court is that parents have a due process right to retain custody and control of their minor children (*Stanley* v. *Illinois,* 1972, 405 U.S. 645, 92 S.Ct. 1208, 31 L.Ed. 551). Furthermore, state action cannot deprive a parent of rights inconsistent with due process (*Lassite* v. *Department of Social Services,* 1981, 452 U.S. 18, 101 S.Ct. 215, 68 L.Ed. 640). The courts have found that the conduct of a peace officer in depriving a parent of a custody and control right is "performance under color of state law" and falls within the meaning of 42 USC Section 1983. The facts of the *Anderson* case make it clear the officer should have done no more than stand by, maintain the peace or status quo, and advise the parties to go to court and get a court order.

In the following civil rights case, a peace officer was jointly and severally liable for an individual's abduction of a child in violation of a court order.

Shields *v.* Martin (Idaho 1985) 606 P.2d 21.

While in the midst of a custody battle with her ex-husband, the mother enlisted aid of a police officer to gain custody of the child. The two went to the day-care center where, making use of a copy of a superseded custody decree, the mother obtained the child and took him from the day-care center. The police officer erroneously advised the day-care center operator that the document was valid and binding and that the child should be relinquished. He also told the day-care operator that she could not call the father before delivery of the child to the mother. Subsequently, after regaining custody of the child, the father sued the police officer for violation of civil rights and the mother for her tortuous deprivation of his right of custody. At trial, the court refused to instruct on the issue of joint and several liability. The jury awarded separate verdicts against the police officer and the mother, but in differing amounts.

The Idaho Supreme Court reversed. The court found, as a matter of law, that the two defendants were joint tortfeasors, whose combined acts caused the father to be denied his right of custody. The mother's flight from the state, with the child, was a wholly foreseeable consequence of the abduction. Thus, the police officer was jointly liable for all compensatory damages awarded against the mother on the state law theory. The police officer could not be held accountable, however, for punitive damages that had specifically been assessed against the mother.

The reviewing court also upheld the father's constitutional claim against the police officer even though the officer's conduct was no more than negligent. Citing U.S. Supreme Court precedent, the Idaho court concluded that negligent conduct may constitute a due process violation where there existed no adequate state tort remedy. Because the Idaho torts Claims Act afforded complete personal immunity to the officer on the state tort theory, the trial court had not erred in allowing the father to submit his due process claim to the jury.

Finally, consider the following story adapted from a newspaper article published in July 1988. The article demonstrates the need for officers to cautiously and correctly act when handling child abduction and custody dispute cases.

City told to pay $3.8 million
Father of missing child wins judgment

A jury ordered a California city to pay $3.8 million Tuesday because police failed to respond adequately to a father's plea for help when his daughter was stolen....The city was found at fault even though the mother who took the three-year-old committed no crime.

The father, a retired New York city attorney still searching for his missing daughter, said the verdict was a clear warning to third parties who assist in child abduction, even through inaction.

"They're going to be held liable," said the father, 60, who was awarded $3.5 million as compensation for the loss of his child. The father represented himself during the trial, assisted by two other lawyers.

"(The money) is going to bankroll me so I can go back to doing what I was doing all along—hiring people who can help me find my daughter," said the father, who suffered a heart attack shortly after his daughter vanished August 26, 1979. The balance of the jury award, $325,000, is to be paid on behalf of the missing child, who will be 12 next month. She is still believed to be with the mother, 48, who is in hiding.

Other defendants in the lawsuit—the private investigator hired by the mother and her friends and relatives who assisted—were dismissed from the case earlier after agreeing to pay the father $350,000.

Attorneys on both sides of the dispute said there is scant state law on the civil liability of third parties in a case where a parent abducts a child.

Lawyers for the city said that if the verdict is allowed

to stand, it would dramatically broaden such liability, placing an unfair burden on police officers intervening in custody disputes between warring parents.

"Its just an absolute travesty," said the attorney who represented the city. "What we're dealing with here is an area where police officers have to exercise their discretion. This is an extremely dangerous area for police to be subjected to liability."

The jury of 11 women and 1 man deliberated more than five days before finding, by a nine-to-three vote, liability on the part of the city and a police sergeant, who was watch commander on the day of the abduction. Nine votes are required to reach a verdict in civil suits.

Jurors said they focused much of their attention on the sergeant's behavior the day of the abduction. They said they concluded that he had failed to take adequate steps to bring both parents into the police station to resolve their dispute over the child.

They suspected the sergeant intentionally failed to act because the private investigator hired by the mother to assist her is a former police officer who knew members of the city police department.

"To a degree they felt—some jurors felt—that there is a strong bond between police officers and ex-police officers," said the foreman.

The private investigator's insurance carrier paid $100,000 to win his dismissal before the trial. Ironically, the jurors, who knew nothing of the dismissal, absolved him of any liability.

Jurors also said they were suspicious that crucial tape recordings of police communication and other records have been lost over the years. Some speculated that there might have been a police cover-up.

At the center of the dispute is an 11-year old girl whose photograph has been circulated nationwide on milk cartons and leaflets offering $2,500 for her return.

The girl was taken from the porch of a mobile home,

where her father was visiting relatives. The father said he saw the private investigator grab the child and drive away with her in a van. The private investigator testified that the mother took the girl while he blocked the father's way.

The father and mother, who never married, retained equal custody of the girl at the time she was taken in 1979, attorneys in the case said. After her disappearance, the father was awarded custody in California, and a warrant was issued for the mother's arrest.

The father said he has spent more than $200,000 looking for his daughter, chasing down leads, hiring private investigators, and pressing his lawsuit.

The city attorney said the city previously had made a "nominal" settlement offer after the judge summoned the city manager into her chambers and urged a settlement. The judge made the request after the sergean''s trial testimony.

A former police chief, called by the father as an expert in police procedures, testified that proper routine for the sergeant would have been to summon both parents to the police department in an effort to sort out the dispute.

Instead, the sergeant testified that he decided, based on a conversation with the private investigator and the mother, who called police from an undisclosed location several minutes after taking the child, that the mother had rightful custody. Although an officer went to the scene and took a report from the father, no further action was taken by police.

The private investigator acknowledged during the trial that he knew many officers on the police department, but he said he did not know the sergeant. The private investigator said he believed at the time that the father previously had stolen the child from the mother where the couple lived together in Florida. If upheld, the $3.8 million judgment would be the largest award paid by the city.

(14.7) Summary

The jury is a sworn body of persons convened to render a rational, impartial verdict and finding of fact on a legal question officially submitted to them, or to set a penalty or judgment in a jury trial of a court of law.

Trial by jury has its origins in England in about 1066, replacing two other forms of trial: trial by battle and trial by ordeal. Early trials used "eyewitnesses" as jurors; later, jurors were unbiased citizens who listened to evidence and decided the verdict. In writing the Sixth Amendment, the framers of our Constitution recognized the value of the jury system

Juries are selected from a random group of citizens of the community in which jurisdiction the trial will be held. In criminal trials, the verdict of the jury must be unanimous for either "guilty" or "not guilty." In civil cases, the jury can render a verdict of a majority of the individuals serving on the jury. The exact number for a majority varies by state as outlined in state procedural codes.

Many of the cases that police investigate can have both criminal and civil litigation issues. Actions of peace officers can also be scrutinized for civil liability suits. Inappropriate police action can result in large sums of money being award to the plaintiff who was injured by poor police decisions. These judgments can be rendered against the officer, his or her agency, and the political entity (state, county, state) that employs the officer.

Discussion Questions

1. What is the number of jurors required in your jurisdiction to arrive at a verdict in your state?
2. How does a civil verdict differ from a criminal verdict?
3. How can a specific case be criminal and civil at the same time?
4. In your jurisdiction, does the jury that determines the verdict in a criminal case also set the punishment for the defendant? If not, what are the exceptions?

15
Sentencing

Farther: as punishments are chiefly intended for the
prevention of future crimes of different natures those
should be most severely punished, which are the most
destructive of the public safety and happiness. . . .
—Blackstone's Commentaries n the laws of
England, Book IV, Ch. 1, p. 16

(15.1) The Sentencing Role

The role of the criminal justice system has traditionally been to
apprehend, convict, and punish offenders. Although our society has
experienced numerous significant changes over the past century, the
system's orientation remains principally punitive.

We draw much of our thinking about law and justice from
systems of the past. So, it is hard to imagine there occurring any
fundamental changes in the administration of justice without making
basic changes in our society. Punishment for the sake of revenge has
never drawn strong support in the United States. Reform and rehabilitation has been the goal of a significant segment of our criminal
justice system.

In earlier times punishment was the aim of our prison system,
and sentences, oftentimes harsh, were a means to this end. These were
the days of hard prison labor, striped convict uniforms, the lock-step,
enforced prisoner silence, and sometimes the lash. Times changed,
attitudes softened, and "rehabilitation" was thought to be the proper
purpose of imprisonment. Penitentiaries became "correctional institutions," guards "correction officers." The idea became widespread
through the criminal justice system that criminals should be

"treated" to cure their criminal tendencies. Correctional institutions became staffed with counselors, psychiatrists, and social workers, all of whom engaged in sincere attempts to rehabilitate prisoners.

Judges adopted the then widely popular indeterminate sentence, with parole boards deciding when the inmate was changed sufficiently to be released into society.

As crime continued to increase and increase, the public's attitudes toward rehabilitation of criminals changed. Parole has been abolished in many jurisdictions, replaced with mandatory sentences designed not to rehabilitate but to "warehouse" prisoners for fixed periods of time and keep them away from society. The death penalty was reinstated. But no form of sentencing has really worked. Conscientious judges are faced with the dilemma of the broadly divergent objectives of attempting to punish and to rehabilitate an offender at the same time.

(15.2) Judicial Discretion

Time and again, judges are forced to make decisions about where and how people will spend years of their lives. The judges, operating with virtually unlimited discretion and unguided by criteria, procedural constraints, or review, often hand down sentences using little or no information beyond the offender's name and the crime of which he or she is guilty. The accuracy and reliability of information provided to the court by presentence reports often goes unchallenged, and sentencing laws in some states are disjointed and confusing. Also, some states have mandatory flat sentence laws that preclude judicial discretion; in others, judges exercise broad discretion in imposing sentences. Sentencing disparity is a major cause of unrest resulting in prison violence.

No uniform sentencing structure exists. Sentencing provisions vary not only from state to state and the federal jurisdiction, but often within a single state, depending on the nature and circumstances of the crime. On the national basis, courts use at least seven major structures when imposing criminal sentences, each with variations.

1. There are "flat" or determinate prison sentences with no maximum or minimum limits. The sentence is required by law for the

specific category of crime with only a slight variation allowed the judge based on mitigating or aggravated circumstances.

2. The maximum and minimum years of confinement are set by the judge subject to legislative outer limits.
3. Maximum terms for each crime are fixed by law, and the court has no discretion in imposing the sentence.
4. The judge sets maximum and minimum terms, but the minimum term cannot exceed some fraction, usually one-third, of the maximum.
5. A minimum term of imprisonment is set by the legislature and must be imposed by the court. However, the judge has discretion in setting the maximum term.
6. Statutory law establishes both maximum and minimum terms, allowing the judge no discretion in assigning penalties in such cases.
7. In the case of a completely indeterminate sentence, the convicted individual may be sentenced to prison for any period of time from one day to life. Under this sentencing structure, the determination of sentence length is removed from the legislature and from the judge and placed elsewhere, usually with parole authorities.

(15.3) Sentencing Disparity

Sentencing disparity can be a consequence of multiple convictions. That is, if defendants are convicted of several offenses or on several counts of the same type of offense, they may be sentenced to either concurrent or consecutive terms. Time served for concurrent sentences begins on the same day, regardless of the number of sentences imposed. In consecutive sentences, however, time served on the second sentence begins only after the first sentence is served.

Sentences of preposterous totals such as five hundred or a thousand years draw media attention, and the judge may gain a reputation as being "tough" on criminals. But the terms run concurrently and will have the same net effect as if the offender had received a single sentence for all the offenses with which he or she is charged.

Sentencing disparities are serious imperfections in the criminal justice system. They adversely affect prisoners who do not know the facts of fellow inmates' convictions and do not understand why they are being treated differently. Further, these inadequacies negatively affect the general public, which is becoming more aware of them, and are calling into question the integrity of the entire criminal justice system. Finally, judges themselves, operating without guidelines for comparison, find it frustrating and difficult to eliminate disparities.

A broad range of sentencing choices exists for identical offenses. The indeterminate sentence, long thought to be a solution to the disparity problem, has been challenged on the grounds of inequities and inconsistencies deriving from disparities among judges in the same jurisdictions administering the same laws and disposing of offenders to the same correctional facilities. No uniform sentencing practices exist that are common to all jurisdictions, and judges vary along a continuum from leniency to severity in sentencing.

In day-to-day court operations, trial judges often have insufficient time to consider all critical aspects of the crime and distinctive characteristics of the offender before imposing sentence. In fact, some judges are inclined to standardize their decision making, pronouncing sentences deemed appropriate to particular classes of crimes without giving much consideration to the offender. This is especially true in cases involving minor offenders, even though these individuals are often good candidates for reform. Frequently, sentencing immediately follows a guilty plea or find, and, if counsel requests a presentence investigation report prior to sentencing, a defendant may be required to remain in jail during the interim, a price many are unwilling to pay.

Many jurisdictions have recently begun to use sentencing guidelines to systematize sentencing and eliminate much disparity. Under such guidelines every crime is weighted according to its severity. Various factors in the offense may be assigned points. The defendant's criminal record is also given point factors. The final number of points computed for the offense gives the judge a minimum and maximum range within which he can pronounce sentence. If the court goes outside the guidelines in its sentence, he must state his reasons for the record, and the sentence (not the conviction) is subject to correction on appeal. The federal guideline system even allows the appellate court to *increase* a sentence made outside the guideline range (18 U.S. Ca. 3742 [e] [B i i i]).

Figure 15.1, Florida's guidelines for the crime of burglary, illustrates a typical guideline arrangement.

Reasons for departure:

_____

_____

_____

| SG5 - effective 7/1/84 | DISTRIBUTION:
White........Court File
Green........Sentencing Guidelines Commission | Canary........State Attorney
Pink........Defendant/Defense Counsel
Goldenrod........Sentencing Preparer |

1. Please print or type the information entered upon the scoresheet and use sufficient pressure to assure that all copies will be legible.

2. Enter the court case, court file, or docket number for the primary offense.

3. Enter the docket numbers for the additional cases presently before the court for sentencing.

4. Enter the name of the county where the sentence is imposed.

5. Enter the name of the sentencing judge.

6. Enter the date sentence was imposed.

7. Enter the defendant's full name.

8. Enter the defendant's date of birth.

9. Enter the defendant's sex.

10. Enter the date of the primary offense. If there are multiple counts of the primary offense, occurring on different dates, enter the earliest date.

11. Enter the common title of the primary offense at conviction with sufficient specificity to distinguish it from other offenses within the same chapter.

12. Enter the statutory felony degree of the primary offense. The following abbreviations may be used.

    L   Life felony
    1pbl first-degree felony punishable by life
    1   first-degree felony
    2   second-degree felony
    3   third-degree felony

13. Check the appropriate box if the sentence is imposed for a violation of probation or community control.

14. Indicate whether adjudication was obtained by plea or trial. If convictions were obtained by trial for some offenses and by plea on other counts, check the trial box.

15. Indicate whether the guideline sentence has been imposed or whether the sentence represents a guideline departure.

Category 5
Burglary

Points	Recommended Range
20–46	any nonstate prison sanction
47–71	Community Control or 12–30 mos. incarceration
72–90	3 yrs. incarceration
91–106	4 years (3½–4½)
107–120	5 (4½–5½)
121–143	6 (5½–7)
144–164	8 (7–9)
165–205	10 (9–12)
206–265	15 (12–17)
266–325	20 (17–22)
326–385	25 (22–27)
386–445	30 (27–40)
445+	Life

The following factors shall be used when counts of primary offense, additional offenses or prior record exceed four. These tables are used only for those counts in excess of four. The point total for the counts in excess of four should then be entered on the face of the scoresheet.

I. Number Primary Offense Counts Above 4

Degree			
Life	_____	X 8 =	_____
1st pbl	_____	X 7 =	_____
1st	_____	X 6 =	_____
2nd	_____	X 3 =	_____
3rd	_____	X 2 =	_____

II. Number of Additional Offense Counts Above 4

Degree			
Life	_____	X 2 =	_____
1st pbl	_____	X 2 =	_____
1st	_____	X 1 =	_____
2nd	_____	X 1 =	_____
3rd	_____	X 1 =	_____
MM	_____	X 1 =	_____

III. Number of Prior Convictions Above 4

Degree			
Life	_____	X 97 =	_____
1st pbl	_____	X 78 =	_____
1st	_____	X 58 =	_____
2nd	_____	X 27 =	_____
3rd	_____	X 9 =	_____
MM	_____	X 1 =	_____

[E1831]

Figure 15.1 Florida's sentencing guidelines for burglary.

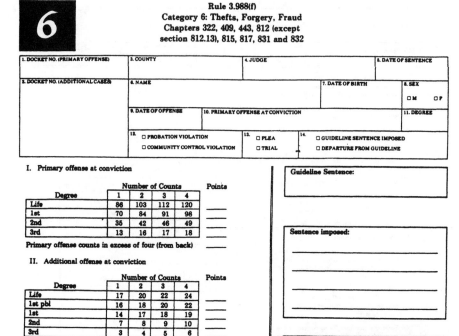

6

Rule 3.988(f)
Category 6: Thefts, Forgery, Fraud
Chapters 322, 409, 443, 812 (except
section 812.13), 815, 817, 831 and 832

1. DOCKET NO. (PRIMARY OFFENSE)	3. COUNTY		4. JUDGE		5. DATE OF SENTENCE
2. DOCKET NO. (ADDITIONAL CASES)	6. NAME			7. DATE OF BIRTH	8. SEX □ M □ F
	9. DATE OF OFFENSE	10. PRIMARY OFFENSE AT CONVICTION			11. DEGREE
	12. □ PROBATION VIOLATION □ COMMUNITY CONTROL VIOLATION		13. □ PLEA □ TRIAL	14. □ GUIDELINE SENTENCE IMPOSED □ DEPARTURE FROM GUIDELINE	

I. Primary offense at conviction

Degree	Number of Counts				Points
	1	2	3	4	
Life	86	103	112	120	____
1st	70	84	91	98	____
2nd	35	42	46	49	____
3rd	13	16	17	18	____

Primary offense counts in excess of four (from back)   ____

II. Additional offense at conviction

Degree	Number of Counts				Points
	1	2	3	4	
Life	17	20	22	24	____
1st pbl	16	18	20	22	____
1st	14	17	18	19	____
2nd	7	8	9	10	____
3rd	3	4	5	6	____
MM	1	2	3	4	____

Additional offense counts in excess of four (from back)   ____

III. A. Prior record

Degree	Number of Prior Convictions				Points
	1	2	3	4	
Life	50	110	180	270	____
1st pbl	40	88	138	216	____
1st	30	66	96	162	____
2nd	15	33	48	81	____
3rd	5	11	18	27	____
MM	1	2	4	6	____

Prior convictions in excess of four (from back)   ____

B. Prior convictions for Category 6 offenses

Number prior convictions _____ × 5 =   ____

IV. Legal status at time of offense

No restrictions   0
Legal constraint   6   ____

Guideline Sentence:

Sentence imposed:

FOR OFFICE USE ONLY

Offense Code _____

T.S. _____

S.P. _____

Prob. _____

C.C. _____

C.J. _____

Sentencing Judge

Figure 15-1, *continued*

Guideline sentencing does have the advantage of more uniformity. It also lets a defendant know what sentence he can expect and so facilitates guilty pleas. Many judges, though, feel that it ties their hands and tries unsuccessfully to reduce sentencing to a formula. The whole guideline system is still evolving and being tested by experience. Meanwhile, the federal guideline system has been ruled constitutional by the United States Supreme Court (*Mistretta* v. *U.S.* 109 S. Ct. 647, 102 L.Ed. 2 714 [1989]).

(15.4) Presentence Investigation

Approximately 25 percent of the states require a presentence investigation report for offenses that provide for imprisonment of more than one year. Approximately 85 percent of the states, however, do prepare some kind of presentence report in felony cases, although extreme variation exists in the reports' quality and usefulness. The presentence report, if properly researched and prepared, can be a valuable instrument for trial judges to use in reaching their sentencing decisions.

A central problem with the sentencing decision is that it requires judges to predict human behavior. Judges must ask themselves whether particular defendants will respond to prison in a positive manner or perhaps benefit more from psychiatric assistance. They have little factual information for guidance.

In the final analysis, most judges reach their decisions based on information in a presentence investigation report, their own intuition, experience, and imagination.

The court's probation officer usually conducts the presentence investigation and prepares the report. Generally, the defense attorney will review the report and may challenge specific details in order to help the judge reach a sentencing decision based on information from all available sources.

The presentence investigation report gives the judge a comprehensive and factual history of the offender, his or her crime, habits, personality, and problems. It also contains recommendations to the court of an appropriate disposition for the case. Judges generally accept the presentence recommendations for probation or for imprisonment.

Presentence investigation reports serve many functions. They are immediately useful in determining appropriate sentencing dispositions. Correctional agencies or institutions use them for classification and program assignments. Probation officers use them in supervising cases, if probation has been the sentence of the court. Presentence investigation reports also follow the offender on parole, where parole officers use them in their supervision efforts. Appellate courts use the reports when considering an appeal of sentence. The reports also provide a frame of reference from which to conduct research on convicted offenders, case flow, and court management.

PRESENTENCE INVESTIGATION

132ND JUDICIAL DISTRICT COURT
PROBATION SERVICES

NAME: Michael J. Mean

ADDRESS: 3421 Archer Ave. Jal, New Mexico

LEGAL RESIDENCE: Same

AGE: 30

DATE OF BIRTH: October 6, 1966

SEX: Male

RACE: White

CITIZENSHIP: U.S.A.

EDUCATION: High School

MARITAL STATUS: Married

DEPENDENTS: Two (Wife and 1 child)

SOC. SEC. NO.:   876–54–3210

FBI NO.:   172649

DETAINERS: None

DATE: **November 28, 1996**

DOCKET NO.:   13218

OFFENSE: Burglary

PENALTY:

PLEA: **November 10, 1996**

VERDICT:

CUSTODY: Personal Bond

PROSECUTOR: J. Edgar Nordmarken

DEFENSE COUNSEL: A. B. Lyncoln

CODEFENDANTS: Axel McCluskey

DISPOSITION:

DATE:

SENTENCING JUDGE: Seymour Justice

OTHER DOCKET NOS.:   None

PRESENT OFFENSE:

On **November 3, 1996** Michael J. Mean was indicted for the felony offense of burglary of a private residence. On

November 10, 1996, Michael J. Mean pleaded guilty to the charges.

On October 12, 1996, Officer Sam Slick of the Winchester Police Department was dispatched to 4321 Oakdale Avenue, Winchester, Texas, in response to a burglary report. Officer Slick contacted the complainant, Mrs. Alma Mater, who reported to the officer that someone had entered her residence by forcing a rear door. She reported the following articles were missing:

1) one VCR, General Electric, valued at $535.00.
2) fourteen video cassettes, assorted titles of recent motion pictures and home-recorded television programs, valued at approximately $300.00.
3) one .22 caliber, Marlin, lever-action rifle, serial number 1122334456, with the initials "RLM" carved in wooden stock, valued at $225.00.

On October 21, 1996, Officer Slick received information from Nicholson Dymes, owner of the Ace of Spades Pawn Shop, that the above described rifle had been offered for sale to him by a person using the name Mike Mean. Officer Slick further interviewed Mr. Dymes and determined that Mean was also attempting to sell or pawn a General Electric video cassette recorder. Following a record check for accurate name and address of suspect, Officer Slick charged Mike Mean with burglary and arrested Mean on Warrant #639 at 10:50 A.M. October 22, at Mean's residence.

DEFENDANT'S VERSION OF OFFENSE:

During interview by the undersigned officer on November 18, 1996, defendant was polite and cooperative; however, he showed no remorse for his behavior. In fact, his attention was clearly focused on efforts to avoid having his probation revoked. He apparently realizes the seriousness of his acts and indicated that he needed professional assistance to overcome his "emotional problems that cause him to steal." Defendant admitted his offense and freely discussed the details during our interview.

PREVIOUS OFFENSES:

3/15/83	P.D. Winchester, TX	Shoplifting	Dismissed Co. Court
6/12/87	P.D. Oak Park, TX	Disorderly Conduct	Fined and Released
6/22/90	S.O. Arbor Co., N.M.	Bootlegging	Fined and Released
11/7/94	P.D. Winchester, TX	Burglary	5 yrs. Probation

PERSONAL HISTORY:

Defendant is a 30-year-old male. He has been in the Winchester County Jail for the offense of burglary since October 22, 1996. According to defendant's own statements and records at the Winchester Police Department and Sheriff's Department, he was born in Espuela, New Mexico, to Oliver G. and Molly B. Mean. His parents, now retired, still reside at Rural Route #1 in Espuela, N.M., where they have lived for 32 years. Defendant states that he has not been in touch with his parents for several years, at least not on a regular basis, since he was graduated from Espuela High School in 1984.

According to defendant, he left during the summer of 1984 and worked for the next two years in the oil fields around Jal, N.M. The investigating officer has been unable to verify this information due to the fact that some of the companies are now defunct, and records are not available. Defendant states that he moved to Notrees, Texas, where he gained employment at a gasoline refinery. About a year later, defendant met and began dating Rita Arbol, age 20, daughter of the plant supervisor. She was employed as a secretary at the same plant. They were married on June 6, 1988. Both continued working at the plant until a son, Larry Joe Mean, was born, August 12, 1990. During this period, defendant was arrested on two different occasions for misdemeanor offenses; in both instances, he was fined and released. On January 20, 1993, defendant resigned from the gasoline plant job and moved back to Jal, New Mexico, where he gained employment with the Sunset Railroad Corporation as a yard hand. His wife, Rita, had resigned her secretarial position about two months prior to the birth of their son, and she did not work outside the home after that. Defendant states that he began drinking frequently and heavily as the family's financial situation went from bad to worse. Increased expenses of maintaining their modest mobile home and additional costs of family expansion apparently brought on the drinking and mental depression. The marital relationship became strained, and the drinking bouts increased in frequency and intensity. Finally, on November 7, 1994, defendant was arrested and charged with the burglary of a tavern, the Kit Kat Klub, Jal, N.M. Defendant pleaded guilty to burglary, a third-degree felony, and received a probated sentence. For the past two years, defendant has worked as an attendant at Hi-Tane Gasoline Service Station, 1212 Pennington Street, DeLeon, N.M., approximately 7 miles from Jal, N.M. According to his probation officer, Al K. Hall, defendant has adjusted well to his situation. The family relationship has been strengthened, and defendant claims that he no longer has a drinking problem. Probation officer Hall states that the defendant regularly reports to him and that defendant's employer considers him to be an excellent employee. Defendant claims that he and codefendant Axel McCluskey were drinking heavily on the night they committed the burglary, for which he has entered a guilty plea.

HOME AND NEIGHBORHOOD:

A neighbor, Jack O. Lantern, 3423 Archer Ave., Jal, N.M., stated that Mike Mean had lived next door to him for nearly four years and that he and Rita were excellent neighbors. He stated that he had never seen Mike Mean intoxicated or otherwise out of order. Other neighbors, Mr. and Mrs. Carlton Bones, 3430 Archer Ave., Mr. and Mrs. Knight Walker, 3412 Archer Ave., and Miss Sally Mander, 3416 Archer Ave., all acknowledge that they know Mike

Mean, but declined to give further information, except that he had always been a "gentleman" when they had observed him.

EDUCATION:

Defendant graduated from Espuela, N.M., High School May 18, 1984. According to school records, his grades were average; his attendance was regular with few absences.

EMPLOYMENT:	**(Information based on defendant's statements)**
June 1984:	Defendant was employed as a roughneck for Lowboy Drilling Co., Jal, N.M. (7 months)
February 1985:	Duster Oil Field Services, Jal, N.M., roughneck (6 months)
July 1985:	Baling Wire Oil Field Equipment Co., Jal, N.M., field hand (8 months)
March 1986:	Spudder Drilling Co., Monument, N.M., derrick hand (2 months)
July 1986:	Petroflex Gasoline Refinery, Notrees, TX, plant yard hand (7 years)
January 1993:	Sunset Railroad Corporation, Dartmouth, TX, yard hand (6 months)
July 1993:	Hi-Tane Gasoline Service Station, DeLeon, N.M., attendant (until present)

FINANCIAL SITUATION:

Defendant, at the time of the interview, had $102.73 in checking account #7865431, Jal National Bank, Jal, N.M. He has no savings account or other source of income besides his job at the gas station. Defendant pays $190 monthly rent on a 2-bedroom mobile home (Old Moon Brand), which includes parking space. Defendant also pays $99.99 monthly on a 1986 brown Oldsmobile, 4-door sedan, license number HRB 321. Records indicate that most of the remainder of defendant's expenses are paid in cash, and therefore no record exists. Defendant's current salary is $1,200 per month, prior to taxes and other deductions; his take-home is $897.12 per month.

HEALTH:

Defendant is apparently in good health. Records reflect that he had one doctor visit about 10 years ago for a job-related accident. Because the company is no longer in business, detailed records are unavailable. Defendant was treated at Jal, N.M., General Hospital emergency room and released. Injury was diagnosed as a "hair-line" fracture of the right arm (ulna) resulting from a fall on a drilling rig. No other medical history.

EVALUATIVE SUMMARY:

Defendant's Strengths:

1. He appears to be in good health.
2. He claims to be skilled in auto service and general repairs.

Defendant's Weaknesses:

1. He has not shown proper responsibility for supporting his family.
2. He has an unstable work record.
3. He freely admits that he has a weakness for stealing and that he needs help.
4. His past record does not indicate a willingness to be law-abiding.

Defendant's Apparent Rehabilitative Needs:

1. Defendant's rehabilitation can best be implemented in a controlled and structured environment.
2. While incarcerated, defendant should receive a psychological evaluation and psychiatric treatment.
3. While incarcerated, defendant should enroll in a long-range vocational rehabilitation program.

RECOMMENDATION:

It is the recommendation of this department that defendant receive a medium sentence at the Texas Department of Corrections.

(13.5) Summary

Sentencing may be regarded as the most important phase of the criminal justice process because the offender's disposition is decided at this stage. In earlier times, retaliation and corporal abuse were standard punishments for wrongdoing. Contemporary criminal justice is still punitive in its philosophy and orientation, but the punishment is justified on several more practical grounds, including deterrence and incapacitation. Sentencing practices in recent years reflect growing support for the correctional philosophy of rehabilitation. Traditional dispositions include fines, probation, and imprisonment, with probation the most common choice. The presentence investigation and report play a vital role in helping courts arrive at appropriate sentences.

Discussion Questions

1. Compare and contrast advantages and disadvantages of the fixed and the indeterminate sentence.
2. Discuss the problem of disparity in sentencing.
3. Discuss the legal steps that must be followed in any sentencing proceeding.
4. What is the usual role of the probation officer in the presentence investigation and report?
5. Discuss the functions of a presentence investigation.

16

Appeals Before the U.S. Supreme Court

You are a licensed attorney (called "counsel") who is about to appeal and argue a case before the United States Supreme Court. Congratulations! But, how do you proceed? The Court outlines and publishes rules for procedural methods to follow, and attorneys should be familiar with these rules. The most recent rules became effective October 1, 2007.[1]

(16.1) Introduction

Individuals seeking to appeal a case before the U.S. Supreme Court must first have exhausted all other avenues of appeal before courts of the highest jurisdiction in the respective entity: generally the highest state court (criminal or civil), or Federal Circuit Court of Appeal. Appeals to the Supreme Court must be veiled in a constitutional issue. These appeals seek the Supreme Court's final opinion, which then becomes not only a precedent for future cases, but also a historical document. In the United States, a writ of certiorari

---

1. www.supremecoutus.gov

is used by the Supreme Court to review questions of law or to correct errors and to ensure against excesses by the lower courts. Such writs are also issued in exceptional cases when an immediate review is required.[1]

The attorneys representing the defendant or plaintiff first submit a petition and briefs requesting that the Supreme Court issue a writ of certiorari. *Certiorari* is a Latin word meaning to be informed of, or to be made certain in regard to. It is also the name given to certain appellate proceedings for re-examination of actions of a trial court, or inferior appeals court. The U. S. Supreme Court uses the term *certiorari* in the context of an appeal.

A petition for a writ of certiorari (informally called "cert petition") is a document that a losing party files with the Supreme Court asking it to review the decision of a lower court. The petition includes a list of the parties, a statement of the facts of the case, the legal questions presented for review, and arguments as to why the Court should grant the writ.[2]

A petition may be reviewed by justices of the Supreme Court. At least four of the sitting jurists must agree that the petition warrants Supreme Court review (this is called the "Rule of Four"). In this case, the court issues a writ of certiorari, which officially calls the case up for review before the Supreme Court. If the Court denies a petition for certiorari, the abbreviated legal citation is "cert. denied." The Supreme Court is the sole authority to decide if a case warrants a hearing. In fact, the Court receives thousands of cert. petitions per year, and denies all but about one hundred. If the court accepts the case, it grants a writ of certiorari.

(16.2) Notification of Counsel

After receipt of the petition, the clerk of the Court will notify counsel when the Court enters an order, noting probable jurisdiction, postponing jurisdiction, or granting a petition for a writ of certiorari.

---

1. www.britannica.com/EBchecked/topic/19835/American-law
2. The following web site provides the basis for material in this chapter: www. techlawjournal.com/glossary/legal/certiorari.html

Counsel is furnished written instructions concerning information on the preparation and filing of the joint appendix and the briefs of the merits. A specification chart that clearly displays the colors to be used for the covers of briefs will also be furnished. Counsel is required to follow the outlined steps provided by the clerk. Any questions regarding the procedures or steps to follow are directed to the clerk through the merits cases clerk. All records are kept by docket numbers, which must be used when seeking information.

The merits cases clerk must be notified immediately of any changes, including any change of counsel. The merits cases clerk relies upon those attorneys listed as counsel of record for all communication, as do parties interested in filing *amicus* (friends of the court) briefs when making their requests for letters of consent. When a party changes counsel of record, or when any party of a multi-party side of a case originally represented by one attorney at the petition stage chooses to separately retain counsel of record, a letter must be submitted to the clerk and all other counsel of record indicating such changes.

(16.3) Records

If the certified record of the proceedings outlined in the next section here has not been previously filed in the Supreme Court, the clerk will request the clerk of the court processing the record to certify and transmit it to the Court. This is generally done upon the Court's scheduling of a case for oral argument. Consequently, if counsel desires to have the record to remain in the lower court for a certain period of time, counsel must notify the Clerk's Office immediately (Rule 16.2).

(16.4) Joint Appendix and Merit Briefs (Preparation: Rules 25, 26, 33.1 and 34)

The time for filing and preparation requirements for the joint appendix is governed by Rule 26. Preparation of the joint appendix may be deferred until after the briefs have been filed upon approval of the clerk. Deferral of the joint appendix is not favored. Parties wishing to dispense with the requirement of the joint appendix must seek leave of the Court (Rule 26.7).

Because the entire certified record is available to the Court for reference and examination, only those significant portions of the record that have not been included within a brief for filing with the Court, and which are directly relevant to the issue or issues for the Court's consideration, shall be included in the joint appendix. A brief may always cite directly to anything contained in the certified record.

Counsel for the petitioner must keep the clerk advised respecting any disagreement on the designations or dates when the designations are made concerning the joint appendix. Copies of the designations need not be forwarded to the clerk.

The time for filing the parties' briefs on the merits is dictated by Rule 25. Content requirements and word limits are governed by Rules 24 and 33.1. Counsel seeking leave to file a brief on the merits in excess of the word limits must do so in the form of an application to the individual justice submitted in accordance with Rule 22 (Rule 33.1(d)). Such applications should be submitted only in the most extraordinary circumstances, and they should be submitted promptly to enable counsel adequate time to modify and timely file their brief in accordance with the rules should the circuit justice deny the application.

It is the responsibility of counsel to read a brief before it is submitted to the clerk and to make appropriate changes as necessary. If a brief has been filed with the clerk and not yet circulated to the Court, counsel may arrange to have a representative come to the Clerk's Office to note the changes in the 40 copies of the brief on file. Counsel should contact the Clerk's Office for instructions as to what method of correction is most appropriate. Opposing counsel must be informed of such changes immediately. After a brief for distribution has been circulated to the Court, the clerk will consider receiving 40 copies of a "corrected" brief for distribution only when a meritorious reason and sufficient time exist.

(16.5) Time (Rules 25 and 30.4)

Absent an order of the Court setting forth a briefing schedule, the time within which to file the briefs on the merits is as set out in the Rules and the due dates do not appear on the Court's docket.

For good cause, the time limit for filing the joint appendix and the opening briefs on the merits may be extended by the clerk pursuant to Rule 30.4. Extensions of time to file briefs on the merits are not favored. Any request for an extension of time to file a joint appendix or an opening brief on the merits should be presented in the form of a letter to the clerk and served on all other counsels of record pursuant to Rule 29.2. The letter should set out the specific reasons why an extension of time is justified and indicate opposing counsel's position on the request. The clerk or the Court may at any time modify a briefing schedule (Rule 25.4).

The reply brief for the petitioner, if any, must be filed within 30 days after the brief for the respondent or appellee is filed, but any reply brief must actually be received by the clerk not later than 2 P.M. one week before the date of oral argument (in this instance, Rules 29.2 and 30.1 do not apply). Counsel should note that if the seventh day prior to the oral argument date falls on a holiday, the reply brief due date moves to the prior business day to allow sufficient time for distribution to and review by the justices.

The clerk is not authorized to extend the time to file a reply brief on the merits. Counsel seeking such an extension must do so in the form of an application to an individual justice submitted in accordance with Rule 22.

(16.6) Filing and Submission (Rules 25.8 and 29)

On the day a merits brief is filed, counsel shall submit a PDF version of the brief on the merits to the clerk and opposing counsel via e-mail. The rules also dictate that a PDF version of *amicus* briefs be submitted to the clerk and to all counsels of record via e-mail (Rule 25.8 and 37.3(a)).

The clerk will not file a brief on the merits after a case has been argued except by leave of the Court (Rule 25.6). In such instances, a motion for leave to file and the brief sought to be filed shall be sub-

mitted as one document and prepared in accordance with the requirements of Rule 33.1.

(16.7) Scheduling and Preparation for Oral Argument

Oral arguments are normally conducted during October through
April each year. There is two-week session held each month, with arguments scheduled on Monday through Wednesday of each week.
Unless the Court directs otherwise, each side is allowed one-half hour
for argument. The Court generally hears arguments for two cases each
day beginning at 10:00 A.M. and adjourns after the argument for the
second case ends, usually around noon. If more than two cases are to
be argued in one day, the Court will reconvene at 1:00 P.M. to hear the
additional arguments.

When a case has been calendared for argument, the clerk sends a
notice to counsel, together with a map of Capitol Hill and an argument
form to be completed and returned promptly. Once the argument
schedule is set, the clerk cannot make chances to the schedule. If
counsel has any longstanding professional or religious commitments
or for some other reason cannot appear for oral argument on any date
in the future (particularly within the two argument sessions following
the due date of the respondent's brief), these matters must be called to
the clerk's attention by letter, with a copy sent to opposing counsel.
To the extent possible, the clerk endeavors to schedule the oral arguments to avoid conflicts. In addition, counsel informs the clerk of any
necessary accommodations (such as a wheelchair) that may be required in order to allow the clerk and the marshal to make suitable
seating arrangements at the counsel tables.

(16.8) Day of Oral Argument

Appropriate attire for counsel appearing before the Supreme Court
is conservative business dress in traditional dark colors, such as navy
blue or charcoal gray. The attorneys arguing the case report to the
Lawyers' Lounge on the first floor of the Court between 9:00 A.M. and
9:15 A.M. on the day of argument. The clerk briefs counsel at this time
on courtroom protocol, answers any last-minute questions that they

may have, and issues counsel and co-counsel identification cards. The attorneys whose cases are scheduled for the afternoon session report to the Lawyers' Lounge between 12:15 P.M. and 12:30 P.M. In the event that the attorneys encounter a line when they arrive at the Court building, they proceed to the front of the line, identify themselves to the police at the entrance, and enter the building.

The attorneys are not allowed to take personal computers, cellular phones, cameras, PDAs, or any other electronic devices into the Lawyers' Lounge or the courtroom. These items must be checked in a locker at the Court. The lockers are located at the front of the building on the first floor (Courtroom level). Coats, hats, and papers of arguing counsel and co-counsel may be left in the Lawyers' Lounge.

The Court has a large residential corps of journalists who follow the dockets closely. No interviews or news cameras are permitted in the court building; however, they are allowed on the front plaza on argument days, where reporters frequently wait to talk to counsel after arguments are concluded.

Transcripts of oral arguments are posted on the Supreme Court's website (www.supremecourtus.gov) on the same day the argument is heard by the Court. Attorneys can obtain a copy of transcript by contacting Alderson Reporting Company, 1-800-367-3376 or 202-289-2260. If the attorneys note an error in the transcript, that fact should be brought to the attention of the marshal of the Court (202-479-3333).

Courtroom artists, who are employed by various news organizations, may be contacted in advance to commission a sketch on the day of oral arguments. The Public Information Office (202-479-3050) may provide the names and phone numbers of such artists upon request.

(16.9) Seating For Counsel

After the attorneys have met with the clerk and received identification cards, the attorneys report immediately to the courtroom officials inside the railing to be assigned an appropriate seat. Four seats are available at each counsel table in the courtroom. When only one counsel is to argue a case per side, the arguing counsel and three co-counsels will be accommodated at the table. If divided arguments have been granted and two attorneys are to argue on the same side, the Court will accommodate only one co-counsel per each arguing counsel at the table. It is appropriate for co-counsel to occupy the arguing counsel's chair when the latter is presenting argument. Except in extraordinary circumstances, co-counsel does not pass notes to arguing counsel during argument.

Once at the table, attorneys may find quill pens at the counsel table; these pens are gifts to counsels as a souvenir of having argued before the highest Court in the land. Attorneys may take the quill pens with them when they leave the Court; they are handcrafted and usable as writing quills.

(16.10) Courtroom Seating

Courtroom seating is extremely limited. Spectators are seated first-come, first-seated, either for an entire argument or on a short (three-minute) rotation to view proceedings. Groups can request reserved seating for up to 15 persons by writing the marshal of the Court as far in advance as possible.

If arguing counsel desires to reserve space in the public section, counsel must contact the marshal's office after completing and returning the argument form to the clerk. A letter concerning reservations, including the names of guests, should be sent to: Marshal, Supreme Court of the United States, Washington, D.C. 20543. Depending on available space, the marshal will try to accommodate as many guests as possible—not exceeding six spaces per side. When two counsels are arguing on one side, those counsels are each permitted a maximum of four spaces, subject to availability.

When guests arrive at the court on the argument day, they should check coats, hats, briefcases, cameras, electronic equipment, and similar items in the cloakroom (Courtroom level) that is located on the first floor by the main door. The guests should proceed to the marshal's office, which is located to the right as a person faces the main entrance to the Courtroom. An attendant, seated at a small table in the hallway outside the marshal's door, will receive the guests. Guests must be escorted through the metal detectors and into the reserved seating area of the courtroom.

Members of this Court's Bar are invited to sit inside the brass railing. Before entering, they will be required to report to the clerk's assistant who is seated adjacent to the statue of Chief Justice John Marshall in the Lower Great Hall on the ground floor. These guests use the north entrance door (Maryland Avenue side of the building) to reach the check-in desk. The north entrance opens at 7:30 A.M. The Supreme Court Bar check-in process normally begins at 9:00 A.M. Guests show the assistant a photo identification card, and his or her name will be checked against the Bar membership roster. Bar members will be issued a pass and directed to proceed to the Courtroom on the first floor. Seating is on a first-come, first-seated basis. Bar members may leave hats, coats, and papers in the Lawyers' Lounge. When the Bar section is filled, remaining Bar members will be seated in the Lawyers' Lounge, where arguments can be heard through a loudspeaker. Bar members are asked to wear professional business attire.

(16.11) Order of Business in the Courtroom

Arguing counsel and co-counsels should be seated in their assigned seats at the counsel table about five minutes before Court is scheduled to commence. The marshal of the Court cries the Court in at 10:00 A.M., and the Justices of the Supreme Court enter the courtroom. After seating, the Chief Justice makes any routine announcements. Opinions of the Court, if any, are then released. The authoring Justice will read a summary of the opinion, and each opinion takes about five minutes. Motions for admission to the Bar occur next. The Chief Justice announces that the Court will hear arguments in the first case for argument that day. The counsel for the petitioner proceeds promptly to the lectern; the attorney does not need to wait for the Chief Justice to issue an invitation. The attorney remains standing at the lectern and says nothing until the Chief Justice recognizes the attorney by name. Once the Chief Justice has done so, counsel may acknowledge the Court by the usual: "Mr. Chief Justice, and may it please the Court..."

Arguing counsel does not introduce him- or herself or co-counsel. In current practice, "Mr." (or "Ms." if applicable) is only used in addressing the Chief Justice. Other jurists are referred to as "Justice (last name) or "Your Honor." Counsel should not use the title "judge" when addressing a member of the Supreme Court. In the event counsel is not certain which Justice he or she is addressing, it is best to use

"Your Honor" rather than mistakenly address the Justice by another Justice's name.

(16.12) Counsel's Argument

Many attorneys find it very educational to attend a Courtroom session before their scheduled argument day. If so, the attorney should go to the Clerk's Office and introduce him- or herself to the clerk and the marshal.

Counsel should remember that briefs are different from oral arguments. A complex issue might take up a large portion of the attorney's brief, but there may be no need to argue that issue. Merits briefs should contain a logical review of all issues in the case. Oral arguments are not designed to summarize briefs, but present the opportunity to stress the main issues of the case that might persuade the Court in favor of the arguing counsel. It has been said that preparing for oral argument at the Supreme Court is like packing clothes for an ocean cruise. A person should lay out all the clothes he or she may think will be needed, and then return half of them to the closet. When preparing for oral argument, eliminate half of what you initially planned to cover. The allotted time passes quickly, especially when numerous questions come from the Court. Counsel should be prepared to skip over much of the planned argument and stress the strongest points.

Some attorneys find it useful to have a section in their notes entitled "cut to the chase." Such notes refer to that section in the event that most of their time has been consumed by answering questions posed by the Justices. This allows them to use the few precious minutes remaining to stress the main points.

In the event that the argument before the Court focuses on a statute, regulation, or ordinance, the attorney should ensure that the law is printed in full in the pleadings so that counsel can refer the Justices to it in order that they may look at it during the argument.

Counsel should not bring numerous volumes to the lectern. One notebook will suffice. Because a legal-sized pad does not fit properly onto the lectern, counsel should avoid such pads. In addition, turning pages in a notebook appears more professional than flipping pages of a legal pad. Depending on how well-versed counsel is in the case material, he or she may argue without any notes; however, this is general-ly a rare occurrence.

Counsel should know the record, especially the procedural history, of the case. The attorney should be prepared to answer questions such as, "Why didn't you make a motion for summary judgment?" Counsel and co-counsel have the opportunity to inform the Justices about facts of which they are not aware. Justices frequently ask, "Is that in the record?" Counsel should be prepared to answer. It is impressive when counsel can respond with the volume and page where the information is located. It is also quite effective to quote from the joint appendix. However, attorneys should not make assertions about issues or facts not in the record.

Attorneys should know their client's business. One counsel repre-senting a large beer-brewing corporation was asked about the differ-ence between beer and ale. The question had little to do with the is-sues, but the case involved the beer-brewing business. Counsel gave a brief, simple, and clear answer that was understood by everyone in the Courtroom. He knew the business of his client, and it showed in his answer. The Justice who posed the question warmly thanked counsel.

The following are excellent sources of information for arguing counsel: *Making Your Case, the Art of Persuading Judges*, by Justice Antonio Scalia and Bryan Garner; Chapter 14, Oral Argument, *Supreme Court Practice* (9th edition), by Eugene Gressman, Kenneth Geller, Stephen Shapiro, Timothy Bishop, and Edward Hartnett; and *Supreme Court Appellate Advocacy: Mastering Oral Argument*, by David Frederick.

(16.13) Limited Argument Time

Generally, the time allotted for counsel's argument is limited to 30 minutes; however, it is not necessary or required to use all of the time allotted. For example, counsel for the respondent in *Whitfield* v. *United States*, 543 U.S. 209 (2005) argued for only ten of the allotted 30 minutes. Counsel for the respondent in *Burgess* v. *United States*, 553 U.S. ___ (2008) argued for only seven of the allotted 30 minutes. Both respondents prevailed in unanimous decisions of the Court.

Unless other arrangements are made with the marshal, a white light on the lectern will be activated when five minutes of the allotted time remains. The red light will be activated when the time has expired. Prior to argument, the marshal will flash the white light at a time requested by counsel.

When the marshal activates the white light, counsel should be prepared to stop the argument in five minutes. When the red light comes on, terminate the argument immediately and sit down. However, if counsel is answering a question from a Justice, the attorney may continue his or her answer and respond to any additional questions from that or any other Justice. In such an instance, counsel does not need to worry about the red light. However, no further argument may be made after questions are completed from the Justices when the red light is activated.

In some cases, counsel and co-counsel may divide the argument. In such an instance, it is effective for counsel to inform the Court of their argument plan. For example, petitioner's counsel might say, "I will cover the Fourth Amendment aspects of this case and counsel for the *amicus* will argue the Fifth Amendment issues." Regardless of how many attorneys argue in a case, only one is permitted to present rebuttal argument. If two attorneys argue for the petitioner, the one who argued first should be the person to present rebuttal. A petitioner's counsel who wants to reserve time for rebuttal should, about five minutes before the allotted time is to expire (white light), say, "If there are no further questions, I would like to reserve the remainder of my time for rebuttal." Petitioner's counsel then sits down and the Chief Justice calls on the respondent's counsel for argument. Respondent's counsel proceeds to the lectern, waits for acknowledgement by the Chief Justice, and then opens with, "Mr. Chief Justice, and may it please the Court." When respondent's counsel has finished and gathered all items from the lectern, petitioner's counsel should return to the lectern and wait for acknowledgement by the Chief Justice. At that time, the Chief Justice should grant counsel the remaining amount of time for rebuttal. Counsel then begins rebuttal argument without repeating the greeting to the court.

Promptly and quietly vacate the front argument table after the Chief Justice announces that "the case is submitted." Counsel at the back-up tables should move to the front table for the next case. In the event counsel wishes to listen to the next argument, he or she may sit at the back-up tables.

(16.14) Protocol

The Supreme Court is not a jury. A trial lawyer tries to persuade a jury with facts and emotion. However, for the Supreme Court, counsel should try to persuade the Court by arguing points of law. The argument should focus only on the question or questions presented in the petition that was granted. Attorneys should not deviate from those points.

Ordinarily, the Justices will know if the attorney is making his or her first argument before the Court. Some first-time arguments have been far superior to presentations from counsel who has argued several times before the Court. As noted, if the argument focuses on statues, regulation, or ordinance, attorneys must make certain that the law is printed in full in one of the pleadings in order that the Justices may refer to it during the argument.

Counsel for the petitioner need not recite the facts of the case before beginning argument. The facts are set out in the briefs, which the Justices have read prior to the proceedings.

Counsel should speak in a clear, distinct manner, and try to avoid a monotone delivery. The attorney speaks into the microphone so that his or her voice will be audible to the Justices and to ensure a clear recording. Avoid having notes or books touch the microphones, because such actions interfere with the recording process. Under no circumstance should counsel read the argument from a prepared script. Counsel should not attempt to fit in more argument by rapid fire, staccato delivery.

Exhibits can be useful in appropriate cases, but counsel should be very careful to ensure that any exhibit used is appealing, accurate, and capable of being read from a distance of about 25 feet. If used, counsel must be certain to explain to the Court the intent of the exhibit as soon as possible. Before appearing before the Court, Counsel must advise the clerk of the intent to use an exhibit. For a good example of an exhibit used at oral argument in Court, see *Shaw* v. *Reno*, 509 U.S. 630, 658 (1993).

Counsel should be knowledgeable about what is and what is not in the records in the case before the Court. Justices frequently ask counsel if particular matters are in the record. If asked a question that will require counsel to refer to matter not in the record, counsel's answer should so state; then proceed to respond to the question unless advised otherwise by the Justice.

Counsel should never interrupt a Justice who is addressing him or her. Counsel must give his or her full attention to that Justice; do not look down at any notes, and do not look at a watch or the clock located high on the wall behind the Justices. If counsel is speaking and a Justice interrupts him or her, counsel ceases talking immediately and listens to the Justice.

If a Justice makes a point that is adverse to counsel's case, he or she should not "stonewall." Counsel should either concede the point, as appropriate, or explain why the point is not dispositive of the case and proceed with the argument. Counsel should not "correct" a Justice unless the matter is essential. In one case, a Justice asked a question and mentioned "waiver." Counsel responded by stating that a "forfeiture" rather than a "waiver" was involved. The distinction was irrelevant, but the comment generated more questions and wasted valuable time.

Counsel should be careful to use precise language. In one case, counsel stated, "The Supremacy Clause does not apply in this case." A Justice responded: "The Supremacy Clause applies in every case. Perhaps counsel meant that the statue in question does not conflict with the Supremacy Clause."

Counsel should be careful not to use the "lingo" of a business or activity. The Court may not be familiar with such terms, even if widely understood within that business or activity. For example, counsel should not say "double-link connector" or "section 2b claims" unless those terms have been explained and/or defined. Similarly, counsel does not use the familiar name of the client during the argument. For instance, counsel might say, "Mr. Clark denied the request" rather than say, "Buddy denied the request."

When referring to an opinion of the Court, counsel should not say: "In Justice Ginsburg's opinion." However, it is appropriate to say: "In the Court's opinion, written by Justice Ginsburg."

If counsel quotes a document verbatim (e.g., a statute or ordinance), counsel tells the court where to find the document (e.g., page 4, appendix B to the petition).

Attempts at humor usually fall flat. The same is true of attempts at familiarity. For example, counsel should not say something like, "This is similar to a case argued when I clerked here." Counsel should not denigrate opposing counsel. It is far more appropriate and effective to be courteous to the opponent in the case.

Avoid emotional oration and loud, impassioned pleas. A well-reasoned and logical presentation without histrionics is easier for listeners to comprehend. Counsel should not argue facts. Counsel should argue the question or questions of law presented in the petition for the writ of certiorari that was granted.

Counsel for respondents are often effective when they preface their argument by answering questions that the petitioner's counsel could not answer or answered incorrectly or ineffectively. This can often get counsel off to a positive start.

If opposing counsel is persuasive on a certain theme during argument, especially one that was not anticipated, counsel should address that issue at the outset of argument or rebuttal argument rather than adhere to a previously planned presentation. Counsel takes great risk if he or she ignores a persuasive point made by the opponent.

Rebuttal can be very effective. However, counsel can be even more effective if he or she thoughtfully addresses it when the opponent has not been impressive. If counsel has a rebuttal point, he or she should make it and then sit down. There is no requirement that counsel uses all of the allotted time.

(16.15) Answering Questions

Attorneys appearing before the U. S. Supreme Court should presume that the Justices have read the briefs filed in the case, including *amicus curiae* ("friend of the court") briefs. Counsel should expect questions from the Court, and make every effort to directly answer their questions. If at all possible, say "yes" or "no" and then expand upon the answer if explanation is needed. In the event that counsel does not know the answer to the question, he or she should so indicate. On one occasion, instead of responding to a question from a Justice, an attorney posed a question to the Justice, only to have another Justice chastise him for doing so; avoid any behavior that may alienate the Court.

Counsel should anticipate what questions the Justices will ask and be prepared to answer those questions. If a case with issues similar to the case being argued was previously argued before the Court, consider reviewing a transcript of the oral argument of that case, which may also help counsel anticipate questions that those Justices who heard the previous case may ask in the case now before the Court.

If a counsel stumbles when answering a question from the Court or does not fully answer it, a good tactic may be to have an *amicus curiae* counsel supporting the counsel's side to begin argument by repeating the question and answering it correctly and completely. The *amicus* counsel will have time to reflect on the initial question and perhaps develop a better answer.

A Justice will often ask counsel seeking to establish a new precedent, "Do any cases from this Court support your position?" Counsel should be ready for the question, but be careful to cite only those cases that truly support the position. Counsel should not distort the meaning of a precedent. The author of the opinion is likely to be a member of the Court and to have a remarkable memory of exactly what the opinion stated. If counsel is relying on a case that was announced by a "plurality opinion," be sure to mention that there was no "opinion for the court" in the case.

In appropriate cases, counsel may suggest to the Court that "bright-line rules" (or setting a standard to avoid ambiguity) should be adopted and suggest what the standard should be in this case.

Counsel should always strive to be polite and accurate. If a question seems hostile to counsel's case, he or she should not respond with a short and abrupt response. Should a Justice pose a hypothetical question, counsel should respond to that question on the facts given therein. In the past, several attorneys have responded, "But those aren't the facts in this case!" The Justice posing the question is aware that there are different facts in the case before the Court, but wants and expects counsel to answer the hypothetical question. Once the hypothetical question is answered, counsel might say something such as, "However, the facts in this case are different," or "The facts in the hypothetical question are not the facts in this case." A "yes" or "no" might be suitable for a narrow question. Nevertheless, counsel's answer should be carefully tailored to fit the question. A simple "yes" or "no" in response to a broad question might unintentionally concede a point and prompt a follow-on question or statement that ultimately may damage counsel's position.

In the event that other Justices ask questions before counsel completes an answer to a prior question, counsel should take a commonsense approach in determining which of the questions to answer first. Counsel might consider responding to the last question, indicating, if he or she believes is proper, that counsel will answer that question first before completing the answer to the prior question. Alternatively, counsel may indicate to the last questioner that, if permitted, responding to the first Justice's question would help in answering the second Justice's question. There is no definite rule of protocol. However, ordinarily if two Justices start to speak at once, the junior Justice will withdraw in deference to the senior Justice. Counsel, by analogy, might respond to the senior Justice's question first, and then address questions from the junior Justices.

(16.16) Decision Process

After a case has been argued, the Court will vote at a conference, and the case will be assigned to a Justice to write the majority opinion. Opinions may be handed down at any time after the argument. Generally, cases argued during the Term are decided before the end of June.

Opinions are released in the Courtroom on any day the Court is sitting, but usually on Tuesday or Wednesday when the Court sits for oral arguments, and on Monday when the Court sits for the announcement of order and group Bar admissions. Counsel should also be aware that in June the Court frequently adds additional sittings to announce opinions. The Clerk's Office or Public Information Office announces the following week's Court schedule on Friday afternoons.

Opinions are typically announced at 10:00 A.M. and are released to the public and news media—in both written and electronic form—as they are read from the bench. When an opinion is announced, an assistant will call arguing counsels and advise them of the ruling. However, because of different time zones, counsel might not be notified until several hours after the media have had access to an opinion. Opinions are available on the Court's website and other websites soon after announcement. Copies of opinions are mailed to arguing counsel and counsel of record on the day of release.

The judgment or mandate of the Court will be issued by the clerk following the end of a 25-day period after the release of the opinion, unless a petition for rehearing has been timely filed (Rule 45).

If the petitioner prevails, the clerk will provide for an award of costs, if appropriate, in the judgment or mandate. Only the costs of printing the joint appendix and the docketing fee may be awarded (Rule 43).

(16.17) General Information

The Supreme Court's website (www.supremcourtus.gov) provides access to the automated docket, slip opinions, Court calendar, argument calendar, transcripts of oral arguments, Bar admission forms, and instructions, rules of the Court, guides to filing paid and *in forma pauperis* petitions, order lists, granted/noted lists, merits briefs in cases to be argued, and other information about the Court. Counsel can also access the clerk's Automated Response System (CARS) at 202-479-3034. Callers should have the Supreme Court docket number available. A recorded voice will provide callers with current case status information.

The Supreme Court is located at the corner of First Street and Maryland Avenue, N.E., directly across from the United States Capitol, and is easily reached by taxi or metro (subway) from Ronald Reagan National Airport. The Union Station rail terminal and the Capitol South Metro terminal are within walking distance. The building is open from 9 A.M. to 4:30 P.M. Monday through Friday. Arguing attorneys and co-counsel may enter through the north door (Maryland Ave. side of the building) after 7:30 A.M. The building is closed Saturdays, Sundays, and holidays. It is accessible to persons with disabilities through the Maryland Avenue entrances. There is virtually no parking available in the vicinity of the Supreme Court building.

Topcoats, raincoats, umbrellas, hats, cameras, cell phones, PDAs, and recording devices are not permitted in the Courtroom. A checkroom and lockers are located at the front of the building on the first floor (Courtroom level). Members of the Bar and spectators in the public section can use writing materials.

There are many hotels in the Washington metropolitan area, and several are in the vicinity of Capitol Hill within walking distance of the Court. A detailed map of the Supreme Court and its immediate surrounding area is available upon request from the Clerk's Office. A map is also included on the Court's website.

Airports serving the Capitol area include Ronald Reagan National Airport, Dulles Airport, and Baltimore-Washington International Thurgood Marshall Airport.

The Supreme Court Historical Society has a gift shop on the ground floor of the Court building. A cafeteria and public telephones are also located on the ground floor.

(16.18) Examples of Recent U. S. Supreme Court Case Issues

In 2009, the U.S. Supreme Court issued several interesting opinions. Examples of these opinions are follows:

• *Voting Rights*: *Northwest Austin Municipal Utility District Number One* v. *Holder, Attorney General, et al*. Argued April 29, 2009; decided June 22, 2009.

At stake was the federal government's authority to prevent discriminatory changes to voting rights through a provision of the landmark Voting Rights Act. This section forces all or parts of 16 states, many in the South, to submit proposed election changes to the Justice Department. In 2006, Congress extended the provision, first enacted in 1965, to 25 more years. The local Texas governing authority challenging the law said the safeguard once may have been needed to prevent discrimination, but no longer can be justified.

The appellant was a small utility district with an elected board. Because it is located in Texas, it is required by Article 5 of the Voting Rights Act of 1965 to seek federal preclearance before it can change anything about it elections, even though there is not evidence it has ever discriminated on the basis of race in those elections. The district filed suit seeking relief under the "bailout" provisions in Article 4(a) of the Act, which allows a "political subdivision" to be released from the preclearance requirements if certain conditions are met. The district argued in the alternative that, if Article 5 were interpreted to render it ineligible for bailout, Article 5 was unconstitutional. The federal District Court rejected both claims. It concluded that bailout under Article 4(a) is available only to counties, parishes, and subunits that register voters, not to an entity like the district that does not register its own voters. It also concluded that a 2006 amendment extending Article 5 for 25 years was constitutional.

The Court held that the historic accomplishments of the Voting Rights Act are undeniable, but the Act now raises serious constitutional concerns. The preclearance requirement represents an intrusion into areas of state and local responsibility that is otherwise unfamiliar to our federal system. Improvements are no doubt insignificant parts of the Voting Rights Act itself, and indicate its success, but the Act imposes current burdens and must be justified by current needs. The Act also differentiates between the States in ways that may no longer be justified.

At the same time, the Court recognized that judging the constitutionality of an Act of Congress is "the gravest and most delicate duty that this Court is called upon to perform." Since 1982, only 17 jurisdictions—out of more that 12,000 covered political subdivisions—have successfully bailed out of the Act. It is unlikely that Congress intended the provision to have such limited effect. The Court reversed and remanded the case.

- *Reverse Discrimination. Ricce et al.* v. *DeStefano et al.* Argued April 22, 2009; decided June 29, 2009

   White firefighters in New Haven, Conn., claimed they were discriminated against when the city tossed out the results of a promotion exam because too few minorities scored high enough. The city said it acted because it might have been vulnerable to claims that the exam had a "disparate impact" on minorities in violation of the Civil Rights Act of 1964. The white firefighters said the decision violated the same law's prohibition on intentional discrimination.

   The Court held that the city's action in discarding the tests violated Title VII. This law prohibits intentional acts of employment discrimination based on race, color, religion, sex, and national origin, 42 U.S.C. Article 2000e-2(a)(1) (disparate treatment), as well as policies or practices that are not intended to discriminate but in fact have a disproportionately adverse effect on minorities.

The Court's analysis began with the premise that the city's actions would violate Title VII's disparate-treatment prohibition absent some valid defense. All the evidence demonstrated that the city's actions rejected the test results because the higher-scoring candidates were white. Without some other justification, this express, race-based decision making is prohibited. Fear of litigation alone cannot justify the city's reliance on race to the detriment of individuals who passed the examination and qualify for promotions. Discarding the test results was impermissible under Title VII, and summary judgment is appropriate for petitioners on their disparate-treatment claim. The case was reversed and remanded.

- **DNA Testing:** *District Attorney's Office for the Third Judicial District et al.* v. *Osborne.* Argued March 2, 2009; decided June 18, 2009

  In a case from Alaska, the Justices examined whether, long after a conviction, defendants have a constitutional right to test genetic evidence that could be used to exonerate them. Alaska is one of a handful of states without a state law providing for DNA testing, which has been used to exonerate more that 200 people wrongfully convicted of violent crimes.

  Respondent Osborne was convicted of sexual assault and other crimes in state court. Years later, he filed this suit under 42 U.S.C. Article 1983, claiming he had a due-process right to access the evidence used against him in court to subject it to DNA testing at his own expense. The federal court first dismissed his claim, holding that Osborne must proceed in habeas because he sought to set the state for an attack on his conviction. The Ninth Circuit Court reversed, concluding that Article 1983 was the proper vehicle for Osborne's claims. On remand, the District Court granted Osborne summary judgment, concluding that he had a limited constitutional right to the new testing under the unique and specific facts presented, that is, that such testing had been unavailable at trial, that it could be accomplished at almost no cost to the state, and that the results were likely to be material.

The Court held that, assuming Osborne's claims can be pursed using Article 1983, he had no constitutional right to obtain post-conviction access to the state's evidence for DNA testing. The Ninth Circuit erred in finding a due-process violation. The Court rejected Osborne's invitation to recognize a free-standing, substantive due-process right to DNA evidence untethered from the liberty interests he hoped to vindicate with it. In the circumstances of this case, there is no such right. Generally, the courts are "reluctant to expand the concept of substantive due process because guideposts for responsible decision making in this unchartered area are scarce and open-ended." There is no long history of a right of access to state evidence for DNA testing that might prove innocence. "The mere novelty of such a claim is reason enough to doubt that 'substantive due process' sustains it." Moreover, to suddenly constitutionalize this area would short-circuit what has been a prompt and considered legislative response by Congress and the states. It would shift to the Federal Judiciary responsibility for devising rules governing DNA access and creating a new constitutional code of procedures to answer the myriad questions that would arise. There are reasons to suppose that federal courts' answers to those questions will be any better than those of state courts and legislatures, and good reasons to suspect the opposite. The Court reversed and remanded the case.

These are but a few examples of cases that can be researched on the Supreme Court's website. Use the Court's search engine and type in a topic (such as Judicial Ethics, Student Strip Search, Detainee Lawsuit) to access recent Court opinions. Students can also view pending cases on the docket and date of pending arguments.

During the summers of 2009 and 2010, President Obama nominated two new Justices who have been seated in place of retiring Justices. The most lasting impression that any president has in his or her administration is an appointment of a Justice to the Supreme Court. Long after the president leaves office, the judgments of these Justices will prevail for most of their lifetimes while they serve in the U. S. Supreme Court.

Discussion Questions

1. How important is time spent in planning and preparation to appear before the U.S. Supreme Court in order to be successful and win your argument?
2. How important may it be to counsel's case if he or she could recognize each Justice and refer to him or her by name when addressing the Court?
3. Do you believe that the Court Justices are swayed by political beliefs or does each member put politics aside in deciding a case before the Court?
4. Research and discuss the finding of cases before the U.S. Supreme Court during the current year.
5. Will the recent appointment of new Justices change the balance in the Supreme Court and will this have any bearing on future rulings of the court?

Appendix A. Rules of Evidence for United States Courts and Magistrates

Article I. General Provisions

Rule 101. Scope

These rules govern proceedings in the courts of the United States, bankruptcy judges, and before United States magistrates, to the extent and with the exceptions stated in Rule 1101.

Rule 102. Purpose and Construction

These rules shall be construed to secure fairness in administration, elimination of unjustifiable expense and delay, and promotion of growth and development of the law of evidence to the end that the truth may be ascertained and proceedings justly determined.

Rule 103. Rulings on Evidence

(a) *Effect of erroneous ruling.* Error may not be predicated upon a ruling which admits or excludes evidence unless a substantial right of the party is affected, and

(1) *Objection.* In case the ruling is one admitting evidence a timely objection or motion to strike appears of record, stating the specific ground of objection, if the specific ground was not apparent from the context; or

(2) *Offer of proof.* In case the ruling is one excluding evidence, the substance of the evidence was made known to the judge by offer or was apparent from the context within which questions were asked.

(b) *Record of offer and ruling.* The court may add any other or further statement which shows the character of the evidence, the form in which it was offered, the objection made, and the ruling thereon. It may direct the making of an offer in question and answer form.

(c) Hearing of jury. In jury cases, proceedings shall be conducted, to the extent practicable, so as to prevent inadmissible evidence from being suggested to the jury by any means, such as making statements or offers of proof or asking questions in the hearing of the jury.

(d) Plain error. Nothing in this rule precludes taking notice of plain errors affecting substantial rights although they were not brought to the attention of the court.

Rule 104. Preliminary Questions

(a) Questions of admissibility generally. Preliminary questions concerning the qualification of a person to be a witness, the existence of a privilege, or the admissibility of evidence shall be determined by the court, subject to the provisions of subdivision (b). In making its determination it is not bound by the rules of evidence except those with respect to privileges.

(b) Relevancy conditioned on fact. When the relevancy of evidence depends upon the fulfillment of a condition of fact, the judge shall admit it upon, or subject to the introduction of evidence sufficient to support a finding of the fulfillment of the condition.

(c) Hearing of jury. Hearings on the admissibility of confessions shall in all cases be conducted out of the hearing of the jury. Hearings on other preliminary matters shall be so conducted when the interests of justice require or when an accused is a witness and so requests.

(d) Testimony by accused. The accused does not, by testifying upon a preliminary matter, become subject to cross-examination as to other issues in the case.

(e) Weight and credibility. This rule does not limit the right of of a party to introduce before the jury evidence relevant to weight or credibility.

Rule 105. Limited Admissibility

When evidence which is admissible as to one party or for one purpose but not admissible as to another party or for another purpose is admitted, the court, upon request, shall restrict the evidence to its proper scope and instruct the jury accordingly.

Rule 106. Remainder of or Related Writings or Recorded Statements

When a writing or recorded statement or part thereof is introduced by a party, an adverse party may require him at that time to introduce any other part or any other writing or recorded statement which ought in fairness to be considered contemporaneously with it.

Article II. Judicial Notice

Rule 201. Judicial Notice of Adjudicative Facts

(a) Scope of rule. This rule governs only judicial notice of adjudicative facts.

(b) Kinds of facts. A judicially noticed fact must be one not subject to reasonable dispute in that it is either (1) generally known within the territorial jurisdiction of the trial court or (2) capable of accurate and ready determination by resort to sources whose accuracy cannot reasonably be questioned.

(c) When discretionary. A court may take judicial notice, whether requested or not.

(d) When mandatory. A court shall take judicial notice if requested by a party and supplied with the necessary information.

(e) Opportunity to be heard. A party is entitled upon timely request to an opportunity to be heard as to the propriety of taking judicial notice and the tenor of the matter noticed. In the absence of prior notification, the request may be made after judicial notice has been taken.

(f) Time of taking notice. Judicial notice may be taken at any stage of the proceeding.

(g) Instructing jury. In a civil action or proceeding, the court shall instruct the jury to accept as conclusive any fact judicially noticed. In a criminal case, the court shall instruct the jury that it may, but is not required to, accept as conclusive any fact judicially noticed.

Article III. Presumptions in Civil Actions and Proceedings

Rule 301. Presumptions in General in Civil Actions and Proceedings

In all civil actions and proceedings not otherwise provided for by Act of Congress or by these rules, a presumption imposes on the party against whom it is directed the burden of going forward with evidence to rebut or meet the presumption, but does not shift to such party the burden of proof in the sense of the risk of non-persuasion, which remains throughout the trial upon the party on whom it was originally cast.

Rule 302. Applicability of State Law in Civil Actions and Proceedings

In civil actions and proceedings, the effect of a presumption respecting a fact which is an element of a claim or defense as to which state law supplies the rule of decision is determined in accordance with state law.

Article IV. Relevancy and Its Limits

Rule 401. Definition of "Relevant Evidence"

"Relevant evidence" means evidence having any tendency to make the existence of any fact that is of consequence to the determination of the action more probable or less probable than it would be without the evidence.

Rule 402. Relevant Evidence Generally Admissible; Irrelevant Evidence Inadmissible

All relevant evidence is admissible, except as otherwise provided by the Constitution of the United States, by Act of Congress, by these rules, or by other rules prescribed by the Supreme Court pursuant to statutory authority. Evidence which is not relevant is not admissible.

Rule 403. Exclusion of Relevant Evidence on Grounds of Prejudice, Confusion, or Waste of Time

Although relevant, evidence may be excluded if its probative value is substantially outweighed by the danger of unfair prejudice, confusion of the issues, or misleading the jury, or by considerations of undue delay, waste of time, or needless presentation of cumulative evidence.

Rule 404. Character Evidence Not Admissible to Prove Conduct; Exceptions; Other Crimes

(a) *Character evidence generally.* Evidence of a person's character or a trait of his character is not admissible for the purpose of proving action in conformity therewith on a particular occasion, except:

(1) *Character of accused.* Evidence of a pertinent trait of character offered by an accused, or by the prosecution to rebut the same;

(2) *Character of victim.* Evidence of a pertinent trait of character of the victim of the crime offered by an accused, or by the prosecution to rebut the same, or evidence of a character trait of

peacefulness of the victim offered by the prosecution in a homicide case to rebut evidence that the victim was the first aggressor;

(3) Character of witness. Evidence of the character of a witness, as provided in Rules 607, 608, and 609.

(b) Other crimes, wrongs, or acts. Evidence of other crimes, wrongs, or acts is not admissible to prove the character of a person in order to show action in conformity therewith. It may, however, be admissible for other purposes, such as proof of motive, opportunity, intent, preparation, plan, knowledge, identity, or absence of mistake or accident, provided that upon request by the accused, the prosecution in a criminal case shall provide reasonable notice in advance of trial, or during trial if the court excuses pretrial notice on good cause shown, of the general nature of any such evidence it intends to introduce at trial.

Rule 405. Methods of Proving Character

(a) Reputation or opinion. In all cases in which evidence of character or a trait of character of a person is admissible, proof may be made by testimony as to reputation or by testimony in the form of an opinion. On cross-examination, inquiry is allowable into relevant specific instances of conduct.

(b) Specific instances of conduct. In cases in which character or a trait of character of a person is an essential element of a charge, claim, or defense, proof may also be made of specific instances of his conduct.

Rule 406. Habit; Routine Practice

Evidence of the habit of a person or of the routine practice of an organization, whether corroborated or not and regardless of the presence of eyewitnesses, is relevant to prove that the conduct of the person or organization on a particular occasion was in conformity with the habit or routine practice.

Rule 407. Subsequent Remedial Measures

When, after an event, measures are taken which if taken previously, would have made the event less likely to occur, evidence of the subsequent measures is not admissible to prove negligence or culpable conduct in connection with the event. This rule does not require the exclusion of evidence of subsequent measures when offered for another purpose, such as proving ownership, control, or feasibility of precautionary measures, if controverted, or impeachment.

Rule 408. Compromise and Offers to Compromise

Evidence of (1) furnishing or offering or promising to furnish, or (2) accepting or offering or promising to accept a valuable consideration in compromising or attempting to compromise a claim which was disputed as to either validity or amount, is not admissible to prove liability for or invalidity of the claim or its amount. Evidence of conduct or statements made in compromise negotiations is likewise not admissible. This rule does not require the exclusion of any evidence otherwise discoverable merely because it is presented in the course of compromise negotiations. This rule also does not require exclusion when the evidence is offered for another purpose, such as proving bias or prejudice of a witness, negativing a contention of undue delay, or proving an effort to obstruct a criminal investigation or prosecution.

Rule 409. Payment of Medical and Similar Expenses

Evidence of furnishing or offering or promising to pay medical, hospital, or similar expenses occasioned by an injury is not admissible to prove liability for the injury.

Rule 410. Inadmissibility of Pleas, Plea Discussions, and Related Statements

Except as otherwise provided in this rule, evidence of the following is not, in any civil or criminal proceeding, admissible against the defendant who made the plea or was a participant in the plea discussions:

(1) a plea of guilty which was later withdrawn;
(2) a plea of *nolo contendere*;
(3) any statement made in the course of any proceedings under Rule 11 of the Federal Rules of Criminal Procedure or comparable state procedure regarding either of the foregoing pleas; or
(4) any statement made in the course of plea discussions with an attorney for the prosecuting authority that do not result in a plea of guilty or that result in a plea of guilty later withdrawn.

However, such a statement is admissible (i) in any proceeding wherein another statement made in the course of the same plea or plea discussions has been introduced and the statement ought in fairness be considered contemporaneous with it, or (ii) in a criminal proceeding for perjury or false statement if the statement was made by the defendant under oath, on the record, or in the presence of counsel.

Rule 411. Liability Insurance

Evidence that a person was or was not insured against liability is not admissible upon the issue whether the person acted negligently or otherwise wrongfully. This rule does not require the exclusion of evidence of insurance against liability when offered for another purpose, such as proof of agency, ownership, or control, or bias or prejudice of a witness.

Rule 412. Sex Offenses

(a) Notwithstanding any other provision of law, in a criminal case in which a person is accused of an offense under chapter 109A of title 18, United States Code, reputation or opinion evidence of the past sexual behavior of an alleged victim of such rape or assault is not admissible.

(b) Notwithstanding any other provision of law, in a criminal case in which a person is accused of an offense under chapter 109A of title 18, United States Code, evidence of a victim's past sexual behavior other than reputation or opinion is also not admissible, unless such evidence other than reputation or opinion evidence is—

(1) admitted in accordance with subdivisions (c)(1) and (c)(2) and is constitutionally required to be admitted; or
(2) admitted in accordance with subdivision (c) and is evidence of—
(A) past sexual behavior with persons other than accused, offered by accused upon the issue of whether accused was or was not, with respect to the alleged victim, the source of semen or injury; or (B) past sexual behavior with the accused and is offered by the accused upon the issue of whether the alleged victim consented to the sexual behavior with respect to which rape or assault is alleged.

(c)(1) If the person accused of committing an offense under chapter 109A of title 18, United States Code, intends to offer under subdivision (b) evidence of specific instances of the alleged victim's past sexual behavior of specific instances of the alleged victim's past sexual behavior, the accused shall make a written motion to offer such evidence not later than fifteen days before the date on which the trial in which such evidence is to be offered is scheduled to begin, except that the court may allow the motion to be made at a later date, including during trial, if the court determines either that the evidence is newly discovered and could not have been obtained earlier through the exercise of due diligence or that the issue to which such evidence relates has newly arisen in the case. Any motion made under this paragraph shall be served on all other parties and on the alleged victim.

(2) The motion described in paragraph (1) shall be accompanied by a written offer of proof. If the court determines that the offer of proof contains evidence described in subdivision (b), the court shall order a hearing in chambers to determine if such evidence is admissible. At such hearing the parties may call witnesses, including the alleged victim, and other relevant evidence. Notwithstanding subdivision (b) of Rule 104, if the relevancy of the evidence that the accused seeks to offer in the trial depends upon the fulfillment of a condition of fact, the court, at the hearing in chambers or at a subsequent hearing in chambers scheduled for such purpose, shall accept evidence on the issue of whether such condition of fact is fulfilled and shall determine such issue.

(3) If the court determines on the basis of the hearing described in paragraph (2) that the evidence that the accused seeks to offer is relevant and that the probative value of such evidence outweighs the danger of unfair prejudice, such evidence shall be admissible in the trial to the extent an order made by the court specifies evidence that may be offered and areas with respect to which the alleged victim may be examined or cross-examined.

(d) For purposes of this rule, the term "past sexual behavior" means sexual behavior other than the sexual behavior with respect to which an offense under chapter 109A of title 18, United States Code, is alleged.

Article V. Privileges

Rule 501. General Rule

Except as otherwise required by the Constitution of the United States or provided by Act of Congress or in rules prescribed by the

Supreme Court pursuant to statutory authority, the privilege of a witness, person, government, State, or political subdivision thereof shall be governed by the principles of the common law as they may be interpreted by the courts of the United States in the light of reason and experience. However, in civil actions and proceedings, with respect to an element of a claim or defense as to which State law supplies the rule of decision, the privilege of a witness, person, government, State, or political subdivision thereof shall be determined in accordance with State law.

Article VI. Witnesses

Rule 601. General Rule of Competency

Every person is competent to be a witness except as otherwise provided in these rules. However, in civil actions and proceedings, with respect to an element of a claim or defense as to which State law supplies the rule of decision, the competency of a witness shall be determined in accordance with State law.

Rule 602. Lack of Personal Knowledge

A witness may not testify to a matter unless evidence is introduced sufficient to support a finding that the witness has personal knowledge of the matter. Evidence to prove personal knowledge may, but need not, consist of the testimony of the witness himself. This rule is subject to the provisions of Rule 703, relating to opinion testimony by expert witnesses.

Rule 603. Oath or Affirmation

Before testifying, every witness shall be required to declare that the witness will testify truthfully, by oath or affirmation administered in a form calculated to awaken his conscience and impress his mind with his duty to do so.

Rule 604. Interpreters

An interpreter is subject to the provisions of these rules relating to qualification as an expert and the administration of an oath or affirmation that he will make a true translation.

Rule 605. Competency of Judge as Witness

The judge presiding at the trial may not testify in that trial as a witness. No objection need be made in order to preserve the point.

Rule 606. Competency of Juror as Witness

(a) At the trial. A member of the jury may not testify as a witness before that jury in the trial of the case in which the juror is sitting. If he is called so to testify, the opposing party shall be afforded an opportunity to object out of the presence of the jury.

(b) Inquiry into validity of verdict or indictment. Upon an inquiry into the validity of a verdict or indictment, a juror may not testify as to any matter or statement occurring during the course of the jury's deliberations or to the effect of anything upon his or any other juror's mind or emotions as influencing the juror's assent to or dissent from the verdict or indictment or concerning the juror's mental processes in connection therewith, except that a juror may testify·on the question whether extraneous prejudicial information was improperly brought to the jury's attention or whether any outside influence was improperly brought to bear upon any juror. Nor may a juror's affidavit or evidence of any statement by him concerning a matter about which the juror would be precluded from testifying be received for these purposes.

Rule 607. Who May Impeach

The credibility of a witness may be attacked by any party, including the party calling the witness.

Rule 608. Evidence of Character and Conduct of Witness

(a) Opinion and reputation evidence of character. The credibility of a witness may be attacked or supported by evidence in the form of opinion or reputation, but subject to these limitations: (1) the evidence may refer only to character for truthfulness or untruthfulness, and (2) evidence of truthful character is admissible only after the character of the witness for truthfulness has been attacked by opinion or reputation evidence or otherwise.

(b) Specific instances of conduct. Specific instances of the conduct of a witness, for the purpose of attacking or supporting the witness' credibility, other than conviction of crime as provided in Rule 609, may not be proved by extrinsic evidence. They may, however, in the discretion of the court, if probative of truthfulness or untruthfulness, be inquired into on cross-examination of the witness (1) concerning the witness' character for truthfulness or untruthfulness, or (2) con-

cerning the character for truthfulness or untruthfulness of another witness as to which character the witness being cross-examined has testified.

The giving of testimony, whether by an accused or by any other witness, does not operate as a waiver of the accused's or the witness' privilege against self-incrimination when examined with respect to matter which relate only to credibility.

Rule 609. Impeachment by Evidence of Conviction of Crime

(a) General rule. For the purpose of attacking the credibility of a witness, (1) evidence that a witness other than the accused has been convicted of a crime shall be admitted subject to Rule 403, if the crime was punishable by death or imprisonment in excess of one year under the law under which the witness was convicted, and evidence that an accused has been convicted of such a crime shall be submitted if the court determines that the probative value of admitting this evidence outweighs its prejudicial effect to the accused; and (2) evidence that any witness has been convicted of a crime shall be admitted if it involved dishonesty or false statement, regardless of the punishment.

(b) Time limit. Evidence of a conviction under this rule is not admissible if a period of more than ten years has elapsed since the date of the conviction or of the release of the witness from the confinement imposed for that conviction, whichever is the later date, unless the court determines, in the interests of justice, that the probative value of the conviction supported by specific facts and circumstances substantially outweighs its prejudicial effect. However, evidence of a conviction more than 10 years old as calculated herein, is not admissible unless the proponent gives to the adverse party sufficient advance written notice of intent to use such evidence to provide the adverse party with a fair opportunity to contest the use of such evidence.

(c) Effect of pardon, annulment, or certificate of rehabilitation. Evidence of a conviction is not admissible under this rule if (1) the conviction has been the subject of a pardon, annulment, certificate of rehabilitation, or other equivalent procedure based on a finding of the rehabilitation of the person convicted, and that person has not been convicted of a subsequent crime which was punishable by death or imprisonment in excess of one year, or (2) the conviction has been the subject of a pardon, annulment, or other equivalent procedure based on a finding of innocence.

(d) Juvenile adjudications. Evidence of juvenile adjudications is generally not admissible under this rule. The court may, however, in

a criminal case allow evidence of a juvenile adjudication of a witness other than the accused if conviction of the offense would be admissible to attack the credibility of an adult and the court is satisfied that admission in evidence is necessary for a fair determination of the issue of guilt or innocence.

(e) Pendency of appeal. The pendency of an appeal therefrom does not render evidence of a conviction inadmissible. Evidence of the pendency of an appeal is admissible.

Rule 610. Religious Beliefs or Opinions

Evidence of the beliefs or opinions of a witness on matters of religion is not admissible for the purpose of showing that by reason of their nature the witness' credibility is impaired or enhanced.

Rule 611. Mode and Order of Interrogation and Presentation

(a) Control by court. The court shall exercise reasonable control over the mode and order of interrogating witnesses and presenting evidence so as to (1) make the interrogation and presentation effective for the ascertainment of the truth, (2) avoid needless consumption of time, and (3) protect witnesses from harassment or undue embarrassment.

(b) Scope of cross-examination. Cross-examination should be limited to the subject matter of the direct examination and matters affecting the credibility of the witness. The court may, in the exercise of discretion, permit inquiry into additional matters as if on direct examination.

(c) Leading questions. Leading questions should not be used on the direct examination of a witness except as may be necessary to develop the witness' testimony. Ordinarily leading questions should be permitted on cross-examination. When a party calls a hostile witness, an adverse party, or a witness identified with an adverse party, interrogation may be by leading questions.

Rule 612. Writing Used to Refresh Memory

Except as otherwise provided in criminal proceedings by section 3500 of title 18, United States Code, if a witness uses a writing to refresh his memory for the purpose of testifying, either—
  (1) while testifying, or
  (2) before testifying, if the court in its discretion determines it is necessary in the interests of justice,
an adverse party is entitled to have the writing produced at the hearing, to inspect it, to cross-examine the witness thereon, and to introduce in evidence those portions which relate to the testimony of the witness. If it is claimed that the writing contains matters not related

to the subject matter of the testimony the court shall examine the writing in camera, excise any portions not so related, and order delivery of the remainder to the party entitled thereto. Any portion withheld over objections shall be preserved and made available to the appellate court in the event of an appeal. If a writing is not produced or delivered pursuant to order under this rule, the court shall make any order justice requires, except that in criminal cases when the prosecution elects not to comply, the order shall be one striking the testimony or, if the court in its discretion determines that the interests of justice so require, declaring a mistrial.

Rule 613. Prior Statements of Witnesses

(a) Examining witness concerning prior statement. In examining a witness concerning a prior statement made by the witness, whether written or not, the statement need not be shown nor its contents disclosed to the witness at that time, but on request the same shall be shown or disclosed to opposing counsel.

(b) Extrinsic evidence of prior inconsistent statement of witness. Extrinsic evidence of a prior inconsistent statement by a witness is not admissible unless the witness is afforded an opportunity to explain or deny the same and the opposite party is afforded an opportunity to interrogate the witness thereon, or the interests of justice otherwise require. This provision does not apply to admissions of a party-opponent as defined in Rule 801 (d) (2).

Rule 614. Calling and Interrogation of Witnesses by Court

(a) Calling by court. The court may, on its own motion or at the suggestion of a party, call witnesses, and all parties are entitled to cross-examine witnesses thus called.

(b) Interrogation by court. The court may interrogate witnesses, whether called by itself or by a party.

(c) Objections. Objections to the calling of witnesses by the court or to interrogation by it may be made at the time or at the next available opportunity when the jury is not present.

Rule 615. Exclusion of Witnesses

At the request of a party the court shall order witnesses excluded so that they cannot hear the testimony of other witnesses, and it may make the order of its own motion. This rule does not authorize exclusion of (1) a party who is a natural person, or (2) an officer or employee of a party which is not a natural person designated as its representative by its attorney, or (3) a person whose presence is shown by a party to be essential to the presentation of his cause.

Article VII. Opinions and Expert Testimony

Rule 701. Opinion Testimony by Lay Witnesses

If the witness is not testifying as an expert, the witness' testimony in the form of opinions or inferences is limited to those opinions or inferences which are (a) rationally based on the perception of the witness and (b) helpful to a clear understanding of the witness' testimony or the determination of a fact in issue.

Rule 702. Testimony by Experts

If scientific, technical, or other specialized knowledge will assist the trier of fact to understand the evidence or to determine a fact in issue, a witness qualified as an expert by knowledge, skill, experience, training, or education, may testify thereto in the form of an opinion or otherwise.

Rule 703. Bases of Opinion Testimony by Experts

The facts or data in the particular case upon which an expert bases an opinion or inference may be those perceived by or made known to the expert at or before the hearing. If of a type reasonably relied upon by experts in the particular field in forming opinions or inferences upon the subject, the facts or data need not be admissible in evidence.

Rule 704. Opinion on Ultimate Issue

Testimony in the form of an opinion or inference otherwise admissible is not objectionable because it embraces an ultimate issue to be decided by the trier of fact.

(*a*) Except as provided in subdivision (b), the testimony in the form of an opinion or inference otherwise admissible is not objectionable because it embraces an ultimate issue to be decided by the trier of fact.

(*b*) No expert witness testifying with respect to the mental state or condition of a defendant in a criminal case may state an opinion or inference as to whether the defendant did or did not have the mental state or condition constituting an element of the crime charged or of a defense thereto. Such ultimate issues are matters for the trier of fact alone.

Rule 705. Disclosure of Facts or Data Underlying Expert Opinion

The expert may testify in terms of opinion or inference and give his reasons therefor without prior disclosure of the underlying facts or data, unless the court requires otherwise. The expert may in any event be required to disclose the underlying facts or data on cross-examination.

Rule 706. Court Appointed Experts

(a) Appointment. The court may on its own motion or on the motion of any party enter an order to show cause why expert witnesses should not be appointed, and may request the parties to submit nominations. The court may appoint any expert witnesses agreed upon by the parties, and may appoint expert witnesses of its own selection. An expert witness shall not be appointed by the court unless he consents to act. A witness so appointed shall be informed of the witness' duties by the court in writing, a copy of which shall be filed with the clerk, or at a conference in which the parties shall have opportunity to participate. A witness so appointed shall advise the parties of the witness findings, if any; the witness' deposition may be taken by any party; and the witness may be called to testify by the court or any party. The witness shall be subject to cross-examination by each party, including a party calling him as a witness.

(b) Compensation. Expert witnesses so appointed are entitled to reasonable compensation in whatever sum the court may allow. The compensation thus fixed is payable from funds which may be provided by law in criminal cases and civil actions and proceedings involving just compensation under the Fifth Amendment. In other civil actions and proceedings the compensation shall be paid by the parties in such proportion and at such time as the court directs, and thereafter charged in like manner as other costs.

(c) Disclosure of appointment. In the exercise of its discretion, the court may authorize disclosure to the jury of the fact that the court appointed the expert witness.

(d) Parties' experts of own selection. Nothing in this rule limits the parties in calling expert witnesses of their own selection.

Article VIII. Hearsay

Rule 801. Definitions

The following definitions apply under this Article:

(a) Statement. A "statement" is (1) an oral or written assertion

or (2) nonverbal conduct of a person, if it is intended by him as an assertion.

(b) Declarant. A "declarant" is a person who makes a statement.

(c) Hearsay. "Hearsay" is a statement, other than one made by the declarant while testifying at the trial or hearing, offered in evidence to prove the truth of the matter asserted.

(d) Statements which are not hearsay. A statement is not hearsay if—

(1) Prior statement by witness. The declarant testifies at the trial or hearing and is subject to cross-examination concerning the statement, and the statement is (A) inconsistent with the declarant's testimony, and was given under oath subject to the penalty of perjury at a trial, hearing, or other proceeding, or in a deposition, or (B) consistent with the declarant's testimony and is offered to rebut an express or implied charge against the declarant of recent fabrication or improper influence or motive, or

(2) Admission by party-opponent. The statement is offered against a party and is (A) the party's own statement, in either an individual or a representative capacity or (B) a statement of which the party has manifested his adoption or belief in its truth, or (C) a statement by a person authorized by the party to make a statement concerning the subject, or (D) a statement by the party's agent or servant concerning a matter within the scope of his agency or employment, made during the existence of the relationship, or (E) a statement by a co-conspirator of a party during the course and in furtherance of the conspiracy.

Rule 802. Hearsay Rule

Hearsay is not admissible except as provided by these rules or by other rules prescribed by the Supreme Court pursuant to statutory authority or by Act of Congress.

Rule 803. Hearsay Exceptions: Availability of Declarant Immaterial

The following are not excluded by the hearsay rule, even though the declarant is available as a witness:

(1) Present sense impression. A statement describing or explaining an event or condition made while the declarant was perceiving the event or condition, or immediately thereafter.

(2) Excited utterance. A statement relating to a startling event or condition made while the declarant was under the stress of excitement caused by the event or condition.

(3) Then existing mental, emotional, or physical condition. A statement of the declarant's then existing state of mind, emotion, sensation, or physical condition (such as intent, plan, motive, design, mental feeling, pain, and bodily health), but not including a statement of memory or belief to prove the fact remembered or believed unless it relates to the execution, revocation, identification, or terms of declarant's will.

(4) Statements for purposes of medical diagnosis or treatment. Statements made for purposes of medical diagnosis or treatment and describing medical history, or past or present symptoms, pain, or sensations, or the inception or general character of the cause or external source thereof insofar as reasonably pertinent to diagnosis or treatment.

(5) Recorded recollection. A memorandum or record concerning a matter about which a witness once had knowledge but now has insufficient recollection to enable the witness to testify fully and accurately, shown to have been made or adopted by the witness when the matter was fresh in the witness' memory and to reflect that knowledge correctly. If admitted, the memorandum or record may be read into evidence but may not itself be received as an exhibit unless offered by an adverse party.

(6) Records of regularly conducted activity. A memorandum, report, record, or data compilation, in any form, of acts, events, conditions, opinions, or diagnoses, made at or near the time by, or from information transmitted by, a person with knowledge, if kept in the course of a regularly conducted business activity, and if it was the regular practice of that business activity to make the memorandum, report, record, or data compilation, all as shown by the testimony of the custodian or other qualified witness, unless the source of information or the method or circumstances of preparation indicate lack of trustworthiness. The term "business" as used in this paragraph includes business, institution, association, profession, occupation, and calling of every kind, whether or not conducted for profit.

(7) Absence of entry in records kept in accordance with the provisions of paragraph (6). Evidence that a matter is not included in the memoranda, reports, records, or data compilations, in any form, kept in accordance with the provisions of paragraph (6), to prove the nonoccurrence or nonexistence of the matter, if the matter was of a kind of which a memorandum, report, record, or data compilation was regularly made and preserved, unless the sources of information or other circumstances indicate lack of trustworthiness.

(8) Public records and reports. Records, reports, statements, or data compilations, in any form, of public offices or agencies,

setting forth (A) the activities of the office or agency, or (B) matters observed pursuant to duty imposed by law as to which matters there was a duty to report, excluding, however, in criminal cases matters observed by police officers and other law enforcement personnel, or (C) in civil actions and proceedings and against the Government in criminal cases, factual findings resulting from an investigation made pursuant to authority granted by law, unless the sources of information or other circumstances indicate lack of trustworthiness.

(9) Records of vital statistics. Records or data compilations, in any form, of births, fetal deaths, deaths, or marriages, if the report thereof was made to a public office pursuant to requirements of law.

(10) Absence of public record or entry. To prove the absence of a record, report, statement, or data compilation, in any form, or the nonoccurrence or nonexistence of a matter of which a record, report, statement, or data compilation, in any form, was regularly made and preserved by a public office or agency, evidence in the form of a certification in accordance with Rule 902, or testimony, that diligent search failed to disclose the record, report, statement, or data compilation, or entry.

(11) Records of religious organizations. Statements of births, marriages, divorces, deaths, legitimacy, ancestry, relationship by blood or marriage, or other similar facts of personal or family history, contained in a regularly kept record of a religious organization.

(12) Marriage, baptismal, and similar certificates. Statements of fact contained in a certificate that the maker performed a marriage or other ceremony or administered a sacrament, made by a clergyman, public official, or other person authorized by the rules or practices of a religious organization or by law to perform the act certified, and purporting to have been issued at the time of the act or within a reasonable time thereafter.

(13) Family records. Statements of fact concerning personal or family history contained in family Bibles, genealogies, charts, engravings on rings, inscription on family portraits, engravings on urns, crypts, or tombstones, or the like.

(14) Records of documents affecting an interest in property. The record of a document purporting to establish or affect an interest in property, as proof of the content of the original recorded document and its execution and delivery by each person by whom it purports to have been executed, if the record is a record of a public office and an applicable statute authorized the recording of documents of that kind in that office.

(15) Statements in documents affecting an interest in property. A statement contained in a document purporting to establish or

affect an interest in property if the matter stated was relevant to the purpose of the document, unless dealings with the property since the document was made have been inconsistent with the truth of the statement or the purport of the document.

(16) Statements in ancient documents. Statements in a document in existence 20 years or more whose authenticity is established.

(17) Market reports, commercial publications. Market quotations, tabulations, lists, directories, or other published compilations, generally used and relied upon by the public or by persons in particular occupations.

(18) Learned treatises. To the extent called to the attention of an expert witness upon cross-examination or relied upon by the expert witness in direct examination, statements contained in published treatises, periodicals, or pamphlets on a subject of history, medicine, or other science or art, established as a reliable authority by the testimony or admission of the witness or by other expert testimony or by judicial notice. If admitted, the statements may be read into evidence but may not be received as exhibits.

(19) Reputation concerning personal or family history. Reputation among members of a person's family by blood, adoption, or marriage, or among his associates, or in the community, concerning a person's birth, adoption, marriage, divorce, death, legitimacy, relationship by blood, adoption, or marriage, ancestry, or other similar fact of personal or family history.

(20) Reputation concerning boundaries or general history. Reputation in a community, arising before the controversy, as to boundaries of or customs affecting lands in the community, and reputation as to events of general history important to the community or state or nation in which located.

(21) Reputation as to character. Reputation of a person's character among associates or in the community.

(22) Judgment of previous conviction. Evidence of a final judgment, entered after a trial or upon a plea of guilty (but not upon a plea of *nolo contendere*), adjudging a person guilty of a crime punishable by death or imprisonment in excess of one year, to prove any fact essential to sustain the judgment, but not including, when offered by the government in a criminal prosecution for purposes other than impeachment, judgments against persons other than the accused. The pendency of an appeal may be shown but does not affect admissibility.

(23) Judgment as to personal, family or general history, or boundaries. Judgments as proof of matters of personal, family or

general history, or boundaries, essential to the judgment, if the same would be provable by evidence of reputation.

(24) Other exceptions. A statement not specifically covered by any of the foregoing exceptions but having equivalent circumstantial guarantees of trustworthiness, if the court determines that (A) the statement is offered as evidence of a material fact; (B) the statement is more probative on the point for which it is offered than any other evidence which the proponent can procure through reasonable efforts; and (C) the general purposes of these rules and the interests of justice will best be served by admission of the statement into evidence. However, a statement may not be admitted under this exception unless the proponent of it makes known to the adverse party sufficiently in advance of the trial or hearing to provide the adverse party with a fair opportunity to prepare to meet it, the proponent's intention to offer the statement and the particulars of it, including the name and address of the declarant.

Rule 804. *Hearsay Exceptions: Declarant Unavailable*

(a) Definition of unavailability. "Unavailability as a witness" includes situations in which the declarant:

(1) Is exempted by ruling of the court on the ground of privilege from testifying concerning the subject matter of the declarant's statement; or

(2) Persists in refusing to testify concerning the subject matter of the declarant's statement despite an order of the court to do so; or

(3) Testifies to a lack of memory of the subject matter of the declarant's statement; or

(4) Is unable to be present or to testify at the hearing because of death or then existing physical or mental illness or infirmity; or

(5) Is absent from the hearing and the proponent of the declarant's statement has been unable to procure the declarant's attendance (or in the case of a hearsay exception under subdivision (b)(2), (3), or (4), the declarant's attendance or testimony) by process or other reasonable means.

A declarant is not unavailable as a witness if the exemption, refusal, claim of lack of memory, inability, or absence is due to the procurement of wrongdoing of the proponent of a statement for the purpose of preventing the witness from attending or testifying.

(b) Hearsay exceptions. The following are not excluded by the hearsay rule if the declarant is unavailable as a witness:

(1) Former testimony. Testimony given as a witness at another

hearing of the same or a different proceeding, or in a deposition taken in compliance with law in the course of the same or another proceeding, if the party against whom the testimony is now offered, or, in a civil action or proceeding, a predecessor in interest, had an opportunity and similar motive to develop the testimony by direct, cross, or redirect examination.

(2) Statement under belief of impending death. In a prosecution for homicide or in a civil action or proceeding, a statement made by a declarant while believing that his death was imminent, concerning the cause or circumstances of what the declarant believed to be his impending death.

(3) Statement against interest. A statement which was at the time of its making so far contrary to the declarant's pecuniary or proprietary interest, or so far intended to subject the declarant to civil or criminal liability, or to render invalid a claim by the declarant against another, that a reasonable man in the declarant's position would not have made the statement unless he believed it to be true. A statement tending to expose the declarant to criminal liability and offered to exculpate the accused is not admissible unless corroborating circumstances clearly indicate the trustworthiness of the statement.

(4) Statement of personal or family history. (A) A statement concerning the declarant's own birth, adoption, marriage, divorce, legitimacy, relationship by blood, adoption, or marriage, ancestry, or other similar fact of personal or family history, even though declarant had no means of acquiring personal knowledge of the matter stated; or (B) a statement concerning the foregoing matters, and death also, of another person, if the declarant was related to the other by blood, adoption, or marriage or was so intimately associated with the other's family as to be likely to have accurate information concerning the matter declared.

(5) Other exceptions. A statement not specifically covered by any of the foregoing exceptions but having equivalent circumstantial guarantees of trustworthiness, if the court determines that (A) the statement is offered as evidence of a material fact; (B) the statement is more probative on the point for which it is offered than any other evidence which the proponent can procure through reasonable efforts; and (C) the general purposes of these rules and the interests of justice will best be served by admission of the statement into evidence. However, a statement may not be admitted under this exception unless the proponent of it makes known to the adverse party sufficiently in advance

of the trial or hearing to provide the adverse party with a fair opportunity to prepare to meet it, the proponent's intention to offer the statement and the particulars of it, including the name and address of the declarant.

Rule 805. Hearsay within Hearsay

Hearsay included within hearsay is not excluded under the hearsay rule if each part of the combined statements conforms with an exception to the hearsay rule provided in these rules.

Rule 806. Attacking and Supporting Credibility of Declarant

When a hearsay statement, or a statement defined in Rule 801 (d) (2), (C), (D), or (E), has been admitted in evidence, the credibility of the declarant may be attacked, and if attacked may be supported, by any evidence which would be admissible for those purposes if declarant had testified as a witness. Evidence of a statement or conduct by the declarant at any time, inconsistent with the declarant's hearsay statement, is not subject to any requirement that the declarant may have been afforded an opportunity to deny or explain. If the party against whom a hearsay statement has been admitted calls the declarant as a witness, the party is entitled to examine him on the statement as if under cross-examination.

Article IX. Authentication and Identification

Rule 901. Requirement of Authentication or Identification

(a) General provision. The requirement of authentication or identification as a condition precedent to admissibility is satisfied by evidence sufficient to support a finding that the matter in question is what its proponent claims.

(b) Illustrations. By way of illustration only, and not by way of limitation, the following are examples of authentication or identification conforming with the requirements of this rule:

(1) Testimony of witness with knowledge. Testimony that a matter is what it is claimed to be.

(2) Nonexpert opinion on handwriting. Nonexpert opinion as to the genuineness of handwriting, based upon familiarity not acquired for purposes of the litigation.

(3) Comparison by trier or expert witness. Comparison by the trier of fact or by expert witnesses with specimens which have been authenticated.

(4) Distinctive characteristics and the like. Appearance, con-

tents, substance, internal patterns, or other distinctive characteristics, taken in conjunction with circumstances.

(5) Voice identification. Identification of a voice, whether heard firsthand or through mechanical or electronic transmission or recording, by opinion based upon hearing the voice at any time under circumstances connecting it with the alleged speaker.

(6) Telephone conversations. Telephone conversations, by evidence that a call was made to the number assigned at the time by the telephone company to a particular person or business, if (A) in the case of a person, circumstances, including self-identification, show the person answering to be the one called, or (B) in the case of a business, the call was made to a place of business and the conversation related to business reasonably transacted over the telephone.

(7) Public records or reports. Evidence that a writing authorized by law to be recorded or filed and in fact recorded or filed in a public office, or a purported public record, report, statement, or data compilation, in any form, is from the public office where items of this nature are kept.

(8) Ancient documents or data compilations. Evidence that a document or data compilation, in any form, (A) is in such condition as to create no suspicion concerning its authenticity, (B) was in a place where it, if authentic, would likely be, and (C) has been in existence 20 years or more at the time it is offered.

(9) Process or system. Evidence describing a process or system used to produce a result and showing that the process or system produces an accurate result.

(10) Methods provided by statute or rule. Any method of authentication or identification provided by Act of Congress or by other rules prescribed by the Supreme Court pursuant to statutory authority.

Rule 902. Self-Authentication

Extrinsic evidence of authenticity as a condition precedent to admissibility is not required with respect to the following:

(1) Domestic public documents under seal. A document bearing a seal purporting to be that of the United States, or of any state, district, commonwealth, territory, or insular possession thereof, or the Panama Canal Zone, or the Trust Territory of the Pacific Islands, or of a political subdivision, department, officer, or agency thereof, and a signature purporting to be an attestation or execution.

(2) Domestic public documents not under seal. A document purporting to bear the signature in the official capacity of an officer or employee or any entity included in paragraph (1) hereof, having no

seal, if a public officer having a seal and having official duties in the district or political subdivision of the officer or employee certifies under seal that the signer has the official capacity and that the signature is genuine.

(3) Foreign public documents. A document purporting to be executed or attested in the official capacity by a person authorized by the laws of a foreign country to make the execution or attestation, and accompanied by a final certification as to the genuineness of the signature and official position (A) of the executing or attesting person, or (B) of any foreign official whose certificate of genuineness of signature and official position relates to the execution or attestation or is in a chain of certificates of genuineness of signature and official position relating to the execution or attestation. A final certification may be made by a secretary of embassy or legation, consul general, consul, vice consul, or consular agent of the United States, or a diplomatic or consular official of the foreign country assigned or accredited to the United States. If reasonable opportunity has been given to all parties to investigate the authenticity and accuracy of official documents, the court may, for good cause shown, order that they be treated as presumptively authentic without final certification or permit them to be evidenced by an attested summary with or without final certification.

(4) Certified copies of public records. A copy of an official record or report or entry therein, or of a document authorized by law to be recorded or filed and actually recorded or filed in a public office, including data compilations in any form, certified as correct by the custodian or other person authorized to make the certification, by certificate complying with paragraph (1), (2) or (3) of this Rule or complying with any Act of Congress or rule prescribed by the Supreme Court pursuant to statutory authority.

(5) Official publications. Books, pamphlets, or other publications purporting to be issued by public authority.

(6) Newspapers and periodicals. Printed materials purporting to be newspapers or periodicals.

(7) Trade inscriptions and the like. Inscriptions, signs, tags, or labels purporting to have been affixed in the course of business and indicating ownership, control, or origin.

(8) Acknowledged documents. Documents accompanied by a certificate of acknowledgment executed in the manner provided by law by a notary public or other officer authorized by law to take acknowledgments.

(9) Commercial paper and related documents. Commercial paper, signatures thereon, and documents relating thereto to the extent provided by general commercial law.

(10) Presumptions under acts of Congress. Any signature, document, or other matter declared by Act of Congress to be presumptively or prima facie genuine or authentic.

Rule 903. Subscribing Witness' Testimony Unnecessary

The testimony of a subscribing witness is not necessary to authenticate a writing unless required by the laws of the jurisdiction whose laws govern the validity of the writing.

Article X. Contents of Writings, Recordings, and Photographs

Rule 1001. Definitions

For purposes of this article the following definitions are applicable.

(1) Writings and recordings. "Writings" and "recordings" consist of letters, words, or numbers, or their equivalent, set down by handwriting, typewriting, printing, photostating, photographing, magnetic impulse, mechanical or electronic recording, or other form of data compilation.

(2) Photographs. "Photographs" include still photographs, X-ray films, and motion pictures.

(3) Original. An "original" of a writing or recording is the writing or recording itself or any counterpart intended to have the same effect by a person executing or issuing it. An "original" of a photograph includes the negative or any print therefrom. If data are stored in a computer or similar device, any printout or other output readable by sight, shown to reflect the data accurately, is an "original."

(4) Duplicate. A "duplicate" is a counterpart produced by the same impression as the original, or from the same matrix, or by means of photography, including enlargements and miniatures, or by mechanical or electronic re-recording, or by chemical reproduction, or by other equivalent techniques which accurately reproduce the original.

Rule 1002. Requirement of Original

To prove the content of a writing, recording, or photograph, the original writing, recording, or photograph is required, except as otherwise provided in these rules or by Act of Congress.

Rule 1003. Admissibility of Duplicates

A duplicate is admissible to the same extent as an original unless (1) a genuine question is raised as to the authenticity of the original or (2) in the circumstances it would be unfair to admit the duplicate in lieu of the original.

Rule 1004. Admissibility of Other Evidence of Contents

The original is not required, and other evidence of the contents of a writing, recording, or photograph is admissible if—

(1) Originals lost or destroyed. All originals are lost or have been destroyed, unless the proponent lost or destroyed them in bad faith; or

(2) Original not obtainable. No original can be obtained by any available judicial process or procedure; or

(3) Original in possession of opponent. At a time when an original was under the control of the party against whom offered, that party was put on notice, by the pleadings or otherwise, that the contents would be a subject of proof at the hearing, and he does not produce the original at the hearing; or

(4) Collateral matters. The writing, recording, or photograph is not closely related to a controlling issue.

Rule 1005. Public Records

The contents of an official record, or of a document authorized to be recorded or filed and actually recorded or filed, including data compilations in any form, if otherwise admissible, may be proved by copy, certified as correct in accordance with Rule 902 or testified to be correct by a witness who has compared it with the original. If a copy which complies with the foregoing cannot be obtained by the exercise of reasonable diligence, then other evidence of the contents may be given.

Rule 1006. Summaries

The contents of voluminous writings, recordings, or photographs which cannot conveniently be examined in court may be presented in the form of a chart, summary, or calculation. The originals, or duplicates, shall be made available for examination or copying, or both, by other parties at reasonable time and place. The court may order that they be produced in court.

Rule 1007. Testimony or Written Admission of Party

Contents of writings, recordings, or photographs may be proved by the testimony or deposition of the party against whom offered or by his written admission, without accounting for the nonproduction of the original.

Rule 1008. Functions of Court and Jury

When the admissibility of other evidence of contents of writings, recordings, or photographs under these rules depends upon the fulfillment of a condition of fact, the question whether the condition has been fulfilled is ordinarily for the court to determine in accordance with the provisions of Rule 104. However, when an issue is raised (a) whether the asserted writing ever existed, or (b) whether another writing, recording, or photograph produced at the trial is the original, or (c) whether other evidence of contents correctly reflects the contents, the issue is for the trier of fact to determine as in the case of other issues of fact.

Glossary

Abandoned property. Property that has been abandoned and belongs to no one. The voluntary relinquishment of possession, right, and claim to something, accompanied by an apparent intention of not reclaiming it.

Accessory. A person who has aided, abetted, or assisted the principal offender, or who has counseled and encouraged the perpetration of a crime.

Accessory after the fact. A person who has knowledge of the crime and assists the perpetrator in avoiding arrest or in an escape.

Accessory before the fact. A person who has aided or encouraged the offense before its commission, but who did not, either actually or constructively, physically participate in its commission.

Accomplice. A person who knowingly, voluntarily, and with the common intent with the principal offender unites in the commission of a crime. The cooperation must be real, not apparent; mere presence coupled with knowledge that a crime is about to be committed, without some contribution, does not raise the liability of an accomplice.

Acquittal. A verdict of not guilty. The certification by a court or jury of the innocence of a defendant during or after trial.

Ad hoc. Specially pertaining to, or for the sake of, this case alone.

Adjudicate. To hear, try, and determine the claims of litigants before the court.

Admissibility. Determination of whether testimony, exhibits, or evidence will be allowed in trial.

Advocacy. The act of defending, assisting, or pleading for another; to defend by argument.

Advocate. One who renders legal advice and pleads the cause of another before a court or tribunal; one who speaks in favor of another. A lawyer.

Affidavit. A voluntary, sworn written statement.

Alibi. A plea by a suspect of having been elsewhere at the time of the commission of the crime.

Amicus curiae. Latin term meaning "friend of the court." The name for a brief filed with the court by someone who is not a party to the case, but who believes that the court's decision may affect its interest.

Ancient document rule. A document is "ancient" if it is twenty or more years old, and the proof of its age suffices as authentication. An ancient document, if relevant to the inquiry and free from suspicion, can be admissible in evidence without the ordinary requirements of proof of execution.

Answer. Defendant's written response to a civil complaint, containing his admission or denial of each of the allegations in the complaint. Cf. Plea.

Appeal. The judicial review of a decision of a trial court by a higher court with no new testimony taken or issue raised. A post-conviction step in judicial proceedings.

Appointed attorney. Legal counsel provided by a court for defendants who are without funds to hire private counsel.

Arm's reach doctrine. Officers can only search without a warrant the arrestee and the area immediately around him where the arrestee can reach or jump over to. This curtailment of the scope of searches evident to a legal arrest was ruled by the Supreme Court in *Chimel* v. *California,* 395 U.S. 752 (1969).

Arrest. To take a person into custody for the purpose of answering to the court. To consummate an arrest an officer must have the authority to make an arrest and an intention to arrest the suspect. There must be some restraint of the suspect, either physical or mental, and the suspect must understand that he is arrested.

Authenticating witness. One who establishes that a writing or document is what it purports to be and that it was made by the party to whom it was attributed.

Authentication. A legal process of proof that is designed to establish the genuineness, not the truth, of the contents of a writing or document.

Bail. To procure the release of a defendant from legal custody by guaranteeing his future appearance in court and compelling him to remain within jurisdiction of the court. Cash or other security may be required.

Ballistics. The identification of the firing characteristics of a firearm or cartridge; the scientific examination of evidence found at crime scenes and connected with firearms; firearms, spent bullets, empty cartridge or shell cases, cartridges, and shells.

Bench. The presiding judge (and his position at the front of the courtroom).

Best evidence rule. The contents of any writing must be proven by the writing itself or the failure to do so must be adequately explained. In addition to documents in writing, the rule is also applicable to recordings, X rays, photographs, and films.

Bill of particulars. A written statement of the facts upon which a charge is brought, that is more specific than the complaint of information, and is produced on the demand of a defendant.

Bright Line Rule. A judicial rule that helps resolve ambiguous issues by setting a basic standard that clarifies the ambiguity and establishes a simple response. It brings clarity to a law or regulation that could be read in two (or more) ways. Often a bright line rule is established when the need for a simple decision outweighs the need to weigh both sides of a particular issue. For example, the court may set a standard of five years or more to determine a valid age discrimination suit to be launched in an employment case (*Knight* v. *Avon Products* 2003, SJC 08876, Massachusetts Supreme Court.)

Burden of proof. The duty of establishing the truth of the issue at trial by such a quantum of evidence as the law requires.

Capias. A writ used to seize the property or person of the defendant; sometimes used to bring in a person for a mental examination.

Certiorari. A discretionary writ from a higher court to a lower one, or to a board or official with some judicial power, requesting the record of a case for review A *writ of certiorari* is a decision by the Supreme Court to hear an appeal from a lower court.

Circumstantial evidence. Facts and circumstances concerning a transaction from which the jury may infer other connected facts that reasonably follow according to common human experience.

Citation. Reference to an authority for a point of law, as a case by title, volume, and page of the report or reports in which the opinion appears and the year it was decided.

Citizen's arrest. Citizens are authorized to make arrests in felonies or breach of the peace without a warrant, when the offense is committed in their presence.

Compensatory damages. Damages assessed for the pain or suffering, humiliation, and defamation of the plaintiff.

Complaint. The pleading that initiates a criminal proceeding; sometimes called a criminal affidavit.

Consensual search. The party in possession of what is to be searched validly consents to a search by police. The suspect voluntarily, without coercion or deceit, relinquishes the right under the Fourth and Fourteenth Amendments to demand a search warrant.

Conspiracy. An agreement between two or more people to commit a criminal act, coupled with an overt act in furtherance.

Contraband. Things that are illegally possessed and that cannot be lawfully owned.

Coram nobis. Writ of error. A petition to fight a criminal conviction to the original court that seeks to set aside a conviction on some alleged error that does not appear on the record.

Corpus delicti. Body of crime.

Corroborating evidence. Evidence that supports and supplements previously offered evidence. It is directed at the same issue as the initial evidence, but it comes from a separate source and is designed to enhance the credibility of the prior testimony.

Criminal act. Any act or omission that is punishable as a crime.

Criminal intent. A guilty or evil state of mind to do an act prohibited as a crime by law.

Cross-examination. The interrogation of a witness by counsel for the opposing party by questions to test the truthfulness and accuracy of his testimony.

Curtilage. The area immediately surrounding a person' s home and all attached structures that has the same constitutional protections as the home.

Declarant. A person who makes a statement.

Declarations against interest. Out-of-court statements by a person that are in conflict with his pecuniary interests.

Declarations against penal interest. Out-of-court statements by a person that are in conflict with his innocence.

Demonstrative evidence. A model, an illustration, a chart, or an experiment offered as proof; real evidence.

Deposition. The testimony of a witness, compelled by subpoena, at a proceeding where counsel, but not the judge, attend. It is a pretrial discovery device.

Detention. A stop of a suspect by an officer; a temporary curtailment of personal freedoms. An officer may detain a suspicious individual to ask him questions about his conduct.

Dictum, dicta. A judicial opinion on some aspect of a case not essential to a court's decision on the issue under review.

Direct evidence. Evidence that comes from any of the witness' five senses and is in itself proof or disproof of a fact in issue.

Discovery. The compelled disclosure of facts, statements, or the production of documents, through subpoena duces tecum, interrogatories, or deposition, prior to trial.

Diversion. Finding alternatives to formal action in the criminal justice system.

Documentary evidence. Tangible objects that can express a fact or that tend to clarify the truth or untruth of the issues in question. Broad category includes private writings, documents, official records, newspapers, maps, or any other objects on which symbols have been placed with the intention of preserving a record of events or impressions.

Double jeopardy. Being tried more than once for the same crime.

Duress. An affirmative defense by a suspect that he was forced or coerced to commit a crime.

Dying declaration. A statement made by a homicide victim about to die without any hope of recovery concerning the facts and circumstances under which the fatal injury was inflicted. This declaration is offered in evidence at the trial of the person charged with having caused the speaker's death.

En banc. All the qualified judges of a court (particularly an appellate court) sitting and hearing a case.

Entrapment. The procurement of a person to commit a crime that he did not contemplate or would not have committed, for the sole purpose of prosecuting that person.

Evidence. Anything offered in court to prove the truth or falsity of a fact in issue.

Exclusionary rule. A rule of evidence that suppresses and rejects oth-

erwise admissible evidence because it was obtained in violation
of the Fourth or Fifth Amendment; applies to direct and derivative evidence, seized as a result of an illegal arrest or search.

Exemplar. A sample of handwriting; a specimen; a model.

Exigent circumstances. An emergency situation. If a true emergency
exists, or is reasonably believed to exist, police officers may enter the premises without a warrant. In most jurisdictions anything seen inside in plain view may be seized without a warrant.

Expert witness. A person who must appear to the trial judge to have
such knowledge, skill, or experience within the particular subject of inquiry that his opinion will be of some aid to the trier of
fact in arriving at the true facts.

Facts. Findings as to what particular occurrences did or did not take
place, which must be proved by evidence.

False arrest. The unlawful physical retainment of a citizen. An arrest
of a civil plaintiff by an officer without probable cause.

False imprisonment. The unlawful incarceration of a person.

Field interrogation. Questioning of a suspect by the police outside of
a police station.

Forensic. Pertaining to or belonging to the courts of justice.

Forensic science. The use of scientific knowledge to investigate and
solve crimes.

Foundation. The preliminary basis required for the admission of certain evidence.

Fresh pursuit. See Hot pursuit doctrine.

Frisk. A limited form of searching; a pat-down of a person's outer
clothing for a weapon.

Fruit of the crime. An object directly obtained by criminal means.

Fruit of the Poisoned Tree doctrine. The application of the exclusionary rule to evidence *derived* from an illegal search.

Grand jury. An accusatory body that inquires into felonies committed
within a particular district.

Guilty. A defendant's plea in a criminal prosecution; admission of
having committed the crime with which he is charged.

Habeas corpus. A writ seeking to bring a person already in custody
before a court or judge to challenge the lawfulness of the imprisonment.

Habeas corpus ad testificandum. A writ directed to the person having
legal custody of an inmate in a jail or prison that orders him to
bring the prisoner to court to testify.

Hearsay. An out-of-court statement offered to prove the truth of the matter contained in the statement. It is only hearsay if it is offered to prove that the statement itself is true.

Hot pursuit doctrine. An officer who chases a fugitive, or is in fresh pursuit, does not need a search warrant to continue his chase into homes or offices, and anything found in the course of the pursuit and is incident to it is an admissible item.

Impeachment. The act of discrediting a person or a thing. Questioning the credibility of a witness.

In camera. In judicial chambers. A hearing in which all but counsel are excluded from the courtroom.

Indictment. A written accusation, provided by a grand jury, charging a person with the commission of a crime.

In Forma Pauperis. (Also known as: IFP) Latin: "In the form of a pauper." This term applies to a person who is without the funds to pursue the normal costs of a lawsuit or criminal defense. It can also refer to a petition filed by a poor person in order to proceed in court without having to pay court costs such as filing fees.

Information. An affidavit, filed by the prosecutor, that initiates a criminal proceeding.

Informer's privilege. Right of the police *not* to disclose the identity of informants to protect them from retaliation and to maintain a confidential source of information about crime.

Inquest. An examination of the cause and circumstances of a violent or suspicious death.

Instructions to jury. A final charge given to the jury by the trial judge. An explanation of the law of the case being tried to furnish guidance to the jury in their deliberations.

Instrumentality. A thing used to facilitate a crime such as a tool or weapon.

Intent. The mental purpose to do a specific thing.

Inter alia. A Latin term meaning: "among other things." It is used to indicate that something is one out of a number of possibilities. For example, "he filed suit against respondents in state court, alleging, inter alia, a breach of contract."

Interrogation. Any questioning likely or expected to yield incriminating statements.

Interrogatories. Written questions by one party to a proceeding sent to the opposing party, which are to be answered under oath; a discovery device.

Inventory. A check of the contents of an impounded vehicle by officers pursuant to departmental regulations or standing custom. It is conducted for the purpose of safeguarding any valuables found in the vehicle, and it protects the officers from liability from mysterious disappearance of the valuables.

Judicial notice. The recognition by the court that a given fact is true without requiring formal proof. The fact must be one that is certain and indisputable, or the fact must be one of common, everyday knowledge in that jurisdiction, which everyone of average intelligence and knowledge can be presumed to know.

Juvenile. A child up to the age of eighteen who is tried in a special court on the issues of neglect and delinquency.

Latent (fingerprint). Present but not visible. A latent fingerprint must be searched for and developed by evidence technicians with special skill and equipment and preserved as evidence.

Lay witness. A nonexpert person who must be able to base his testimony upon his ability to observe, recollect, and explain to others. He may testify only to facts that he has acquired through his own senses.

Leading question. A question that suggests the desired answer to the witness.

Malicious prosecution. The actual prosecution of criminal charges against an accused person when there is no probable cause and when the charges were brought for malicious reasons.

Mens rea. An evil intent; criminal state of mind.

Modus operandi (m.o.). Method of operation; the characteristics of a particular criminal conduct or technique.

Motion. An application made to a court or judge to obtain an order.

Motion to suppress. A motion made by the defendant prior to the actual start of his trial to exclude evidence under the theory that it has been "tainted" by being seized or obtained in violation of the Fourth or Fifth Amendment.

Motive. The moving power, the reason for doing something.

Ne exeat. A writ ordering the detention of a person until he posts an appearance bond in a civil case that will "guarantee" his appearance.

Nolle prosequi. A formal entry on the record, by the prosecutor, that he will no longer prosecute the case.

Nolo contendere. A plea of "no contest" having the same effect as a plea of guilty.

Objection. A protest against a determination by the court, especially a ruling upon the admissibility of evidence.

Open field doctrine. Officers may enter private outdoor property to look for evidence, without a warrant or other justification, and anything seen in the course of their expedition falls within the plain view rule.

Peace officer. A public officer such as a policeman, sheriff, deputy sheriff, marshal, constable, or state investigator; a "sworn" officer.

Per se. By or through itself.

Physical evidence. Items, things, and traces found at a crime scene; suspects or other persons or places concerned with a criminal investigation.

Plain view rule. Readily observable things seen by an officer (in a place where he has a right to be) that are not the product of a search and are not subject to exclusion from evidence.

Plea. In criminal cases, the official answer to the charge brought against him. The usual pleas are guilty, not guilty, and nolo contendere.

Plea bargaining. The process whereby a defendant and the state bargain a plea of guilty for a reduced sentence. The "agreement" is supervised by the court prior to approval.

Plurality Opinion. This is the controlling opinion of the Court when no majority opinion exists. It is written when only majorities of the majority of judges agree on the reasoning behind the decision. For example, in the Supreme Court, five of the justices believe that the one side should prevail, but only four of them agree on the reasoning behind that decision.

Posse comitatus. Male, and in some jurisdictions female, adults whom a sheriff or other officers may summon to their assistance. Citizens who may be deputized to assist officers in making an arrest.

Preliminary hearing. A judicial examination of witnesses to determine whether or not a crime has been committed and if the evidence presented against the accused is sufficient to warrant bail or commitment pending trial.

Presentence report. A report compiled under court direction by a probation officer on the social and criminal history of a convicted defendant with a recommendation to the sentencing judge of the best corrections program for the offender.

Presumption. The drawing of a particular inference of one fact from the existence of a related known or proven fact.

Prima facie. First view. Evidence in a criminal case that on its surface is sufficient to prove the charge.

Privileged communication. A communication between persons in a confidential relationship, such as husband and wife, attorney and client, confessor and penitent, or doctor and patient. Under public policy the court will not allow such information to be disclosed or inquired into.

Probable cause. A conclusion of law that an offense probably was committed and the suspect probably is guilty thereof.

Public place. A place exposed to the public where people gather together and pass to and fro and where whatever occurs would be seen by a number of persons.

Punitive damages. Damages awarded by a jury to "teach and punish" the civil defendant. In most jurisdictions neither cities nor insurance companies will indemnify an officer for punitive damages, and they cannot be discharged through the bankruptcy courts.

Real evidence. Tangible objects presented in the courtroom for the trier of fact to view. Something directly connected with the incident out of which the cause of action arose.

Rebuttal. The answer of the prosecution to the defense case in chief.

Rebuttal evidence. Evidence disputing or answering that given by the opposite side. Evidence that denies any affirmative fact that the adverse party has endeavored in any matter to prove.

Rejoinder (surrebuttal). The answer of the defense to the prosecutor's rebuttal.

Relevancy. Relevant evidence is that evidence which "advances the inquiry"; that is, it proves something.

Replevin. A civil action to recover things wrongfully possessed by another, such as stolen goods. Also brought by acquitted defendants for return of property illegally seized.

Res gestae. Exclamations and statements made by the participants, victims, or spectators of a crime immediately before, during, or after the commission of the crime, where such statements were made as a reaction to, or utterance inspired by, the occasion and where there was no opportunity for the declarant to deliberate or fabricate a false statement.

Return (search warrant). A statement in writing of police action taken while executing a search warrant, including a description of the place searched and an inventory of property seized.

Rules of evidence. The laws that determine what evidence may be used to prove facts. These laws are not concerned with what the outcome will be once the facts are finally decided (as most laws are), but instead are only concerned with the admissibility of various evidence that is offered to prove facts.

Rules of law. Once the facts are determined from evidence presented, certain rules are then applied to those facts that determine the outcome of the case.

Search. The seeking of something not in plain sight, in places where the object (or person) sought might be concealed.

Search warrant. A legal process, issued by a judge upon a supporting affidavit, that authorizes a peace officer to search a person or place for evidence of an offense, contraband, instrumentalities, and fruits of a crime.

Secondary evidence. See Circumstantial evidence.

Special damages. See Punitive damages.

Stare decisis. To abide by, or adhere to, decided cases. Policy of courts to stand by precedent and not to disturb a settled point.

Statement. Oral, written, or even nonverbal conduct that conveys a message.

Stipulation. The admittance of proof by agreement of the opposing attorneys.

Stop and frisk. The right of a police officer to detain suspicious individuals temporarily and to frisk (pat-down search) those who appear dangerous. Upheld by the landmark case *Terry* v. *Ohio,* 392U.S. 1 (1968).

Subpoena. A process to cause a witness to appear and give testimony, commanding him to lay aside all pretenses and excuses, and appear before a court or magistrate therein named at a time therein mentioned to testify.

Subpoena ad testificandum. A technical and descriptive term for the ordinary subpoena.

Subpoena duces tecum. A process by which the court, at the request of a party, commands a witness who has in his possession or control some document or paper that is pertinent to the issues of a pending controversy to produce it at the trial.

Suppression hearing. A formal motion by a defendant's lawyer to suppress and reject either tangible or intangible evidence that was allegedly illegally obtained.

Testimony. Spoken evidence given by a competent witness, under oath or affirmation; as distinguished from evidence derived from writings and other sources.

Tort. A civil wrong committed to the person or property of another and resulting in some damage or injury.

True bill. A grand jury indictment.

Venue. A neighborhood, place, or county in which an injury is declared to have been done, or fact declared to have happened. Also, the county (or geographical division) in which an action or prosecution is brought for trial, and which is to furnish the panel of jurors. In a criminal case the defendant has a constitutional right, which he can waive, to be tried in the district in which the crime was committed.

Verbal act. An action by words. A statement that shows the motive, character, and object of an act.

Vital statistics. Data relating primarily to health, such as the registration of births, marriages, and deaths, which have been compiled under public authority.

Voir dire. The examination of prospective jurors or witnesses before the trial begins to determine if they have the necessary qualifications to be fair and impartial.

Voluntary statement. A statement that is free of duress and coercion, but is usually elicited by questioning.

Volunteered statement. An utterance made without elicitation, frequently a spontaneous statement.

Weight of evidence. The believability of evidence. Evidence may be technically legal and, thus, admissible in court, but the question remains as to whether or not it should be given any value or weight.

Witness. One who, being present, personally sees or perceives a thing; a beholder, spectator, or eyewitness.

Table of Cases

Index